SUCCESSION

SEASON THREE

SUCCESSION
SEASON THREE

The Complete Scripts

faber

First published in 2023
by Faber & Faber Limited
The Bindery, 51 Hatton Garden
London EC1N 8HN

Typeset by Brighton Gray
Printed and bound at CPI Books Ltd, Croydon CRO 44Y

The right of Jesse Armstrong, Jon Brown, Ted Cohen, Georgia Pritchett, Tony Roche,
Susan Soon He Stanton and Will Tracy to be identified as authors
of this work in accordance with Section 77 of the
Copyright, Designs and Patents Act 1988

A CIP record for this book
is available from the British Library

978-0-571-37976-7

Printed and bound in the UK on FSC® certified paper in line with our continuing
commitment to ethical business practices, sustainability and the environment.
For further information see faber.co.uk/environmental-policy

4 6 8 10 9 7 5 3

Contents

Introduction

One Last Pitch

What happens in the room?

I've been asked that a lot. It's a good question, it makes me panic: what *does* happen in the room? I suppose a group of writers, between eight and twelve, a mixture of Brits and Americans, comic and tragic, gather for five or six hours a day, for a few months, chat and mock and giggle, discuss lunch at length, and leave. But that can't be it, can it? Because then, how does the show happen?

I suppose the most honest answer I can give is that 'the room' is the setting, the time and place, where all the possibilities of a show exist, and then gradually, carefully, sometimes surreptitiously and sometimes decisively, those possibilities are narrowed, sculpted, discarded or embraced, into the shape of a season.

Exactly how that happens depends on the personalities in the room, any process that's been imposed, and most importantly, the showrunner, who sets the tone and the dynamic. Jesse Armstrong has always talked about running a room as being like throwing a party: that you're responsible for the guests and the atmosphere and ensuring people want to come. He was excellent at it.

I found myself in the *Succession* writers' room through a combination of personal failure and Britain's decision to leave the EU. My career was languishing after some failed projects and a breakdown that I won't bore you with. On the night the results of the EU referendum were announced in the summer of 2016, I was in a bar in Westminster after attending a free workshop about writing sitcoms, something I had been trying and failing to do. Jesse was there having given the session. Writers chatted, nervously, as the referendum result came in. No one expected it. I think Jesse recognised something in my politics and my sense of humour that felt familiar and could be useful. Turns out we had the same agent who recommended me for *Succession* anyway. But I like to think my job on the show was the only good thing to come out of Brexit.

The *Succession* room was always in London. Although, it's important to say there was a writers' room on location every day as we filmed. Jesse believes in having writers (a minimum of two, usually three, and sometimes more) present every day on set and that meant a version of 'the room' travelled. Sometimes it would be the kitchen of a Manhattan restaurant, sometimes the basement cinema of a millionaire's mansion. It depended where we were shooting. But the real room, the main writers' room – where the season was planned, storylined, designed – was always in London. Maybe that seems an odd choice for a show so decisively set in New York. But I believe something special occurred as a result of our far-away status. No writer arrived in the room feeling like an employee in immediate debt to some executive overlords waiting patiently (then impatiently) for scripts. We weren't in intimidating environs that stressed the pressures of prestige television. Early on, we were a far-flung and not much overseen satellite office, with a sense of having been forgotten about, which provides an excellent situation for creativity to flourish.

There was the first room, soulless and anonymous, in an office block near Oxford Circus. The one with incessant drilling. Well, not incessant, occasional, which is worse. If it had been incessant, we could have addressed it, worked around it, complained about it. But it was occasional. Sometimes we'd be halfway through a day before the drilling began. And it would come in the middle of someone's sentence and they'd drop their head into their hands as we all realised that we hadn't even appreciated the lack of drilling and now it was too late. Now, there was drilling. I don't think I've ever laughed as hard in my life as I did that first year in the office near Oxford Circus. But I can't be sure, I couldn't hear over the fucking drilling.

There was the second season room in Brixton, where our excellent writers' assistant Shiv (yes, Shiv) stapled carpets to the walls to stop the cavernous echoes when we spoke, only to realize as summer struck that they made the room unbearably hot. For seasons three and four we decided to return to the safety of corporate soullessness in a shared office block in Victoria, a room with such little soundproofing that we had to come up with codenames for plot points in case the very loud businessmen next door were *Succession* fans with access to the internet. (A crucial event in season four became referred to as 'Larry David' in all conversation. 'Is this before or after Larry David?' we would ask.)

The room had huge white walls on which Jesse would stick swathes of blank paper, with character names as headings. He would write underneath each character any ideas from the room that stuck, from the fun, small nonsense like 'Afraid of sharks?' under Roman, to what turned out to be the arc of a whole season under Kendall, like 'Beaten Dog' (season two) or 'Goes Beyond' (season three). Eventually, what survived would get loaded into a massive mega-chart type thing on the largest wall, with character names horizontally across the top and episode numbers running down the left-hand side on the vertical. The basic beats of the season were plotted within.

Normally, Jesse would arrive in the room with a clear sense of the end of a season, but be open to total invention as to how we got there. For season three, he had a feeling that the siblings would band together to take on their father, and he was certain that Tom should break a trust by betraying that to Logan, but how we got there was totally up for grabs. I always loved this. The room resonated with 'maybes': Maybe this? Maybe that? Writers tend to be riddled with doubt. (Thank god, or we'd be directors.) A trick of writing is to stay open until you absolutely have to close down the narrative, decide for sure, just so you don't miss that last possible moment of magic, that idea that solves everything. So you stay alive to promise till the very last minute. I remember one of the actors saying at a season one readthrough how he'd never seen scripts with so many 'maybes'. 'Maybe Connor does this', 'Maybe we see a glimpse of . . .', etc. Perhaps it's a British thing, self-effacing, embarrassed to be tyrannical, but I think it was also an overhang from the room. The occasional maybe is no bad thing. It's not always uncertainty or lack of confidence. It's an offer, it's a kindness, it's a gesture to another artist: 'Here's how I picture it, but how do you picture it? Do you have a better idea? There's room. You're involved. You're here too.' That's how I felt in the room. Now I always keep the maybes in.

We had often toyed with the idea of Logan selling Waystar. It came up a lot, and in the room there were different opinions. Some thought that was antithetical to the whole show. Logan would never sell. The company was all that mattered to him. It wasn't real. 'But it *is real*!' others would say, 'Murdoch literally did it, it's *more real*!' An appeal to reality over the mythic was always the most powerful pitch in the room, only occasionally losing out to whatever was the most funny.

This may make the room sound competitive, but it never was. It was gentle, silly, funny, my favourite stage of making the show. It was where everything was possible. Where you could move a table of writers with a delicately told pain from your own history that would help inform a character's past, or riff on a joke so much you might make the funniest man in the world, Tony Roche, vibrate enough with laughter he'd slowly start to cry, a gift given maybe once a season.

The necessary mode of voicing ideas is called 'pitching' in the room. Which is really just a wanky way of saying 'suggesting.' When I would pitch early on, I would always preface it by saying, 'This is shit but –' thus making everyone sit through a suggestion I had just told them was shit. It took me a while to realise that I was not only instructing people not to listen, but also wasting time, insisting people comfort my needy narcissism before responding to my idea. Did it really require an acknowledgment of self-loathing every time I spoke? Surely they knew I loathed myself already, I was in a writers' room.

Pitching is a practice that bestows terrible privilege on the articulate. It relies on very quickly being able to gather people into your point of view. 'See! It would be like this!' The room is a particularly testing ground for writers, as an inability to verbally express what they mean might well have been the thing that led them to write in the first place. If you can directly convince someone of your point of view, why on earth would you bother to write it?

I found a particular niche for myself helping build the bones of the story, by starting from something vivid, pulpy, sometimes tragic. Instead of negating the idea before I said it, I'd contextualise it, beginning by saying, 'This is the trashy version' or 'I know this is vivid, but . . .' 'Not this, but maybe – Something *like this.*' We were all aware that *Succession* was a show in which things got withheld. Sometimes emotion, often truth, always love. But by starting from the vivid, the tragic, we could pull it back while still retaining the dramatic flavour. When planning Kendall's party, for example, we enjoyed sitting around (like the hangers-on do in episode eight), coming up with ideas for his fortieth birthday. There was a vivid suggestion that he might kill himself in front of everyone; that the party's theme was forty and out. Slowly, this became an idea that he might 'pretend to kill himself', as a piece of party performance art. And then eventually, in a very *Succession* journey, the story point became that Kendall backs out of sort of 'pretending to kill himself' by deciding against appearing onstage at the party, on a crucifix, singing. Pitching is the way in which you work out what the show isn't, as well as what it is.

For a short while, we talked so much and laughed so hard about Tom going to jail that we began to wonder, should Tom go to jail? Were we the sort of show who could cut to Tom in jail? It seems absurd now. It's so right and so clear that Tom should get away with it, as so many corporate criminals do, to show how the system works, to facilitate a further crisis in his marriage, as well as to prompt one of the funniest scenes in the whole show when Tom explodes with relief in Greg's office. But for a while there, for a playful couple of hours, we were a show where Tom *went to jail*. And we cut to it. And I love that. I love that show too. I love all the shows we never made. Each season, as the room would come to an end, I would find myself bothered by two sadnesses. One, the loss of all my friends I'd see every day. Two, the loss of all the other shows that could have been.

In your hands you have season three of the show that was. I guess I just want you to know that before this book, before the show, before we shot and produced and edited, before any acclaim, there was the room. And – this is too folksy, too vivid – I know. But. Those were the best of days.

Maybe?

Something like that.

Lucy Prebble
April 2023

Note on the Text

This book contains the scripts as they stood when we started to film each episode. Reading them, you'll discover that they are quite often a little different from what made it to screen. These departures occurred for one of several reasons: a choice we had to make on what to lose in the edit; a new line myself and my fellow writers offered on set; or a bit of improvisation or extemporisation by an actor.

You'll also find a few footnotes scattered through the following pages. I've tried to limit the footnoting to those spots where the reason for a change might not be self-explanatory. Where they occur, I've sometimes also included a little flavour of the research that informed the show. Any errors, failure of memory or omissions are entirely mine.

Jesse Armstrong
March 2023

SUCCESSION

SEASON THREE

SUCCESSION
SEASON THREE

Executive Producers	Jesse Armstrong
	Adam McKay
	Frank Rich
	Will Ferrell
	Kevin Messick
	Jane Tranter
	Mark Mylod
	Tony Roche
	Jon Brown
	Lucy Prebble
	Will Tracy
	Scott Ferguson
Writers	Jesse Armstrong
	Jon Brown
	Tony Roche
	Georgia Pritchett
	Will Tracy
	Susan Stanton
	Ted Cohen
	Francesca Gardiner
	Lucy Prebble
	Alice Birch
	Jamie Carragher
	Lucy Kirkwood
	Will Arbery
	Jonathan Glatzer
Directors	Mark Mylod
	Cathy Yan
	Shari Springer Berman
	Robert Pulcini
	Kevin Bray
	Andrij Parekh
	Lorene Scafaria
Supervising Producer	Dara Schnapper
Produced by	Gabrielle Mahon
Associate Producers	Callie Hersheway
	Nathan Elston
	Lauren Salvia
	Maeve Cullinane

First Assistant Directors	Christo Morse
	John Silvestri
Directors of Photography	Patrick Capone
	Christopher Norr
Editors	Ken Eluto, ACE
	Jane Rizzo
	Bill Henry
	Brian A. Kates, ACE
	Ellen Tam
Composer	Nicholas Britell
Production Designer	Stephen H. Carter
Costume Designer	Michelle Matland
Casting Director	Avy Kaufman, CSA
Original Casting by	Francine Maisler, CSA
Script Supervisors	Lisa Molinaro
	Holly Unterberger
Gaffer	Andy Day
Key Grip	Brendon Malone
Property Master	Dierdre Kane
Set Decorator	George DeTitta Jr.
Supervising Sound Editor & Re-Recording Mixer	Nicholas Renbeck
Re-Recording Mixer	Andy Kris
Music Editors	John Finklea
	Todd Kasow
Production Sound Mixer	Ken Ishii
Hair Dept Head	Angel DeAngelis
Make Up Dept Head	Nuria Sitja
Location Manager	Paul Eskenazi

Episode One
SECESSION

Written by Jesse Armstrong
Directed by Mark Mylod

Original air date 17 October 2021

Cast

LOGAN ROY	Brian Cox
KENDALL ROY	Jeremy Strong
GREG HIRSCH	Nicholas Braun
SHIV ROY	Sarah Snook
ROMAN ROY	Kieran Culkin
CONNOR ROY	Alan Ruck
TOM WAMBSGANS	Matthew Macfadyen
FRANK VERNON	Peter Friedman
COLIN STILES	Scott Nicholson
KARL MULLER	David Rasche
GERRI KELLMAN	J. Smith-Cameron
WILLA FERREYRA	Justine Lupe
RAVA	Natalie Gold
KAROLINA NOVOTNEY	Dagmara Dominczyk
HUGO BAKER	Fisher Stevens
JESS JORDAN	Juliana Canfield
NAOMI PIERCE	Annabelle Dexter-Jones
DAYTIME PGN ANCHOR	Rana Novini
MICHELLE-ANNE	Linda Emond
BERRY SCHNEIDER	Jihae
COMFREY PELLITS	Dasha Nekrasova
LISA ARTHUR	Sanaa Lathan
KEITH	Jordan Lage
STEVE COX	Wayne Pyle
DELTA PIKE	Sharla McBride
RAVA'S HOUSEKEEPER	Sol Marina Crespo
LISA'S ASSISTANT	Shannon Moore

DAY ONE

EXT. HELICOPTER – DAY

A helicopter descends over a European landscape. Music plays.

INT. HELICOPTER – DAY

Logan looks out. He is deep in thought. It's hard to read his thoughts but he looks like he's seeing the world afresh from up here. The game of it all. A little pleasure at the fight—

INT. HOTEL BATHROOM – DAY

9 a.m. On an animated breathing aid. Out of vision, Kendall makes a guttural noise – he's calming himself. But his head is fizzing. He swipes to another breathing aid. Another.

He makes some more noises, trying to get things out of his head. He growls. Makes noises he recalls from a workshop. Yelps and shrieks.

INT. HOTEL SUITE – DAY

Outside the bathroom: Karolina, Jess and Greg. We hear some of the noises from their POV. They look at one another: WTF?

EXT. SMALL CROATIAN AIRPORT – AIRFIELD – DAY

3 p.m. Logan gets out. Keeping his own counsel. Followed by Gerri and Frank and Karl. Some ground crew meet them and offer hands and arms to guide them towards a passenger van.

Logan walks alone – radiating bristling internal calculation. Hugo comes to greet Logan.

> HUGO
> Hey, hey, hey! Sir!

From behind—

> GERRI
> *(calling to Hugo)*
> Where's the plane? Can we go?

> HUGO
> Jet's en route back. And we're chartering. Should be no more than an hour. And where we headed, sir?

Logan walks on past Hugo, to one of the waiting vans. Roman, Shiv and Tom, Connor and Willa emerge from their helicopter.

> *(after Logan)*
> I've got us a nice space to wait?
> *(to Karl and Frank)*
> I mean it's not that nice. But it's the nicest I can source— Where are we going, do you know?

> GERRI
> Either New York or Geneva or London or Singapore or LA.

Confused, Hugo heads over to Logan. Gerri, Frank and Karl wait for Shiv and Tom and Roman to catch up. They look over at Logan studying his phone.

> SHIV
> So, what's he been saying?

> GERRI
> Um not much.

> TOM
> Right – like what's he thinking?

> GERRI
> Yeah, he was talking about his mom a little bit.

> ROMAN
> Yeah? I mean, what's the play?

> KARL
> I dunno. Lot of interesting ideas flying around.

> FRANK
> I got fired.

(*re Karl*)

He got fired.

(*re Gerri*)

She got promoted. I got rehired. She got demoted, right?

KARL

He was – he was saying maybe he and Kendall should just meet in Central Park and wrestle it out?

SHIV

Okay?

FRANK

I mean he was kidding but—

LOGAN
(*leans out, shouts*)

C'mon!

Gerri looks at Roman: Can you talk to your dad?

ROMAN

Dad?

Logan's distracted.

Dad? You want me to ride with you, talk things through?

LOGAN

Huh? You wanna suck my dick?

Logan's door closes. Hugo climbs in with Logan, he's ready to go. Car moves off for the terminal.

ROMAN
(*to Shiv*)

I dunno. I mean that's a question I often ask myself.

Looks all round: Is Logan handling this okay?

As Shiv and Tom ready to get in a car, Tom looks around, they've hardly had a moment privately.

TOM

Hey. So, you okay?

SHIV

Fuck knows. Yeah. I guess?

> TOM

Right? Because. This is— I mean this is really really really really bad, right? I mean this is just a terrible situation. The sacrificial lamb just shat all over the – temple and – and I mean, what the fuck is going to happen? Who's going to carry the can? How quickly are the fucking FBI coming, Shiv?

> SHIV

Tom? Easy.
> (*then*)
I mean, what are you thinking?

He looks at her – can they talk frankly or is this business?

> TOM

I'm not taking a position, Shiv, I'm just saying.

> SHIV
> (*coolly*)

Let's just keep calm, okay?

As they are joined by others they clam up.

INT. HOTEL BATHROOM – DAY

Greg is outside the bathroom.

> GREG
> (*off*)

You okay, dude?

Nothing.

If you're okay will you say 'okay' because otherwise I will have to break the door in. And I'm not sure I'll be able to but—

Kendall opens the door of the bathroom.

> KENDALL

Okay. Action stations, let's fucking go! Let's get into this.

INT. SMALL CROATIAN AIRPORT – BAR AREA – DAY

In the provincial/small-scale/military Croatian airport. Hugo has found a part of a bar/lounge to use as a waiting area. It's large enough for little gangs to form.

Connor and Willa are last to arrive into a weird atmosphere. Shiv, Tom, and Roman are there with Gerri, Frank and Karl. Everyone quiet – aware of the king, monitoring phones . . .

Roman starts to own the space – looks at the selection of beverages in the little bar.

Gerri gets a call and goes to a separate part of the room to talk privately. Then Karl gets one.

On the far side of the room, Logan is positioned away from everyone else – facing out over the airfield. He watches Kendall's press conference again on a phone. He can't quite believe it, mixed emotions.

Shiv gets a call. Looks at Roman and Karl and Tom.

> SHIV
> *(re the call, to Roman)*
> I'm getting a lot of board action. You?

> ROMAN
> Yeah, people are suddenly super-curious about their liability. D&O insurance. And whose names are on those papers?

> SHIV
> *(re Gerri and Karl)*
> Frank? I think they need to be on the same page before they talk to the board?

> FRANK
> Er, not talking to the board I don't think.

Frank gets a call and excuses himself—

> I should take this.

Frank heads off. Shiv figures out who they're all talking to—

> SHIV
> Ugh. Everyone's fucking lawyering up!

Shiv marches over to be near Gerri, who is listening intently. Gerri turns away. Tom catches up.

TOM

And should – we, take a view on our own positions? I mean what *is in* those papers?

He makes eyes. They both know what they could be. An anger has been growing inside Shiv. It bursts out sharp and loud—

SHIV

I don't know. I don't know, I don't fucking know!! Jesus. What a fucking disaster!

Logan barely reacts. The rest of the room grows even tenser.

ROMAN

Hey. He'll have a plan.

Roman's phone goes. Shiv paranoid, is hard in—

SHIV

Who's that?

ROMAN

This? It's Kirsty-May Fuck You.

Roman heads off to a corner. Shiv watches him go, suspicious.

HUGO
(*tentatively calls to Logan*)
And, sir? Logan? As I coordinate, the travel plans, in terms of, the charter – where might we be—? Just, in terms of the knowledge, for strictly my brain, where might we be flying you to?

Logan doesn't respond. Connor's call is over.

CONNOR
(*tentative*)
Um, Dad, in case you're interested Ivo Yates wants to say hi and sorry for your troubles, can he connect?

SHIV
(*groans*)
Urgh. *No.* That fucking little insider-trading kiddie-fiddler?

CONNOR

The message actually is, you can use his boat if we want to get out of the spotlight?

ROMAN
We have a fucking boat.

CONNOR
He's actually a nice guy and it has a missile system apparently?

SHIV
No. Con. And make sure everyone knows he never spoke to Dad.

She approaches Logan and, soothingly, to get him to focus—

Dad, do you want to huddle on our message to the board and also talk about a lawyer for you personally in case things move fast?

But he's deep in thought. Grunts. She backs off – is he okay?

EXT. HOTEL EXIT AREA – DAY

Karolina and Jess and Kendall and Greg get ready to head out of the hotel through press to a waiting Suburban.

KAROLINA
And where are we going, Ken—?

KENDALL
Waystar, plant a flag, fix on my lawyer, PRs, get some independent directors shaking, and maybe right in to see the fucking feds?

Kendall motions and they head out through the press.

GREG
No comment! No comment! No comment!

KAROLINA
(*aside*)
You don't need to say that, Greg – just don't comment, yeah?

INT. KENDALL'S CAR – DAY

Into the car. Karolina is last—

KAROLINA
It's just this is a company vehicle?

Kendall ignores.

> Look, I don't have a dog in this fight.
>> (*as they drive off*)
> But – you just – clearly opened the company to investigation and lawsuits? So, I imagine you are no longer working for the company?

> KENDALL
> Well no, because I was acting in the best interests of the company.

> KAROLINA
> Yeah? Violating your duty of confidentiality? Your fiduciary duties as a director?

> KENDALL
> Continuing in silence was untenable from a legal and moral point of view.

> KAROLINA
> But this is a Waystar vehicle.

> KENDALL
> This – *this* is Waystar now.

He motions to the group of them in the car. Outside on the street photographers surround the vehicle in slow-moving traffic. Kendall looks at Karolina.

> Look. I need a sealed unit here, Karolina. I need a clean jar. Are you in for this revolution?

> KAROLINA
> Well, it's exciting. I just think I just have to – to—
> Contractually—

Her phone goes.

> KENDALL
> Hey. No. Keep looking at me, okay? Don't answer the phone. Are you with me, yes or no?

> KAROLINA
> Why did you do it like that, Ken?
>> (*to Greg*)
> I mean, did you know?

                          GREG
Me? No.
                    (*the line:*)
No I had no prior warning and I was surprised at his comments,
but now I am obviously concerned and interested to hear more.

She looks at Greg – too practiced and slick?

                       KAROLINA
Okay?

                        KENDALL
You're at a fork in your life, Karolina. Do you want to join the
good team?
                   (*ready to push*)
You know he makes jokes about you? Do you want to hear
what he says about you? He calls you the 'Sausage Grinder'
and—

                       KAROLINA
I'm pretty tough, Ken—

                        KENDALL
Do you wanna be able to look your kids in the eye? *This* is the
righteous vehicle.

                       KAROLINA
I hear you. I do. I do. It's just—

But he hasn't got the commitment he needs—

                        KENDALL
Okay. Stop the car.

                       KAROLINA
Ken?

                        KENDALL
Out. Please. I need to make calls. I can't have weevils in the
fucking flour sack, okay? Out. Now.

                       KAROLINA
Ken?

*He's serious. She gets out. He looks out of the window at her
standing on the pavement in Midtown. A pack of photographers on
foot have followed them through the traffic.*

KENDALL

Everything you've heard today is privileged. Repeat anything
and I'll sue you out your ass. Goodbye!

KAROLINA

Greg? You coming, Greg?

Greg doesn't know quite what to do.

GREG

I just gotta— Um, I'm getting a ride with these guys thanks!

*As they head off, out on the street there are photographers getting
shots of Karolina.*

KENDALL

Good kid!

GREG

Oh fuck. Oh, man. Here we go!

INT. SMALL CROATIAN AIRPORT — BAR AREA — DAY

*Shiv and Roman watch business news, regular news for reactions.
Maybe we see some memes of the press conference? Shiv shows
Roman a picture of Karolina curbside. The NYT are live-updating
the story under a 'Roy Family Civil War' headline. Roman nods. He is
watching PGN with Connor—*

DAYTIME PGN ANCHOR

. . . delivered an electrifying denunciation of his father – and the
values and practices of ATN owner Waystar Royco.

*Roman mutes it. Looks at Shiv, gets in close so he can talk. Looks
over at their father.*

ROMAN

So. Look. What are you actually thinking here?

SHIV

What am I thinking?

ROMAN

Yeah, what are you thinking?

SHIV

As in—? In terms of? What?

ROMAN
In terms of – the fucking – situation?

SHIV
(*eyes him*)
Well, what are you thinking?

Roman looks at her.

ROMAN
Oh, right, like I'm going to tell you what I'm thinking.

SHIV
Fine. Okay. I'll tell you what I'm thinking.

She leaves him hanging a beat.

I'm thinking what you're thinking.

ROMAN
Fuck you.

He looks at her.

SHIV
I'm thinking we just have to back Dad right now and I can't believe anyone would be thinking anything else?

ROMAN
No sure of course.

SHIV
But you mean, what am I *actually* thinking?

ROMAN
(*gets closer*)
Yeah?

SHIV
I'm thinking: Is he toast?

ROMAN
Fuck you. You are? Really?

SHIV
Well yeah, why, what are you thinking?

No reason not to be a little honest—

ROMAN

I dunno, yeah, I guess. Fuck. I'm trying to get it in proportion.
But I guess, I was thinking: 'Should I be thinking, is he toast?'

Tom joins them. And then Connor joins the gang.

TOM

Is he okay? I really think we need to react?

ROMAN

By George, I think he's on to something!

Gerri comes over to Roman as Shiv speaks to Tom privately.

GERRI

Hugo's got the planes. Is he okay?

CONNOR

He's not asleep is he? Rome, should you check if—?

ROMAN

Fuck you.
                    (*nodding to Karl, Frank*)
What are they saying?

GERRI

Well, you know, they're antsy. Karl was saying if this goes
'maximum-monkey' now might be a time to take a moral stand.

ROMAN

Oh Jesus. Karl? *Karl* takes a moral stand?

Shiv comes back to them.

Guess what, Karl might have found his moral compass.

SHIV

Did he pull it out of an intern's asshole where he buried it in
1976?

GERRI

We're not getting much guidance. But no, I think they're
basically solid.

SHIV

They look solid. When they're not shaking like shitting dogs.

Frank and Karl come over with Hugo, who keeps his voice low.

HUGO

Hi, listen I'm drowning in calls and I want to deny – you know – 'speculation'. So just checking we're obviously all good if I, if I just say as a starter, that he never hurt anyone, and he never touched anyone, personally?

Shiv and Roman look like: No of course not, come on.

Good.

(*then*)

I mean, do we need to ask him, just before I go on the record on that?

ROMAN

Come on, man?

HUGO

Sure. No. Fine . . . It's just the one thing you don't want to do, PR-wise, is recant. So should someone just ask . . .?

SHIV

What, 'Hey Dad you ever rape anyone?'

HUGO

No – just—

SHIV

Here's a suggestion: how about we assume my father isn't Rape Van Winkle?

GERRI

You can reassure on that, Hugo.

HUGO

Right and these papers. I guess the question is: What's in those papers? I mean he's not gonna have put his name on anything that's gonna send him to prison. Right?

Then, out of nowhere—

LOGAN
(*calls over*)

Did you know?

(*without looking round*)

Shiv? Roman? Con? Did you know?

They approach.

                                  ROMAN
    What's that?

Maybe Logan seems surprisingly sanguine.

                                  LOGAN
    Did you know he was going to do that? I was wondering.

                                  ROMAN
    Well – obviously not, Dad.

It's unclear whether Logan believes them or not.

                                  LOGAN
    Uh-huh.

                                  ROMAN
    Kendall's mentally ill. He's insane.

                                  LOGAN
    Uh-huh.
                                  (then)
    Where's my phone?

INT. KENDALL'S CAR – DAY

*Kendall has his feet up. All on their phones. Kendall searches Twitter.
Looking at different reactions, memes that are already springing up.*

                                  KENDALL
    I think I want Lisa Arthur as my personal lawyer, but can you
    call Remi to hit me up with other names?

                                  JESS
    Uh-huh.

                                  KENDALL
    Greg – if I get taken out on other shit, I might need you to take
    my cultural temperature. Okay?

                                  GREG
    Uh-huh. Got it.
                                  (then)
    As in—? What does that—?

KENDALL

Before I get my media monitoring in place you might need to slide the socio-political thermometer up the nation's ass and take a reading, okay? I'll get seasick. Feed me the metadata, anything that's going to move the market on me reputationally, yeah?

GREG

Oh yeah. Yeah. Sure. Media monitoring department over here.

Kendall's like: Sorry man. Incoming text.

KENDALL

Everyone is telling me Lisa Arthur. Did you get her avails for me, Jess?

Then his phone goes. Bolt of electric. He looks at it buzzing. 'Dad'. He considers. Kendall gives Jess his phone. She looks at the name.

JESS
(*you want me to answer?*)

Yeah?

KENDALL

You're my ear.

His phone buzzes.

I should know what he's saying but I'm not sure it's wise for me to hear it, legally.

JESS

Okay.

He nods. She composes herself, answers.

Jess Jordan on Kendall's phone.

KENDALL
(*to Jess*)

Is it him?

JESS
(*nodding to Kendall*)

Hi.

KENDALL
(*to Jess, whispered*)

Just – listen.

23

                              JESS
   Kendall's just attending to other matters but I can pass on your
   thoughts.

We can hear indistinct noises: Logan through the receiver.

                              KENDALL
   What's he saying?

Kendall looks at Jess's face. Jess covers the receiver.

                              JESS
   You wanna know (what he's saying)—?

                              KENDALL
   Is it bad?

                              JESS
                    (*listens, then to Logan*)
   Okay. I'll tell him.
                         (*reports*)
   He says this could get ugly for him. You played a decent move.
   If you retract, say you were unwell and you misspoke, then
   maybe there's a deal here?

Kendall is tempted to take the phone. Almost praise.

                              KENDALL
   Tell him legally it's not wise for me to talk to him. But I'm going
   to be in contact with the government. This would be a good
   moment for him to step down.

Jess goes to report but—

                              JESS
   Okay, he heard.
                         (*listens*)
   He says in that case he's going to 'grind your bones to make his
   bread'.

Too weird to take seriously.

                              KENDALL
   Okay? Well tell him I'll run up off the fucking beanstalk.

Jess looks like: Really? Kendall nods: Go on—

                              JESS
Logan? Yeah, he says in that case then he'll 'run up the
beanstalk'?
                        (*hand over phone*)
He's kind of laughing. But not very nice laughing?

                            KENDALL
He should step back and cooperate. I don't want to see him
behind bars. He may no longer be a father to me, but I don't
want that.

*Logan hears this too. It flips something in him. Pours his reaction into
Jess's ear. Maybe we stay with Kendall and only hear from there or
maybe we see a little of Logan.*

                             LOGAN
That's bullshit, that's fucking sanctamonious horseshit. It was a
fucking play. It was a play, it was a fucking move, so don't act
like a stuck-up cunt to me because it won't fucking wash!

*Over the phone, we can't hear all the words but Logan is getting
louder and more horrible. Then silence as call ends.*

                            KENDALL
What did he say? Any actual physical or legal threats?

                              JESS
Um?

                            KENDALL
You know what? I don't need that in my head. Put it in an email
and send it to yourself, in case it comes up, okay?
                           (*then*)
Okay. Jess. Lisa Arthur! And let's start talking to PR outfits.
I like Clowd Mayflower, okay?

INT. SMALL CROATIAN AIRPORT – BAR AREA – DAY

Logan has ended the call. Everyone else is freaked.

                             LOGAN
Okay. Action stations. I gave him a chance. Gerri. Let's go.

The group begin to gather around him. Gerri's been thinking.

GERRI

Great. So. I suggest I call the DOJ and right away let them know
how *horrified* we were to learn about these, um, allegations
and that we intend to appoint a special committee and tell
them which of the white-shoe law firms – I have ideas – we are
considering to thoroughly investigate and promptly report back
on their findings.

LOGAN

Right. But do we cooperate?

Gerri didn't see this.

GERRI

With the government? Well there's 'cooperation' and
cooperation.
(*oh fuck*)
But we have to cooperate? I mean, we were under pressure
anyway—

ROMAN
(*interrupting*)
Well, unless we don't?

GERRI

Yeah, but real world? As a public company? We don't know
what they have or what they might get. There is really only one
play here – launch an internal, get a dialogue going with the
government, calm things down? Then maybe—
(*aside, private*)
throw in the wrenches.

LOGAN

And if I don't want to pull my panties down so fast?

ROMAN

Pull up the drawbridge. It's politically motivated, 'Come get us,
motherfuckers.' And we get—
(*coughs*)
shredding.
(*then off everyone's shudders*)
If we even need to.

LOGAN

Uh-huh?

GERRI

That's—

(*nuts*)

very aggressive.

LOGAN
(*to Roman*)

What's our story?

ROMAN

Our story is: 'It's sad he's exploiting these poor women.
You were grooming him for the top. But guess what? He's
a pathetic junkie and he blew up. He's a bitter fuck-up who
needs psychiatric help. And of course you're the big baddie, so
everyone's jumped on board.'

SHIV

And these papers?

ROMAN

Fakes. Stolen. If they even exist. Are you worried about the
papers?

Gerri looks at Logan. He shrugs, like: Probably.

Go after him for theft of corporate property. It's not nice to say
about your son – but maybe you chop him into a million pieces
and throw him in the Hudson? Destroy Kendall, it falls apart.

LOGAN

What do we think?

People are wary. Gerri won't meet his eye.

How's the price?

*Logan looks at Karl who doesn't want to break cover too much, but
has to tell the truth—*

KARL

Well, net-net it's steady.

FRANK

But – it's, I mean it's a ball of snakes. Institutions are dumping in case this kills us and arbs are buying in case Sandy and Stewy win.

GERRI

DOJ, SEC, Senate Commerce, they're all going to get into this.

SHIV

I'm afraid Ken's changed the game. Non-cooperation, now, I think it's just too hot out there. It's very high-risk.

ROMAN

Well, everything's high-risk, if you're a pussy?

SHIV

Hey I eat red meat. But the – repercussions?

ROMAN

You're looking too small. We'll do a dance – the DOJ will lean on us, Waystar resists . . . we bide our time until the election. ATN anointy-nointy the Raisin for a second term? New attorney general. By then it's all getting stale, Kendall will self-destruct because that's his favorite. It all fades the fuck away.
(like Bob Marley 'legalize it')
'Politicize it, don't criticize it.'

LOGAN

Does it track? Do we fly home and push that?

Roman and Logan are kind of high on this. Others are worried. Frank and Gerri look away. Maybe the storm will pass?

CONNOR
(eager to please)
I mean I like the aggression?

Logan looks at Tom. Gerri's looking at Tom: Say something.

TOM

I'm not sure I can love it, but I can definitely like it.

Everyone follows Logan, who looks at Frank. He hates it but can see which way Logan is leaning so . . .

FRANK

I mean I can't recommend it. But it's clear.

Gerri hates it. She pushes reservations a bit further . . .

> GERRI
>
> Sure but will the board wear it? What if we get a defection from a top-tier investor? The Ulsterman, Park?

> ROMAN
>
> We cooperate, outsiders come in. We lose control of the situation. 'Fuck you' is high-risk, but it's high reward?

Logan thinks.

> LOGAN
>
> I start saying sorry, picking at scabs, who knows where we end up. Class actions from opportunists. Admissions of wrongdoing, billions out the door.

> ROMAN
>
> I mean, fuck. Maybe you call up the attorney general right now?

> KARL
>
> Well careful. You don't take a swing from the canvas, Roman. Only kick a man when he's down.

> CONNOR
>
> The gentleman's way.

> ROMAN
>
> If he was to call up the AG and shout at him, could we find out if that would be okay?

> FRANK
> (*calling over*)
>
> Hugo, can you find out what would happen if Logan called the AG?

> LOGAN
>
> Get the Raisin. Let's go to the top. Get the president. But gentle. Okay? Anything else?

> KARL
>
> Do we want to order some lunch?

> LOGAN
>
> Lunch? Swallow. We're on fucking saliva and adrenalin till we get on a plane. Alright? No local food. I get the shits, we're fucked. No illness!

> SHIV
>
> I'll be in touch with the microbes.

> LOGAN
>
> Hugo, let's go. C'mon, we've fucking lingered long enough, let's get back!

As the group splits to exit, Frank's phone goes – he takes it and keeps his face fixed as he walks with Logan and the others . . .

Intercut with:

INT. KENDALL'S CAR – DAY

Kendall sits with his feet up on the phone. Greg is 'media monitoring'. Looking through tweets. He gives an update quietly, as Kendall dials—

> GREG
>
> Okay. You're the number-one trending topic, ahead of tater tots. There's basically way too much stuff to even track. The Pope followed you.
> (*looks at phone*)
> Okay – not the real— Is this the real—? No I think this isn't the Pope? No. It's a pope.

> KENDALL
>
> Hey. Frank? You don't need to speak. I just want to say. Sorry I didn't talk to you before but I just want to let you know – you just need to tell him time's up, okay? He steps back and we can cool this down. Someone like you steps in, lot of respect, you know? Lot of folks would put in a shift for you? Steady the ship together. I did this for you, man. For the old guard. This is exciting, Frank.

End of call.

Frank looks scared. Deletes the call record.

> KENDALL
> (*cont'd*)
>
> Gerri. Get me Gerri.

Jess dials on another phone.

JESS

Voicemail.

EXT. SMALL CROATIAN AIRPORT – DAY

Vans are waiting on the tarmac.

*The gang emerge. Gerri is on a call. Puts Michelle-Anne on hold.
Logan and the rest of the group (minus Karl) are on the move,
walking across the hot tarmac. Gerri reports to the group as they
approach the van—*

GERRI

So. The president is basically supportive but they think it might
be best for there not to be a call with you on the White House
log today?

SHIV

Like he can't make a private fucking call?

GERRI

We got offered Michelle-Anne?

SHIV

His fucking welcome mat?

GERRI

I got her if you wanna—?

*Logan thinks, looks at Shiv and Roman. Different faces. Shiv looks:
Yes. Roman looks: Maybe.*

LOGAN

No. Fuck it. No. I don't talk to the babysitter. You sound her
out.

GERRI
(*into phone*)

That would be great.

*Logan looks at Frank who nods like: Smart move. Logan clocks
something's amiss.*

LOGAN

Where's Karl?

FRANK

(*enjoying landing Karl in it*)

Really feels he needs a sandwich.

Logan shakes his head.

I tried to tell him.

Over with Willa and Connor. Willa's looking at an email on her phone.

WILLA

Ooh! Uptick in ticket sales.

Connor looks.

For my play?

CONNOR

Okay well that's good, why, I wonder?

WILLA

'Why'?

CONNOR

I mean. I know why. People are finally getting it. I mean it took me a while to get it.

WILLA

Yeah well I put in a number of deliberate obstacles, you know? I never wanted to be like – 'blah blah – funny funny, oooooh what's gonna happen next?'

CONNOR

Yeah no sure, I hate that.

Gerri gets connected. They climb aboard the van.

GERRI

Michelle? Gerri Kellman. How you doing? Listen just wanted to say it was all nonsense and we know the president will be supportive but we just wanted to offer to answer any questions he has?

Logan nods for her to put her on speakerphone.

MICHELLE-ANNE
(*on speakerphone*)
Hi, yeah, Gerri, I think he just feels for Logan at this difficult time?

GERRI
Great well, let him know we don't want to interrupt him with this – funky chowder.

MICHELLE-ANNE
Well that's appreciated. And is Logan okay?

GERRI
He's great. Yeah. Kendall's just going through some stuff and we're sad he's exploiting these poor women is our thing.

MICHELLE-ANNE
Right. Okay. Well I'll pass that on. Good to connect.

GERRI
And look, we don't need favors—

MICHELLE-ANNE
We hear you.

GERRI
We just wouldn't – simply in terms of resources – want for DOJ to follow Kendall off down his rabbit hole of bitterness.

MICHELLE-ANNE
Okay, well, you know how much the president respects Logan. Okay?

Is that the offer of a deal?

GERRI
Great, so off the record, what's the temperature at Main Justice, any danger of them or Southern District going Batman on this?

That's a bit of a push . . .

MICHELLE-ANNE
The attorney general is very smart.

GERRI
We all love Bhavick. He'll see through this, right?

> MICHELLE-ANNE

It's just the DAG likes to think she's something of a 'straight shooter'. Marilyn's prickly. So that's your only issue: Marilyn.

> GERRI

Well, maybe you should just fire her!

Everyone laughs.

> MICHELLE-ANNE

It's just a question of political capital. You know? We have challenges and Kendall's allegations are vivid, Justice can't do nothing.

Static buzz.

> GERRI

Well they could?

> MICHELLE-ANNE

It's out of our hands.

> GERRI

Unless you grab it?

No response. Logan looks at Gerri: Don't fuck this up.

Okay, well look we don't want to fall out with him.

> MICHELLE-ANNE

Well no, he's the president.

> GERRI

No sure. But, do we want to get, the old guys on the blower so they can just chat for five?

> MICHELLE-ANNE
> (nope)

This will all be great, Gerri. Just find me whenever, on anything, okay?

Logan puts a finger across his neck: This call is over.

> GERRI

Okay I appreciate getting a read. Many thanks.

Logan looks downbeat. Heavy atmosphere. That didn't go well.

Yeah. Good?

FRANK

Good work. Basically supportive. Feels good.

Shiv looks at Roman, dubious.

LOGAN

Uh-huh.

Everyone is quiet. Hugo arrives at the door of the van.

HUGO

Okay we're fueled and tooled. We all set for New York City and a fuckfest?

Shiv gets a call. Gets out and away. Logan looks a bit scared as Shiv looks back at Logan, who is looking at the aircrew – a pilot by the plane door laughing with the hostess.

INT. KENDALL'S CAR – DAY

Kendall is feeling positive – all sing-song and insinuating—

KENDALL

Oh, Shiv? Shivvy? How you going there? You ready to come over? I got a spot for you? Everything's coming up roses, Shivvy! Just stay quiet and I'll talk—

Shiv ends the call. Kendall isn't too bumped.

Okay. Jess. What we got?

JESS
(*looks*)
Independent directors. Opinion-shapers, A-list. Then you got: Ewan, Laird, your mom, Greg's mom, Marcia?
(*then*)
Greg – how's—?

GREG

Um, I mean – headline: The internet is big obviously, and I haven't— I couldn't read it all, but – overview is – there's a lot about you. A ton. That's the big picture right now from here at media monitoring.

KENDALL

But is it positive?

GREG

Super-positive. The negative stuff does tend to stick in the mind because it's quite, uh, visceral. But yeah. Basically great.

Kendall makes a call on his own phone as Jess lines up his next call.

KENDALL

Nay? Hey. I've got a million calls, but I wanted to say hi.

NAOMI
(*on speakerphone*)

Hey. Well, fuck me.

KENDALL

You're on speakerphone.

NAOMI

Well, why, pencil-dick?

No reason, he likes the drama of the public interactions—

KENDALL

Fuck you. Because it's – simpler. Did you see it?

NAOMI

Uh-huh. Seems like maybe you're the best man in the world?

KENDALL

Yeah fuck you.

NAOMI

I mean but maybe you are?

KENDALL

Okay, 'hahahah', sure. But what if I am?

NAOMI

Right. Funny. But maybe you are?

KENDALL

Sure, sure. But joking aside perhaps I am though, have you considered that?

NAOMI

No sure.
(*then*)
But just seriously for a second here, what if you really are?

JESS

Ken? We're nearly—

They're approaching Waystar. Jess gets a text or email.

KENDALL

Nay. I'm arriving at Waystar. Can you come see me?

JESS

Um, I— Remi says they might be trying to suspend your access?

KENDALL

Later, Nay. I love you.

(*end of call*)

Well, they can't.

JESS

Sure. But they maybe did?

KENDALL

Do I want pictures of me not being let in? As my next visual?

He looks at Greg. Greg shrugs. Kendall thinks.

Fuck it, keep driving. There's press at my place, yeah?

JESS

Yeah. Where are we going?

GREG

Fuck. This is like – this is like OJ. I mean except if OJ never killed anyone.

KENDALL

How'd you know I never killed anyone?

Greg smiles, unsure.

Capitalism, baby! You don't get to be ultra-high-net-worth without a few wage slaves throwing themselves out of windows in Guangdong on my account. Right? Yup! For my sake Indians fucking toil on Brazilian coffee plantations and young dreamers are muscled out of their patent rights, boyee!

Kendall laughs, high and self-ironizing. Greg smiles, maybe high-fives.

EXT. CROATIAN AIRFIELD – DAY

Now everyone is standing around on the tarmac by the jet. Gerri, Frank and Roman with Logan. Hugo is nearby, handling logistics with airport staff.

Connor and Willa – she's looking at messages. Tom is on a phone call – ends it. Returns to Shiv who ponders to herself, post-call, looking at the groups.

> TOM

Hey. You okay?

> SHIV

Uh-huh. I guess. I guess.

> TOM
> (*sympathetic*)

Wondering if you've maybe cuffed yourself to the *Titanic* here?

She looks at him.

And there's this little, fucking lifeboat called Kendall spinning donuts while we sink?
> (*then*)

Are you thinking about life jackets?

She looks at him, doesn't quite feel able to be totally frank – as he gets a call from Cyd—

> SHIV

I need to look after my dad, Tom.

On Willa and Connor. She looks sad.

> CONNOR

Which plane you want? I like lefty? You okay?

> WILLA

Yeah. Just the play. The tickets.

He looks at her.

The sales are up because – people are hate-watching it. Apparently it's saying on social media it's become a hate-watch?

> CONNOR

What's a hate-watch?

> WILLA

Well what do you think?

> CONNOR

Is it when you hate something but you watch it?

> WILLA

Correct.

> CONNOR

Oh. Oh honey. Honey, I'm sorry.

> WILLA

It's fine. You know Van Gogh died unrecognized, so, hate-watch
me, fine. You're still actually getting—
> *(motions to a fizzing head)*
zapped with all my messages. So. I win. Ha-ha.

Shiv walks over to Roman and Frank.

> SHIV

So we loading up—?

*Frank warns her with his eyes, Shiv stops – there is confusion and
unease.*

> FRANK

Just one moment, Shiv.
> *(with a warning:)*
'We' are just thinking.

*The 'we' is Logan. He is looking at his phone and talking to Gerri
who scribbles on paper, phone at her ear.*

Shiv looks: What? Roman looks back: Easy, Dad's fragile.

> ROMAN

We might want to drug-test the pilots. He doesn't like the look
of the aircrew.

Gerri is returning to the group—

> SHIV

We okay, Gerri?

                    GERRI
                    (no)
Uh-huh. Yup. Great. All good. I'm just gonna talk to Hugo.
Because we're thinking of going now, in the first instance, to
Sarajevo.

                    SHIV
Sorry, what the fuck. To *Sarajevo*?

                    CONNOR
Great, because all good things start in Sarajevo?

                    GERRI
Think he got a little freaked by Michelle-Anne.

Gerri discreetly hands Shiv an envelope with names scrawled on.

Got a few options to consider?

Shiv looks at them. Roman reads.

                    ROMAN
'Bahrain, Bosnia, Kuwait, Lebanon, Maldives, Morocco, Qatar,
Saudi Arabia, the Vatican'?

                    SHIV
                    (a thought lands)
Okay. Fuck.

Roman doesn't see it.

What do all those countries have in common?

                    ROMAN
They're all made up? They're all lands with dragons?

                    SHIV
I imagine none of them have an extradition treaty with the US?

Gerri nods as she goes off.

                    ROMAN
Oh. Okay. Fuck.

Tom gets off the phone, returns.

TOM

One thing we could do is discreetly dangle some juicy contributor contracts down the line for the more 'responsible' prosecutors?

SHIV

We might be going to Sarajevo.

TOM

To Sarajevo? Excuse me the fuck?

ROMAN

It's fine. Shut up.

TOM

Oh sure. Sounds – normal. Nothing to see here.

CONNOR

Hey archduke, let's go to Sarajevo.

ROMAN

Might just be for lunch?

TOM

Right. The longest fucking lunch. Logan Polanski.

LOGAN

Hey?

Shiv, Tom and Roman, Connor go over for a private counsel. Gerri too.

Look, I'm not sure how much cover I have. What you think? Am I fucked?

Silence. Will anyone speak up? Gerri judges now might be the moment to say what's on her mind.

GERRI

Honestly. Look, I just don't know about non-cooperation. We're a Fortune 500. We can't play corporate jazz. The shareholder meet coming up? Sandy and Stewy will be rubbing their hands.

Logan looks around, at Roman.

ROMAN

I still like saying fuck 'em and killing my brother. It just feels so right.

CONNOR

This is a can of worms for me, Pops. I'll give you counsel, but it has to be in a lead-lined room.

Logan looks like: Thanks, later. Looks at Shiv.

SHIV

I dunno. My gut is cooperate. But my gut isn't your gut.

Logan looks at Tom.

TOM

You're gonna win this, Loge. It's just what is the cleanest win?

LOGAN

I need to talk to a lawyer on my position. Who's a tough bastard?

TOM

Sort of Layo Upton-type motherfucker?

GERRI

A woman would be great right now. Like a Lisa Arthur?

Frisson – few people glance at Shiv, who looks down.

LOGAN

She did the hookers? Right.

GERRI

She repped the trafficked sex workers yes, be great to have her credibility.

FRANK

There are three or four good women, but Lisa has an excellent brain. She's a winner?

GERRI

You go with Layo, people will be like he's going scorched earth, 'Maybe he can fight it.' You get Lisa, people will be like 'Gee, maybe this is bullshit.'

Logan looks around.

LOGAN

Could I get her?

TOM
(*does she want to say?*)
Well Shiv— Right?

SHIV
Um, Lisa? I know her yeah. Yeah, she's a pretty— She's a friend.

LOGAN
Could you get her for me?

SHIV
Um. I dunno. She loves money and she fucking loves winning.
She's great. I just don't—

Logan considers. He angles his body to talk to just Shiv.

LOGAN
Listen, cooperate or not, to keep the board sweet, I'm thinking
I might have to take a step back?

*She wants him to be safe. But calculates, maybe it would be good for
her if she could put some distance between them?*

SHIV
Right. So, who, who would . . .?

It's like he hasn't heard this.

LOGAN
I don't want to go back right now. You think that plays?

*Is this a watershed moment – is it best for her to start distancing
herself? Shiv answers by tenderly stroking his back.*

SHIV
I want you safe, number one.

Then—

LOGAN
(*to the group*)
Okay. Gerri and Shiv and Roman are going back to manage
New York. Make contacts. No need to go running back like a
slapped girl, looks weak.

FRANK
You want me to go—?

> LOGAN
> (*'friendly'*)
> No, I can't trust you, you stay with me, and Karl for board
> liaison. Tom here on ATN. Okay? I'll make a call on the lawyer.
> I like Layo but let me think. Council of war on the plane!
> (*to Roman*)
> Go on, get the fuck back there, Tumbledown Dick.

*Logan motions for his gang to head to the other plane. He gives
Roman's head a ruffle. Connor looks disconsolate at being left out.
Willa nudges him. He looks like: No.*

> WILLA
> And, ahem, Logan? Do you need—?

> LOGAN
> Con? Yeah. Very important. Can you – hold the fort here? Can
> you keep this – all secured?

> CONNOR
> Hold the Balkans with just two divisions? I can try.

People head to planes.

Thanks.

Willa smiles: It's nothing.

> And, listen, my guy was in touch and they wanted to know if we
> wanted to do a marketing push, on the play.

> WILLA
> Okay?

> CONNOR
> On the hate-watch angle, like get together all the worst reviews
> like 'kill yourself if you get a ticket' and um, the one about—

> WILLA
> Yeah I know them, Con—

> CONNOR
> Right. Jump on the irono-cycle and turn it into a thing for the
> hipsters and the dipshits? We could get a nice little return?

WILLA

Oh. Okay? Uh-huh. Sure. Yeah. I mean. Yeah. That sounds –
exciting.

CONNOR

Yeah? Hate-watch hit, bank the bile?

WILLA

Sure. Why not. Yeah. Really funny.

They both look sad as everyone heads off.

As Shiv goes, Tom comes for a word before she goes.

TOM

Uh-huh. Look, we can talk about – things, I guess when we're
back yeah?

SHIV

Right. Sure. Okay. Cos, look, I love you.

TOM

Uh-huh. Thank you.

*But he hasn't said it back, she notices. But she refuses to look needy.
She looks at Logan. Tom sees her look.*

You know, it's okay. You will see him again.

SHIV

Well obviously I'll see him again.
(*then*)
Why would you even say that?

TOM

I'm being nice, Shiv. If you're worried he won't be able to come
home, that's unlikely.

SHIV

Well I know that. Thanks.

TOM

Well, good. Great. It's fine.

Beat.

SHIV

Did Ken call you?

                              TOM
                             (*yes*)
   Me? Did he call me? No. No. Not to speak. Why, did he call
   you?

Can she tell he's lying? Maybe that's what makes her adjust?

                             SHIV
   No. Not – not— No. I just wondered. Okay. Look after him
   yeah? Stay in touch?

They kiss briefly as they part.

*Karl hurries towards the plane eating a sandwich, or carrying food
and drink.*

EXT. NEW YORK – RAVA'S PLACE – DAY

*Jess is outside the car, briefing a couple of guys from a security firm
that she has been in contact with.*

*Kendall finishes up a call and heads into the house, followed by Greg.
Let in by a housekeeper Kendall knows.*

INT. NEW YORK – RAVA'S PLACE – DAY

                            KENDALL
                           (*calling*)
   Hey?!

*They make it in, or up, and Rava comes to greet him. She's been
working from home.*

                             RAVA
   Hey. You okay, how you doing?

                            KENDALL
   I'm good. I'm good. Yeah.

                             RAVA
   Good.
                             (*then*)
   Wow? Huh? You really did it, huh?

                            KENDALL
   Yeah, well, it's been in the mail.

RAVA

It has been in the mail.

KENDALL

You know, you always said— So. It was either this, or you
know, go to Mount Athos and become a monk.

RAVA

Right, monastery on Mount Athos. Is it a tax haven now? So.
What did you come for? A pat on the back?

*They smile. She respects his move. His inability to challenge Logan
was a big deal between them.*

KENDALL

Press are swarming my place and I need a hidey-hole. Plus
I actually just wanted to see you and the kids? You know, I –
kind of, I mean, it was kind of for you guys?

RAVA
(*c'mon*)

Yeah well.

*Behind them Jess is coming in with the two security guys. Jess knows
Rava well – they say hi.*

KENDALL

Is it okay if I bring in the guys?

RAVA

Uh-huh? Are they – vetted?

KENDALL

They're legit, right, Jess? All the Emirati use the firm.

RAVA

Amazing.

KENDALL

Is this okay? To do a few calls? I wouldn't ask if I had options?

*She knows what is being asked, not crazy about it. But this sort of
goes deeper.*

RAVA

Of course. Sure. Go ahead.

> KENDALL

Thank you. Thanks, Rava.

He has a warm feeling of home, of respect. Rava and Kendall walk towards what will be his war room.

> RAVA

I didn't see, I'm up against it with work but people are saying you did great?

> KENDALL

Whatever, I don't know. I mean you might want to watch it.
> (*looks at her*)

I'm talking to Lisa Arthur?

> RAVA

Great. Well she's famous.

> KENDALL

Yeah. Well. Do you think it's going to work? Can I win?

> RAVA

I don't know, Ken.

> KENDALL

No. Right. Right.

He almost laughs at himself for wanting the reassurance.

INT. LOGAN'S PLANE – DAY

On their plane, Frank, Tom and Karl look over at Logan.

> KARL

How you feeling?

> FRANK
> (*not telling you*)

I'm 'looking forward to seeing more of the Balkans'.

> KARL

Uh-huh.
> (*then*)

Is this the worst?

FRANK

Well there were the tabloid suicides? When we nearly
went kablooey because of Argentina? The Tiananmen
Accommodations? The Black Cloud after Sally-Anne? I don't
know. He's the comeback kid.

KARL

Uh-huh but Senate, FBI, SEC? Class actions. Plus Sandy and
Stewy? I mean that's a twelve-foot sub of poisonous tree frogs.

HUGO

Gentlemen?

He's summoning them over to Logan. Logan's energy has changed—

LOGAN

So. This is where I'm landing. For Waystar, three white-shoe
firms on retainer. And the next best five, let's play footsie, see if
we can tie them up with conflicts.

KARL

Okay.

LOGAN

Once I have my personal legal position figured out they'll
coordinate with corporate legal and crisis PR.

HUGO

Uh-huh.

LOGAN

Calls in to my brother, Marcia. You two touch base with Senate
and house surrogates, payroll commentators and friends.
(*then*)
I want everyone lawyered up. Set a joint defense meeting with
my counsel, and the Waystar lead firm to lock down our list of
counsel for individuals.
(*then*)
Tom, me to see editorial on anything on this across ATN
and global cable and print outlets. We pressure-point other
operations, the line is, don't lean on this it's bendy as fuck. Play
it smart today and you won't look a cunt tomorrow.

(*then*)
Karl, I need to talk to the top-twelve shareholders in the next thirty minutes. Emergency board meeting ASAP and they're going to be rolling for the next week, okay?
(*nods*)
Hugo, I imagine most of that is obvious and in train, right?

HUGO
(*kinda*)
Largely in hand. Largely in hand.

FRANK
Great and in terms of cooperation or—?

LOGAN
It's war. Fuck off. Good?

Everyone takes it in – not great.

TOM
Good.

LOGAN
But we throw them this.
(*then the big one*)
I'll step back as CEO.

FRANK
Okay, fuck.

TOM
Are you sure?

LOGAN
(*with a smile*)
Obviously on operational matters I will expect to have informal input.

This clearly has a double meaning.

So as I step back, temporarily. Who do we like as CEO?

They all consider what to say. Silence in the court.

I don't give a fuck. It's nameplates. C'mon. Brain dump. Speak. Let a hundred flowers bloom! No comeback.

KARL

(after a beat and a cough)

Well. I have to say I look good?

Chuckles.

What? I like me. Why not?

FRANK

Just the fresh face we're looking for.

LOGAN

Karl, if you've got cleans hands it's only cos your whorehouse also does manicures.

Laughs. Pally and very male – Tom's excited to be in on this.

FRANK

I mean I imagine you're looking at a kid. Or Gerri?

Logan looks at him.

But if you want – if you want someone short term, who knows the place inside out—

LOGAN

Frank? You're not trusted. You're mashed potatoes.

FRANK

Okay. Uh-huh. Yep can see that.

LOGAN

I'd like a kid obviously. So Roman or Shiv. But we'd love a woman, so Shiv or Gerri. But I'd like experience so Roman or Gerri?

Tom gets up to use the bathroom.

INT. SHIV AND ROMAN'S PLANE – DAY

On their plane – Shiv's answering her phone.

SHIV

Hello?

Intercut with:

INT. LOGAN'S PLANE – BATHROOM

Tom's in the plane bathroom sitting on the closed toilet.

> TOM
>
> So listen. They're playing fucking dice with God next door? He's picking a new CEO in real time.

> SHIV
>
> Hold on. Let me check that?

She gets up and moves away. Heads to another section.

> Okay, what? Interim?

> TOM
>
> Sure. But you know, how long will this last? VW was like five years. Walmart took a decade.

> SHIV
>
> And what's the temperature?

> TOM
>
> It's free-form, 'let a hundred flowers bloom'?

> SHIV
>
> Oh sure! But listen, do you want it?

The thought has crossed his mind.

> TOM
>
> Me? What? Are you crazy?

Line buzzes.

> Shiv. No I don't think that's even, with the hearings and cruises? No I think. I mean. I think—

> SHIV
>
> So you're okay to push me?

> TOM
>
> Well sure. That's what I wanted to know. He's gonna fight, he says. You wanna be the face of that?

> SHIV
> (*thinks*)
> You can get too fucking clever with this, right?

Knock knock.

> HUGO
> (*off*)
> You having problems in there, buddy? Can't find a vein?

> TOM
> (*to Hugo, savage*)
> Watch it, fuckhead!
> (*then to Shiv*)
> I gotta go. But look, if it's going, you want it?

> SHIV
> Oh fuck! I don't wanna get buried like Miss Havisham with a bonnet full of clever fucking stratagems. Yes. Yes. Okay. Yes! Get in there and hustle, baby, hustle!

INT. RAVA'S PLACE – KENDALL'S WAR ROOM – DAY

Greg is on the phone, on hold. Two women wait to see Kendall. Crisis PR professionals – Berry and Comfrey. Berry, high status, is doing three other things. Comfrey politely smiles at Greg.

> GREG
> Hey. I was doing his media monitoring for a while but I guess? Yeah?

Comfrey smiles.

> COMFREY
> Yeah that would be us.

> GREG
> I wrote down a lot of tweets, but, I'm not sure that's useful to hand over?

> COMFREY
> Uh-huh. We can probably find those.

> GREG
> (*explaining*)
> On hold.

(then)

Yeah. Just – just cancelling my mom's credit card.

COMFREY

Okay? Nice.

GREG

No. I mean. When my grandpa cut her off – long story –
I guaranteed her gold card but now after Ken's press conference,
she's under the impression that Waystar is going down and she's
panic-buying NutriBullets and *a lot* of Kruggerands. And she
never even drinks the smoothies, so?

COMFREY

Sure.

GREG

(gets through)

Hi. Hi.

Comfrey looks at him, like: Not great. He looks at Comfrey. Then, for her benefit—

You know what, it's fine. It's fine. Wave it through, yup, all of it.

And . . . Kendall is there.

KENDALL

Hey, hey, hey! Berry fucking Schneider! Come in – sit, sit. How
you doing?

BERRY

Great. Great. Good to see you, Ken. This is Comfrey? Can we
just say, right off, some jobs are money jobs, some are heart
jobs.

COMFREY

We loved what you did.

BERRY

We'd love to work with you.

KENDALL

And I'd love to work with you, but if it's cool and I know you
guys are the best, but is it okay if it's still a pitch?

> BERRY

Of course! So. We have a lot of thoughts: communication planning and positioning thoughts. How we can leverage our relationships with significant writers at major outlets. Prepare to prime and amplify some impressive secondaries.

> KENDALL

Great, great shall I talk or will you?

> BERRY

Well we want to hear your thoughts, but you wanna hear just like our five points?

> KENDALL

Sure, you go.

(but just to add)

But I think the headline needs to be fuck the weather – we're changing the cultural climate. But you go.

> BERRY

Great I mean—

> KENDALL

For context, I'm talking to the *Times* about an op-ed. Draft an alternative corporate manifesto. Drop a – rapid-reaction TEDx.

> BERRY

Well, that's great.

> KENDALL

It's cheesy as fuck but, I need people to see this was part of a coherent philosophy, not just punching an old guy in the fucking nose, right?

> BERRY

Right. Right. That's, in line with our thoughts.

> KENDALL

I realize I'm talking too much. You guys jump in, but I was thinking a really significant donation, to a an addicts' shelter, like today? They'll hit me with my history in that area for sure. I'm sorry.

> BERRY

No go on – I think that's great. That is.

>   KENDALL

Yeah well I may as well say, on a dumb level, I'd like my Twitter
to be off the hook. This could all get super-earnest, so I was
thinking of hitting up some *BoJack* guys, some *Lampoon* kids
to just smash that shit, make my feed a little powder keg people
need to check in with?

>   BERRY

Like cool tweets that position you?

Kendall looks at her.

>   KENDALL

Yeah that would be the straight-leg chino way of putting it.
'Cool tweets'.

>   BERRY

Fuck you!

>   KENDALL

I'm kidding. I know you guys are the best. I'm sorry, let's get
into this. I want to work with you if you can work with me?

>   BERRY

Sure. Well we think you're going to win this and we like
winners!

INT. SHIV AND ROMAN'S PLANE – DAY

Shiv returns from the bathroom.

>   ROMAN

Interesting call?

>   SHIV

What? Oh. No. No, just bullshit.

>   ROMAN

Oh 'just bullshit'? Right. So boring.

He lets her read her phone for a beat, staring at her.

I hate boring shit, don't you?

>   SHIV

What?

ROMAN

I just hate boring phone calls about bullshit. They're so boring, aren't they, Shiv?

She looks at Gerri, clocks something is going on.

Yeah because Gerri just heard from Frank? Dad's live-picking a new CEO.

SHIV

Oh? Okay.

ROMAN

'Oh okay'. Tom didn't mention that?

SHIV

Oh, no, okay. Right. Now you mention it, maybe he did?

ROMAN

Fuck you!

Shiv looks at Gerri.

SHIV

How come Frank told you and how come you told him?

GERRI

I'm just a very straightforward person, Shiv.

SHIV

So, what have you heard?

GERRI

Well, I have heard that there are a number of names in contention.

ROMAN

Wanna make it interesting, put a little money on the table?

SHIV

You know what, I'm already pretty fucking interested so I think I'm good?

EXT. SARAJEVO – EVENING

Arrival in Sarajevo. Logan deplanes to waiting cars.

Logan heads into the hotel.

INT. SARAJEVO HOTEL — EVENING

Logan, Tom, Karl, Frank sit around discussing.

> LOGAN
>
> Gerri is clean, right?

> FRANK
>
> Well, I mean. Up to a point?

> LOGAN
>
> She was nowhere near cruises was she when – when, you know?

> FRANK
>
> She was in the UK on all that regulatory shit I think during the time in question.

> TOM
>
> I have to say, I do like Gerri.

> LOGAN
>
> Oh you like Gerri?

Logan looks at him, scoping him out.

> TOM
>
> Uh-huh. I do.

> LOGAN
>
> You playing the reverse banjo, son? You trying to black-spot her?

> TOM
>
> Nope. No. I do. Very stolid. And I like Roman.

> LOGAN
>
> Oh you like Roman? And what about yourself, Tom?

> TOM
>
> Oh me? What?!

> LOGAN
>
> Kind of like family? Kind of new blood?

> TOM
>
> Yeah, well that's very— But no. No. I think – that's a little – rich for my blood just yet.

LOGAN

Uh-huh. What about Shiv?

TOM

Well, Shiv's great.

FRANK

I like Shiv. But no experience. And Roman, great, *but*—

LOGAN
(*to Frank*)
You don't think Roman's ready?

FRANK

Do you?

LOGAN
(*could be*)
Is anybody ready? Was I ready?

FRANK

Sure. Sure.

LOGAN

He's not all fucking 'meh meh meh'. Plus I'll be pulling the strings. Right?

Karl sees which way the wind is blowing.

KARL

I like Roman.

TOM

I like Roman.

FRANK

Of course I like Roman.

LOGAN

Sure you do! He'll fucking fire you on day one!

His phone goes. He answers—

Uh-huh?

Intercut with:

INT. SHIV AND ROMAN'S PLANE – TOILET – DAY

Roman in the bathroom or a separate area. He's nervy.

> ROMAN
>
> Dad. Can I speak for one moment?

> LOGAN
>
> Sure.

> ROMAN
>
> Look, it's already getting out what you're thinking about so can I just throw a couple of things in the – old lobster pot?

> LOGAN
>
> Uh-huh.

> ROMAN
>
> I think it should be me.

> LOGAN
>
> Okay?

> ROMAN
>
> It's my time. I think I can do it, I want it and I think I can. So.

Logan likes this. It's right there for Roman. But how long can he wait for his dad to speak? He can't see Logan's face and the silence is killing him . . .

> LOGAN / ROMAN
>
> Okay— / But—

> ROMAN
>
> What? You say?

> LOGAN
>
> Nothing – you go.

> ROMAN
>
> Okay. Well I think it should be me. *But.* If you don't think I'm ready, okay, which I would understand and I'm not saying I agree, but you know, a couple of years under the wing of an older, hen, could, you know, see me crack out of the old egg? So can I just say, I know you've been sweet on Shiv, and I love her,

like a brother, haha, but I just don't think this is the time. You know? All bitterness aside, I do wonder if it isn't Gerri time. Let the, stone-cold bitch do it? She's tough, she's got the good chromosomes. So, if it ain't Romey time maybe it's croney time, right?

LOGAN

Uh-huh.

ROMAN

I hope I haven't offended?

A certain sadness from Logan.

LOGAN

Nope. Thanks, kid. Thank you.

ROMAN

Have you made a decision?

LOGAN

You've given me food for thought.

ROMAN

Okay. Well. I'd love it but you know, I understand. But I do want it. Okay? But, you know. No hard feelings. So. Listen, I'm gabbling. I love you.

LOGAN

Uh-huh.

End of call. Roman breathes. Good job. Logan looks at phone.

Roman's out.

EXT. TETERBORO AIRPORT – DAY

The plane lands.

INT. SHIV AND ROMAN'S PLANE – DAY

Inside, as the plane taxis, Shiv and Roman and Gerri wait, checking their phones. A call to Shiv. 'Dad' on the display.

GERRI

Who is it – is it him?

Roman watches intently as Shiv takes the call.

> SHIV

Hey.

> *(listens)*

Okay. Okay, Dad. Well great thanks. Thank you. Sure I can do it. I can.

She ends the call.

> ROMAN

What?

Roman studies her face – she gives a little smile.

> *(feeling sick)*

Oh fuck! Fuck! Go on.

> SHIV

He wants me to get Lisa.

He looks at her – can tell it's the truth.

> ROMAN

You fucking bitch.

Shiv smiles a smile of her innate confidence.

> SHIV

Uh-huh. He said, you two just wait airport adjacent – he might need someone, on investors. You might have to go to Boston to see the Ulsterman. Or, you know, hijack a plane and fly him to Cuba?

> ROMAN

And he didn't say – about CEO?

> SHIV

Oh yeah no, he said, it's me.

He looks at her.

> ROMAN

Yeah, fuck you.

EXT. SHIV'S CAR – DAY

Shiv rides into the city. She looks out.

INT. LISA'S LAW FIRM – LOBBY – NIGHT

Shiv goes through security and into the elevator.

INT. LISA'S OFFICE – NIGHT

Shiv is shown in, Lisa takes charge of the room.

> SHIV
>
> Hey, Lisa! How you doing, goddess?!

> LISA
>
> Hey, Shiv.

> SHIV
>
> How's things, this place is amazing – how's everything, how's—?

> LISA
>
> Great, yeah, so listen, I'm just going to jump right in because I don't want this to be difficult with a friend and I hope I've not wasted your time because—

> SHIV
>
> Yeah the message came through. You can't act for my dad.

Okay? New vibe. But Lisa is being careful. She's had a call from Kendall's office.

> LISA
>
> Right. I don't think I fit so—

> SHIV
>
> Okay but, cards on the table. I want to talk to you about something else.

> LISA
>
> Oh, okay?

> SHIV
>
> Yeah. I'm thinking about my own position.

Lisa looks at her.

> And honestly, I could do with a friend. A discreet friend with legal training. A consigliere. A, a smart savvy woman who can help me navigate the position I find myself in.

                            LISA

Right, that's kind – but that's not the kind of role I normally
take on.

                            SHIV

Look. Honestly, honestly, I just have nowhere to fucking – turn,
Lise? My husband is a player in this. One world I could be in a
position to come out here as CEO. Or I might have to leave the
operation to preserve my reputation. I don't know what my dad
did or my brother did or the firm did and, I'm in a fucking –
fuck pie here. Can I clean it up? I don't know. I have a plan,
but I could easily get fucking crushed between these men, and,
and I need to game shit out and I need to do that with someone
who can give me a read, legally, culturally, politically, socially,
because it's a lot. And I trust you and—

*This is getting difficult for Lisa now, she might want to take the gig
with Kendall.*

                            LISA

Okay look – stop. Shiv.
                    (*then*)
I can't give you legal advice and you should not give me any
confidential information. Okay?

Lisa gives poker face. Uncomfortable. Shiv studies her. A realization.

                            SHIV

Oh. Okay. Fuck. Jesus. Okay? Right? Does that mean what
I think it means?

                            LISA

Are we done?

                            SHIV

Okay well. I would just say, think about who you want to hitch
your wagon to, honey, because a lot of wagons are going in the
ditch.

                            LISA

Right. Thanks ,'honey'. Shall we draw this to a close?

                            SHIV

You'd actually consider working with that disingenuous little
fuck-doll? Because he's not on the level, Lisa.

LISA

Shiv. I am not available to help you. If for some reason that changes I will let you know. Okay?

Shiv looks at her.

SHIV

Oh sure. Sure. Well. Thanks, *pal.*

INT. RAVA'S PLACE — NIGHT

Kendall comes out of his war room to make a request. Rava is through in the kitchen or other room beyond, talking to the housekeeper.

KENDALL
(*calling through, checking*)
Hey Rav? I got more folks?

Rava waves: Sure thing.

And just as an FYI, is it cool if, Naomi Pierce comes up?

Rava comes to talk to Kendall.

RAVA

Sure, she is the – is she the Pierce person?

KENDALL

Yeah. And you know we had, have, a little thing going?

RAVA

Fine. Yeah. I heard.

KENDALL

She's really good for me, Rav. Is it cool? Not weird?

RAVA

Sure.

Rava nods.

KENDALL

Look at us, huh? Ah? And I saw the razors, so, yeah?

RAVA

What?

KENDALL

In your bathroom, whose are those?

RAVA

Why were you in my bathroom?

KENDALL

Why? Because – I don't like to take a dump where the staff go?

RAVA

Right? Ken, those don't actually mean—

KENDALL

No? Male razors?

RAVA

Um – well – no. They're less expensive.

KENDALL

Oh, so I'm not giving you enough money for gender-appropriate razors now?

RAVA

Ken – I'm not having this conversation.

KENDALL

I'm kidding. This isn't that conversation. I'm kidding.

Jess is bringing up Lisa and Keith, another lawyer.

Hey, Team Genius!

KEITH

Too kind.

The lawyers head into the war room as Kendall bows, courtly.

KENDALL
(*to Rava*)

It'll just be four or five hours?

RAVA

It's fine.

Then Naomi makes it upstairs. She has takeout bags.

KENDALL

Okay. Incoming. Here she is now! Here she is!

(then, introducing)

Rava – Naomi.

They don't know what to say. Naomi is friendly, but doesn't push herself on the kids.

> NAOMI
> *(to Rava)*
> Hey. Good to meet you. And—
> *(re having her in her home)*
> Thank you.

> RAVA
> Oh, you know, not at all.

Rava is backing away, heading out of the area with a smile of forbearance. Kendall's phone goes with a text.

> KENDALL
> Greg – I should, I need to— Can you, help us yeah?

Greg, who is on his phone, takes his orders – he will aid Naomi. They head through.

Kendall heads in to see Keith and Lisa.

He's still in Europe! He's scared! My dad's gone to Sarajevo.

This lands with Lisa.

Lisa!

> LISA
> Hey so I should make it clear this is just a preliminary – so no confidential information?

> KENDALL
> Sure. Sure. Well, listen, what can I tell you? My dad's the devil, he runs a crime ring and I would love to hire you because you're a superstar and I think you can take down my dad and, and this will be the case of the century and the highlight of your career.

> LISA
> Okay. Okay. Well that might be—

> KENDALL
> I'm serious. They'll make a movie about you. *We* should make a movie about you!

Lisa smiles.

> LISA

Right. And how would that look?

> KENDALL

It would look amazing, because it would be brilliant!

> LISA

Okay look, this is quite a complex situation to progress because – as I understand it you want to help take down your dad but without implicating yourself?

> KENDALL

Correct.

> LISA

And without damaging the company to the extent that you lose control at your shareholder meeting.

> KENDALL

Who will play you in the movie you think?

> LISA

And you know that Shiv and I did have a – friend – relationship?

> KENDALL

Yeah well, that might work out anyway.

> LISA

Okay, well that's for you two, but – first things. Has the government reached out to you or have you received a subpoena for the documents yet?

> KENDALL

No. And look – to be clear. I will do whatever you tell me to do. I am your puppet.

> LISA

Well in the first instance, we need to make sure that you are in the clear with our friends at One St Andrew's. So first thing is to make sure your head isn't on the block, okay?

> KENDALL

Lisa, I feel like you're my lawyer? Are you my fucking lawyer, Lisa?!

Then there's a shout.

RAVA
(off)

Oh for fuck's sake!

(then)

Ken?

Kendall smiles – goes out. Kendall heads through to where Greg is with Rava. He has a big bottle of wine, a magnum of expensive thirty-year-old Rioja. Naomi is off elsewhere on her phone.

KENDALL

We okay?

RAVA
(pissed off)

It's fine.

GREG

Rava, I'm really, really sorry.

RAVA

It. Is. Fine.

KENDALL

What?

RAVA

It's fine, that was one my godfather gave me—

GREG

Naomi told me to open it, Ken?

KENDALL

Take a photo of the label, Greg. I'll get you a case, Rav. I'll get you twenty cases.

RAVA

Yeah well you can't get this bottle back. He gave it to me after—
I was saving it for a special occasion—

Naomi appears with a tray with plates and glasses.

NAOMI

Shall we eat?

                              KENDALL
                          (*re the wine*)
We'll stopper it?

                               RAVA
Drink it, it's fine. It's good. It's like when someone breaks
something beautiful and it reminds you that nothing lasts—

Naomi looks at the bottle.

                              NAOMI
Thanks, Rava. You know, this is a good wine?

                               RAVA
Yes, I am aware.

Rava retreats – Naomi takes the tray. Kendall chuckles to himself.

                             KENDALL
Look at all these brilliant fucking women, Greg. Ah? Look at
them.

Looks round at Rava and Jess and, through the door, Lisa.

I must be doing something right? Ah? Right.

INT. NEW YORK – AIRPORT HOTEL SUITE – NIGHT*

*Roman and Gerri reading and looking at papers. A text comes in to
Gerri. Roman stops, looks at her reading.*

                              ROMAN
Any vibes?

                              GERRI
On what?

                              ROMAN
'On what'? The whole will-my-dad-go-to-jail situation? Who's
climbing Mount Olympus to be the new Dr Zeus?

Gerri shrugs.

* This is a recapitulation of a scene first written for episode ten of season two.
The plot shape and flow of events in this episode allowed it to find a spot to
nestle more comfortably.

You know I put in a word for you.

GERRI

Well, that's very kind of you.

ROMAN

What's going to happen, you think?

GERRI

It's all up in the air. It's a complicated time, Roman.

He looks at her.

ROMAN

Fascinating. You're really letting me in here.

Beat. They both look at laptops. Look at their phones.

Look at us here. Waiting.
                              (*then*)
So fucking – hot.

She ignores.

GERRI

If it's you, you think you're clean?

ROMAN

Obviously – there is that bed through there?
                              (*then*)
Wanna give it a go? Jigga-jigga? Hubba-bubba?

GERRI

The pipeline was still sending cruise girls out west when you were in LA right?

ROMAN

That was mostly over. There's deniability, Frank thinks. We essentially didn't even know. It's all on the little guys – and Mo.

GERRI

Uh-huh? What about the satellite launch, accelerating it?

ROMAN

I'd lay you badly, but I'd lay you gladly?

She looks at him.

> GERRI

Can I remind you that so far as I am concerned nothing has ever happened between us other than of a professional nature?

> ROMAN

Just once though?
> (*cockney*)
'Give us a try won't ya, Her Majesty, I'm ever so eager!'

She looks at him.

> GERRI

Suppose I was interested. How does that play out? What does that look like for me in a week? In six months. In three years?

> ROMAN

You must be curious though? Young fighter, in his prime, technically raw, but hungry.

> GERRI

I am quite a successful person, Roman, and I have remained so by avoiding – complications.

> ROMAN

We're going to sit here for an hour, Gerri. It's essentially irrelevant whether we do it or not? No one will ever know.

The moment stretches. Her phone goes. She answers.

> GERRI

Hey Logan. Okay. Great. Okay. Well. Okay. Well – yes. Yes.
> (*then*)
Sure, I'll let him know. I'll tell him. Thank you.

He hopes it is him . . .

> ROMAN

So?

> GERRI

It's me.

> ROMAN

You're kidding.

> GERRI

It's me.

>   ROMAN
> Are you kidding?

>   GERRI
> I'm not kidding.

>   ROMAN
> It's actually you?

>   GERRI
> It's me. Shiv blew it with Lisa.

>   ROMAN
> Okay? Shit a pony, so, what, you're the boss of me?

>   GERRI
> Well—

>   ROMAN
> Well, congratulations . . . You fucking – bitch.

>   GERRI
> It's just an administrative position, largely. So?

>   ROMAN
> You know, I think I probably swung that for you, you know
> that?

>   GERRI
> Well thank you.
>   (*then*)
> I mean, it'll probably all blow up and kill me. I'm basically
> jumping on a grenade.

>   ROMAN
> Sure. Quite a lucrative fucking grenade? A Fabergé grenade.
> Does Shiv know? Can I tell her? I'd like to tell her, it would be
> nicer coming from me?

INT. SHIV'S CAR – NIGHT

Shiv rides through the city. Her phone goes.

Intercut with:

INT. NEW YORK – AIRPORT HOTEL SUITE – NIGHT

> ROMAN
>
> Yeah we lost Lisa. You fucked it. Your friend doesn't like you! And Gerri got the job. He wanted me to let you know. So, I got a song for you and it goes like – Shiv sucks ass ah ah ah ah, ah ah ah ah, ah ah ah ah ah—

Shiv kills the call. Looks out through the window. Makes a decision.

INT. SARAJEVO HOTEL – NIGHT

Logan paces.

> LOGAN
>
> Where's Shiv?

> TOM
>
> I'm trying.

> KARL
>
> Looks like the Gerri CEO news might have leaked?

Logan mumbles, pissed off – this is the sort of thing that happens when you start to cede power and he doesn't like it.

> HUGO
>
> And I got Simon from the board lined up.

> LOGAN
>
> Uh-huh.

> HUGO
>
> Do you want a room?

> LOGAN
>
> Yes I want a fucking room. I'm about to eat dick for three hours straight, so yes I want a fucking room.

Logan's phone goes: 'Kendall'.

> I don't need that.

He passes it to Frank. Frank answers.

> FRANK

Right. Sure, well, whatever.

End of call. Logan takes the phone back.

> LOGAN

What now?

> FRANK

Nothing.

> LOGAN

Go on, fucking say.

> FRANK

It's not a big deal.

Logan stares him down.

Lisa Arthur is going to represent Kendall.

> LOGAN

Huh. Fine. Fine. Get me Layo. Let's beast them. We're going full fucking beast, alright?

EXT. SARAJEVO HOTEL – NIGHT

Logan walks out. We stay with him.

Impassive – but creaking under the pressure.

Does he stumble on a step but catch himself? He's preoccupied, under siege. He makes it out into some fresh air – a balcony.

An aircraft is landing. The howl and screech are overwhelming. He's a little disorientated. His phone goes.

> LOGAN

How the fuck did you get this number now? You're not a journalist. Who are you? Who the fuck are you? I've never heard of you. 'How does it feel to no longer be CEO?' How does it feel to know your boyfriend fucks a moron who just flushed her career down the toilet? Ah? How fucking dare you!

He throws his iPhone off, skimming it away like a stone.

All is not well. He's alone. He goes and picks up the scratched phone with difficulty, we can hear him breathe as he bends.

75

INT. SHIV'S CAR – NIGHT

On Shiv as she makes her way through the city. Looking out.

Episode Two

MASS IN TIME OF WAR

Written by Jesse Armstrong
Directed by Mark Mylod

Original air date 24 October 2021

Cast

LOGAN ROY	Brian Cox
KENDALL ROY	Jeremy Strong
MARCIA ROY	Hiam Abbass
GREG HIRSCH	Nicholas Braun
SHIV ROY	Sarah Snook
ROMAN ROY	Kieran Culkin
CONNOR ROY	Alan Ruck
TOM WAMBSGANS	Matthew Macfadyen
FRANK VERNON	Peter Friedman
COLIN STILES	Scott Nicholson
KARL MULLER	David Rasche
GERRI KELLMAN	J. Smith-Cameron
WILLA FERREYRA	Justine Lupe
RAVA	Natalie Gold
KAROLINA NOVOTNEY	Dagmara Dominczyk
HUGO BAKER	Fisher Stevens
JESS JORDAN	Juliana Canfield
EWAN ROY	James Cromwell
STEWY HOSSEINI	Arian Moayed
SOPHIE ROY	Swayam Bhatia
IVERSON ROY	Quentin Morales
SANDY FURNESS	Larry Pine
BERRY SCHNEIDER	Jihae
COMFREY PELLITS	Dasha Nekrasova
REMI BISHOP	KeiLyn Durrel Jones
LIA	Gabby Beans
LISA ARTHUR	Sanaa Lathan
OLIVER NOONAN	John Sanders
CELESTE	Paris Benjamin
SANDI	Hope Davis
ROGER PUGH	Peter Riegert
GRAHAM	Don Stephenson
KEITH	Jordan Lage
RAVA'S HOUSEKEEPER	Sol Marina Crespo
SACHA	Talia Thiesfield
SHIV'S DRIVER	Frank Bal

DAY ONE

INT. SHIV'S CAR – NIGHT

On Shiv. Thinking. Looking out at the city as she is driven.

Something grand plays, like Haydn's Mass in Time of War.

On an iPad, coverage of the family dispute plays – sound off. But maybe we can see a package of news – footage of Kendall's press conference, photo of Logan with a chyron: '"Full and Thorough" Investigation into allegations promised'. 'Where is Media Mogul Logan Roy?'

Her phone goes: 'Dad'. She's set the icon to display a picture of Saddam Hussein. She watches it buzz, and buzz – doesn't answer.

INT. SARAJEVO HOTEL – NIGHT

Logan is ending the call.

>   LOGAN
>   (*shouts over to Tom*)
>   Tom, where is she? Ah?

>   TOM
>   I'm sure she's just in transit, or a tunnel.

Karl has called Roman—

>   KARL
>   Roman.

Gives Logan the phone.

>   LOGAN
>   (*into phone*)
>   Where's Shiv? Where are you? What the fuck's going on? What's
>   everyone saying? I need to know where everyone is and what
>   everyone's thinking.

Imtercut with:

INT. ROMAN'S CAR – NIGHT

Roman is heading home.

> ROMAN
>
> I don't know where she is, Dad.

> LOGAN
>
> Where are you?

> ROMAN
>
> Heading for a shit, a shave and a shower.

> LOGAN
>
> No. I need Connor steadied. I need Marcia. I need Shiv. I need Ray and Cyd and fucking . . . I need you showing your face for me, son.

> ROMAN
>
> You want me to go talk to him, to Ken?

> LOGAN
>
> No! Fuck that. No one talks to the snake. No. Keep Gerri close. Keep an eye on, ah? I trust you.

> ROMAN
>
> Uh-huh. Well, thank you.

Roman has a call: 'Kendall'. He cancels.

> LOGAN
>
> You know, it just had to be Gerri? For right now, for today, yeah?

> ROMAN
>
> Sure. Uh-huh, I get it, Dad.

INT. RAVA'S PLACE – HALLWAY – NIGHT

Kendall makes a new call and is leaving a message while welcoming a friendly executive in, Remi Bishop, who's accompanied by an assistant who has a shirt in its shop wrapping. Kendall nods and they unwrap it for him and he changes into the fresh shirt.

KENDALL

Oh, Shivvy? This is it, sweetheart. Tomorrow the wine and roses, but today the necessary murder!

He ends the call. Looks at his other phone. Greg is there, in some makeshift spot, looking at an iPad, concerned.

Okay! Greg, let's game a call with your grandpa because I'd like us to get Ewan squared off?

GREG

Oh. Okay? Yeah. Oh yeah. I mean, you probably ought to . . . to do that, right?

KENDALL

You okay, dude?

Greg looks worried. Kendall sees – time to sprinkle some sugar.

You wondering if you tied your dick to a runaway train here?

GREG

What? No. No. No. I mean.

KENDALL

You aren't Judasing are you, Greg?

Greg wonders if he can tell the truth, opens up—

GREG

I am a little bit scared, Ken? I don't really want to go back to Congress. I'm kinda young to be in Congress so much, you know?

KENDALL

My dad get to you?

GREG

Tom keeps calling. But I'm not picking up. They want to know where you got the papers and what's in them?

KENDALL

I'm not going to burn you, kiddo. Okay?

Greg nods.

I don't even have to tell the government where I got the papers.

This is a subtle shift, that Greg spots—

GREG

Well you told me you wouldn't say?

KENDALL

And I'll stick by that. Could have come from a million places. I could've found them on a photocopier, could have got sent them? You did the right thing.

GREG

I want to do the right thing.

He's clearly wobbly. Kendall considers.

KENDALL

Listen, let's settle your stomach. Let's set you up with a lawyer. I'll talk to Lisa, she'll give you the name.

GREG

Lisa. Your lawyer?

KENDALL

She's the fucking best. And I'll cover that shit off, okay?

He winks. But Greg is not reassured.

GREG

Yeah. I guess my hope was to not to have to take sides in all this?

Kendall laughs indulgently.

KENDALL

You fucking piece of shit!
(*then*)
Fine. Fine. Look, Greg. I'm pretty sure I'll be victorious, but maybe not? Go on, take a walk and have a think: Do you want to be on the side of – like, good or evil?

GREG

Okay. Thanks. I'm with you, I am, I just, you know, the factoring, of the factors. But totally. You know?

Greg is in a state of confusion. He starts to head out.

In the background, Jess shows Kendall a text—

JESS

Um, Ken?

> KENDALL

Fuck yeah! Okay. Jess, can you figure this out?

Jess calls for the hallway and the war room to get cleared.

We stay with Greg as he heads downstairs and out – past a flurry of activity. Maybe a changeover of security – some PR and legal people arriving. A large wooden horse sculpture being delivered.

EXT. RAVA'S PLACE – NIGHT

Greg makes it outside and sees as he goes out – Shiv, a little way down the street or coming in through a back entrance with her driver.

Greg keeps moving. Shiv waits and then makes a move into/through the building when she thinks no one can see.

Greg gets a call and takes it.

> TOM
> *(from phone)*

Hello, *Gregory.*

> GREG

Tom? This isn't the Tom number.

Intercut with:

INT. SARAJEVO HOTEL – NIGHT

Tom paces – in view of Logan but out of earshot.

In the background, during the call, an intermediary, a Bosnian official makes contact with Frank and they have a discreet discussion.

> TOM

I know. Aren't I clever? Hey, Gregory. Is it true you have a saucy secret?

> GREG

I don't— Hello, Tom?

> TOM

Do you do your house chores in the nude?

GREG

Hello? What?

TOM

What the fuck's going on, Greg? Logan is pissing blood.

GREG

I'm just an observer. I'm not – in this.

TOM

Okay? Because Logan is very interested what you're up to? You should be shitting your whack, buddy. You don't come home to us, you're going to end up in a work camp. Logan's going to fire a million poisonous spiders down your dicky. You better crawl into an animal's corpse and hide.

GREG

I'm not a part of this, necessarily, Tom.

TOM

O-kay?
(nervous too)
And the papers?

GREG

I maybe don't even know what they are or where they came from.

TOM

Uh-huh. That's gonna be your thing, is it?

GREG

Yeah. That's what I'm saying.

TOM

Okay. Okay. I guess that works?

GREG

That keeps us – keeps us clean, right?

TOM

So, what, you're open for offers, you dirty fucking little slut?

GREG

I mean, I'm staying out of things. I want to do the right thing?

TOM

Okay. Fine. Well, I'll see if he'll buy that.

Then . . . Greg thinks, what might he have to offer Tom?

> GREG
> I mean, I can say, did you know Shiv's over there?

> TOM
> At Kendall's?

> GREG
> Yeah. Did you know?

Tom isn't about to admit he was out of that loop.

> TOM
> Obviously. But let's keep that under the old Stetson, shall we, cowboy? Okay?

End of call.

> LOGAN
> (*calls over*)
> Any Shiv news?

Tom considers. He walks over. Could he gain some credit and traction with a betrayal? Would be a big roll of the dice—

> TOM
> Um. What? No. No luck there. As yet. I'll keep checking.

Frank heads over. Leaves the officials in suits off in another part of the room.

> FRANK
> Um, Logan. That gentleman is from the Office of the High Representative for Bosnia and Herzegovina?

> LOGAN
> (*not quiet*)
> Impressive. Did he come in a chauffeur-driven tractor?

> FRANK
> They're just enquiring how long we plan to be staying? They're politely suggesting we might be more comfortable elsewhere?

> KARL
> Like the Hilton?

                              FRANK
    Like China.

INT. RAVA'S PLACE – HALLWAY – NIGHT

Jess has cleared the area.

                              JESS
    Okay?

Kendall regards the cleared hall.

                            KENDALL
    Okay.

                              JESS
    Also, I called Stewy and asked, and this came from him. It's—

*She motions to a package. It's visible in the hallway. Kendall looks –
an Ancient Greek horse model, from wood. Real horse size.*

                            KENDALL
    What is that? A Trojan horse? Is that a joke or—? Who's the
    Trojan horse here?

                              JESS
    You want me to check inside it?

                            KENDALL
    What? No. It's mind games. Send it back. Fill it with – fucking
    mousetraps and feta and send it back, okay? Barrel-aged. And
    set something, I need to see him.

                        SHIV'S DRIVER
                        (*off, calling up*)
    We good?

                              JESS
    We're good!

And up the stairs to the first-floor landing area hallway comes—

                              SHIV
    Hi.

*Kendall straightens himself up, prepares to greet her. Slowly, Shiv and
Kendall regard one another.*

(*looking him over*)
So. Here he is, the little man who started this big war.

He smiles, she doesn't.

KENDALL
How you doing? C'mon, let's talk.

SHIV
Can we get out of the sunlight please?

Kendall and Shiv are in a lobby/corridor area. He bounces them into the war room, all high and perky – she is much more circumspect.

INT. WAYSTAR – GERRI'S OFFICE – NIGHT

Roman is in at the office, walking through as people look at him.

He makes a cursory knock but walks in to find Gerri watching business news – an information crawl bar with a leak: 'Report: Waystar General Counsel Gerri Kellman to Assume Interim CEO Role to "Steady the Ship"'.

It's a small announcement on the crawl. But Gerri is taking a photo of it.

ROMAN
Awww.

GERRI
Yeah, well, for my daughters.

ROMAN
That's so cute. How they doing? You got pictures?

She looks at him: Easy there.

GERRI
Don't talk about my daughters.

ROMAN
Okay, good for you to let me know sensitive areas. You know me, I'll be very respectful.
(*looks around*)
So this is it? It's happening.
(*looks at her*)
The fucking – odor prevails. The gas also rises.

GERRI

I'm well aware of the context of my elevation.

ROMAN

No. I'm proud. Who would have thought it?

She half smiles.

'The nothing woman of Idaho'. The Cleaning Woman. The Potato State.

It's not affecting Gerri, who is looking at her phone. Roman is irritated not to get a reaction.

Look at you smiling, it's so pathetic, it's heartbreaking.

GERRI

Thank you.

ROMAN

Are you happy? You must be happy, right? Are you physically happy, Gerri? It's hard to tell.

GERRI

Well you know, when you have lists of popes and emperors there are some with asterisks by their names? So— But yeah. You know?

ROMAN

And I wanted to check, are you concerned about – this at all?

She looks back, blank. He motions between them.

GERRI

I don't know what you're talking about.

ROMAN

I just hope you're not anxious that you've – chained yourself to a fire hydrant that spews out cultural insensitivity and sperms?

She rolls over that—

GERRI

Look, I'm not kidding myself about anything. I need family support. So I am very open to cooperation and input.

ROMAN

Right?

GERRI

You have good instincts, I mean you have bad instincts too, not cooperating is a fucking disaster but – you know, you have a good finger on the pulse in terms of, of—

ROMAN

You mean I sometimes 'surf the web'.

GERRI

Yeah on news and culture you – you – you have an instinctive—

ROMAN

Look, I'm thinking: You should put together an executive committee to guide things in this interregnum.

Gerri immediately weighs the advantages and disadvantages.

GERRI

I don't want to dilute my potency?

ROMAN

Yeah but big calls, you dip everyone's hands in blood. But you and me run it to fuck?

GERRI

I was thinking first I'd work you into the quarterly earnings calls? As a signal?

ROMAN

Uh-huh. Likey likey. That's good.

GERRI

But. Let me think on the executive committee? That has good angles, like he's irreplaceable? It takes six of us to replace him?

ROMAN

Yeah.

Warily, they can see they are on the same page.

GERRI

Okay.

ROMAN

Okay? 'The rockstar and the – the – the molewoman'. It's happening, baby.

> GERRI
> Well, congratulations. Here we go.

That feels good.

> Your apprenticeship begins!

That feels less good.

INT. RAVA'S PLACE – KENDALL'S WAR ROOM – NIGHT

Kendall comes in with coffee/drinks for them.

> KENDALL
> So. So, okay, okay! How we doing?

> SHIV
> Look, at you, so fucking – merry. Is Lisa here?

> KENDALL
> So, I have an offer.

She takes her time, looks around.

> SHIV
> Yeah, that's not why I came here.

> KENDALL
> I'm not going to fuck around. I want you to join me. I want you
> on my team.

> SHIV
> Look. I'm not here to cozy up.

She leaves it a beat.

> But, for the record, I would say, what Dad asked from you, the
> sacrifice, was cold.

He looks at her for a while. He's figuring out her angles.

> KENDALL
> (*coolly*)
> Well, I dunno. From his point of view, it made sense.

> SHIV
> Uh-huh?

KENDALL

I mean who else was he going to choose?

She wonders – how much does he know or has divined about her betrayal of him – choosing him over Tom? She stays calm.

Unless, you know, he took responsibility himself?

They both look a bit like: Like that would ever happen. Smiles. Slight connection over this almost-joke.

SHIV

So, I get it, you were angry but that was a fucking snake move, okay? You should have talked to me.

KENDALL

Yeah, well the situation was the situation. I felt I had no choice.

SHIV

That was self-aggrandizing bullshit. It was a peacock fuck-show.

He looks at her.

KENDALL

I get it, sis. You're angry with yourself.

SHIV

I'm sorry?

KENDALL

You know I did the right thing and you're angry with yourself for never doing it.

SHIV

Oh come on, fuck you.

KENDALL

That's just what I would say is going on here. But if you don't see it that way, fine. Shall we talk?

She stalks the room.

SHIV

That is not it.

He shrugs: No biggie. Infuriating to Shiv.

You fucked the family.

> KENDALL

Or, I saved the family? Depends if you think the family is Dad?

Now it's her turn to just look at him.

> SHIV

You dragged our reputation through the mud, that was Medici shit. That presser is his whole obituary now.

> KENDALL

Maybe it deserves to be?

> SHIV

You reduced him to a – a – a caricature, of a version, of his worst aspects.

> KENDALL

Well, I dunno, Shiv, maybe don't let the guys rape the girls?

> SHIV

Oh c'mon!

> KENDALL

You may say I'm a dreamer, but I'm not the only one.

> SHIV

Like you give a fuck about any victims.

> KENDALL

I have a daughter, Shiv.

> SHIV

Okay. You have a *daughter*? Wow. And that's really sort of clarified your position on sexual assaults? You're definitely against now?
> > (*then*)
> You're acting out a personal grudge against Dad.

He considers – to rebut, or let her in?

> KENDALL

Shiv – I don't know. Honestly, I don't know. People aren't one thing. I think I did a good thing. But yeah, maybe from a mixture of motives?

SHIV

On TV? America isn't your therapist, Ken. It was just so, fucking – unclassy.

KENDALL

Well I'm sorry, Anna Wintour, next time I take down a crime ring dressed up as a Fortune 500, I'll wear a turtleneck.

It's complicated – she doesn't want to diminish the crimes. But also, it's bullshit how he is portraying things.

SHIV

'Crime ring'. Look, we are all, since this thing broke, we have all been, I think, trying to chart a way through this, through conflicting loyalties – without getting too binary. And that's difficult. And if, through some inflexibility of mind, you can't navigate that, and you have to turn fucking – Jacobin – that's not my affair.

He looks at her.

KENDALL

You tell yourself you're a good person. But you're not a good person. Right now, I'm the real you.

That really pisses Shiv off but she holds it, feels it burn, then—

SHIV

Sure. You're the real me and I'm the real you and we're both Dad, and Mom's a sea monster. What-fucking-ever.

INT. SARAJEVO HOTEL – NIGHT

For a long beat, Logan looks at a shitty Balkan room service. He pushes the items around. Stewing. Boiling up inside.

Frank, Karl and Hugo are picking at theirs. Inertia. Logan calls to Hugo.

LOGAN

Where is she? Ah?

(to Hugo)

Have you spoken to Marcia? Is someone connecting?

                              HUGO
She's available, we hear. You want to reach out?

Logan turns steely.

                              LOGAN
Yes I want you to reach out, Hugo.

They're not getting it.

I am stuck in quicksand. My family have disappeared. The
world is wobbling here – does no one understand what the fuck
is happening? I am losing juice. I can't get the right fucking
lawyer. The sky is falling in, so when I say something – it
fucking *happens*! We have to act on the fucking world, we have
to act!

Everyone bristles. Tom makes a call.

                              HUGO
Yes, sir.

                              LOGAN
Get her up. And Con. My brother. And get me some options,
solid fucking options on where we can fly. I'm not getting
smuggled out in a fucking packing case, okay?

Hugo starts to dial.

                    (*calls over to Tom*)
You got her?

Tom is talking, waves a hand: No, I'm trying.

Karl has a phone. He's dialed and hands it to Logan.

INT. NEW YORK – CONNOR'S CAR – NIGHT

Connor is in a car with Willa. Looking at his phone.

                             CONNOR
You see this, the ticket numbers? For your play?

                             WILLA
                           (*subdued*)
Yeah. Yeah. I did.

CONNOR

It's good huh? I mean it looks like we're not just getting
the hate-watchers. We're also getting a fair number of
rubberneckers.

WILLA

Rubberneckers?

CONNOR

Yeah. Rubberneckers. They've heard it's a disaster but they want
to see it unfold. The rubberneckers are ogling the hate-watchers.

WILLA

Oh right, good.

CONNOR

I mean I was worried it might have been a little languid for a
hate-watch.

WILLA

Sorry you thought my play was too boring to hate?

Connor is shaking his head as a call comes in.

Intercut with:

INT. SARAJEVO HOTEL – NIGHT

LOGAN

Con. How ya doing?

CONNOR

Oh I'm great. We flew back scheduled, so, that was *just
delightful.*

Logan's on his best behavior, bites his tongue.

LOGAN

I'm sorry, son. That's – tough.

CONNOR

I can take it. I'm no hero. I'll ride the nose cone for you.

LOGAN

Well, thank you. And, look, I just wanted to say hello, you
know, and thanks for holding the fort?

CONNOR

Sure. Operation: Thumb-Twiddle. No problem.

LOGAN

But look. Now we have a moment, about those words, maybe harsh words, on that tin can, on the boat, you know?

CONNOR

Uh-huh.

That is an apology as far as Logan is concerned.

LOGAN

Yeah. So. No harm done? I mean I'd like to help you out.

CONNOR

You were pretty rude, Dad?

Logan doesn't respond.

I mean, are you saying, you've reconsidered and I am presidential material?

LOGAN

Well, uh-huh. Anything can happen.

Connor lets him hang.

And just to say, you know, with everything, good to know I can rely on you, with Kenny going nut-nut?

CONNOR

Well, yeah, you know. Yeah.

The silence stretches.

LOGAN

No one talks to him, okay? You're number one, kiddo, you know that.

That is still nice to hear. The call ends. Connor can't help being pleased.

CONNOR

'Number one', ah?

Connor dials his business lawyer.

Yeah, well, sure. I mean when he says it he means it but—

Phone connects.

Hey Steven, he made contact. Can you call Gerri and let them know I would like to be supportive but I might need some sugar in my fucking bowl here?

WILLA
(*whispered while he's on the line*)
Con. Do I have to be a hate-watch? I'm not sure I want to be a hate-watch?

CONNOR
Oh. Honey. We gotta make our nut back? I mean, I have to? That's kind of the law.

INT. RAVA'S PLACE – KENDALL'S WAR ROOM – NIGHT

An impasse. Shiv and Kendall look at one another.

SHIV
So, look. Where are these famous papers?

KENDALL
Safe. Getting copied.

SHIV
(*testing*)
Uh-huh. You know – lose those, all this goes away. Burn them. Go say sorry to Dad? Beg for mercy?

KENDALL
Sure. What, say I had some deli sushi and everything went hazy? Shiv? C'mon, I'm going for this and I want you on my side.

She doesn't respond.

SHIV
Then show me the papers.

KENDALL
Well I can't unless you come on board with me obviously.

Beat of silence. He looks at her for a while. Kendall considers. Then, Jess knocks and puts her head round the door.

JESS
Um, Kendall, you have a visitor?

Jess goes and tells Kendall privately.

> KENDALL
> Okay! *Now* we're talking! Romey!

> JESS
> Shall I send him up?

> SHIV
> Does he know who's here?

> KENDALL
> (*to Jess*)
> Does he know *she's* here?

> JESS
> Er, I didn't mention?

> KENDALL
> Okay!
> (*to Shiv*)
> You wanna let him up?

> SHIV
> (*not necessarily*)
> Well, I mean. Um.

> KENDALL
> You're the one I want, Shiv. I want you.

> SHIV
> (*thinking*)
> Uh-huh.

She looks at Kendall, she's not unavailable, but nor is she about to jump in. So, to play for time and because she thinks looking ahead she kind of has to, she says—

We should bring him in, of course.

Kendall sees her moves—

> KENDALL
> Okay. Jess – show him up!

Jess's phone beeps.

JESS

And Lisa. Needs two minutes?

Shiv reacts – Lisa! He goes out.

INT. GREG'S APARTMENT – NIGHT

Greg is with a pal, Lia. He's getting them both a beer.

GREG

Okay, so, Kendall wants to pay for my lawyer. And I just think— Well, you say, what do you think legally?

LIA

I haven't even finished first semester, Greg?

GREG

I just need someone to talk to, Lia.

The door buzzer goes. He gets up.

Oh god. Oh, man. What now?

Greg opens the door. A well-dressed guy, Oliver (forties).

Hello?

OLIVER

Hi. Oliver Noonan. Gerri Kellman said you'd agreed that I could come talk to you?

GREG

Oh. Right? Who buzzed you in—?

OLIVER

I met you during the Hill hearings?

GREG
(no clue)

Oh? Yeah, hey. Good to see you.

OLIVER

There were a lot of us, right! I'm from Arbuthnot Weiss. And I just wanted to check in and say hi and see you're doing okay?

GREG

Okay. That's nice. Um, yeah. I mean just to, sorry to ask but am I paying for this here?

> OLIVER

No, Greg! My fees are paid by Waystar. Shall I come in and explain?

> GREG

You're – from Waystar, from Logan?

> OLIVER

No. No, I'm from Arbuthnot Weiss, Greg, keep up! Haha no, I'm just checking in to see if the FBI has been in contact and answer any questions?

> GREG

Right? Because. Okay and you're, like—

> OLIVER

I'm your lawyer. Right? So I'm gonna call Gerri to tell her we are squared away, and if the government calls, she can tell them that I represent you. We can do the written retainer and all that shit later. Good?

> GREG

Fuck yeah. Cool, I mean, yeah, cool, but just one moment.

He goes out and round to Lia—

So there's a lawyer here, Lia? And so he is saying he's my lawyer.
(*then*)
Do you think he's probably my lawyer?

> LIA

Er, well, I don't know.

> GREG

Do you think you could you ask him?

> LIA

He can't be your lawyer unless you want him to be?

> GREG

Right. No. No. You'd think so, right?
(*then*)
But – would you ask him?

She looks at him.

I'm, just a little embarrassed. I mean we were getting on and
I don't want for him not to trust me?

LIA

I think you probably need to be able to ask your lawyer if he's
your lawyer?

GREG

Right.

(thinks)

He couldn't sue me or— Not arrest me, but subpoena me or—
I don't properly know what any of it means you know?

She shrugs, Greg returns to the door.

Hey, man! Sorry, this all sounds great but just to check. Do you
choose me, or do I choose you?

OLIVER

Hahaha. Well you choose, Greg!

GREG

Right. And I don't want to be rude, but like – would you be
working for me or for Waystar—?

OLIVER

You'd be my client. My sole loyalty would be to you. My role is
to look out for your interests.

GREG

Okay. And so – I mean I like you, *a lot* obviously, in the time
I've known you here. But would Waystar pay for any lawyer
I choose?

OLIVER

Greg. You can check my references, this is what I do. But if you
want to choose someone else, would the company pay for that?
I'm gonna have to check. I honestly don't know.

GREG

Okay. Okay.

OLIVER

So are we good, shall we say go on this?

> GREG

Okay – Oliver, I'm going to close the door now but not in an
unfriendly way, I just need to think. Okay? So – see you soon.
Not that, that constitutes a legal promise!

As Oliver objects, Greg closes the door.

INT. RAVA'S PLACE – HALLWAY PRIVATE AREA – NIGHT

Kendall approaches a room on the phone—

> KENDALL

Hey Marcia, it's Kendall. Listen, I've been thinking about Dad
and you and I never liked the way he treated you. So, can you
give me a call, I think we might share some interests right now?

He enters to see Lisa.

> LISA

Okay. So I know you have things on but I'm going to need you
for like eight to ten hours very soon. You could get a subpoena
anytime, we need to be ready. I need to start to go through
everything. Okay?

*Kendall nods to Jess. She has an envelope. He takes it from her and
writes something on a piece of paper, puts it in the envelope and gives
it back to Jess.*

> KENDALL

I can't do that right now. I have bigger fish.

> LISA

Bigger fish than staying out of prison? Look. I'll message
you a time. And ahead of our interview I need to look over
these papers. In detail. Then we can talk through what the
government gets and when.

> KENDALL

Uh-huh, uh-huh, let me think.

> LISA

You don't think, I think. Ken, the FBI may show up at your door
now. They could be getting a search warrant for your apartment.

Kendall doesn't agree but isn't about to push back right now.

> KENDALL

Sure. But like, big picture what are you hearing?

> LISA

Well, your dad is pushing political buttons. There's talk he might play hardball and not cooperate. Which would be amazing. I mean that's just a really terrible, terrible decision.

> KENDALL

What if he shuts this all down?

> LISA

He can't shut this all down.

> KENDALL

Well he might. My dad speaks to the president every other day, Lisa. We might need to call the state police to arrest the FBI, we might need a plan to fly me without a tail number to Frankfurt or Venezuela? I'm not serious, okay, but I am serious?

> LISA

I get it. But so far, in my experience, in New York State, we're not yet in Italy so—

> KENDALL

We are in Italy. We're in Sicily, Lisa, what look like walls aren't walls, okay?

INT. RAVA'S PLACE – KENDALL'S WAR ROOM – NIGHT

Jess comes in, with some papers as Shiv's phone goes.

> SHIV

Hey.

Intercut with:

INT. SARAJEVO HOTEL – NIGHT

Jess puts an envelope that looks like the envelope of documents from the previous episode – important – on top of a bunch of other papers on Kendall's pile. Jess looks at Shiv, who pretends to be absorbed with her call. Jess hesitates. Heads out.

> TOM

Hey, how goes it?

> SHIV

Um, good. Why? What's going on?

> TOM

Just – wondering where you are?

> SHIV

Me? I'm just taking five. I'm home.

Why is she lying? Shiv goes round to the pile of papers. Looks at the envelope that Jess brought in.

> TOM

Well I was just checking in. How you're doing. Do you mind about Gerri?

Shiv pulls the papers out of the envelope – Kendall has scrawled in Sharpie on a blank sheet: 'Fuck you Shiv!'

> SHIV

Yeah well, just another humiliation. I dunno.

> TOM

Okay. Well talk to me if there's big stuff?

> SHIV

Will do. And – thanks for checking in. And – Tom. I love you.

> TOM

Thank you.

Beat, a buzz.

> SHIV

And – you know, do you—?

Beat.

> TOM

Why?

> SHIV

'Why'?

> TOM

Yeah, why do you wanna know?

                    SHIV
Well because, I guess it seems pretty important if you do or not?

                    TOM
              (*playful but not*)
You know you can't take my love and bank it, and take a view
of the love market and see if you want to invest in me?

Static.

But – yeah. I do. I do.

                    SHIV
Okay. Because I do love you.

                    TOM
Thank you. Good to know we don't have an unbalanced love
portfolio.
              (*then*)
I love you.

End of call.

INT. RAVA'S PLACE – NIGHT

*Just then Roman is shown in by Jess. Shiv gives Jess a sharp look
about the papers deception. Jess plays it dumb.*

                    ROMAN
Okay! Well now, looky-looky here! Who's this then, ah?

                    SHIV
Hey.

                    ROMAN
Well fuck me. I wondered— But— Okay!

                    SHIV
How is Dad?

                    ROMAN
How is he? He is wondering where the fuck you are. Why aren't
you picking up?

                    SHIV
I've had my phone off. No agenda.

ROMAN

Oh sure, *no agenda*. None at all.

SHIV

How is he?

ROMAN

He's fine. I guess. Gerri's looking at how it works to buy a private island in the Philippines. Regular stuff. So, what the fuck is your game?

SHIV

Well, what's yours?

ROMAN

I'm just here looking for you.

SHIV

Oh, sure. *Sure.*

They eye one another – as Kendall comes in.

ROMAN

Okay, here he comes! The coward of the county!

KENDALL

Hey, Rome! How you going?

ROMAN

Yeah great. Just a great few days all round. How about you?

KENDALL
(tries to answer honestly)
Okay. Yeah. I feel pretty good, certain amount of regret but, you know, pretty cleansed.

ROMAN
(pretending to take him very seriously)
Uh-huh. Interesting. Really interesting. I mean I guess to hear what you're really thinking, I'll have to wait for you to call a – you know – a fucking national press conference – and you'll be like 'No! I *said* I was fine but *actually* I *wasn't* fine and Roman's a dick and he made me feel bad because he didn't even bring anything from the airport! So I'm taking this whole thing down!!'

Kendall takes it, maybe even smiles.

I actually got you some of the Danish cinnamon things, from wherever. I think you like them, so far as I recall.

He has a box of cinnamon rolls from a specialist Nordic bakery. As well as thinking he's a complete jerk, Roman feels bad for Kendall.

KENDALL
That's nice. That's very kind.

ROMAN
Bleurgh. Whatever. I don't know.

Kendall looks at 'the papers' – smiles – looks at Shiv.

KENDALL
You take a look?

SHIV
'Fuck you.'

KENDALL
Uh-huh. So. Look, can we clean-slate this? You didn't like how I did what I did to Dad. Sure. Whatever. I'm sorry. That's for me and him. But here's the thing: He's over so let's work together to take over and help him move on out?

A lawyer knocks and enters to show something to Kendall. Roman and Shiv look at one another.

ROMAN
(*partly for the lawyer's benefit*)
I am literally only here to spy on her.

SHIV
And I'm just here to get you to back down.

Kendall sees they are uncomfortable. The lawyer leaves.

KENDALL
I'm sorry.

Jess comes in with a message on a phone to show Kendall.

ROMAN
What's with all the humans, dude?

> SHIV
>
> Look, I want to tell you what a fucking prick you are but can we please do it somewhere where we don't have to fold in Rava's, fucking, dog walker. Okay?

INT. LOBBY – NIGHT

Lobby of the offices of a charitable foundation. Greg meets Ewan.

> GREG
>
> Hey! Gramps. Thanks for this.

> EWAN
>
> Hello, Gregory.

> GREG
>
> Wow. Gramps. So great you're in the city. What are you doing?

> EWAN
>
> I am putting my affairs in order.

Graham, a friend and aide, comes out to get Ewan.

> GRAHAM
>
> Ewan? People would love to get home eventually. Can we sign off on the bequest sequencing?

> EWAN
>
> Well shall we do this fast or shall we do it right?

Ewan nods him away – Graham heads back in.

> Your publicity-shy friend, the shrinking violet, has been calling. What does he want?

> GREG
>
> Kendall? Oh I think, you know, you saw what he did?

> EWAN
>
> Naturally.

> GREG
>
> Yeah, well so he's very much I think on the same page as you, in terms of – wanting, wanting, if it doesn't sound too basic, to be – like – 'good'? I think. Make the company, nice and so on? Which I guess is your thing?

Greg maybe motions around them.

                    EWAN
I thought his performance was histrionic and meretricious.

                    GREG
Tell me about it.

                    EWAN
The man is a self-regarding popinjay.

                    GREG
No sure, I know everything's more complicated – than it seems
but—

                    EWAN
I don't like seeing dirty laundry washed in public.

                    GREG
Right, that's actually what I wanted to chat about? Because I'm
pondering on my position in all this and just wanted to ask your
advice on something my old—
                    (rarely/never used)
my 'gramper'?
                    (pushing on)
Just thought I would check in with, your wizened old head
there.

                    EWAN
Do you know what 'wizened' means?

                    GREG
Like wizardy? Like wise? Right?

                    EWAN
Right.

                    GREG
Yeah, because my thing is, I'm trying to chart the right course
and Logan is offering me a lawyer and Kendall is offering me a
lawyer and I just, could do with like – independent legal advice,
you know?

                    EWAN
Why do you need a lawyer, Greg?

GREG

Why? I mean, I haven't done anything wrong. It's just if everyone else is like going into battle in armor, I feel kinda exposed here in my loincloth?

Ewan looks at him hard for a long while.

So—?

EWAN

Shush.

GREG

Sorry I was just checking you hadn't – stalled or – crashed?

EWAN

Yes.

GREG

Yes?

EWAN

Yes. I'll set you up with independent counsel. I can back you, Greg.

GREG

Oh god. Thank you! Thank you, Gramps!

He goes to kiss him but Ewan subtly evades and Greg backs off.

INT. RAVA'S PLACE – SOPHIE'S BEDROOM – NIGHT

Kendall moves them into Sophie's bedroom, or a spare room.

KENDALL

So. Okay, it's pretty simple. Let's gang up on Dad and take him down.

Roman opens the door, looks outside to see if anyone is still listening.

SHIV

Why didn't you come to us before? Ah? This is so— It's just a real fucking mess now.

KENDALL

Uh-huh. It came together for me in my head late and— It wasn't, I mean I knew what I was going to do but—

ROMAN

That was spontaneous?

KENDALL

Well, I spoke with a lawyer.

That's news – seems to somewhat contradict Kendall's version.

ROMAN

Oh, okay, so you spoke to a lawyer?

KENDALL

Yeah, but they advised, against, essentially. I can't rehash it all, but I was effectively, acting alone.

ROMAN

Right a spontaneous, heartfelt outpouring of thoroughly lawyered emotion?

KENDALL

It was not actually what they advised. But – look – you can think whatever you want, in the end, of me.

Kendall takes it in, looks at Shiv.

SHIV

You've made this very hard.

Roman looks at Shiv: Are you considering this?

She looks like: No. Are you?

He looks like: No.

But I'm here to find out what you want and to talk you down.

ROMAN

On Dad's behalf.

They can stick to that line if they need to.

KENDALL
(patronizing)

Oh right. Right?

(then)

So if I say I'm taking him down and I'm not interested in any deals with him, you call him, tell him and – just leave?

Jess puts her head in.

                          JESS
He's here.

                         ROMAN
Who?

                        KENDALL
Connor.

                         ROMAN
Right, I thought I heard a clown car pull up.

                        KENDALL
                        (to Jess)
Send him in. Ideally I'd like to make a media appearance all four
of us.

                         ROMAN
Great and will we all be wearing costumes that you've designed?

                          SHIV
That's not happening in any event.

Connor comes in.

                        CONNOR
Okay! Here we all are!

                          SHIV
Con.

                        CONNOR
You know Dad's looking for you two?

                          SHIV
We're just here on Dad's behalf.

But Connor's not that dumb.

                        CONNOR
Oh sure thing honey, me too, all about Dad. That's what we're
all here for.

Kendall gathers himself for his pitch.

                        KENDALL
Okay. Can we close the doors and turn off the devices and get
into this?

He has a whole theory of everything that's been cooking a while.

Okay my thing is: If this shit was just epiphenomenal maybe it could be ridden out. But these incidents are symptomatic of a foundational sickness within our father and his company.

Roman is considering, but covers—

ROMAN

Don't he use that tongue prettier than a twenty-dollar whore?

SHIV

What's your point?

KENDALL

My point is – the milk is going sour.

CONNOR

Well that explains it.

KENDALL

The great whites. From politics to culture, they're rolling off stage. It's our time.

ROMAN

What you mean *us*? This multi-ethnic, transgender alliance of twentysomething dreamers we have right here?

KENDALL

Big picture. We're at the end of the long American century. Our company is a declining empire, inside a declining empire, right?

CONNOR

Amen, brother.

KENDALL

There is a problem. We are in the richest society in the existence of human history and – our life expectancy is going down. You know why?

ROMAN

Is it something to do with grapefruit?

KENDALL

It's unbearable. What we've built. People are killing themselves with guns or dope so fast that we're losing pace.

> SHIV

Unsubscribe.

> KENDALL

We're, you know, we're fat-fingered fucks and we can only live on cream.

> ROMAN

Can you pass me that bong, dude? He's the wisest cat in the whole dorm!

> KENDALL

So, general analysis: US supremacy is waning. How will it go? Two ways: Slow, then fast. What I think is, within that context, we can become omni-national and reposition. Because actually we are not tied, culturally or physically, so we are actually in a great position to leapfrog tech. Information is going to be more precious than water in the next hundred. Combine all our news operations, become *the* global news information hub. Amazon is a quarter of a century old. Gates is an old geezer. Detoxify our brand and we can explode.

Shiv and Roman look at one another.

So, are you interested?

> ROMAN

Yeah there's just something about betraying our father that doesn't sit well?

> KENDALL

Rome. He's a central player in a rotten cabal that has eaten the heart out of American democracy?

> ROMAN

Hmm. Impressively wordified linguafication.

> SHIV

He won't be on trial for that.

> KENDALL

Well maybe he should be?

> ROMAN

If he hadn't done it, someone else would have made the same dollar doing the same shit.

KENDALL

Maybe. Maybe we're all irrelevant. Maybe there were always going to be death camps and maybe the planet is going to fry and there's nothing we can do? Or. Maybe people make a difference? I don't know. Do you think human beings matter?

ROMAN

I'm just going to say, right out, I'm a spy, I'm going to go right back and tell him everything. I'm with Dad. Fuck you.

KENDALL

Fine. I don't actually give a fuck. You know? I can perfectly well do this alone – I am actually just trying to be open-hearted and, and invite you in here. I mean it would probably be simpler to go alone but I want to offer you a – fucking ticket to the escape pod.

Roman looks at Shiv: That's pushing it, right? But Shiv won't engage. She's considering.

I mean you're happy he went over your head and put in *Gerri*?

ROMAN

Gerri's a good choice.

SHIV

Well . . .?

ROMAN

What?

SHIV

Rome, defend Dad, fine? But Gerri can look after herself.

ROMAN

I was simply saying—

SHIV

You can't hide under the covers with Mummy.

ROMAN

Fuck off, Siobhan.

SHIV

You love showing your peepee to everyone but you know someday you'll actually have to fuck something?

ROMAN

Fuck you. Fuck you. Fuck you. Bitch.

Roman heads out the door.

Silence.

CONNOR

Fine. I'll— That was low. That was— Let's, you know, can we try to keep this nice? Yeah?

Connor goes out after Roman.

Shiv looks at Kendall. After a beat he smiles at her, they share a naughty shared smile of the higher-status siblings.

SHIV

Maybe I was a little—?

KENDALL

Nah. He loves it. He'll be out there jerking off wearing my ex-wife's panties.

EXT. SARAJEVO AIRFIELD – NIGHT

A helicopter is arriving. Marcia descends. A distinguished woman with her.

INT. SARAJEVO HOTEL – NIGHT

Marcia arrives from ground transportation with her companion. Logan waits at the door with Karl and Frank and Hugo.

Logan walks to greet Marcia. As Karl and Hugo and Frank watch and comment—

HUGO

Great. Return of Napoleon Bonyheart.

But Frank and Karl know better.

FRANK

Water for the root. Lead in the pencil.

KARL

Even a rock needs a rock.

Out there – Marcia gives Logan a kiss on the cheek.

> LOGAN
>
> Thank you.

> MARCIA
>
> Those fucking kids of yours.

> LOGAN
>
> I know.

> MARCIA
>
> Are you alright?

> LOGAN
>
> I'm okay.

> MARCIA
>
> And what's in these papers?

> LOGAN
>
> Oh I don't know. I'm not, you know, I'm not perfect. But I'm not a monster, so . . . can't be that bad.

> MARCIA
>
> I know.

> LOGAN
>
> What do you think? Am I toast?

He's more vulnerable and unsure than she's seen him.

> MARCIA
>
> You're strong.

> LOGAN
>
> It's not a good time to be estranged, Marcia. The boy. Proxy battle?

> MARCIA
>
> I was very hurt.

> LOGAN
>
> Uh-huh. I know.

> MARCIA
>
> So?

She looks: Are you going to say sorry?

119

> LOGAN

You know I can't eat shit, Marcia. I just can't. But—

He makes a gesture, gives a smile that is as close as he can approximate.

She looks at him.

> MARCIA

You're a fool.

> LOGAN

I can sometimes – get distracted.

But she reaches and takes his hand and gives it a brief squeeze. She's willing to come back. But—

> MARCIA

Of course I might like to have a short conversation with somebody?

Logan understands. He nods to Hugo.

INT. RAVA'S PLACE – SOPHIE'S BEDROOM – NIGHT*

Connor comes in with Roman.

> SHIV

'Sorry'.

> ROMAN

What? I went to the bathroom. I don't give a fuck.
> ('*friendly*')

You whore.

They smile at one another.

> KENDALL

Look, this is how I see this: Dad is complicated. He did, or let bad stuff happen. And now it's a part of us and our sickness, and we have to take responsibility, because we knew, and this is our chance to pay our dues and wash our hands. For absolution.

---

* The wolfpack-speculation material that felt extraneous when we tried it in episode ten of season two felt more germane and sprung-in here.

Despite their moment of closeness, this lands wrong with Shiv – feels accused of something of which she is innocent.

SHIV

Right, well I didn't know.

KENDALL

Sure. Whatever but—

SHIV

Did you – Rome?

ROMAN

Well, no I didn't know. No.

Kendall looks weary.

KENDALL

No?
(*then*)
The fucking 'pipeline'? Of sad dancers who'd got used and abused and promised some Hollywood bullshit, we fucking knew.

ROMAN

I knew, I knew that they had—
(*'had a bad time'*)
But I didn't know—
(*about sexual assault and rape*)
I didn't – I really didn't.

Kendall looks at Shiv. She won't look at him. He looks at Con—

CONNOR

Oh c'mon, we knew.

SHIV

What?

KENDALL

We fucking knew and I don't like bullshit, okay, I'm done.

ROMAN

What did we know?

CONNOR

I'm not saying you were responsible, Shiv. But – the guys, Dad, Mo, the wolfpack—

KENDALL

We knew, the jokes and the vibe, to women and to the fat-asses who took the cruises, the blind-eye and the pay-offs and the hush-hush about Dad's pals or foreign workers who got crushed like meat in a fucking grinder with zero training and 'clean out the rats in the hold', and no it wasn't our fault, and you wanna pretend, go ahead, but we – we—

CONNOR

We knew what those guys in Dad's study were laughing about.

SHIV

I did not know that dancers were fucking for their jobs and I didn't know they threw fucking migrants off boats and I did not know we covered that up as a matter of secret company policy. I did not know what they were laughing about.

CONNOR

'Don't get into the pool with Mo.'

SHIV

I didn't get in the pool with any of those fucking creeps.

KENDALL

Because he let a gang of creeps run cruises.

SHIV

No because I was fifteen.

Kendall can feel himself getting sucked into an argument that doesn't actually advance his desired outcome.

KENDALL

This isn't, fucking, this is a sidebar. All I am asking is for us to move forward from a position of truth?

He's dissatisfied, can't help acting like she is lying to herself.

SHIV

And are we excluded from the Kingdom of Heaven unless we accept the one true truth?

Kendall just breathes. Gets a text.

> KENDALL

Look, the kids are— I wanna hug my kids. Okay? I'll be back—
We don't even need to get into this, okay, this is side shit.

INT. RAVA'S PLACE – HALLWAY – NIGHT

Kendall heads out. Closes the door. Then to Rava who is nearby. Lots to say but she can see he's right in the middle.

> KENDALL

Hey Rav, so grateful. Are they back?

> RAVA

Kitchen. Sophie's making TikToks at Bella's.

> KENDALL

Great. Um, and just so you know, I asked Naomi to go home?

> RAVA

Oh. Okay. Well, thanks for letting me know?

> KENDALL

It's nothing. I just wanted to let you know. Just felt kinda – you know? Little bit?

Kendall heads through. Iverson in his capoeira outfit.

Hey hey hey! Come here. This is great, is this your capoeira uniform.
>   (*checking on a rule-change he's not agreed*)
So your sister stays out late on school nights huh?
>   (*and he's out*)
I love this! Look at you. I'll see you in five okay?

He runs downstairs.

INT. SARAJEVO HOTEL – NIGHT

Hugo talks with Marcia and her lawyer, Celeste.

> KAROLINA
> (*on speakerphone*)
Everyone's so happy you're back, Marcia.

> MARCIA

Good. I am very happy.

> KAROLINA

We were thinking we could discreetly agree, some words in terms of where you've been and where the relationship is at?

> MARCIA

Of course.

> HUGO

Great! And in terms of the optics on this, if you'd find it acceptable we would love to get back visually to the Logan everyone knows and— We're hoping his kids, hugging and kissing and – his wife back by his side so if we fly—

> MARCIA

Obviously I have some requests.

> HUGO

Oh. Okay? Right.

Marcia speaks with her lawyer—

> MARCIA
> (*in French*)

Shall I present the demands or will you?

> CELESTE
> (*in French*)

You do as you choose, I will get into details, so you go ahead in the first instance.

Hugo smiles politely.

> MARCIA

I was quite humiliated by his infatuation with that woman.

Marcia looks at Hugo, who doesn't want to say too much.

Hugo looks at the lawyer who is making a note.

> HUGO

Karolina? Do you wanna—?

> KAROLINA
> (*fuck you*)

No you go, Hugo.

> HUGO

I mean I think Logan's – position, and it's the truth—

> MARCIA

I was humiliated. And things must be made right.

> HUGO

is that nothing, needs to be said—

> MARCIA

He was led by his prick.

Hugo winces.

> HUGO

Because we really would say nothing happened?

> MARCIA

She's a whore and it's not my problem if she wouldn't finish him.

> HUGO

Uh-huh. Got it. Got the message.

> MARCIA

So, for my return to be public I will need my role on the trust finalized. Amir's prospects assured, my daughter looked after, and improvements in my financial position. Celeste will deal with the details.

Marcia gets up. Hugo and Celeste watch her as she walks over to Logan and rubs his shoulders – he appreciates the gesture. She holds all the cards.

> CELESTE

Now. The numbers I am going to propose will sound like very very large numbers. But if you consider them in terms of the difficulties it would present Mr Roy to have an acrimonious divorce announced ahead of a contested shareholder meeting, then they start to seem like very reasonable numbers.

INT. RAVA'S PLACE – SOPHIE'S BEDROOM – NIGHT

Rava and Sophie knock on the door.

> RAVA

Um – guys – someone else needs the room I'm afraid.

Kendall, Roman and Shiv, all looking at their phones, head out, each giving Sophie a ruffle on the head and smiles as they think and text.

> ROMAN
>
> Thanks, kiddo. Great room, five stars.
> *(to his sibs)*
> Perfect for planning a family murder.

EXT. STREET – NIGHT

As Kendall comes down, Stewy is there. Standing outside a car.

> STEWY
>
> So. What the fuck? Did you have an aneurysm?

> KENDALL
>
> Thanks for the horse, man.

> STEWY
>
> I wanted to send a real horse – well a severed head – but you wouldn't believe the paperwork.

> KENDALL
>
> Look, man, sorry I couldn't – you know, fold you in, or alert you on the press conference.

> STEWY
>
> Dude. I got to watch the Vietnamese monk set himself on fire. I got a ticket to the greatest freak show on earth.

> KENDALL
>
> So. Look, how does this play from the point of view of—?

> STEWY
>
> Do you have an actual case?

> KENDALL
>
> Yes, I can kill him.

> STEWY
>
> Good then, I guess as a figure – you're, I dunno. I mean, we're all ears but I don't see it dude.

Stewy nods – they get into the car.

INT. STEWY'S CAR – NIGHT

Sandi, Sandy's daughter, sits in the car. Stewy sits in too.

> KENDALL
> Hey. Sandi, thanks for coming over.

> SANDI
> It wasn't terribly convenient.

> KENDALL
> No, well sure. I guess nor would losing the proxy vote for you or your dad?

Sandi nods and an assistant up front hits a phone.

> SANDI
> Dad, you're on.

> KENDALL
> Hey Sandy!

> SANDY
> (*on speakerphone*)
> Hello.

> KENDALL
> Look, so I give you two hours, two minutes or two words.

> STEWY
> Shorter's better?

> KENDALL
> Back me.

> STEWY
> Maybe a *little bit* more?

> KENDALL
> Look, Sandy, we all know you are kind of, not-really-but-yeah-really, doing this, to beat my dad.

The line buzzes with silence.

> SANDI
> My father doesn't operate that way.

> SANDY
> (*on speakerphone*)
> I'm in this because of the business fundamentals.

But they all know he does.

> KENDALL
> Sure. Well, the offer we made you in Greece, Stewy, we stick
> with all that, but plus – my dad's gone?
> (*beat*)
> And when my dad offers you the board seats and all, one way or
> another, he's going to sideline you, right? But not me. When my
> team offers a strategic review, we mean it. So you can call off the
> dogs. We have a reform-minded senior management who will
> invite you in with an open heart, unlike my dad who fucking
> loathes you.

> SANDI
> What's your standing? Do you even work there now?

> KENDALL
> My standing is that I am a witness in the investigation of my
> dad. Most likely, as I see it, he gets smart and steps away. I'm
> getting my siblings on-side and I think the board will support
> us. My relationship with other key shareholders, the Ulsterman,
> Aaronson, is great. So I just think, you know, our time has come,
> and I want to know when we kick Dad upstairs, we have a way
> through here that is cooperative.

*He's pushing hard. It's not total bullshit. Stewy looks at Sandi. There
are a hell of a lot of assumptions in there.*

> SANDI
> And what's in these papers?

> KENDALL
> I'm pretty sure Dad will fold.

> STEWY
> So what do you want today?

> KENDALL
> I just want the conversation. And an understanding, if we push
> him out, then we can avoid a contested shareholder vote?

INT. RAVA'S PLACE – KENDALL'S WAR ROOM – NIGHT

Connor is on the phone in the background—

CONNOR

Well I do worry. I was assured that yours was the best facility for the storage of fine wines, but now I'm looking at a geological survey and it's worrying me.

In private, Shiv looks at Roman. Roman looks at Shiv. They are considering it. But neither wants to jump first.

SHIV

So?

ROMAN

So what?

SHIV

Where are you at?

ROMAN
(*after a beat*)

Just – hear him out and report.

Right?

SHIV

Right. We need to protect Dad.
(*then, the real part*)

Because, if we knifed him now, it is true he would bleed out. So.

She looks at Roman with meaning. There's something there if they want to consider—

ROMAN

Well, I don't know about that?

SHIV

Well that's just true.

ROMAN

I'm not sure I want to speculate.

She makes a face: Come on, you know what's on the table here.

SHIV

Rome, that is just a statement of fact.

ROMAN

Yeah?

SHIV

Yeah.

ROMAN

Then why are you making fucky eyes at me?

SHIV

I am not making fucky eyes at you.

ROMAN

Well, yeah you are.

SHIV

I am not.

ROMAN

Well, yeah you were.

She was, they both know. She's pissed off.

It's not necessarily even true, Shiv. Dad's fucking Moby Dick. He could take us all down even with his back bristling with harpoons.

SHIV

All three of us? And Con? No. We all back Ken? He's toast.

Roman waggles his head: Maybe.

He just is. I'm not saying we should do it, but it's no good shirking. I mean fine, you can if you want, but we better know what the fuck we're doing because this is a moment.

Roman looks at her—

ROMAN

I mean what do you think?

SHIV

First it was Rhea, Gerri now? That's not great?

Connor ends his call.

ROMAN

I don't think Dad would go anyway, do you, Con?

SHIV

He's not infallible, Rome.

ROMAN

No. Sure. I just don't think he has ever failed. Or ever will.

SHIV

He missteps all the time, he's not what you think he is. He's not Dad, not when he was – you know?

CONNOR

It's very hard to imagine him surviving if we allied and backed Kendall.

SHIV

If we did that and we squared Frank. Karl? He would be toast.

ROMAN

I don't know. Maybe.

SHIV

Yes-be.

ROMAN

It's his board.

SHIV

Well, lot of fresh blood. Lot of fear. We pull the pin today, I think tomorrow, we could win a spooked board, take over. Which is— It's interesting.

Roman doesn't respond, then—

ROMAN

I guess, my only other concern, is, if it might actually kill him?

Kendall arrives back.

KENDALL

Okay! How we doing?

Shiv and Connor and Roman look at one another. Shiv is liking it but she has a concern.

SHIV

Look. You win this, take Dad out, we risk losing control in the proxy battle. Shareholders don't like confusion. I'm not sure the family comes through in control.

> KENDALL

Nope. We give Dad the revolver and show him to his office. The proxy battle is over. Sandy and Stewy would back down. I've spoken with them.

> ROMAN

Busy fucking bee.

> KENDALL

No vote. We'd have a settlement.

> SHIV

Really?

> KENDALL

I think if Dad went fast, yes.
> (then)
Look. I dunno. I dunno what I think about Dad. I love him, I hate him, me and my therapist can work on that. But he was gonna send me to jail. You know? He'd do that to you, Rome. And Con. Shiv, I dunno – I dunno. Maybe. So. What do you owe him here? Really?

Roman is considering. Shiv and him look at one another. The world is teetering.

> ROMAN

And what's the shape of this fucking, new reality, with us leapfrogging Amazon?

> KENDALL

Well, we're looking at three-twenty-three BC.

> ROMAN

Uh-huh, of course.

> KENDALL

Alexander is dead. I take Asia, you take Egypt, Shiv takes Europe. Con, rest of the world.

> ROMAN

Uh-huh?

KENDALL

Separate divisions. I could oversee, as CEO on paper, as we shift
to these spheres of influence and evaluate what is core as we
move forward.

ROMAN

Oh, *you'll* oversee us?

KENDALL

I'd offer my leadership initially as a necessary part of a
transformative process.

ROMAN

You'd do that?! You are one *generous motherfucker*!

SHIV

Okay, no. In your position that just doesn't work.

CONNOR

It's a stretch.

ROMAN

A 'stretch' – him? It's a fucking, scrotum across a timpani drum.

SHIV

No. If I were to back you against Dad, you'd need to let me take
over.

ROMAN

Whoa, Nelly!

KENDALL

No, because you don't have the experience, so that's not possible
right now. I wish it was, but it isn't.

SHIV

You're a busted flush, I'm the only person who can reform.

KENDALL

You're too divisive. You're still seen – I don't see you this way –
but you're still seen as a token woman wonk woke snowflake.
(*beat*)
I don't think that but the market does.

SHIV

Bullshit.

> ROMAN
> (*with pretend phone*)
> I just spoke to the market, that's exactly what the market thinks.

> KENDALL
> Interim chair. New directors. Clean broom. And then we can figure out how to split the spoils?

They look at one another.

> SHIV
> I need to make some calls.

> ROMAN
> Well I do actually need to make some calls. So?

> KENDALL
> Fine, take five, take a moment.

> SHIV
> But this stays in here?

> ROMAN
> Absolutely.

They all look at one another.

EXT. RAVA'S PLACE – ROOFTOP – NIGHT

Shiv is on the line with Tom.

> SHIV
> Can you talk?

Intercut with:

INT. SARAJEVO HOTEL – NIGHT

Tom makes a noise and moves to safety and looks over at Logan.

> SHIV
> So, listen, Tom, I'm with Ken.

> TOM
> (*pretending*)
> Oh. Okay. Wow? You are?

But she picks up his tone.

SHIV

Did you know?

TOM

Um, no I, no. Why would I know?

SHIV

He's offering an alliance. Me, Rome and Con, we take Dad down?

TOM

Okay? Shit. *Shit.*

SHIV

Yeah.

TOM

And what do you think?

SHIV

How is Dad?

TOM

He's okay. The Bosnians might want us to leave.

SHIV

Fuck. Is he okay?

TOM

He's actually better. Marcia's here.

SHIV

Okay? Wow?

TOM

Yeah so, he's steadied.

How does Shiv feel about that? Not great.

SHIV

Uh-huh. But what do you think? Maybe we get you? And
Frank?

TOM

Right. That's terminal I guess? But then? Who ends up King Potato?

SHIV

Exactly.

> TOM

Is it you?

> SHIV

Maybe. But, I'm nobody is the thing. Never worked in the company. I mean what the fuck is my job title? I don't have one. But I don't know? I don't know. It's sort of— You can see it, right?

INT. RAVA'S PLACE – ROOF LOWER TERRACE – NIGHT

Roman looks at Shiv and makes sure she can't hear—

> ROMAN

Hey, Ger. Okay. So I'm gonna just put my dick right in your mad, scheming scissor-hands here.

Intercut with:

INT. WAYSTAR – GERRI'S OFFICE – NIGHT

Gerri's at her desk.

> GERRI
> (*a warning*)

Roman—

> ROMAN

I'm at Ken's and he wants us to join up with him and take down Dad.

Gerri thinks – oh fuck. But plays her cards close.

> GERRI

Uh-huh?

> ROMAN

So yeah, nightmare for you if it happens. But, put that aside – which you obviously can't. But if I do it. What happens?

> GERRI

Um. You and Shiv? I think— I don't know. And Connor? You all come out and work the board yeah – honestly, I think that zaps your dad.

ROMAN

Right. And who takes over? Kendall – or me? Or Shiv?

Gerri thinks again – she has to keep trust but also doesn't want him to do what he's suggesting, but knows she'll be much more persuasive if she tells the truth—

GERRI

Um. No I don't think any of you come through. It's snake linguine. Maybe Sandy picks? Maybe – I don't know, but I think you all get burnt.

ROMAN

Uh-huh. But obviously I can't trust you?

GERRI

Hmmm.

ROMAN

I mean your advice is so compromised as to be worthless.
(*then*)
But what's your advice?

GERRI

Stick with me, Roman, we have something going. Our interests coalesce. And I'm an incredibly dangerous enemy to whom you've just imparted prejudicial information.

ROMAN

Don't threaten me, Gerri. I don't have the time to jerk off.

GERRI

So. What you gonna do?

Roman looks like: Not gonna tell you right now.

ROMAN

Thanks, Gerri.

INT. RAVA'S PLACE – KENDALL'S WAR ROOM – NIGHT

As Shiv heads in Lisa is coming out of a side space with Keith. Surprised to see Shiv. Shiv plays it cold.

SHIV

Oh, hi, Lisa. How you doing?

> LISA

Yeah, hey, Shiv.

> SHIV

Wow, how funny, seeing you here. How interesting. What are you doing here?

> LISA

Yeah well, I'm not the dog walker obviously.

> SHIV

Oh you're repping my brother? Well this is awkward. What with us being old friends. Still – great that you've handled it so clean, you know, waiting to bump into me here on the stairs to let me know?

> LISA

Hey. We're busy people, right, Shiv?

But then Roman arrives with Shiv, they look at each other. It's right in the balance. Lisa and Keith move on.

They head in. Connor is there with news.

> CONNOR

Dad sent donuts.

Box of fancy donuts on the table.

> SHIV

What the fuck?

> CONNOR

Dad has sent some perfectly innocent and I am sure safe-to-eat, donuts.
> *(he has a card)*
He wants us to 'all have a nice tea party'.

> KENDALL

It's fine. He's gonna know. Of course he is.

> SHIV
> *(to Kendall)*

Did you tell him?

> KENDALL

Shiv? C'mon.

SHIV

Oh fuck. What?

Everyone looks at the donuts. Connor goes to take one.

Well I wouldn't eat one.

CONNOR

No?

SHIV

I mean, sure but, I mean?

CONNOR

You think he would – send poison donuts to the house of his grandchildren?

ROMAN

I'm like ninety-eight percent sure they won't be poisoned.

KENDALL

Okay, these are irrelevant. So—

ROMAN

Well, no I'd say those are relevant donuts.

Kendall looks at Connor.

KENDALL

So, you wanna—? I'll make the call. Right now. We'll say it tonight. It's over. We're in. New dawn.

Roman and Shiv look at one another. Con is studying the donuts and card. Spooked.

Con. Stop looking at the fucking donuts, man. It's – just— Okay, focus.

CONNOR

I'm out.

KENDALL

Well fine. You're irrelevant.

CONNOR

Hey fuck you.

KENDALL

Go on. Go.

CONNOR

No because—

KENDALL

You're not wanted. You're not wanted, you're not wanted,
you're not wanted.

ROMAN
(*to Connor*)
You love this don't you, this is your dream?

CONNOR

Carry on, I can take it.

Kendall looks a little out of control.

KENDALL

Rome?

ROMAN

Sorry, bro.

KENDALL

Why?

ROMAN

A number of reasons.

KENDALL

Like? What, you think I can't win? No. *We'll* win. Come on,
man, what I eat don't make you shit, there's enough for us all.

ROMAN

I have made a decision to stick with Dad.

KENDALL

You're a fucking, moron. Shiv.

SHIV

No, I'm with Dad.

KENDALL

Why?

SHIV

Because I am.

KENDALL

Why?

SHIV

Why? I don't have to tell you.

KENDALL

Well yes you do. Have you been spooked by fucking donuts, that's pathetic, Shiv. You owe me an explanation.

SHIV

Yeah, because you've always been so careful to keep me fully informed.

Kendall can see Roman won't jump if Shiv doesn't. When Roman won't return his gaze, Kendall returns his anger and focus to Shiv.

KENDALL

Why? You don't believe me? Obviously, you believe me. So you're literally choosing the wrong thing over the right thing? That's what you're doing?

SHIV

I know you're angry but don't project your own disappointment on to me, okay?

KENDALL

There – are, times, to be someone. It's high tide.

SHIV

I ought to go.

KENDALL

Is it cowardice or avarice? I'm intrigued? It's because you don't take over – is that it? Well, good luck with sleeping on that, Shiv.

SHIV

Fuck you, Armani Jesus.

KENDALL

You're a piece of shit.

SHIV

Oh right, I was the only one that mattered, I was the only one you wanted?

We might clock this lands with Roman. Sounds plausible that Kendall said this.

> KENDALL

Yeah only cos you're the girl. Girls count double now, didn't you know?

> SHIV

Yeah yeah, I know. I fucking know.

> KENDALL

It's only your teats that give you any value, so you know.

Shiv picks up some things.

You're calling it wrong. And you're fucking over the victims and you're fucking renewal at the company and and therefore in the country and on the planet. So well done, dipshit.

Jess pops her head in, looks at Kendall who flashes angry.

> CONNOR

I don't want to destroy Dad. I'm a national figure. It's not good to kill one's father. History teaches us that.

> ROMAN

I think everything teaches us that.

> KENDALL

Yeah you're a prick. You're a bunch of pricks. Goodnight!

Kendall walks out. Jess is there.

What?

INT. SARAJEVO HOTEL — NIGHT

Logan is looking at news footage: 'A House Divided: Family Civil War'. He looks at Marcia.

> LOGAN

I think I need to get back to the city. People need to see a little family unity.

> MARCIA

Of course.
> (*then*)
And you do have things, you could say, no, to stop him?

She looks at him.

142

LOGAN
You drop some bombs, you get burnt too, you know?

Hugo arrives with phone.

Shiv?

HUGO
Roman.

LOGAN
(*into phone*)
Uh-huh. Romulus?

Intercut with:

INT. ROMAN AND SHIV'S CAR – NIGHT

Roman is in the back seat with Shiv.

ROMAN
Hey, Pop.

LOGAN
You got her?

ROMAN
Who? The one who matters? Yeah. I'm with her.

LOGAN
Was she there? Was she wobbling?

Shiv looks at Roman. Roman hesitates. The beat lives.

ROMAN
Nah. No. She was trying to get to Kendall, to push him off course.

LOGAN
Uh-huh.

Logan takes it in. Roman lets the moment hang without giving an explanation, then—

ROMAN
She was dark cos she was all-in on trying to get to him, trying to talk him round. To like burn the papers. But she couldn't change his mind. He's gone bananas . . .

143

Logan soaks it all in.

LOGAN

Uh-huh.

Does he believe Roman?

Is she solid?

*Does Roman let Logan know, in the subtlest way, with his voice, that
Shiv was in play?*

ROMAN

Oh yeah. Yeah. She's solid.

Shiv looks at him.

LOGAN

Uh-huh. Okay. Well, thank you, Tumbledown. I'm getting out of
this shithole. We should be together.

End of call. Shiv looks at Roman.

SHIV

Thanks.

ROMAN

What for?

*But she wants to let him know he could have done better at covering
for her—*

SHIV

For nothing.

ROMAN

I just told the truth, right?

SHIV

Sure. I mean you did a bit of positioning but—

ROMAN

I did not do any positioning! I did the fucking business.

Beat, but she won't quite let that stand.

SHIV

Well, you *kind of* did the business.

They smile as they drive, they both know the game.

INT. CONNOR'S CAR – NIGHT

Connor gets in with Willa. She's there with a laptop.

> CONNOR
> Hey. Thanks for coming.

> WILLA
> No worries. I've only been writing. And crying.

> CONNOR
> How are the hate-watch numbers?

> WILLA
> Yeah I mean fine. I guess it's hard to be a really big hate-watch hit. But, I guess, gotta make that nut back?

He looks at her.

> It's fine. I mean, it's my fault. So. I'm a laughing stock. 'Haha'.

Connor thinks. Looks at her.

> CONNOR
> Yeah. Let's kill it. Let's pull it.

> WILLA
> Yeah, Con. They've sold the tickets?

> CONNOR
> Yeah well, fuck 'em. Find something else to hate, dickwads. No one laughs at you. You're fucking amazing.

Willa looks at him. That's not nothing.

DAY TWO

EXT. NEW YORK – DAY

Dawn breaks.

INT. LAWYER'S OFFICE – DAY

Greg is with Ewan at a lawyer's office. Posters and photos, mementos of progressive causes and issues.

> GREG
> Er Gramps? This isn't the lawyer I had recommended?

EWAN

Pugh's a good fellow. He's helping me set my estate in order.

An older lawyer, Pugh, comes in with a coffee.

PUGH

Hey there. Just getting a double black eye.
(*to Greg*)
Strong filter with a double espresso shot. Fire up Charles
Babbage's Difference Engine here!

Taps his head.

GREG

Oh. Oh right. Nice.

*Ewan greets his old acquaintance with a smile and one of the slogans
of their youth—*

EWAN

America is always right . . .

PUGH

. . . Never left.

They smile a shared smile.

EWAN

I think you're going to like Pugh. He's incredibly intransigent.

GREG

Right? Good. Yeah. So may I enquire, do you have much
experience in this realm?

PUGH

Gregory, Gregory. Gregory Hitch.

GREG

Hirsch.

Pugh looks at a file.

PUGH

Right you are. So. Priority one: Your well-being and a
satisfactory outcome.

GREG

Good. Okay. Yes. Yes.

PUGH

Priority two: Expose the structural contradictions of capitalism as reified in the architecture of corporate America.

GREG

Uh-huh. Good, also good.

PUGH

You're our little wedge, Greg. A nice little wedge to open the hood and have a poke around in at Waystar.

GREG

Okay. Good, I guess I am quite focussed on like – my position, and me in particular not getting fired or going to jail – if that isn't too selfish?

PUGH

Eyes on the prize, Greg. Eyes on the prize.

GREG

Uh-huh. Uh-huh. Good.

EXT. TETERBORO AIRPORT – DAY

A line of vehicles. Shiv is waiting in one of the cars.

A private jet plane comes in to land. Logan looks out the window.

Tom and the rest of the gang head down the steps. Tom heads over to the car, gets in and kisses Shiv.

There are photographers a discreet distance away.

INT. LOGAN'S PLANE – DAY/EXT. SHIV'S CAR – DAY

Inside the plane, Hugo is on the phone, peering out. Logan is waiting in his seat.

HUGO

Will she get out?

Karolina gets out and walks past Roman, who is waiting, to the window of Shiv's car.

INT. SHIV'S CAR – DAY

> KAROLINA
>
> Is she gonna get out?

> TOM
> (*reporting*)
> Um, we think it's a little chilly?

> KAROLINA
> (*into phone*)
> They're eager to wait till he gets in the car.

> HUGO
> (*into phone*)
> We'd love it, if she'd greet him outside?

> TOM
> (*to Karolina*)
> We could maybe crack the window?

> KAROLINA
> (*into phone*)
> They could crack the window?

> HUGO
> (*into phone*)
> We would love that outdoor hug?

Shiv shakes her head to Tom. Tom makes a face to Karolina.

> KAROLINA
> (*into phone*)
> It's not happening.

Then: Logan heads down the steps.

There are photographers in evidence who get shots of him.

Roman is there with Gerri. Roman gives Logan a handshake-hug.

Logan is met by PRs and lawyers. He goes to Shiv's car and gets in the back.

INT. SHIV'S CAR — DAY

As they travel into the city the vibrations between father and daughter are complex.

> LOGAN
> You couldn't get out for your old man?

> SHIV
> I'm sorry, I didn't know.

> LOGAN
> Uh-huh. Good to see you Pinky.

> SHIV
> Good to have you back, Dad.

He leafs through newspaper cuttings that Karolina has prepared. News stories about yesterday's press conference.

> LOGAN
> Woulda been nice to get the hug?

> SHIV
> Thanks for the donuts.
> *(then)*
> I think they got shots of me through the window anyway.

> LOGAN
> Not for the shot. For the – for the hug.

Probably not true, is it?

> SHIV
> Sure. 'Captain Cuddles'.

He smiles. She smiles. They quite like the fencing.

Maybe she gives his hand a touch.

> LOGAN
> So, what do we need to do here?

> SHIV
> I dunno?

> LOGAN
> I'd like to get you in now. Before the shareholder meet. High level. 'President'.

> SHIV

Uh-huh. What does it mean?

> LOGAN

It means whatever you want it to mean.

> SHIV

So, made-up?

> LOGAN

Someone at the top with – credibility.

> SHIV

Uh-huh. A mascot?

> LOGAN

My eyes and my ears, Shiv. At the heart of everything through this shitstorm, but wearing a full chemical and biological suit going by the name of Gerri Kellman?

He smiles.

As we end we cut between the three kids—

INT. LISA'S OFFICE – DAY

Kendall in at Lisa's office with her and Keith and the team. Is he winning?

INT. SHIV'S CAR – DAY

President Shiv. Smiling next to her father. Is she?

INT. ROMAN'S CAR – DAY

Roman plotting with Gerri.

All have a plausible route to the throne.

Episode Three
THE DISRUPTION

Written by Ted Cohen & Georgia Pritchett
Directed by Cathy Yan

Original air date 31 October 2021

Cast

LOGAN ROY	Brian Cox
KENDALL ROY	Jeremy Strong
MARCIA ROY	Hiam Abbass
GREG HIRSCH	Nicholas Braun
SHIV ROY	Sarah Snook
ROMAN ROY	Kieran Culkin
CONNOR ROY	Alan Ruck
TOM WAMBSGANS	Matthew Macfadyen
FRANK VERNON	Peter Friedman
KARL MULLER	David Rasche
GERRI KELLMAN	J. Smith-Cameron
KAROLINA NOVOTNEY	Dagmara Dominczyk
HUGO BAKER	Fisher Stevens
JESS JORDAN	Juliana Canfield
NAOMI PIERCE	Annabelle Dexter-Jones
NATE SOFRELLI	Ashley Zukerman
KERRY CASTELLABATE	Zoë Winters
COLIN STILES	Scott Nicholson
BERRY SCHNEIDER	Jihae
COMFREY PELLITS	Dasha Nekrasova
LISA ARTHUR	Sanaa Lathan
REMI BISHOP	KeiLyn Durrel Jones
MICHELLE-ANNE	Linda Emond
CELESTE	Paris Benjamin
TANA	Melissa Miller
REECE	Drew Ledbetter
DAVIS	William Connell
FRONT-DESK SECURITY GUARD	Michael Paul Smith
SECURITY GUARD 2	Louis Holmes
SOPHIE IWOBI	Ziwe
EXECUTIVE PRODUCER	Stephanie Janssen
PRODUCTION ASSISTANT	Regan Moro
RECEPTIONIST	Nic Inglese
LAWYER	Gabriel Marin
EMCEE	Cory Stonebrook
DYLAN	Will Tracy

RAY	Patch Darragh
MARK RAVENHEAD	Zack Robidas
SONAM	Tenzing Kalden
CATHLEEN CARMICHAEL	Kelly Nash
DELTA PIKE	Sharla McBride
JUNE	Taylor Rae Almonte
GALA PHOTOGRAPHER	Daniel Lalor
LAWYER	Gabriel Marin
SOCIETY PHOTOGRAPHER	Osiris Valerio
GALA REPORTER	Allyson Woods

DAY ONE

INT. HOTEL RESTAURANT – DAY

Kendall talks with a journalist, Tana.

> KENDALL
>
> —Yeah it's a shit show over there apparently.

> TANA
>
> Yeah?

> KENDALL
>
> Oh yeah, advertisers bailing. Gerri Kellman in charge? I'm sorry, Gerri's great. I actually love Gerri. But Gerri is a time-server who's way out of her depth. Meanwhile, the DOJ and I are in contact about the terms of my immunity deal. So, yeah. Does not look good for them.

> TANA
>
> Wow. Right.

> KENDALL
>
> As we said – all that's on background I'm afraid, lot of moving parts. But please – let's dive in!

She hits record on her phone and puts it on the table.

> TANA
>
> Okay!

A waiter sets down plates.

> KENDALL
>
> So will this be in the piece? 'Kendall Roy ordered a Cobb salad and picked at it inquisitively'?

Tana smiles.

> TANA
>
> You're quite concerned with how you're going to come across?

KENDALL

Not really. No.

(thinks)

I dunno. Maybe. Look, I come from a world of, of image. That's the family business I guess. But the path I'm on now is about saying, 'You know what? Let's cut the bullshit. This is me, this is what I believe.'

Then Kendall hits a note of gentle self-mockery to re-emphasize how incredibly frank he is being—

That's the new image I'm selling.

TANA

And how does that feel? To be outside the image thing?

KENDALL

Great. I'm not trying to prove anything anymore, right? Did you see the Sophie Iwobi monologue?

TANA

Umm—

KENDALL

Yeah she did a bit – 'Oedipussy'. Funny right? But it doesn't hurt now because, I am who I am. And I have an aim or mission, to be like, if it doesn't sound too naive, to be – good. And to plant a flag – I want to physically get in and plant a flag for that inside my family's business.

TANA

And in terms of family business, one question that people have is about your siblings? Where are they in this? Have you managed to stay close with them?

KENDALL

(no)

You know, sure. There are issues but – essentially, yes. We'll always have our connection.

(beat)

I'm just really happy in my headspace. And I hope they're happy in theirs?

DAY TWO

INT. WAYSTAR – BULLPEN – DAY

Shiv reads something on her phone as she walks. She shakes her head in annoyed disbelief. Roman catches up.

> ROMAN
> Hey. El Presidente. How's your headspace? Are you happy in it?

> SHIV
> Ugh. You like the ending?

> ROMAN
> 'Ooh, I love my kids, what are their names again? Blur Face and Who Cares?'

Shiv heads off towards Logan's office. Roman to see Gerri—

INT. WAYSTAR – GERRI'S OFFICE – DAY

Gerri's office – Gerri, lightly wearing her enhanced status, looks at Roman approaching. She is in with Karl and Karolina.

> GERRI
> And let's press go on that sale – the Israeli machine-learning operation.

> KARL
> *(he has doubts)*
> O-kay?

> GERRI
> What?

What about Logan?

> KARL
> Nothing, good. Let me get into that.

> GERRI
> Fuck you, Karl. They're losing five mil a year on zero revenue. It's board approved.

Karl looks over to Logan's office.

> Look at me.

I am!

As Roman stops by.

ROMAN
Action stations. Strategy meet. Time to go tickle my dad's balls. The job we hate to love!

INT. WAYSTAR – LOGAN'S OFFICE – DAY

A way off, Logan is looking over towards Gerri's office, Gerri with Roman and Karl and Karolina.

LOGAN
I just hope our Acting CEO isn't getting too fucking acting.

Tom and Frank are in his office waiting. Shiv has grabbed Hugo to talk in the area outside his office.

FRANK
I tell you what's a scary story we should maybe reboot? *Pinocchio*. A puppet that comes to life.

Logan smiles. Tom does an insinuating laugh.

LOGAN
Where the fuck is everyone? C'mon, let's start – they can catch up, what's on fire?

Roman arrives.

ROMAN
Hey. Dad, how's your headspace?

Karolina arrives with Hugo and Shiv—

A guy with a headband walks past, eating. Logan clocks him as he passes.

LOGAN
Who's this, Mr fucking Headband having a cronut on my time?

Now Karl makes it in.

I hear Gerri is looking at the Israeli outfit?

KARL

Oh, uh, it's pretty insignificant.

LOGAN

No. I have, I have a shape of things in mind for that. GoJo, streaming and— Just kill that, thanks.

Karl is uncomfortable, hesitates.

You wanna check the chain of command?

Gerri enters, doesn't know quite where to locate herself. Maybe there is a too peripheral seat she doesn't know whether to take.

What does he mean, 'plant a flag', ah?
                    (*to Gerri without looking*)
Please don't fucking hover.

TOM

There's talk Kendall might be planning to come in?

LOGAN

Are you kidding? In here? That rat sets one foot inside this building, I'll punch him in the nose. Okay?

ROMAN

Well that seems like a grown-up solution that keeps everyone happy?

LOGAN

Find out what this fuck is planning, I don't want him between my teeth right now.

Shiv has an idea.

SHIV

I can – I can scope that out.
                    (*then*)
But what are we doing to counter?

LOGAN

Yes! The rest of you, you should be out there, call him out on this!

Shiv and Roman maybe avoid eye contact with Logan. Not sure they want to do that.

> SHIV

Well we did discuss the town hall event?

Logan is just about agreeable, makes a growl of assent.

> GERRI

I like it. Something to bring everyone together. Open, anonymous questions. Employee-facing.

Logan maybe makes the wanker sign.

> SHIV

I'm happy to lead that if we want, if it's about change?

Gerri feels slightly sidelined, she and Roman share a look.

> ROMAN

Now who's planting a flag?

> FRANK

A town hall is timely. I heard the flooded floors in the executive washroom was maybe a protest.

> ROMAN

I think it was just one of your mega-turds, Frank. But I guess someone wants to turn that into Silkwood?

Karolina, attentive as ever, picks up Shiv's baton.

> KAROLINA

In terms of getting proactive. Hugo had Frankton's put together some full-page responses.

> HUGO

There were a couple we liked.

Hugo has some artwork to lay out – a couple of full-page ads. Waystar logo, some pledges and big text: 'We Get It'.

Full page. With a number of like, pledges – we can figure out the verbiage – and the tagline 'We Get It'.

> LOGAN

As in?

> HUGO

As in you, know, 'we get it', as in, 'it's okay, we hear you and we get it.' I thought it was quite – funky.

ROMAN

'We get it'. A bit like those ladies on the cruise ships got it?

HUGO

Gerri liked it?

SHIV

Yeah. 'We Get It' yeah could sound kind of like, 'Yeah, yeah, we get it already, stop moaning about the rapes.'

LOGAN

Fine. Fine. But—

(to Karolina)

let's talk about what media to put the kids in. Okay?

Shiv and Roman eat it with queasy nods.

What else?

TOM

Um – I think I need to do a dinner for our blue-chip ad buyers. They're spooked.

ROMAN

Did you see him tagging their accounts on Twitter? I'm so embarrassed.

LOGAN

Sure. You want me to – come by, sprinkle some fuck-dust?

Tom doesn't want him there.

TOM

Um . . . Could you?

Logan can sense it.

Kerry comes in.

KERRY

Logan, um, we have agents on the phone asking if Waystar will accept service of a document subpoena?

LOGAN

Tell them to fuck off.

Chuckles.

                              KERRY
Okay . . .

                              GERRI
Kerry, hold on. He's kidding.

                              SHIV
Dad?

But Logan remains resolute. Gerri nods discreetly for Kerry to not go just yet. But who will speak up?

                              GERRI
I just wonder if we might start playing ball, Logan? I mean everybody cooperates.

                              LOGAN
Maybe I don't do that dance?

                              GERRI
How – does that feel in regards to the shareholder meeting?

Logan shrugs.

We don't accept service, in an hour, they'll send two agents to serve us. While they're at it, they could subpoena you to the grand jury.

                              LOGAN
Fuck 'em.

                              KERRY
Logan?

Looks all around.

An expression from Shiv: What's the point?

                              LOGAN
They can fuck off.

A couple of people look to Shiv as a new weighty figure in the room.

                              SHIV
Whatever.

                              KARL
Uh-huh. Ballsy.

ROMAN

Still works. It does work.

GERRI

Look, fine, if that's the call, that's the call.

Gerri and Roman exchange a glance.

INT. WAYSTAR – GREG'S OFFICE – DAY

Tom enters.

TOM

FBI, hands up!

Greg is startled but recovers.

GREG

Heh, how's it going?

TOM

To be honest?
(*sighs*)
Not great, Greg. It's looking pretty bad with the investigation, and Logan says we have to take these.

Tom shakes two white tablets out of a container in his pocket and places them on Greg's desk.

Cyanide pills. The whole team.

Greg buys it for a millisecond, but then—

It's a mint, you doofus. Take one, your breath does stink.
(*then*)
Listen. Can I show you something?

INT. WAYSTAR – MEZZANINE – SHABBY OFFICE – DAY

Tom and Greg enter a small shabby office.

TOM

So I was thinking, 'Greg, my chief of staff – leggy princeling of ATN – he deserves a new office.' What you think?

GREG

It's – I mean, it's not very nice?

TOM

Well that's rude, rude boy. It's your new office.

GREG

But this is the travel department?

TOM

Nice folks. High fliers. The wits have designated it the Pet Cemetery I believe.

GREG

Okay. I see. This . . . Is this punishment? Is this because of me not taking the company lawyer? Am I getting demoted?

TOM

Of course not, Greg! In the middle of an investigation? No. This is just part of a totally standard office rationalization. No! Do whatever you like. Hang out with Kendall. Take any counsel you want!
(then)
I hear you have a great lawyer. Is it true you can find him anytime day or night . . . ?

GREG

Umm . . . ?

TOM

. . . because he has one of those bow ties that lights up and spins round?

GREG

He's actually really good. I'm very very happy.

Tom looks around. Makes sure door is closed.

TOM

Uh-huh. Look, on the level, buddy. There's a million knives being sharpened. The DOJ is gonna be a combine harvester in a wheat field of dicks. So. Look, I can see this is tough. I've gone Waystar. I think that's safest. *But*. I'm actually seeing a pal tonight? To get an objective take on my situation. If you want I can fold you in?

GREG

Tonight? Okay. Right—

TOM

Thought over a beer, we could, just kick back and recall what happened. Check we both *remember it exactly the same way?*

GREG

Fuck. Okay?

But Tom can see Greg is unsure.

TOM

What?

GREG

Um, no. No. It's just – Ken—

TOM

Fuck Ken.

GREG

Yeah. No sure. But . . .

TOM

What?

GREG

It's tricky, Tom, he's figuring me out a watch to say thanks. I dunno. He needs me.

TOM

'He needs me.' Fuck him. I need you.

GREG

Can I come along later?

Tom looks at him.

I'm in a difficult position, Tom. I'll try to come. I want to come.

TOM

You sold your ass for a watch? I'll buy you a watch, dickwad. Fucking come over. You don't have to be 'Gregory the Accessory the Boy with the Unfortunate Trajectory'.

Tom heads out. Greg looks around. Shit.

INT. WAYSTAR — KENDALL'S OFFICE — DAY

Hugo and Karolina have invited Shiv and Roman in for a chat. They are using Kendall's office. The siblings side by side.

KAROLINA

So look, your dad wants, wanted, to get you – there and he has asked us to talk with you – how to, how to—

HUGO

to deploy you.

SHIV

Uh-huh. Like tanks? Or army men?

HUGO

Positive stuff is notably absent. The public discourse about your dad feels really, one-sided.

KAROLINA

So we would love to get your help with more dimensions. Your experiences of him.

The siblings look appalled.

SHIV

Uh-huh.

KAROLINA

Very controlled – business interview – with some softballs at the end.

HUGO

So, Shiv, or someone like Shiv, talking about him. Sharing some memories, feelings about your father.

SHIV

Me?

HUGO

Well, you or someone like you?

SHIV

Right, and who is like me would you say?

HUGO

Your dad just wondered? To help gently – pump some humanizing material into the culture?

SHIV

I think I'm best placed neutralizing Kendall.

She's not going to do it.

KAROLINA

Well we'd love to get some more positive stuff floating around the media environment. From you or – yeah someone like you?

Roman looks between them – it's down to him.

ROMAN

Fine fuck you I'll go out and say I love Dad, sure. Why not? I do. So. Fuck you.

SHIV

Look at you. The cutest cheerleader in high school. Is it true you let the track team finger-bang you for lunch money?

INT. KENDALL'S LIMO – EVENING

Later – on Greg. Sipping champagne. Looking around. He and Naomi and Kendall and Comfrey are giggly. Reece, Kendall's watch guy, is showing Greg a watch.

GREG

I like it. I do. What do you think, Ken?
(*holds up the watch*)
I mean it's very expensive. And I usually use my phone for my time needs.

KENDALL

Fuck it, man. You deserve it.

REECE

Dude, your phone is a widget. It's a straw, a button – it's fucking air. Every janitor in America has one. The watch is your *Mona fucking Lisa*.

Elsewhere in the car, a sense of wild, buzzed giddiness.

KENDALL

Okay, Reece, shut the fuck up, are we ready? Ladies and gentlemen, because it is game time! And the game is . . . Good Tweet/Bad Tweet!

Laughs and cheers.

You crazy fuckers better have these ready when I call them out. You ready?

NAOMI

Jesus, just start already!

KENDALL

Okay, aaaaand . . . GOOD TWEET!

Naomi stifles a laugh while reading a tweet from her phone.

NAOMI

Okay . . . @BowlerBomb tweets: 'Allies don't always come in the form we like. But what Kendall Roy did was important and brave.'

KENDALL

Boom! That's that shit!

The limo explodes with cheers.

Greg mockingly tries to kiss Kendall's ass.

All right, all right, all right. You guys ready? BAD TWEET!

GREG
(reads from phone)
'Kendall Roy is not a hero, fam. He's bootleg Ross with a daddy complex.'

KENDALL

YES! Love it. LOVE IT!

Everyone laughs. It's like he's indestructible.

Keep 'em coming, motherfuckers. GOOD TWEET!

COMFREY
(reads from phone)
'Maybe it's just cos he's murking his shitty dad, but I kind of want to fuck Kendall Roy?'

KENDALL

Oh hells yeah! Booya!

Huge cheers.

Yo, what time is it y'all?

> EVERYONE
> (*chanting*)
> BAD TWEET! BAD TWEET! BAD TWEET!

> KENDALL

Hit me, yo!

> COMFREY
> (*reads*)
> 'He clearly has mental health issues and crazy guilt coupled with
> addiction. That's all this is. And it's sad.'

That one wasn't very funny. A mini beat. Then—

> KENDALL

Boooooo!

> EVERYONE
> BOOOOOOOOOOO!

> KENDALL
> (*starting a chant*)
> That! One! Sucked!

> EVERYONE
> THAT! ONE! SUCKED! THAT! ONE! SUCKED!

EXT. FANCY HOTEL – EVENING

*A sign for the Committee for the Protection and Welfare of
Journalists (CPWJ) benefit.*

*They all get out of the limo. Greg doesn't really want to be seen out
with Kendall – keeps out of things. There are six or seven society
and news photographers. Kendall's one of the more exciting names.
They snap photos and call his name. He likes it. Berry is there to meet
them. She and Comfrey try to usher him in . . .*

> KENDALL
> (*spotting someone*)
> Yo, what up, kid? Stay free.

Photos flashing all around Kendall.

> > (*to Berry*)
> Should I give them something?

Berry looks like: Shall we just go in?

> > (*yells out to photographers*)
> Fuck the patriarchy!

Kendall and his crew giggle at their thrilling transgressiveness as they head inside.

INT. FANCY HOTEL — EVENING

A large gala event with tables, champagne, appetizers. A liberal New York media-elite vibe.

Berry is there with Comfrey. Kendall clocks their air of disapproval. He can't have anyone not love him right now, so tries to move on but comes back—

> KENDALL
> What? You guys are mad at me now?

They maybe all head in.

> BERRY
> Of course not. It's a photo and a joke. We just talked about scarcity value and bidding up your cultural price?

> KENDALL
> Uh-huh, I just think that's a really lame strategy.

> BERRY
> Well, fine.

> KENDALL
> I'm kidding, no, I say that with respect, because I want to be real here, because it's an honor to have three totally badass women in my corner. Which sounds corny, but whatever. So.

> COMFREY
> No, thank you.

> BERRY
> It's just the headspace interview? We had a *long call* with Lisa about her need for oversight.

KENDALL

Lisa *my* lawyer. Who I'm paying? This is a full-spectrum situation okay? The legal theater is maybe not even the main theater. I dropped a bomb. The whole world is watching for my next move.

They look at him uncomfortably. That's not quite it. Kendall heads over to Naomi or she drifts to him.

Hey. Nice huh? Your natural habitat?

NAOMI

I have a tremendous urge to set fire to everything.

KENDALL

You smell crazy good.

NAOMI

Fuck off and get schmoozing.

KENDALL

You know what, it's actually cool to be with people who give a shit.

NAOMI

Yup, they really give a shit. About their overall deals.

KENDALL
(*smiles*)
Ooh, Ms Cool Girl's seen it all, folks.

A waiter passes with champagne. He gets one for Naomi.

Can I get a water with cayenne pepper, lemon juice, and maple syrup?

He sees Shiv. They look at one another. A crackle around. Other people look at them clocking one another.

With Shiv as she and Kendall make eye contact. Perhaps Kendall does a cheers with Naomi's drink. Then, from another direction, Shiv is blindsided by Nate.

NATE

Shiv fucking Roy? Great to see you here.

SHIV

I always come.

> NATE

Committee for the Protection and Welfare of Journalists? You're into that, but you like to keep them protected, in hutches, correct? With the, little feeding bottles, kind of like hamsters?

> SHIV

Hehe. You know what, we do keep more newspapers alive and employ more journalists worldwide than any other company. So I guess we're doing our bit?

> NATE

Uh-huh. Soviet Union employed a ton of journalists too.

> SHIV

Wow we got to Stalin fast. Is Gil still turning up on *Russia Today* 'by mistake'?

Nate waves at Kendall, who has the balls to come over and join the pair.

> NATE

Oh hey, Ken! Wow. 'It's a family affair.'

> KENDALL

Hey. Hey, man.

Kendall hugs and backslaps Nate quickly. Nothing for Shiv.

> SHIV

Mhm. Hey.

> KENDALL

Wow I didn't think you'd be here. I thought the 'President' of Waystar Royco would be too busy?

> SHIV

I'm on the advisory. Whereas you're – the newest attraction at the zoo. Half man, half Nobel Prize.

They feel people watching.

> KENDALL
> (to Nate)

I wanted to talk to you, actually, about Gil. Some public questions, someone needs to keep an eye on strings getting pulled. There has to be proper oversight.

SHIV

Wouldn't it be amazing if you had an opportunity to do that in a public forum, like in Congress?

Nate knows he's being used as a Shiv-needler but doesn't mind.

NATE

Hey he's welcome in. We're always looking for new members. Like Costco.

SHIV

Or the Khmer Rouge.

Nate takes his leave. Fake, mean smiles with Shiv. Leaving her with her brother.

KENDALL

So how is he? Is he all, like, angry hog at the state fair, rolling in shit and snapping at kids?

SHIV

He's fine. Worried you might come in.

KENDALL

Let him worry.

SHIV

Yeah well that would just be dumb. We all need for us to win the shareholder vote. You too. Just wait a week, okay? And cool it on the interviews. That's just smart all round.

KENDALL

Uh-huh. Well, maybe. I'm not a suicide bomber.

She looks at him.

I wanted to say, um, just – at Rava's, I think I'm right, I am right, but, I maybe threw a couple of ugly rocks in there.

SHIV

Uh-huh.

KENDALL

I'm just trying to be – thoughtful now. So.

SHIV

Look. I actually think we have the same aim here is the truth. Big picture. I'm tired of all this too. And I'm pushing for change.

Like is there a world where maybe if you stop being gross and throwing stones, we can acknowledge, and rebuild. Truth and reconciliation. And, maybe we find a way to actually fucking fix things, from inside, which is the only place anything ever gets done?

Kendall looks at her, clocks why she's here.

> KENDALL
> They made you get all dressed up for this?

> SHIV
> Or do you not actually give a fuck? And is it all just ego?

> KENDALL
> Look at this. It's you now. I'm sorry for you, Siobhan.

Competitive pity. Infuriating.

At the podium, an MC is in the midst of introducing Kendall as a presenter.

> EMCEE
> Ladies and gentlemen! To present our next award, a man who's used to owning the news rather than making the news . . . Kendall Roy.

Kendall bounds up to the podium and launches into it—

> KENDALL
> Thank you for that, semi-respectful intro. I was very pleased to be invited. And, no, it's true though, I—
> (*sees someone he knows*)
> Oh hey. Sorry, um, yeah. It's been a crazy week. I am so touched to be here, in a place that's so untouched by hypocrisy and greed and dishonesty . . . mostly. Really! It's very refreshing for me . . . !

Feeling attacked, Shiv heads out.

INT. WAYSTAR – ROMAN'S OFFICE – EVENING

Roman is doing interview prep, feet up. A producer, Davis, sits nearby.

>   DAVIS

So, thanks for making time and when we do it, first section will
just be the South Asian streaming stuff, we'll have to ask the
shareholder-meeting question . . .

>   ROMAN

Uh-huh. Very confident. Massive optimism.

>   DAVIS

Great. Great – and then, as you know, I think you know there's
this idea everyone—
>   (*he's been ordered to do this*)
everyone thought would be really kind of fun, after everything,
if we might crack open the door on some family stuff a little bit?

Roman pretends to retch.

I know. We won't overdo this, so we'll keep it loose and it will
be fun to freewheel it?

>   ROMAN

Tell me precisely every single word they are going to ask.

Davis has all the questions.

>   DAVIS

Well I couldn't disclose specific questions because of our policies
at ATN Business and that would be ethically . . . you know—

Roman just looks at him as he peters out. Davis has a way out—

But, it might be something like . . . 'Logan seems like a business-
orientated guy, what's something special that you and your dad
enjoy doing together?'

>   ROMAN

Nope. Next question.

>   DAVIS

Okay? Sure. Um . . . second one could be like, 'What was a time
your dad came to your aid when you really needed him?'

>   ROMAN

Mmmmm, no. Not doing that.

                              DAVIS
Right. How about . . . 'What is your most cherished father–son
memory?'

                              ROMAN
So far these are very bad.

                              DAVIS
Sorry. Just trying to find a launching point. Maybe . . . 'What's
something silly about Logan Roy we might not know?'

                              ROMAN
Are you fucking kidding me?

                              DAVIS
Or could you lead? Is there a childhood story you could tell?

                              ROMAN
I mean, I got one in the bank. 'Fly-fishing in Montana'. If you
want me to wheel that out?

                              DAVIS
Sure. Sure. Thank you.

INT. LOGAN'S APARTMENT – NIGHT

*Marcia is sitting with Karolina and Celeste and one of Logan's
lawyers. Marcia looks through a list of terms they've agreed, nodding:*

                              MARCIA
Uh-huh. Uh-huh. Yes, yes, yes, yes.

                              KAROLINA
So. Are we happy? Can I tell him we're done?

Marcia lays the list aside.

                              MARCIA
One thing, which does not need to be written down, but for
which I need an understanding, is my physical needs.

                              KAROLINA
Uh-huh? I mean – I probably don't—

                              MARCIA
I need it understood I am free to have that appetite satisfied as
I see fit. I have healthy appetites.

> KAROLINA

Uh-huh, I mean, is that something where I need to be involved in the discussion?

> MARCIA

I would be discreet. But I would need to know it is understood.

Karolina thinks, that's going to be a fun conversation. Maybe she can see Logan out through the door.

> KAROLINA

Right okay. And if I raise that, the idea would be Logan too could seek his own—

Marcia shrugs.

> MARCIA

A cactus only needs a little water.

Outside. Logan peers in as he greets Shiv.

> KAROLINA

Well I can pass that along then.

> MARCIA

And I don't want him hovering around me on this.

> KAROLINA

Certainly, understood.

> MARCIA

I come and go where I please, with whom I please. My business, yes?

> KAROLINA

Uh-huh, well I will pass that on as well.

Their negotiations continue in the background.

> SHIV

You okay?

> LOGAN

Love and marriage.

> LOGAN

I can feel another million drain with every cluck from that henhouse.

                              LOGAN

Lala.

*Maybe Shiv and Marcia say hello through the doorway as Logan
leads Shiv to where he wants to sit.*

                              LOGAN

So, did you see him?

                              SHIV

I did.

                              LOGAN

Is he gonna come in?

                              SHIV

I don't know. I don't think so. I think he gets it.

                              LOGAN

Uh-huh. Thank you. You know every day I don't see you out
there saying something, I think, does Shiv even like me?

                              SHIV

Isn't Roman—?

                              LOGAN

Yeah but my daughter? My only daughter.

                              SHIV

What is it exactly you want me to do?

                              LOGAN

I dunno. Maybe I'd like you to draw a circle round him? Declare
that your father isn't some . . . dirty bastard. The truth maybe –
about him.

                              SHIV

The truth, but horrible, right?

                              LOGAN

I mean, do you trust me?

                              SHIV

Yes. Of course.

                              (then)

On what?

                             LOGAN

On all this – hullabaloo.

                           SHIV

'Hullabaloo'? Yeah.

                           (then)

I don't know.

                           (then)

Yeah.

                           (then)

I mean. We can talk?

                             LOGAN

Yes we can talk.

                           SHIV

We're a big company. But how bad – is—? What is the worst thing that could be in those papers?

                             LOGAN

Not even that bad. Health and safety, compliance. Few bad apples.

Okay, he's lying to her. Her face falls.

                           SHIV

Uh-huh.

                             LOGAN

What?

                           SHIV

Well I know that's not true.

He makes a face like: Really?

Tom was in cruises, Dad, Bill told him. I know there were black ops, there was targeted intimidation of whistleblowers and victims, there was—

                           LOGAN

Fine. Maybe there were some salty moves.

                           SHIV

You can't just change your story . . .!

LOGAN

I want to keep you clean! I put Gerri in, but I can't trust her.
She's optics. I need you.

That provokes a range of feelings. Nice, but really?

Look, I didn't know about any of the – shit.

SHIV

Well, you're on emails?

LOGAN

You know how many emails I get a day? I don't read my emails.
I get action points.

SHIV

Yeah I know—

LOGAN

Shiv. The world is fucking rough. We ran a cruise line out of tin-
pot ports registered in bongo-fucking-bongo hovels and—

The racism is too much—

SHIV

Dad—

LOGAN

And we poured millions in. And sure, did we play rough with
the odd fucking union boss? Or some Moaning Minnie repeat
litigant? I dunno, it was quarter of a century ago a lot of it. So
yes, I've fought, for you and your brothers, but you're not going
to find a piece of paper that makes you ashamed of me. Okay?

SHIV

Uh-huh?

She looks sad.

LOGAN

Christ, it's just a position, Shiv. There's a million ways through
this.

SHIV

Such as?

LOGAN

I dunno. Bus employees to picket in DC. Run ads in media. Rally surrogates on television. Persuade opinion-formers we're getting spatchcocked. Attack the administration in general. Go after the prosecutors individually.

SHIV

Uh-huh.

LOGAN

I'm not saying we go that way, but let's have a walk round the fucking buffet.

SHIV

The government has an unbelievable amount of leverage at its disposal. The law.

LOGAN

The law is just people and people is politics and I can handle people, okay?

She looks at him.

You help us score some baskets, I'll work the refs. Ah?

He turns on a smile and, despite herself, she does give him a smile.

INT. KENDALL'S APARTMENT – LIVING ROOM – LATE NIGHT

A late-night after-party at Kendall's place. Hip hop, some J Hus, drinks. His crew plus some recruits from the benefit.

Greg is wearing a watch. Shows it to Comfrey. They are a little high. Maybe some discreet powder they've been sharing.

COMFREY

It's – nice. It's a nice watch.

GREG

I have always felt self-conscious about my wrists, so it could address that?

COMFREY

You have totally normal wrists.

GREG

Well that's very kind of you to say. I guess I just have a lot of wrist. Maybe too much?

REECE

Great. So shall we get it figured out – you wanna transfer now? It's forty K.

GREG

Oh no – I think – I think this is a gift situation.

REECE
(*calling over*)
Er, Ken? Are you buying him this?

KENDALL

What? No. I just said I'd hook you up, kiddo.

Greg looks at Kendall, puppy eyes.

What? Don't get weird. I'm not the fucking sugar daddy, cheapskate!

Kendall gets a text.

Hey! Hey hey! Guess what, Sophie Iwobi did me again tonight!

Greg is dying.

GREG

Forty thousand dollars, of money? No, I, I – need to give this back.

REECE

Well no, it has your patina now. We agreed – we've exchanged. Right?

Greg looks at Comfrey. Who shrugs in an entitled way: Yeah, sure, buy it.

Kendall plugs his TV's HDMI cord into his smartphone or connects his phone to TV by a Wi-Fi dongle.

KENDALL

Yeah, she did a segment. Tore me one! 'Oedipussy Two', this time it's a whole seggy!

He turns the music off. Weird party-killing vibe.

Okay, c'mon, buckle up!

COMFREY

Um, shall we – do this tomorrow? We can get you the bullet points—

KENDALL

C'mon, fuck that, we gotta see this!

He plays the clip. On TV: a Samantha Bee-style late-night host, Sophie Iwobi, does her monologue. A picture of Kendall is in the OTS graphic box to her right.

SOPHIE IWOBI

. . . so let's turn for a moment to Kendall Roy. Snitchy Rich. Or as you may know him a jar of mayonnaise in a Prada suit.

The photo of Kendall changes to a funny mock-up of a jar of mayonnaise wearing a nice suit. Kendall smiles, chuckles.

KENDALL

Ha! Okay! Ha!

SOPHIE IWOBI

Boy tweeted earlier today . . .

We see the tweet on screen.

'We must overthrow the culture of corruption that silences women.' The fuck? That's like your dog saying:

ON TV: *funny mock-up of a dog.*

'You guys, you guys, we have to punish whoever ate coffee grounds out of the trash and then shit on the sofa. HASHTAG SOFA JUSTICE!'

Lower third on TV: '#SofaJustice'.

Huge laugh from Kendall.

KENDALL

She's good. That's fine. That's route one. But it's good.

SOPHIE IWOBI

Actual progressives have been embracing this dude. *Why?* This is the guy who told Congress like a month ago that the investigation into his father was a witch-hunt!

Kendall laughs, even though it wasn't a joke.

> And he's also the fail-bro who once posed in this photo flashing a gang sign outside Jean-Georges.

ON TV: Iwobi shows a photo of a younger Kendall making a 'Blood' sign outside a fancy restaurant.

> Poor Kenny. Dude looks like Lil Wayne's tax attorney.

COMFREY
I think she's reaching. You were being tongue-in-cheek.

She looks at Greg but he's just looking at the watch.

KENDALL
That is from Joon's Insta. I think I should go on. Comfrey, can you touch base? What do you think? I think I go on.

SOPHIE IWOBI
See, the problem is, Kendall Roy suffers from a severe case of what doctors call Caucasian Rich Brain.

An anatomical drawing of a human brain. As Sophie explains, animation shows the neural pathways constricting.

> What happens is, genetically inherited wealth and whiteness cause neural pathways in the brain to constrict and make the patient believe he's woke when really he's just a total fucking jackass.

COMFREY
We should talk to Berry. There's a few ways to counter backlash.

KENDALL
This isn't backlash.

COMFREY
Oh – no, I know, but?

KENDALL
This is being in the conversation. This is great.

He watches more. Smiling.

INT. SHIV AND TOM'S APARTMENT – NIGHT
Shiv comes home. Tom is drunk.

TOM

Shivvy!!

SHIV

Hey? Did you have a good night. Did you see your guy?

TOM

Yup. And when I got in, Mondale had eaten some of your
pantyhose and I had to pull them out of his ass.

SHIV

Oh, I'm sorry.

TOM

You shouldn't leave them on the floor, Siobhan. Not once the
help have gone.

SHIV

Are you okay?

TOM

Mondale's not well. Mondale is unsettled. Is Kendall coming in?

SHIV

I don't think so. I went to see my dad and— Yeah, I dunno.
How was your guy?

TOM

How was my guy? Well, yeah I outlined, everything – that might
have happened to a theoretical 'John Doe' divisional head and
you know, we talked about – if what's likely to come out, does
come out, in terms of the investigation and he said, 'It's difficult
to see a world where John Doe doesn't go to jail.' So.

SHIV

Right. Fuck.

(*then*)

Tom, it'll be okay.

TOM

Uh-huh.

(*then*)

I mean, what evidence do you have for that, I'm curious?

SHIV

Tom?

He lets her show some bit of physical affection, a touch or hug.

> TOM
>
> I did have one dumb idea.

> SHIV
>
> Uh-huh?

> TOM
>
> I did think, could it be good to get out front of it?

She looks at him.

> If prison is likely. Could I find in that any benefit?

> SHIV
>
> I don't—?

> TOM
>
> Well if life's going get me raped – do I try to make – rapenade?

> SHIV
>
> What cooperate?

> TOM
>
> Not with the DOJ. Your dad. Go to your dad and offer myself up as the – beating post?

> SHIV
>
> Fuck. I don't think you can do that though, Tom. You're drunk.

Probably what he wants to hear. He would let it go, but—

> But it's smart. It's— I mean that is kind of a win from a no-win?

> TOM
>
> You think?

> SHIV
>
> I mean it's punchy. And I guess there's still a real chance no one goes to prison.

> TOM
>
> Uh-huh. Yeah.

> SHIV
>
> Either way, you bank gold with my dad? Right – the offer? It's kind of genius?

Tom nods, but he's stunned.

TOM
All being well, with a fair wind, I could be done in less than a
year.

SHIV
Oh Jesus. But no. Tom, you can't. You can't. He's got everyone
doing fucking somersaults for him right now.
(*beat, then*)
I just guess, if you did, afterwards, we could do something?

TOM
Like what?

SHIV
I don't know. Get married!

TOM
But we are married?

SHIV
I'm kidding. There was just so much going on last time. We
could do it again. Just us. Renew or whatever, a month in Maui
just us smoking weed and cuddling?

Does sound nice.

DAY THREE

INT. KENDALL'S APARTMENT – BEDROOM – LATE MORNING

*Next morning. Kendall watches Sophie Iwobi on his phone with a
fixed and knowing smile.*

*On the TV, ATN is playing rolling news on mute. He sees Michelle-
Anne on. She's smiling and giving administration talking points about
the day's news.*

Suddenly, he gets out of bed, full of purpose. Makes a call.

KENDALL
Hey. Jess. So I'm going in.

JESS
(*from phone*)
Oh, okay? To the office? When?

> KENDALL

Now.

> JESS
> (*startled pause*)

But you said—

> KENDALL

Yeah. That was a false thought. Make sure my office is ready, I'll ping you before I arrive? Good?

He hangs up and finishes dressing. He makes another call.

Greg. I'm going in.
> (*then*)
I might want to roll deep. Keep it on the down-low, okay? I want to see the shock waves.

INT. ATN STUDIO – DAY

Logan is outside a studio, or in the wings even, waiting with Colin and Kerry.

> TOM

She'll be out momentarily.

> LOGAN

Uh-huh.

> TOM

You okay, sir?

Logan shrugs. Tom speaks at a private volume or angles them so he can discuss things discreetly.

Because I have, ahem, been thinking . . . what is it that you really need right now? And how can I help?

> LOGAN

Uh-huh?

> TOM

Yeah, if it goes – how it could go. Maybe there's no – repercussions. But if not. There'll probably be a cash number and there will probably need to be a face or two, behind bars, right?

                    LOGAN
What's your angle, Tom?

                    TOM
None. No. Just, I'm probably in the firing line. And I wanted
you to know, if you need to strategize. I can be that guy.
                  (*to clarify*)
I'd— step up and go down.

                    LOGAN
Well, it won't come to that.

                    TOM
Of course.

                    LOGAN
But that's it? You don't want anything?

                    TOM
No. That's just there. If you need it. I won't wriggle. Just clonk
the trout on the head and put it in your pouch.

Logan looks at him with a trace of new-found respect.

                    LOGAN
Okay. Well it won't come to that. But thank you. Thank you,
Tom.

Tom stands. Some respect from Logan for the first time ever.

                    TOM
Not a problem.

*Tom walks off – away and round a corner and into his ATN satellite
office near the studios, or a spare empty office.*

INT. ATN – TOM'S OFFICE – DAY

He sits down at his desk. He sits for a moment.

*Then he pulls out his phone and a piece of paper he has somewhere
with a number scratched on it. Dials.*

                RECEPTIONIST
                  (*from phone*)
Bergman, Hendon, and Weiss?

> TOM

Hi. Um . . . yes, hello. So, I was referred this number by a friend of mine. I'm wanting to— I would like to schedule an appointment with Rex Hendon?

> RECEPTIONIST

This is for a consultation?

> TOM

That's right.

> RECEPTIONIST

And can I ask the nature of your visit?

> TOM

Um, do I need to say?
>> (*then*)

Divorce? Or, the possibility thereof.*

Another call comes in on his office line.

Um, can you hold for one moment?
>> (*other line*)

Greg?

> GREG
>> (*from phone*)

Um, so I have something you guys might want to know?

> TOM

Oooh, okay, some intel from the incel?

INT. ATN STUDIO — DAY

Michelle-Anne emerges from her interview with a couple of aides.

> LOGAN

Hey! So. How you doing?

> MICHELLE-ANNE

Great. Are you—? What are you doing down here?

---

* In the edit we took out the direct reference to divorce. Although perhaps still implied, the overt mention seemed to cast too heavy a shadow over subsequent events. A close viewer might spot that Rex Hendon is revealed to be a divorce lawyer in the season finale.

> LOGAN

You were on with Mark right? Isn't he the fucking best?

> MICHELLE-ANNE

Sure. Yeah.

> LOGAN

Yeah, just, as ever, great to have you contribute.
> (*then*)
And could we do five – on what we're gonna do here?

There is a room, she consents to the offer. They enter.

INT. ATN – PRIVATE ROOM – DAY

> MICHELLE-ANNE

Sure, how are things? Look at you, the tough guys! You wouldn't even accept service of a subpoena, right?

> LOGAN

My son stands up and waves his dick in the air and the world's meant to rearrange itself according to his liking. I don't think so, right?

> MICHELLE-ANNE

Right. I see. But are you gonna get more cooperative now that you've set the table?

> LOGAN

It's a witch-hunt. Prosecutors are gonna regret any time or money they spend on it.

So no, he's not going to cooperate . . .

So. What does the old man think?

> MICHELLE-ANNE

Well, he's got poll numbers dancing in front of his eyes morning, noon and night. Someone shits in Wisconsin he's worried it'll float down the Mississippi and hurt his numbers in Iowa.

Logan laughs.

> LOGAN

Relax. We've got his back!

MICHELLE-ANNE

Yeah well. That's – great.

(*then bit of reality*)

I guess, you know, when this thing broke the whole thing was, 'Logan Roy's going down.'

(*then*)

But then you got this thing, some of our folks are like, 'There's no way Roy's going down. President is gonna protect him. THE SYSTEM IS BROKEN!'

LOGAN

People, they have no idea, right? They have these paranoid fantasies.

MICHELLE-ANNE

Yeah, you know, he's always had a connection issue with the base so his room for maneuver is limited.

LOGAN

I mean I don't want you to do anything.

MICHELLE-ANNE

Right.

LOGAN

What I want is – is nothing. Normal consideration and not to become the focus of some bullshit.

MICHELLE-ANNE

Right.

LOGAN

Not favors.

MICHELLE-ANNE

Right.

Now Logan is getting pissed off with her not saying anything.

LOGAN
(*mimicking*)

'Right right right right.'

MICHELLE-ANNE

What?

                              LOGAN
Look, the fact is I never ask for anything because that's not the
way I operate. But I would like to know no one's gonna shit
their pants if I hang tough?

She looks at him.

                          MICHELLE-ANNE
Facebook is full of photos of you and the boss at CPAC and
Davos. All the nice things you've said about each other? It hits
demographics we have to worry about.

He looks at her, sees what way this is blowing.

                              LOGAN
If that Raisin hangs me out to dry I am quite willing to do the
same to him.

                          MICHELLE-ANNE
Well if we're going to be real maybe the president has not been
feeling like your coverage has been very helpful or truthful
lately?

                              LOGAN
Well it could get a lot fucking worse?

Beat. They both breathe.

I did not want this to go like this.

                          MICHELLE-ANNE
We have the same – interest here. Can you lower the
temperature? And I'll see what I can do.

                              LOGAN
Sure. That's all I want, that's all I need.

*Tom is there outside visible, waving, distracting Logan – miming that
Kendall is coming in.*

Uh, what now?

INT. WAYSTAR – GERRI'S OFFICE – DAY

*Roman and Shiv are with Gerri, Hugo and Karolina, going through
questions for the town hall.*

HUGO

We asked everyone to submit concerns and questions
anonymously via the intranet—

KAROLINA

Which has some drawbacks – Shiv, we wanted you to be aware
if you're going to be up there. We'd plan to put these on a screen
and—

SHIV

What are they asking?

HUGO

Well it's fine the general tenor is—
(reading from document)
'What the hell is going on?' A lot of those. Also: 'Is Kendall Roy
telling the truth?' 'I'm embarrassed to say to my mother I work
at Waystar. Any advice?' 'What did Logan Roy know?' 'Who is
in charge now?' 'What do I say to the police if they talk to me?'
'Please tell us anything at all about what is happening here?'

ROMAN

Wah-wah. Did they write their questions in crayon?

SHIV

I mean I have my speech all set – do we need to do questions?

KAROLINA

We did say we wanted to answer any questions?

Shiv looks at more questions.

SHIV

Dad can't see this one. Or this.

Roman looks.

ROMAN

Fuck no. This one would make his head explode.

SHIV

I think there might be about three here we can use.

Roman is looking – he points—

ROMAN

Can we please find out who asked this one?

KAROLINA

They were meant to be anonymous. Ask anything?

ROMAN

Sure but this is just rude. It's not really a question. It has a huge agenda. I don't think people should be thinking things like this who work here.

HUGO

Let me ask. I think we can make it less anonymous if we really want to.

ROMAN

Can we get more questions? Like less – questiony? Because these are horrible questions.

KAROLINA

Hugo and I have prepared a set of questions that are – are more the sort of things that people would actually want to know?

Hugo has some questions.

HUGO

I mean these, we feel, are people's real questions.

He hands over copies of their made-up list to Shiv.

KERRY

We've got a problem.

INT. KENDALL'S CAR – DAY

Kendall is on his way into the office. With Jess, she's made a call.

JESS

Lisa.

She puts it on speaker—

KENDALL

Lisa! The Regal Legal Eagle. How you doing your majesty?

LISA
(*on speakerphone*)
Kendall? I hear you're going in – what the fuck?

> KENDALL
>
> I can't let him dominate the battle space. Wheels are moving.
> My sister is grabbing the crown and I can't just watch it happen.
> What's the story on my immunity?

> LISA
> (*on speakerphone*)
> I'm figuring out a 'Queen for a Day' situation, Kendall. I have to
> have control here.

> KENDALL
>
> Uh-huh. But we're losing the momentum. What about a raid?
> Can we get a raid?

> LISA
> (*on speakerphone*)
> We can't 'get' anything.

> KENDALL
>
> No sure. But really? We hit the right buttons – 'Has the
> Government Gone Soft-Cock on Big Corp?' Push photos of my
> dad and the president? It's binary, but it works? I'll call you in
> forty, Lisa. You're the boss here!

He hangs up.

> (*to Jess*)
> And let's commit to Iwobi. Yeah? Call Noah and get me some
> jokes. Not jokes. Funny-as-fuck shit but not in that bullshit joke
> way.

INT. WAYSTAR – LOGAN'S OFFICE – DAY

Gerri, Tom, Logan. Gerri looking out of the office.

*Shiv comes in with Roman and Hugo and Karolina. Tom feels odd
when he looks at Shiv.*

> SHIV
>
> Is it right, he's on his way?

> LOGAN
>
> Fucking rat. I'm gonna jam a Montblanc down his fucking
> throat.

(*calling out*)

Kerry!

SHIV

He'll eat up any drama, Dad.

Shiv notices Tom staring at her.

What?

TOM

Nothing.

GERRI

Look, we just let him come on in and ignore him.

Kerry enters.

LOGAN

Get us Colin, get us building services. If he comes for me, I want him fucking cuffed.

KERRY

Okay.

LOGAN

He's fired!

GERRI

HR is discussing him stepping back from his duties, but firing? You'd be handing the DOJ a gas can. It would be a PR disaster.
(*then*)
Do you want me to get outside counsel on the line?

Kerry pops her head in.

KERRY

Front desk says he's pulling up.

LOGAN

I don't want people seeing him. Keep him the *fuck* out!

Hugo and Karolina run out.

EXT. WAYSTAR – DAY

Kendall exits the car. Jess and Remi hurry out to meet him.

> JESS

So, I tried to get things set up, but you might still run into a few – issues?

> KENDALL

Issues are fine. We crush issues.

They enter the building. Kendall nods to Remi, who starts filming events on his phone.

INT. WAYSTAR – LOBBY – DAY

Kendall walks confidently through the lobby, even smiling and nodding at people he passes.

> KENDALL
> (*to passer-by*)

Hey, how are you?

He approaches the security gate, gives the front-desk security guard and Sonam, the Waystar receptionist, there the eyes. They look at one another and the front-desk security guard moves into action—

> FRONT-DESK SECURITY GUARD

Sir, sorry. Um. I'm sorry?

> KENDALL

Oh yeah? Yeah?

Kendall pulls out his keycard. He swipes, but the gate won't open.

> FRONT-DESK SECURITY GUARD

Your keycard has expired.

Kendall smiles and chuckles.

> KENDALL

Expired? That's weird.

Hugo and Karolina make it down with two PR flacks.

> HUGO

Hi, Kendall. Bit of a crazy morning here.

> KENDALL

Oh is it?

HUGO

Yeah – if you like we can head out to 43 North and I can fill you in. Might be more comfortable there?

KENDALL

Not going to the satellite office, thanks. My card doesn't work, so I'm gonna hurdle the gates there and have Remi film it?

Doesn't sound great. Karolina assesses. Remi has his phone.

KAROLINA

Ken, we'll head up with you? We'll swipe you in.

Calling to the receptionist at the desk—

KENDALL

You guys wanna sync up? Cos they said—

SONAM

He can't go up.

KAROLINA

No. He can go up.

FRONT-DESK SECURITY GUARD

They've told us he can't go up?

KENDALL

Sorry, who's telling you?

FRONT-DESK SECURITY GUARD

Don't let him up!

KAROLINA

I am letting him up . . .

HUGO

Let's just keep this moving okay?

KENDALL

This is great.

HUGO
(*to Kendall*)
Shall we go grab coffee while they figure this one out?

KENDALL

Fucking mess, eh, Hugo?

INT. WAYSTAR – LOGAN'S OFFICE – DAY

They've got a lawyer on speakerphone talking them through. Frank has also joined.

> GERRI
> We probably can't keep him out of the town hall, correct?

> LAWYER
> (*on speakerphone*)
> You can discourage him from attending in light of his position?

> ROMAN
> Could we discourage him with a taser shot directly into his peni or scrummage sacking?

Kerry pops her head in the room.

> KERRY
> He's headed for the freight.

> LOGAN
> Fine. Send him up in the fucking dumbwaiter like a hamburger.

INT. WAYSTAR – LOADING DOCK – DAY

Kendall shakes the hands of a passing dock employee.

> KENDALL
> Hey, man.

INT. WAYSTAR – LOGAN'S OFFICE – DAY

Roman practically has his nose pressed up to the glass wall of Logan's office. Logan drums his fingers at his desk. Colin is there, he is making contact with other security operatives.

> LOGAN
> Where is he? Is he there?

> ROMAN
> I don't see him yet? With his stupid walk.

> LOGAN
> Tom, I want Sam and Ray, and IT, make sure he doesn't get fucking cute with IT.

Tom heads out.

INT. WAYSTAR – DAY

Kendall, Jess, Remi and one other executive walk through reception and the bullpen. Hugo and Karolina follow, Kendall loves it. Passes a stunned guy he knows.

KENDALL
Hey. Good to see you, man.

Tom walks through. He sees Kendall coming and sees it is going to be hard to avoid him – there's nowhere to go.

Hey, man.

TOM
Oh. Hey.

Tom looks around. Slight feeling that they're on a stage.

KENDALL
Weird, right? How's it going?

TOM
Pretty weird. Yeah. But you know. Life goes on.

KENDALL
Buddhist. Nice. Life does go on, doesn't it? So what's going on in my dad's office? He got any back-channel White House contacts in there or what?

Tom smiles.

I'm joking. You can't tell me that!

TOM
Right? And have you got an immunity deal with the DOJ?

KENDALL
Good we can kid around like this.
            (*then, sudden depth change*)
But look, man, you're in a difficult position. No fun being the last fucking eunuch in the forbidden city.

TOM
I'm doing fine.

> KENDALL

I like you. I have no beef with you, Tom.
> *(whispers to him)*

Another life is possible, brother.

And moves off.

INT. WAYSTAR – LOGAN'S OFFICE – DAY

Roman maintains lookout, reporting.

> ROMAN

Trying to kiss or nibble Tom.

> SHIV

Can we please not turn this into the invasion of Normandy, okay?

> LOGAN

He walked into my building.
> *(furious beat)*

I'm gonna kill him!

Logan suddenly gets up and moves to the door. It's scary and real. Multiple people have to stop and block his way.

> FRANK

Whoa, whoa, whoa, easy—

> SHIV

Dad! Stop.

Shiv stops him. Leads him over to his desk. They share a private moment. Low volume. No one else can hear.

> LOGAN

It's just – so, insolent.

> SHIV

I know. I know. But let's keep it cool.

He leans right in to her ear.

> LOGAN

No one's on my side in this. I need you to protect me, Pinky.

He's making a direct request.

INT. WAYSTAR – KENDALL'S OFFICE – DAY

Kendall is about to enter his office. Turns to address the bullpen—

KENDALL

Hey, everyone! Morning. Just want to say hi, no drama. We're good. Open-door, yeah? No stress, no worries, keep it up. The revolution will be televised!

Kendall and Jess enter the office.

Okay! Here we go. Let's do it.

He taps in his login, but it's changed. No access.

Does it feel cold to you in here?

JESS

Is it?

Kendall waves his arms around to get the motion lights to go on, nothing. He feels the vent.

KENDALL

They've hacked my AC.

JESS

I think this is – I think this is sixty-eight, how you like.

KENDALL

This isn't sixty-eight, no fucking way. This is sixty-five, sixty-two. That's fine. But this is cold. This is doing a number.

REMI

It feels maybe a little cool?

KENDALL

It's cold it's definitely cold. It's clearly cold, Jess. No?

They all try to feel the temperature.

Jess texts. There is a suited security guard now taking up position outside Kendall's office. Kendall opens the door.

Is there a problem?

SECURITY GUARD 2

No, sir.

> KENDALL

I guess you can go then?

> SECURITY GUARD 2

I'm here for your convenience and protection, sir.

> KENDALL

Well you are authorized by me to fuck off, that would be very convenient, okay?

Security guard doesn't say anything.

> SECURITY GUARD 2

My instructions are to stay with you, sir, for your convenience and protection.

Kendall smiles. He's almost enjoying the fuckery.

> KENDALL

So kind of you, man.

He closes the door.

Remi, I'm airdropping you a shopping list. And we need to figure out how to get rid of this goon for me, okay?

Remi heads out. As he does, Colin walks in.

He walks round to Kendall. He comes and stands right by him. Unnerving. Looks at Kendall.

> KENDALL
> (cont'd)

What?

Colin doesn't say anything.

What?

Then Colin leans in.

> COLIN
> (whispered)

You're so small to him.

> KENDALL

Excuse me?

COLIN

Excuse what?

KENDALL

Are you talking to me?

Colin looks at him.

What?

Colin just looks at him.

What?

Kendall backs away. Colin walks after him a little.

COLIN

I know you.

KENDALL

What does that mean?

COLIN

I know you.

Colin looms close and looks at Kendall into his eyes. Then heads out.

INT. WAYSTAR – ATRIUM – DAY

Setting up for a town hall.

INT. WAYSTAR – SHIV'S OFFICE – DAY

Shiv is looking at prompt cards. She's all ready and pumped. Has a couple of her execs there. Karolina enters with Hugo.

KAROLINA

I think we're all set. You good? You like all the questions?

SHIV

Sure. Good.

KAROLINA

Great, so you'll give your introduction as President, Corporate Values, new face of Waystar, then hand off to interim CEO who will do like three mins, then into the vetted Q&A. So, if you're ready?

>   SHIV
> And will Dad be nearby? Undermining my authority?

>   KAROLINA
>   (yes)
> He'll be nearby. Emphasizing your authority.

INT. WAYSTAR – BULLPEN/CORRIDORS – DAY

Shiv leads the group out – a visual signifier of her new power in the company. A couple of her assistants join her.

>   KAROLINA
> The live-feed is being streamed through the building and to all major offices globally.

>   HUGO
>   (so he's not overheard)
> Anything you need, I'm here. And congratulations. I was always pushing for you to be brought in, in my own little way. I think this is really smart.

Maybe Shiv feels a mixture of divine right and nervousness as she feels the power and peril of her new position.

Maybe her and Kendall exchange a look as she passes his office? Or maybe Shiv glances at Kendall but he deliberately doesn't look her way.

INT. WAYSTAR – ATRIUM – DAY

An all-hands company-wide town hall.

Maybe there's a temporary stage. A screen or backdrop with the Waystar logo. Maybe a lectern. Shiv walks to the microphone. Senior execs are arrayed along the front row together: Gerri, Frank and Karl. And Logan. Roman is close enough to Gerri to talk. Kerry and Colin nearby for Logan.

Behind are a row of senior managers including Tom and Ray.

>   SHIV
> Hey thanks, Karolina. So hi, everyone. Thank you, all. Um, so this is basically really, really straightforward. A senior executive,

who happens to be a senior brother of mine – I think I can legally say that – has made some really serious allegations.

Okay. She's pretty good at this. Able to speak straightforwardly to people. If we can sense anything some smiles and warmth about her brother joke.

And as we take those allegations really, really seriously, there is you'll understand a fair bit we can't talk about legally, but this is still a family operation in spirit and you're all part of that family . . .

Does Roman manage to make eye contact with Gerri and rolls his eyes or make a sick sound? She keeps power face but lets him know she agrees.

. . . and as much as we can tell you, we want to tell you. So. I'm Siobhan Roy, Waystar's new President of Domestic Operations. And I'm paying particular and specific attention to corporate responsibility because I think that's actually going to be great for the growth of our core businesses. And we know change is necessary – as it always is at a dynamic company. And I know many of you have concerns. And I'm here to say to you – you know, 'We Get It'. And if mistakes have been made at cruises historically . . .

As Shiv speaks, 'Rape Me' by Nirvana starts to play. Some confused looks in the crowd. Hugo and Karolina exchange a look – and send assistants scampering off to find the source.

Shiv presses on.

INT. WAYSTAR – BALCONY – DAY

On a empty-ish terrace of the atrium, a series of big wireless boomboxes, three or four, are on desks. The music is coming from elsewhere too.

Employees who are looking over the side turn and react to the noise: WTF?

INT. WAYSTAR — ATRIUM — DAY

As the lyrics play some people are confused. Some snicker as it becomes clear this is some sort of prank.

> SHIV
> Um. I don't. Some – some – people might think this – the issue – is a joke, but let me assure you, we take it very seriously— Can we kill that? Sorry. Look, later, there'll be a chance for you to air any issues you want to discuss, and for us to listen . . .

The music gets louder.

> . . . in a non-judgmental environment.
> (*losing her cool, to Hugo and Karolina*)
> Can we do something about that?

Hugo and Karolina break from their panicked discussion. Hugo goes to the mic.

> HUGO
> Apologies, I think we might have to break momentarily.

He leads Shiv away from the mic. She's enraged but trying not to show it.

Gerri makes eye contact with Roman – what a shame Shiv's big moment got spoiled!

INT. WAYSTAR — BALCONY — DAY

Where the boomboxes are, an assistant arrives with security. They try to kill the music.

INT. WAYSTAR — KENDALL'S OFFICE — DAY

Shiv comes in but there's no sign of Kendall.

Just the empty packaging left from where a number of boomboxes were unpacked.

She walks the room. She goes to Kendall's desk. A monogrammed black notebook. No one can see in. She opens it.

Ideas and notes. She presses it open.

Then, like a child, she summons some saliva and lets a string of drool lower onto it. As much as she can manage.

Then she smears it round. Exits.

INT. WAYSTAR – LOGAN'S OFFICE – DUSK

Logan's there as Shiv comes in.

> LOGAN
> I'm sorry, Pinky. Now do you see? Ah?

INT. SHIV AND TOM'S APARTMENT – EARLY EVENING

Roman arrives. Tom greets him as he prepares to leave.

> TOM
> First floor for the fuckery!

> ROMAN
> Not staying?

> TOM
> Me. Nope. Nope.

> ROMAN
> Nice. Keep out of the – bloodbath? The fucking, jacuzzi of gore.

> TOM
> Actually, I'm going out to eat shit for three hours straight so you can continue to fart through silk for the rest of your natural life?

EXT. TV STUDIO – EARLY EVENING

Kendall, Comfrey, Naomi, Greg and a security guy get out of a car and head for a TV taping, past the little gaggle of autograph hunters and celebrity spotters gathered near the talent entrance.

INT. TV STUDIO – GREEN ROOM – EARLY EVENING

Kendall is with his PR team and Naomi in the Sophie Iwobi guest green room. Kendall is looking at index cards, different colors for different jokes, as a make-up artist touches him up.

He looks for a beat at the live-feed flat-screen on the wall that shows what's happening on the floor: they are rehearsing a bit with a guy in a panda suit. Through the scene we maybe might catch the guy miming 'making love' to a variety of stuffed animal toys.

KENDALL

What time is it?

GREG

(looks at watch)

It's like the eighteenth century or something when watches didn't work.

COMFREY

It doesn't work? Why did you get it?

GREG

Why did I get it? You encouraged me.

COMFREY

What?

GREG

You made a look like 'get it'? You shrugged like it was reasonable.

COMFREY

Not for one that doesn't work.

GREG

It's fine. It's okay. I'm a custodian. A piece like this will often have to go to Switzerland for six months. To hold its value.

COMFREY

Are you sure it's broken. Maybe it self-winds?

Over with Kendall.

NAOMI

You nervous, bud?

KENDALL

Little yeah. I have this funny bit – this bit about how for the special committee of the board, and the white-shoe firm that will handle their investigation, how my dad's put pressure on them to hire a firm who will help him cover up and it's like – it's like, um—

> NAOMI

Uh-huh?

> KENDALL

No?

> NAOMI

I'm like a media heiress who's been talking to you day and night for forty-eight hours and I only *think* I understand, so? I'd go with the *Love Boat* vids.

Kendall smiles. A young production assistant pokes her head in the door. Greg is rocking his wrist to try to wind his watch.

> PRODUCTION ASSISTANT

Hey! Because we pushed taping for you, we're still filling out the audience. But shouldn't be long?

> KENDALL

Cool. Thank you.

> PRODUCTION ASSISTANT

You need anything? You guys good?
> (*to Greg, re his wrist action*)
Are you okay?

> GREG

Oh yeah, good, just a little metaphysical CPR.

> KENDALL

He's jerking off his invisible friend. So, where the writers at?

> PRODUCTION ASSISTANT

Cool, um—? Generally writers and guests don't, really—

> KENDALL

No, generally, but I knew a guy at the *Lampoon* who knows Dylan. Can I just find them to say hi? I might pitch a couple of areas for the gigglebots?

> PRODUCTION ASSISTANT

Oh, well—?

Kendall gets up and squeezes past her through the door.

> KENDALL

It's cool, I'll find them.

PRODUCTION ASSISTANT
(*sort of blocking him*)
Well, but maybe not? Just because—

Kendall brushes right past her.

KENDALL
Excuse me.

As he proceeds quickly down the hall, the PA speaks quietly into her shirt mic—

INT. SHIV AND TOM'S APARTMENT – EARLY EVENING

Roman enters. Connor is reading off Shiv's laptop. Drinking his wine, mulling.

CONNOR
Hey, Rome, how you doing?

ROMAN
Uh-huh just been you know, on TV waxing lyrical about me and Dad, out murdering trout and singing sea shanties round the old marshmallow hole.

Shiv has put out sushi.

CONNOR
Have you read it?

Shiv hands Roman a printout. He reads fast.

SHIV
Now, I talked Dad down. He wanted us to do a talk-show appearance. I thought us all on a couch would be very gauche. So I drafted this to land, and end debate. Dad wants us all to sign it.

CONNOR
It's extremely – vivid.

SHIV
That way it's not . . . contestable. It's not one person's reputation on the line, it's facts we are *all* saying.

ROMAN
(*rereading*)
Oh, man. This is . . . quite a rich brew.

SHIV
I think a formal response, it draws a line under it and— I'm sure you're getting asked, so this is just us clearly saying we're not a part of Kendall's – thing.

But Roman finds it hard to read—

ROMAN
Urrgghh . . .

SHIV
You would have to say it's accurate?

CONNOR
Yeah, accurate like Oswald was accurate.

SHIV
I want us to sign up for release to all media tonight?

ROMAN
It's, really pretty. It's kind of—

CONNOR
It's a greeting card from hell. It's a Times New Roman firing squad.

ROMAN
It is very very horrible.

SHIV
It's all, basically, verified.

CONNOR
Yeah, . . . 'drug addict'? 'Serial liar'? 'Absentee father'? 'History of own problematic relations with women'?

SHIV
Which of those isn't true?

ROMAN
(*reading, pained*)
Mmmmmmm. Ahhhh. Gurrrr. I mean, sure, fuck him. But this is out there forever?

CONNOR

PGN still pulls out that photo of me with my ponytail whenever they want to make me look untrustworthy?

SHIV

But he's, he's on a mission. He won't stop unless we take his legs out.

ROMAN

Did Dad ask for us all to do this?

SHIV

(not saying)

It's much more powerful if it comes from all of us.

ROMAN

Yeah look, I'm sorry, but I already gave at the office. I'm not signing this.

SHIV

Why not?

ROMAN

Because it makes me feel unwell and I don't want to. And he taught me how to aim into the toilet.

SHIV

Well that's not a reason.

ROMAN

Uh-huh then take me to reason court and sue me.

SHIV

We all do things we don't want to, Roman.

ROMAN

Yeah but I try to keep it down to like six a day. And I'm not sure this is in my best interests.

SHIV

Con?

CONNOR

What do I get out of it?

SHIV

Con, come on. Dad really wants this. It's all true.

CONNOR

That may be. And I don't want to be a bitch. But my signature is valuable real estate and I'm not giving it away for free.

SHIV

What do you want?

CONNOR

I want consideration, I want a little suck-suck on my dicky-dick.

ROMAN

Same. I'm feeling brutally unsucked right now.

SHIV

God you're such babies.

Shiv stares at them for a beat.

You know, fine. This is pathetic. I'll sign it on my own.

She goes to her laptop and begins to email the letter to Karolina for distribution. Roman and Connor eye each other. Do they stop her?

Thanks for being such a fucking help, as always.

Roman and Connor exchange an uneasy glance. The missile has launched.

INT. ATN STUDIO – EVENING

Tom is entertaining a group of fifteen or twenty senior execs from firms with big advertising spends. They are having drinks before a meal. Lots of ATN talent – they have tried to invite lots of women.

The studio monitors and giant video walls are flashing viewer letters and tweets of support, impressive stats on ATN's audience size and reach. Photos of happy female Waystar employees.

Tom is making an informal speech to reassure—

TOM

Look, we get it. Okay? We get it. That's what I want to say, we hear you, we know our hosts can get a little spicy, but the audience gets it, and I hope you guys get it. And whatever else is happening up in the clouds, where the gods are a little rough-and-tumble, down here, it's very much business as usual.

INT. TV STUDIO — HALLWAY — EVENING

Kendall walks confidently through hallways he's probably not supposed to be in, searching for the writers.

He finds a spot where four or five writers, including head writer Dylan, are huddled on couches and around a table with colored script pages, writing alts.

> KENDALL
>
> Here we go, the geniuses at work! Scribble, scribble, write and nibble!

The writers smile and laugh uncomfortably.

> DYLAN
>
> Oh – hello?

> KENDALL
>
> Dylan? I knew Pat at the *Lampoon*? He says you're a funny dude. I just wanted to drop by and let you guys know you do awesome work – very smart, very satirical.

A security guard kind of hovers on the perimeter, in case.

> DYLAN
>
> Cool. Thanks, man.

> KENDALL
>
> And I want you guys to hit me. Just, Rickles the fuck out of Oedipussy here? I can take it. Give me the treatment okay?

> DYLAN
>
> Okay, well, it's just – it's just the show, so. Yeah.

Comfrey approaches Kendall.

> COMFREY
>
> Hey, can I grab you for a sec?

Comfrey hands Kendall the phone as they walk back to the green room.

> So, I'm not sure how wide this has gone, I'm just seeing it now?

It's Shiv's letter. We stay on Kendall's face as he reads. He looks gutted, but trying to keep his game face.

> KENDALL
> (*in a rush*)

I mean, so? So, so, what do I do—? What do we do with this?
Because, this is actually, really, sort of nothing I think?

He is caught for a second. As they walk, he looks.

Fuck. She's— Do we just treat it like it's nothing? Because it's
bullshit.

He thinks.

Is the world seeing this or just, basically, us?

> COMFREY

Yeah the whole world.

> KENDALL

Uh-huh. Can we ask them not to use it tonight – will they
mention it?

> COMFREY

I think they will mention it.

> KENDALL

But it's private.

> COMFREY

Right. Yeah. I mean, it's not private.

> KENDALL

Okay. Well, I think they'd understand why I can't go on?

His phone goes.

Hey. Yeah. I'm here.
> (*listens*)

Well I don't know about that, Lisa. Well, yeah I've seen it. No.
I don't have – I don't have time—

End of call.

She says, Lisa says she might have second thoughts about
repping me if I go on. Should I go on? What do you think?

*Comfrey knows he shouldn't go on, she just needs to persuade him
gently to do the right thing.*

INT. TV STUDIO – HALLWAY – EVENING

Kendall talks to the EP of the show in an empty hallway.

> KENDALL
>
> I think it's fine – it's the kind of thing where we just maybe steer away from it, you know?

> EXECUTIVE PRODUCER
>
> Uh-huh? My concern is it might be weird if we don't mention it?

> KENDALL
>
> Sure. Uh-huh. Absolutely.

> EXECUTIVE PRODUCER
>
> Good. But look, it's big of you to come here, and we want to be fair—

> KENDALL
>
> Totally. And I'm game.

> EXECUTIVE PRODUCER
>
> Great.

> KENDALL
>
> There's just a possibility, with all the legal of it, that I might have to bow out, but we're good.

> EXECUTIVE PRODUCER
>
> Right . . . We tape in fifteen minutes.

> KENDALL
>
> Sure, no, and I'd help with that.

> EXECUTIVE PRODUCER
>
> How would you help with that?

> KENDALL
>
> I know people.

> EXECUTIVE PRODUCER
>
> You're going to call Jay-Z and get him on the show in fifteen minutes?

> KENDALL
>
> A name. I can do that.

> EXECUTIVE PRODUCER
> I think you're overthinking this. It's a comedy show. We're going to have fun. Sophie is tough, but she's fair, I mean – you're our *guest*.

> KENDALL
> No, I know. You're right.

> EXECUTIVE PRODUCER
> We good? Yeah?

> KENDALL
> Okay. Yeah, no, for sure. Okay.

> EXECUTIVE PRODUCER
> Great.

The producer leaves. Kendall walks in the other direction.

And we stay with Kendall as he walks – back past his green room – up a corridor. There are a couple of technicians but they don't look interested in him. On he walks, maybe a technician comes through a door with a keypad and Kendall walks through into a quiet after-hours area, down a corridor, past some empty edit suites and past unlabeled doors.

He tries one. Locked. Then the next. Thinks about going back.

Needs to collect his thoughts. Opens the next door. He's in a small machine room full of computer hardware with blinking lights.

He paces. Thinks. Considers going back out. Sits on the floor in the corner.

INT. WAYSTAR – LOGAN'S OFFICE – NIGHT

> LOGAN
> (*into phone*)
> You did the right thing.

He looks out across the empty exec floor. Roman is crossing.

INT. SHIV AND TOM'S APARTMENT – NIGHT

Shiv, on the phone, smiles. But it doesn't feel great.

INT. WAYSTAR – LOGAN'S OFFICE – NIGHT

End of call. Logan shouts over.

LOGAN

Hey?

Roman approaches.

Hey. What you in for?

ROMAN

Me? Just running some numbers with Gerri. On, you know, the fucking— Getting the distribution deals with these fucking— It's murder.

He's getting into the detail, finally.

LOGAN

Good kid.

ROMAN

Uh-huh.
(*then*)
And sorry about the – the letter or whatever. I just—

LOGAN

Keeping your nose out, ah?

ROMAN

No it was just—

LOGAN

Smart cookie, ah? Smart little fucking cookie, are you?

Is it praise? It might be.

ROMAN

Well, you know?

LOGAN

I saw your little interview.

ROMAN

Right. We don't have to dissect it.

LOGAN
(*mocking*)
'Oooh, I wuv my daddy.' Hehehe.

                    ROMAN
Ha, yeah.

                    LOGAN
'He's so gweat. I wish I could snuggle him.' I never figured you
for a nancy.

Roman tries to chuckle along.

I'm fucking kidding. What was the fishing thing? I don't
remember.

                    ROMAN
Yeah, Connor. Connor took me on that. But you know, single
multi-use happy childhood memory. So.

Just then – Gerri comes out of her office and runs to his.

*Then Kerry is up, and Colin is coming, and Frank and Karl in the
distance – panic.*

INT. TV STUDIO – MACHINE ROOM – NIGHT

Kendall paces. Now sits – watches.

In the corner there is a monitor playing a feed from the taping—

                    SOPHIE IWOBI
Oh my god. Such sad news. Guess what, we're a guest down.
Oedipussy ghosted my ass.

On TV: photo of Kendall.

Guys, I'm like, heartbroken. Because we had so many names we
were going to call him: Wokestar Royco, Benedickhead Arnold,
Paranoid Kendroid. But honestly, nothing could be as brutal as
the open letter his own sister has released—

On Kendall sitting watching in the corner of the machine room.

                    (reading)
' . . . I am deeply concerned for the well-being of my brother.
Our entire family has supported him through his many attempts
at rehabilitation for his multiple addictions. But the events of the
last days have made it clear that our hopes for his recovery were
misplaced. I've now been a direct witness to his misogynistic

rants and comparisons to world historical figures that were suggestive of grandiose and disordered thinking and I would ask that people give my brother privacy and consideration during this difficult time . . .'

He tries to find a volume control turns it down, then up.

And look, I'm not shaming this dude for having addiction issues. I'm shaming him for being shameful! Which everyone suddenly forgot he was because he sorta did the right thing, once, for about twenty-three seconds after an entire life being one of the biggest assholes in the world, but yeah, you know, they were a somewhat cool twenty-three seconds, so—

Kendall's sort of weirdly calm watching it like a dream/nightmare.

But imagine having a sister who'd write a letter like this?

His phone starts to buzz. And his other one. Masses of incoming alerts and calls and texts.

INT. WAYSTAR – LOGAN'S OFFICE – NIGHT

Gerri arrives – as others come and wait.

GERRI

The FBI is downstairs.

LOGAN

What?

GERRI

Yeah.

LOGAN

Tell them to fuck off.

GERRI

Yeah these are the ones who don't fuck off. This is a search warrant.

KERRY

What do they do at the front desk?

LOGAN
(to Gerri and Frank)
What happens if—? Do we, can we call Southern District? Or—

>   (*to Kerry*)
get Layo, get, get – get—?
>   (*to Gerri*)
Can we stall? Shall I call Michelle-Anne?

GERRI

No! No, I think the deputy attorney general got spooked by you talking to Michelle-Anne.

LOGAN

What did she do? She's got no fucking acumen.

Gerri is angry but has held it in, but she can't help—

GERRI

Well, I guess the government isn't a Pez dispenser. You push a button and something just pops out the other end?

Logan looks at Gerri coolly.

LOGAN

Uh-huh. I am aware.

>   (*then*)
What if we say come back tomorrow?

GERRI

Logan, they're coming up, and if we don't open the door, they kick it in and if you don't open the filing cabinet they pull out the crowbar. This is a show of resolve and there will be cameras outside and they do not need to see the FBI meeting any kind of resistance.

KERRY

What do we say?

Logan is stuck. He hesitates. He thinks. He hates it.

LOGAN

Cooperate. Open up, show them in.

GERRI

(*relief*)
Okay. I'll call down and I'll talk to the lead agent and we can work this out.

LOGAN

Okay.

GERRI

We're cooperating?

He sees there's no other way.

LOGAN

We're cooperating. Get the special committee to switch legals.
We're cooperating.

INT. ATN – CORPORATE DINING ROOM – NIGHT

Tom is talking.

TOM

Guys, people watch our channel for so long we had to animate
our logo. It was burning, into, their screens. That's how loyal
our viewers are. Listen. You need eyeballs. We have eyeballs.
Let's have an eyeball party!

Hugo approaches, wants to talk. Tom looks like: No.

HUGO

Yeah.

TOM

And we'll survive this too, because of our strength, because
of our depth of talent and because of our values – our true
values . . .

*Hugo gives him a note. 'The FBI is raiding the building.' Tom looks at
Hugo: Will you tell everyone? Hugo looks at Tom: Nope – you.*

Um, guys. Just a little heads up. This is not something I want
us to get out of proportion. Or spoil our evening. But some
agents of federal law enforcement are, with our blessing and
cooperation, raiding the premises. So, if you see them, that's
what that is.

(*then*)

End of newsflash!

INT. TV STUDIO – MACHINE ROOM – NIGHT

*Kendall watches PGN on his phone. FBI agents arriving at Waystar.
An intervention! Like magic!*

INT. SHIV AND TOM'S APARTMENT – NIGHT

Shiv is watching the raid on TV.

INT. WAYSTAR – LOBBY – NIGHT

FBI agents – twenty or so – move into the Waystar reception area and the lead agent starts to talk to the receptionist and security guard, who quickly open all the barriers.

INT. WAYSTAR – LOGAN'S OFFICE – NIGHT

As Kerry and others hurriedly prepare Logan's office for the arrival of federal agents, his allies depart. Logan stares out the window and awaits the inevitable.

Episode Four
LION IN THE MEADOW

Written by Jon Brown
Directed by
Robert Pulcini & Shari Springer Berman

Original air date 7 November 2021

Cast

LOGAN ROY	Brian Cox
KENDALL ROY	Jeremy Strong
GREG HIRSCH	Nicholas Braun
SHIV ROY	Sarah Snook
ROMAN ROY	Kieran Culkin
CONNOR ROY	Alan Ruck
TOM WAMBSGANS	Matthew Macfadyen
FRANK VERNON	Peter Friedman
COLIN STILES	Scott Nicholson
JESS JORDAN	Juliana Canfield
KARL MULLER	David Rasche
GERRI KELLMAN	J. Smith-Cameron
KAROLINA NOVOTNEY	Dagmara Dominczyk
STEWY HOSSEINI	Arian Moayed
HUGO BAKER	Fisher Stevens
SOPHIE ROY	Swayam Bhatia
IVERSON ROY	Quentin Morales
KERRY CASTELLABATE	Zoë Winters
LISA ARTHUR	Sanaa Lathan
BERRY SCHNEIDER	Jihae
COMFREY PELLITS	Dasha Nekrasova
MARK RAVENHEAD	Zack Robidas
WANDA	Danielle Skraastad
JOSH AARONSON	Adrien Brody
KARA	Megan Byrne
JUSTIN	J. Stephen Brantley
WANDA	Danielle Skraastad
REMI BISHOP	KeiLyn Durrel Jones
KITTY	Evelyn Twarowski
	Olivia Twarowski

EXT. KENDALL'S APARTMENT – MORNING

With his morning coffee, Greg walks past the new King Kong statue towards a glass tower – Kendall's apartment building. A text stops him momentarily. He glances at it, confused, then continues towards the tower.

INT. KENDALL'S APARTMENT – MORNING

Kendall with Berry, Comfrey, Jess, Greg, with laptops. On the table – coffee, breakfast bowls, a twelve-outlet power strip loaded with chargers, two iPads streaming live news. Kendall relentlessly scrolling. Looking at a 'Leeroy Jenkins Takes Waystar' meme from Twitter.

Maybe we're from Greg's POV watching the action.

> KENDALL
> (re his phone)
> More good shit on the Waystar raid. You all seeing this? Berry, can we content farm this with the meme-team?

Greg gets a text message. He reads it – unexpected news.

> Also, the like is gone again. I think.

> COMFREY
> The like—?

> KENDALL
> I liked a tweet of my dad as the devil with a trident made of dicks and the like is gone. Maybe they're sandblasting my likes somehow? I'm going to re-like now with you all present and can we have someone monitoring the like?

> BERRY
> Sure. Comfrey, do you want to get on, the, trident, made of dicks?

Kendall's eye is drawn by a nearby iPad, now showing PGN coverage of the raid. Chyron: 'Waystar Raid: "Treasure Trove" of Documents Seized'.

KENDALL

Look at that. You glad you're not on their team, huh, G?

But Greg's still not present, still looking at his phone.

GREG

Uh-huh. Oh yeah. Totally.

KENDALL

What?

GREG

Nothing, no. Uncle Logan's just asking to see me. Like, right away? At his apartment. Like, now?

KENDALL

Sure. It just means you have weight, bro. You're an asset, a player.

GREG

Uh-huh. I just keep having this stupid worry that he'll have goons or stooges or rough-jacks there to administer a beating?

KENDALL

He'll try to turn you against me and that's fine. Are you going to turn against me?

GREG

What? No. No, man. I'm sturdy. I'm a sturdy . . . birdy?

KENDALL
(with a smile)

That's right. Say it three times before the cock crows, brother.

As Greg gets ready to leave, Jess gets an alert on her phone.

GREG
(no idea)

Cock-a-doodle-doo!

JESS

Ken – they're here?

KENDALL

Great.

(yelling out)

Hey, kids? Kids?!

Bianca, the nanny, brings in Iverson and Sophie. Jess goes out to get something.

Hey, sweethearts, I know it's an early start for you guys but I just wanted to say thank you for being so incredible through all this. Now I know you don't want anything, that's just who you are but— Jess?

Jess returns, her arms now filled with a very large Continental Giant rabbit, that she's just about able to carry. It weighs around 30lbs and has a large red bow on it. Sophie and Iverson react—

JESS

Look who I just found out in the hallway?

KENDALL

Yeah—? Fun right? That's how much I love you.

SOPHIE

He's huge!

IVERSON

Whose is he?

Jess's phone goes. She checks it. A voicemail. She listens.

KENDALL

He's both of yours. He's going to stay with me here but you can see him anytime. We'll buy him an iPad, you can FaceTime him. Big big iPad.

JESS

Um. Hey, Ken—?

Kendall talks to Jess, away from the kids.

They just said super-high importance. Scheduled in five.

She hands him a note. Kendall thinks on it.

KENDALL

What the fuck? You think they're firing me? Can you gloop me?

233

(*then*)
Hey, guys, I'm going to need the command pod.

Kendall gestures. People start gathering their things.

With Greg, apprehensive, as he picks up his stuff, heads out of the room, nodding to Comfrey, and out through the apartment towards the elevators . . .

INT. KENDALL'S APARTMENT — MAIN SPACE — DAY

Kendall, now with a glass of gloop, dials the number from the note. Puts his phone on speakerphone, ready to prowl. Then—

> AUTOMATED FEMALE VOICE
> (*from phone*)
> Please enter your sixteen-digit participant code followed by the—

Kendall impatiently plugs in the dial-in code from the note.

Please say your name after the tone.

Beat. A tone—

> KENDALL

Little Lord Fuckleroy.

> AUTOMATED FEMALE VOICE

Please hold while we connect you to your conference.

Intercut with:

INT. WAYSTAR — GERRI'S OFFICE — DAY

Roman is there with Gerri, just the two of them.

> KENDALL
> (*voiceover, recorded*)
> 'Little Lord Fuckleroy—'

> AUTOMATED FEMALE VOICE

—is now joining the call.

> KENDALL

Hello—?

> GERRI

Kendall—? You're on with Frank, Karl, Roman, Siobhan, Karolina, Hugo – um – and – and—?

> JUDY

Judy Orbach, sitting in from investor relations.

> KENDALL

Holy shit. Gang's all here, huh? It's like the fucking *Sgt. Pepper* of broken corporate America.

Silence. Nothing at all back on that one.

> ROMAN

Mmm. Conference call jokes are the best jokes.

> KENDALL

So now I'm thinking maybe I should terminate and dial back in with my own counsel—?

Intercut with:

INT. LOGAN'S APARTMENT – DAY

Shiv, on the phone.

> SHIV

It's just a conversation, Ken.

> KENDALL

Oh hey, Shiv—? Thanks for the letter. First-rate composition. Really fucking horrible. Yeah.

> SHIV

I didn't say anything that wasn't true.

> KENDALL

Well I hope it was worth it. I don't know if me and you come back from that.

> SHIV

Okay, sure – Mom.

In Gerri's office Roman is getting comfy, maybe he takes his shoes off.

> GERRI

So if we can turn to the next topic of conversation—

                              KENDALL
                         (*disregarding her*)
So how's this going to work, Siobhan? Can I tell *Vanity Fair*
about the infidelities? You still fucking your way around the city
like some cum-drunk Ukrainian model?

                                SHIV
You okay, Ken—? Cos you're sounding a little slurred.

                              KENDALL
Ha. You sure you picked the right side, Shiv? Ooh too late.

                               GERRI
If we can just steer this back—? Excuse me, excuse me, excuse
me. Kendall, we have a situation. Uh, Frank, Karl? Can you talk,
Frank's going to speak now.

Intercut with:

INT. WAYSTAR – LOGAN'S OFFICE – DAY

*Frank is with Karl, Hugo, Karolina in Logan's office across the
bullpen from Gerri's.*

                               FRANK
Hey, Ken. Yeah the temperature of the DOJ investigation, the
raid here – it's caused serious blowback from investors.

                                KARL
So thank you for that, Kendall—

                              KENDALL
Hey. Accountability's a fucker. The feds find the nipple clamps in
your desk tidy, Karl?

                                KARL
Specifically Josh Aaronson and his four percent holding—

                               ROMAN
The chiseling little fuck—

                               FRANK
He called Gerri direct. He's thinking of switching to Sandy and
Stewy, and noisily.

KARL

His finger's on the big red button, Ken.

FRANK

We've talked to him about what we can do and he's playing
hard-to-get but he was interested in time in the room with you
and your dad.

*Roman is pulling his socks off and doing something transgressive in
Gerri's space – putting his bare feet up on her desk. She doesn't like it.*

KENDALL

Together? No.

FRANK

His thing was I guess to know how this goes—

KARL
(*cutting across him*)
He wants his pound of flesh.

GERRI
(*cutting across him*)
He just wants to know the family business can still function.

*Roman waggles his toes and Gerri pushes them off her desk. He
thinks it's a game but it's not a game to her.*

KENDALL

Well obviously I can't meet jointly with Dad.

FRANK

It's just a half-hour in a lawyer's office, later.

KENDALL

Yeah? Skywalker on lead guitar, Darth Vader on slap bass.
That's not a good band, Frank.

KAROLINA

Kendall. We'd understand the need for discretion. We'd lock it
down.

Kendall making fast calculations. Prowling, trying to process.

GERRI

We're four days out from the shareholder meeting, Kendall.

> KARL

It's control of the company. The vote's on a razor's edge. We need his four percent. Unless you see a bright future for any of us with Sandy and Stewy in control of this firm?

Kendall can't argue with that. Frank pushes it.

> FRANK

Glass Lewis is calling against us. Not to sound dramatic but – they're feeding us, legs spread, onto a buzz saw.

For the first time, we cut to reveal Logan's been on the call the whole time, in his apartment with Shiv. He sits, impassive. Then—

> KARL

So he's suggesting in four hours but we could push that probably . . .

> KENDALL

No. You don't railroad me. I need to run this by my team. Me and Dad together, the optics are janky as fuck.

> SHIV

For what it's worth I agree with Ken.

> KENDALL

Oh you do—?

> SHIV

You're right. Smart move is, Dad cuts you dead. He goes in with me or maybe Roman – tells Aaronson we're building a future without you and we tough it out.

> KENDALL

Ooh nice mind-fuck, Shiv. It's like you got your wang in my brain and you're just waggling it about.

> ROMAN
> (*dry; under it*)

Wow, thanks for the namecheck, Siobhan.

> FRANK

We're just trying to unfuck a relationship with a major shareholder, Ken.

> LOGAN

Come. Behave appropriately. Leave.

Logan's voice sends a chill through the call.

> KENDALL
>
> Oh. Hey, Dad. Come on? When have I ever not behaved appropriately?

> ROMAN
> (*then*)
>
> Once again, great joke, Ken.

Karolina and Karl look at Frank – he has the best relationship with Kendall, can he seal it?

> FRANK
>
> So. Where you sitting on this, Ken? We're all swallowing some lumpy gravy right now and we need to get back to him. Can you do this, for the big picture?

Kendall, prowling—

> KENDALL
>
> This just doesn't work for me, at all. Fuck you and god bless.

Kendall sharply hangs up.

Back with Gerri.

> KENDALL
> (*voiceover, recorded*)
>
> 'Little Lord Fuckleroy—'

> AUTOMATED FEMALE VOICE
>
> —has left the call.

> GERRI
>
> Thanks, everybody. We'll keep hitting the institutional investors, our team will be continuing to look for a settlement with Sandy and Stewy and we'll talk to Josh and – um—

Roman sees she is trying to be a leader and mockingly makes a solemn face – like she is a great leader.

> I'm sure, I'm sure we'll find a way through this, so – onwards!

We cut around the call as they hang up.

INT. WAYSTAR – MEETING ROOM – DAY

But also to a room with ten Waystar lawyers, PR people, etc., sitting around a conference table with a speakerphone. They hang up.

INT. WAYSTAR – GERRI'S OFFICE – DAY

> ROMAN
> (*aside to Gerri*)
> Amazing, Mrs Churchill.
> (*then*)
> Hey, Dad? One thing. Will you stay on?

> LOGAN
> What?

> ROMAN
> Um, is it just us? Hello?

No response

> (*eager*)
> Yeah, I've been digging around and I've got something, on Ken, good leverage. Shrink his halo into a cock ring.

What is it? Logan just breathes. There's one thing he doesn't want to get into . . .

> I'm just keen that I do my share, of the fuckery, you know? After the letter and whatnot?

> LOGAN
> Sure.

Call is over. Roman picks at his feet, looks at Gerri.

> ROMAN
> Okay, can we strategize? Because I've got potential gold and I need your read on how to deploy.

Gerri looks at his feet.

> GERRI
> Roman, can you please put your socks on? For this to work, there need to be – boundaries and—

He toys with them like stockings in his mouth.

240

                    ROMAN
What I can't take my shoes off?

                    GERRI
It's just—

                    ROMAN
And I can't masturbate at a time and place of my choosing? This
is a police state you're building, Gerri.

                    GERRI
See. That – that will kill us.

                    ROMAN
Listen, here's the thing – I've found tattoo-man.

                    GERRI
'Tattoo-man'—?

                    ROMAN
Yup. Funny story. Like, fifteen years ago, Kendall's bachelor
party, New Orleans. We did an ironic bar crawl on Bourbon
Street and got chatting to a friendly hobo and there was some
talk of various disgusting endeavors – 'would the hobo eat a
deep-fried deck shoe?' – before we finally settled on a rather
'indecent proposal', which was to get the homeless man to have
Kendall's name tattooed on his forehead.

                    GERRI
What?

                    ROMAN
Yeah, we got Kendall's initials tattooed on a rando.

*Gerri thought she'd heard it all from these entitled assholes but
nothing surprises her now.*

                    GERRI
Right. Go on.

                    ROMAN
I know. Horrible right? We *monogrammed* a hobo. Shameful.
                    (*then*)
So anyway, I told Sam who told the black-ops team.

                    GERRI
They've found him?

> ROMAN

It was surprisingly difficult considering we tattooed a name on him. I mean we basically filed him for later.

> GERRI

And you think this is a good idea, to dredge this up?

> ROMAN

On Kendall? Woke-ahontas? Using a poor's forehead as a Post-it? 'Need milk'. 'Take down Dad'.

But Gerri sees many angles to this shape.

> GERRI

Hm. I don't know?

Gerri starts gathering her things to leave.

> ROMAN

So. Let's talk it out over lunch. Tactics, TikToks and dick pics?

> GERRI

Not today, Roman. I have a date.

> ROMAN

A date? Excuse me. You have a 'date'—?

> GERRI

A lunch date, yes.

> ROMAN

A date at *lunch*. Fuck off—? With who? Montgomery Clift? The Ghost of Christmas Past?

> GERRI

Laurie. He's ex-DOJ, worked the Arthur Andersen prosecution. I want to see if there's a back channel there.

> ROMAN

Well, 'Laurie'. My god. Well he sounds fucking cool. Laurie. You want Laurie to *back-channel* you, in the parking lot?

> GERRI

Yeah well, I'm dating, so that's something that needs to be understood.

She looks at him dead-on. Roman prepares to leave. Socks, etc., back on.

> ROMAN

No I get it. You're drawing a line? Or what, Laurie might knock my jolly old block off, if he can find his sword stick and fire up his motorized bath chair?

> GERRI

Yeah he's fifty-six, so.

> ROMAN

Sure he is.

Roman heads out. As he goes, a functionary passes.

Hey how's it going—? Did you know Gerri has a date – exciting!

Gerri looks a little despairing as Roman leaves.

INT. LOGAN'S APARTMENT – DAY

Shiv and Logan. Logan's in a low mood.

> SHIV

If he won't go is it bad?

Yes. Logan shrugs.

> LOGAN

Sandy and Stewy will settle. They still want a deal.

She looks at him, doesn't quite believe him. Does he believe it himself?

> SHIV

Uh-huh. I'm hearing the raid was a warning shot. Should calm down now we're playing ball. Law firm and Gerri are ready to pour tons of chicken feed in. Gum up the investigation, buy us time.

> LOGAN

Uh-huh. I think I need more people. More protection.

> SHIV

Dad. You have two former deputy AGs. The former head of fraud at Main Justice. Ex-head of the FCPA unit. Former Crime Chief at SDNY. These are all-stars, Dad. The Harlem Globetrotters. Westchester Judge-Fuckers.

243

> LOGAN

The Raisin owes me everything. And now I need a bit of fucking cover, the forgetful cunt's gone AWOL.
>> (*with meaning*)

I'm starting to feel we have perhaps been insufficiently rigorous, journalistically, on the president?

> SHIV

You think he'll respond well to pressure.

> LOGAN

Every time I call I get Michelle-Anne telling me 'be patient the cavalry will come'. I need leverage. Just the question, is he losing focus. How's his grip?

Shiv gets it. Logan's assistant Kerry comes in. Logan's in no mood—

> KERRY

I have Connor, again?

> LOGAN

Ugh. Everyone sees I'm in a corner and they all want a piece.

> SHIV

Connor's not a problem. Offer him VP of Shitting His Pants.

> LOGAN

Everyone's out of their box. Everything's coming up fuck. You're my eyes and ears, Shiv. I want you on fire-watch. Okay?

Shiv likes it. Feels empowered.

> SHIV

Okay, Dad. Absolutely.

> LOGAN

Watch the negotiations. Karl's a sharp bastard, but he wants to be liked. It's not good.

Logan gets a text. change of location for the meeting with Josh.

Fuck's sake!

> SHIV

What?

LOGAN

Christ. The only place I'm not getting fucked right now is in the bedroom.

SHIV

Whoa, okay! Okay.

LOGAN

Oh don't be so fucking prim. You wanted courtside seats, these are courtside seats!

INT. LOGAN'S APARTMENT – ELEVATOR – DAY

On Greg – heart starting to race. He throws some punches. Growls. Shouts some exhortations to himself. Game time!

INT. LOGAN'S APARTMENT – DAY

Greg emerges. Shiv is leaving. She's heard him.

SHIV

Are you okay, Greg? Were you – shouting?

GREG

Oh. Just – man – stuff.

Greg nods farewell, quite formally. Logan's housekeeper is there to show him through. Greg wipes sweaty palms on his trousers as he ventures on—

INT. LOGAN'S APARTMENT – DAY

Greg enters to find Logan's by the whisky decanters. He hasn't yet seen Greg. He has a beat to straighten, prepare.

LOGAN

Ah, Greg. Drink?

Greg's confidence immediately vanishes.

GREG

Of, of alcohol—?

Obviously.

Uh-huh. Sure. I mean. Early but – I actually think I'll have me a nice glass of—

(*what the fuck*)

rum and Coke?

Logan looks at him for just a fraction of a beat – has Greg overplayed his hand already? Logan crosses to the phone.

> LOGAN
> (*shouts into intercom*)
> Kerry, can we get Greg some 'Coca-Cola'?

> GREG
> You know, it's fine, it's fine. I—

> LOGAN
> No no, what Greg wants, Greg must have. So. How are we doing?

Greg and Logan sit facing each other.

> GREG
> Sorry, what level are we on here? Are we meeting as—? Not as equals but—?

Logan just looks at him.

> LOGAN
> We're just talking.

Kerry comes in with a can of Coke. She fixes Greg's drink.

> GREG
> Thank you. Like – so kind, ridiculous.

> LOGAN
> You're hanging around with Kendall a lot, correct?

> GREG
> Oh. It's purely social, you know. He introduced me to his watch guy—
> (*raises his wrist*)
> What do you think, is it too much?

> LOGAN
> The thing is, your position at Waystar, it becomes complicated if you get too associated with him. You can see that?

GREG
(*re drink*)
Um. Strong. Nice and strong. Strong for a man!

LOGAN
You know the FBI have been poking around in my office. Greg, you've probably never been through something like this. We are all very concerned about you. I don't want to see you get hurt. We need our lawyers all working together, one big happy family. A joint defense agreement. Big strong umbrella, keeps you dry.

GREG
That's interesting. I mean I'd need to talk to Pugh my lawyer but he is often unavailable, during – days.

LOGAN
Well I have the paperwork here for you to sign up.

Ambush!

Then – summoning up the courage from somewhere, voice quavering – Greg asks—

GREG
Right. So, I guess my question would be, what's it worth, potentially? In terms of the 'me' of it all?

LOGAN
'What's it worth'?

GREG
(*trying hard not to fold*)
Uh-huh. What's in it for me?

Can Greg take it? The Logan stare. He almost squeaks with anxiety. Then—

LOGAN
Well. What do you want?

GREG
What do I want—? Well. I mean what can I get?

LOGAN
That's not how it works.

Does he dare? He's very scared, at any moment Logan might blow . . .

> GREG

Well maybe it is?

> LOGAN

Look at you, shaking like a fucking leaf! Listen, you've got some leverage, just a little, so why don't you fuck off, think what you want to ask for to come on-side, and I'll see what I can do, okay?

Logan gets up – Kerry is there. It's time for Greg to go.

> GREG

Fair. Okay.
> (*re drink*)
I'm not gonna down this. Shall I leave it? I'll leave it.

> KERRY

He's here.

Logan nods. He has another visitor. He stands.

> GREG

Already got a little buzz on there. How did you guys do it in the sixties, ah? Different times. Different times indeed. Better times? Not for all.

Logan's not paying any attention, he's walking into another room.

INT. KENDALL'S APARTMENT – DAY

Kendall sits scrolling. Comfrey and others working around him. A second phone goes. Kendall takes it.

> KENDALL

Yo, what's up, Ancient Grains?

Intercut with:

INT. LOGAN'S APARTMENT – DEN – DAY

> FRANK

Just wanted to see where your head's at?

> KENDALL

I don't get railroaded. Not going.

A nearby iPad calls. Kendall checks it, hands it off to Jess.

> (re iPad, aside)

Rabbit-cam, for the kids—

Jess takes the iPad – what the fuck? She exits to FaceTime with the rabbit, as Kendall steps out onto the balcony.

> JESS

Of course.

> FRANK

Ken, say this all blows up the way you intend – your dad's gone. You're going to need the big beasts in your corner afterwards?

> KENDALL

Josh Aaronson is a lock for me. He's always been a lock, right back.

> FRANK

That's not what he says to people.

That's a little bump.

> KENDALL

Uh-huh?

> FRANK

Look. It's smart to do this. You know it is. It's smart for now because you can't have Stewy and Sandy win. Right? That just nukes everything.

That is true.

> KENDALL

They'll settle, in the end. Right?

> FRANK

But also it's smart for tomorrow because it would be fun, if, if your dad has to step away, for you to have backing from major shareholders. No?

Kendall thinks on it.

                         KENDALL
Well obviously I have factored that into my response.

                          FRANK
                    (*insinuating tone*)
Recalculate. You get to show Aaronson who you are.

                         KENDALL
When and where?

                          FRANK
Change of venue, it's all last-minute. Josh's daughter is sick so
he's requested you go out to his island.

                         KENDALL
Uh-huh.

                          FRANK
That's a bonus, right? Discreet. There's a suggestion you convene
with your father for ten minutes on the tarmac just to, you
know, agree the approach, flush out any awkwardness? Are you
in?

Kendall thinks.

                         KENDALL
Uh-huh. Okay. Listen. Fine. I'm in. And – thanks, Frank.

*Reveal that Frank is sitting with Logan. Frank gestures to Logan:
Positive, I think he'll come. Logan nods.*

INT. KENDALL'S APARTMENT – DAY

*Kendall sits, processing. Off in the background, the sounds of the
children calling out to the rabbit through the iPad.*

INT. LOGAN'S APARTMENT – DEN – DAY

Kerry comes in. Time to prepare for departure.

EXT./INT. LOGAN'S TOWN CAR – DAY

Logan and Kerry and Colin.

EXT./INT. KENDALL'S TOWN CAR – DAY

Kendall, Remi and Jess driving in a separate town car.

EXT. HELICOPTER PAD – DAY

Two helicopters sit ready and waiting. A town car pulls up.

INT. KENDALL'S TOWN CAR – DAY

Back inside Kendall's town car.

> JESS
> We're being asked to hold for a second.

Beat. Then a second town car pulls in. Colin opens up to Logan. Logan doesn't look over at Kendall's car as he heads across the tarmac.

EXT. HELICOPTER PAD – DAY

With Colin and Logan.

> COLIN
> Sir, you're this way—

Logan looks over at the helicopter requisitioned for him.

> LOGAN
> No. For the Judas, I'll take this one.

Logan changes path and heads with Kerry to the other helicopter, leaving the travel coordinators to deal with it.

INT. KENDALL'S TOWN CAR – DAY

Back with Kendall and Jess in the town car. Once Logan has boarded—

> JESS
> Okay, we're good.

Only now is Kendall finally allowed to disembark. One helicopter then the other takes off.

INT. LOGAN AND KENDALL'S HELICOPTERS — DAY

We cut between Logan and Kendall in their helicopters, mid-flight.

EXT. AIRFIELD — DAY

Two private jets sit waiting. Logan's helicopter has recently come in to land.

Kendall's helicopter has just followed it in. Kendall exits his helicopter and crosses the tarmac towards the jets with Remi.

> REMI
> They've asked we take the first jet?

Kendall takes this in.

> KENDALL
> Uh-huh. Doesn't want to wait at the other end.

EXT. AIRFIELD — DAY

Two private jets, one lined up behind the other, in a queue to be cleared for take-off.

INT. KENDALL'S PRIVATE JET — DAY

Kendall, taking off.

INT. LOGAN'S PRIVATE JET — DAY

Logan, working. He has his big book of numbers from all the worldwide divisions. Looking at figures. He's on the phone.

> LOGAN
> Karl, this looks like padding on Italian distribution costs. Make sure everyone knows I'm still watching everything, everywhere.

INT. WAYSTAR — TOM'S OFFICE — DAY

Tom sits with a binder of printed materials. Shiv enters.

SHIV

Hey so, listen, Dad wants a host out criticizing the
administration. What do you think about Mark? You wanna tell
him or Cyd?

TOM

Well, that's not really how it works, Siobhan. We would have to
handle that sort of pivot very delicately.

SHIV

Well yes, Tom, I know that, but since I thought I was talking to
my husband, I thought I could be a little more direct?

Tom looks at papers.

It's not a 'release the hounds' situation just a bit of barking from
the kennels. Let the Raisin know how it feels when we get a
little less friendly.

*Tom determinedly looks down at materials he's looking at. He wants
her to ask him about it.*

TOM

Uh-huh. As I say, it's a complex situation so . . .

SHIV

What's—?

TOM
(*poor me*)

Just ranking the facilities. Still on the look-out for my dream
prison.

SHIV

Tom. That's – that's not going to happen.

Tom the martyr.

TOM

Oh, sure. But if it does I'm leaning towards FCI Otisville, as my
number one?

SHIV

Otisville? That's the prison in Maryland—?

TOM

No, Shiv. No. Cumberland is the prison camp in Maryland.
Otisville is Orange County. The Jewish jail?

SHIV

Yes. Right. Right. Sorry.
                    (re phone)
Dad and Ken just landed.

TOM

Just hearing a lot of good things. Kosher vending machines.
Sturdy bunks. No pool, but still.

SHIV

It's an 'if'. Tom. Big fucking 'if'.

TOM

Apparently they're calling me Terminal Tom, down on seven,
because I've got 'cancer of the career'.

Shiv's appetite to indulge Tom has been exhausted.

SHIV

So – who tells Mark we want to send a shot across the bow?
Will you make it happen?

TOM

Ravenhead has his own battalions. He – values his
independence.

SHIV

He's a little bitch. Once he gets it, he'll do what my dad wants.
Where's he gonna go? Stormtrooper FM gonna pay him thirty
million a year?

TOM

Well he's not going to like it.

SHIV

But you'll handle? Thanks.

Beat. She looks at him. He's not happy.

TOM

I mean, I'll do it.

(then)

But. Just in terms of – you know, of corporate governance and optics, and – I probably shouldn't take – like orders from you. Much. Because of corporate governance.

SHIV

'Corporate governance'?

TOM

Yeah and in terms of the org chart. And my . . . masculinity?

SHIV

If you carve out from me it undermines me.

TOM

But it undermines me if I look at the wall and the organizational chart suggests, 'You are being fucked in the ass by your wife.'

SHIV

Taking direction from a colleague is not being fucked in the ass by them.

TOM

No sure.

(then)

But really it is?

SHIV

(out of patience)

Tom – I'd like you to handle Ravenhead. Thanks.

Empowered Shiv, with a harder edge. Tom backs down.

TOM

Okay. Sure. I'll speak to him.

SHIV

(checks time)

And can you thumbscrew Greg? We want him under the joint defense. Check in later, yeah?

Shiv exits. Tom watches her go.

EXT. AIRFIELD — DAY

Logan, Kerry and support staff are disembarking the jet. Kendall's jet already standing nearby. Logan looks around as he descends. Something occurs to him—

LOGAN

Where is he? Where's his car?

Kerry isn't sure. She takes her phone.

KERRY

Trying him now—

Intercut with:

INT. KENDALL'S CAR — DAY

Kendall in his car. His phone goes.

KENDALL
(into phone)

Yeah—?

KERRY
(from phone)

Um, Kendall—? I have Logan for you. We're holding on the tarmac for the catch-up . . .

KENDALL
(cutting across her)

Hey so look I think it's pretty obvious what we need to say so I'm heading straight to Josh's compound.

Silence. Kerry is unsure what to do with that information.

Tell Dad 'meep meep'. It's Roadrunner!

Kendall hangs up. They drive on. A smile.

Back with Logan on the tarmac. Kerry's just hung up. She's unsure how to relay this information to Logan.

KERRY

Ummm—

Logan glowers back.

256

INT. WAYSTAR – SHIV'S OFFICE – DAY

Shiv enters looking at her phone. Connor sat waiting.

CONNOR

Look at you, sis, all 'rushing into your next meeting'. So grown up!

SHIV

Thank you.

CONNOR

'President Shiv'. 'Four more years. Four more years!' Nice office! My god.

SHIV

Ha! Yeah. So. What can we do for you here?

Shiv taking control. Connor wants to hold his own.

CONNOR

Well, at this time of trouble, you know, I want to be a good little boy and I want to be useful. But I guess I need me some pie here!

SHIV

So, shall I go or will you? We're all very excited about the idea of working more closely with you.

CONNOR

Great. So look, politically, a lack of real-world experience is sometimes leveled at me. Now, even with the rumors, the Raisin is likely gonna win again. So, I'm looking at four till I make my move. Therefore, I wouldn't be uninterested in coming inside, hitting three, four major achievements then getting out.

Connor's only just getting warmed up – he brought notes—

SHIV

Oh, you have notes—?

CONNOR

Environment. Streaming. I crack the uncrackable nut of South-East Asia. Then, if I've got time, movies. I head to LA, put up a tent pole or two, and then I Mary Poppins. Umbrella up and off I fuck.

257

Shiv needs to manage expectations here.

> SHIV
>
> Okay, cards on the table, we were thinking of offering you
> Gourmando?

> CONNOR
>
> Gourmando—? I don't see myself at a food network.

> SHIV
>
> You could do a wine-tasting show?

> CONNOR
>
> You think me spitting out Rioja on camera is going to help me
> win the Rust Belt?

> SHIV
>
> I'm not sure we can give you a high-level executive role in the
> current climate.

*Shiv checks her phone. Attention only half on him. Connor smiles. He
resents her dictating terms. The use of 'we'.*

> CONNOR
>
> Listen, sis. I don't like having my boot on the old man's throat
> but I do. I got me some juice.

> SHIV
>
> Well, up to a point.

> CONNOR
>
> Because I can take out the old megaphone any time I want—
> (*megaphone with his hands*)
> 'Hey guess what, I recall actually my dad was a nasty, racist
> neglectful individual who kind of put my momma in the
> nuthouse over one too many vodka tonics'?
> (*then*)
> What did they used to say? 'No blacks, no Jews, no women
> above the fourth floor'?

This sounds dangerous. Shiv in deeper than she expected.

> SHIV
>
> You already have our attention, Connor. I just think a lifestyle
> network or a stock situation might be easier to—

CONNOR

Remember when you had that play post office and you'd stamp all the mail coming into the house? This is a little bit like that, isn't it, Shiv?

SHIV

Let's stay civil, Con.

CONNOR

I don't think I want to deal with you, Shiv.

SHIV

Look, I get that this is uncomfortable but I have Dad's direct authority.

CONNOR

I'd like to talk direct with Popa, mano a mano, okay?

Shiv smiles. Meets his look. Brinksmanship. Starts to dial.

SHIV
(*into phone*)

Dad – sorry. It's me. Connor says he wants something bigger than Gourmando.

We don't see Logan. A half-beat.

LOGAN
(*on speakerphone*)

He can fuck off.

CONNOR

Hey, Dad—? I can't negotiate with my little sister, Dad, it's too weird. Okay?

LOGAN

It's Gourmando or fuck off.

CONNOR

Well. In that case I will consider the options.

End of call. Shiv and Connor look at one another.

See that's a proper 'fuck off', from a proper person.

Another item ticked off. Shiv already on her feet.

EXT. JOSH'S COMPOUND — PRIVATE ISLAND — DAY

Kendall pulls in. He gets out of the car and heads up some steps on the side of the house, where staff wait.

INT. JOSH'S COMPOUND — LIVING AREA — DAY

Kendall enters, guided by staff. Josh is there. A finger in the paperback he was just reading.

KENDALL

Hey! Josh. What's up?

JOSH

Kendall. How are you? You okay, man?

They embrace.

Thanks so much for coming out here.

KENDALL

Are you kidding? Just had to say the word. How's Kitty?

JOSH

Oh, better, it was dumb, she had a fever and I just didn't want to come to the city. Is that okay? How's your—
    (he checked on his phone three minutes ago)
Iverson?

KENDALL

Yeah, he's great. I just bought him a giant rabbit. So now he's googling where he can buy the world's biggest carrot.

JOSH

Hilarious. Fucking hilarious, man. C'mon, take a look.

Josh heads out onto the rear deck, with Kendall following.

EXT. JOSH'S COMPOUND — REAR DECK — DAY

Josh heads out, followed by Kendall.

JOSH

So where's the big man?

KENDALL

It's all good. He had to take a call. He sent me ahead.

JOSH
'It's all good'?

Kendall considers – decides on some calculated frankness—

KENDALL
I dunno, sure. It's all terrible, it's all good. You know.

Josh looks at him. Maybe there are some drinks out there.

JOSH
I mean – I guess that's my whole question?

KENDALL
We should probably wait for the old man.

Kendall grabs his opportunity to move first without Logan—

But yeah, I still love him, I'm still his son. It's a fuck pie. But it's not that complicated. I'm better than my dad. But my dad is still better than Sandy and Stewy.

Josh scopes him out – does Kendall believe this?

JOSH
He is, is he?

KENDALL
My dad or Sandy? Sure. They're basically the same shitty business guy. But my dad is a smart psychopath who's off the chart, whereas Sandy is a vengeful little middling prick.

JOSH
Uh-huh. Or frankly, you know, my other option is just get out?

KENDALL
Well. The comet is coming but we're working on the biodome. You've seen our streaming offering?

Josh nods.

Bullshit. Myriad reasons – infrastructure, loss of key talent. But – a single acquisition and we buy in an oven-ready UI. Machine-learning, social media, super-app dinges. We buy GoJo.

JOSH
Uh-huh. Little overpriced.

KENDALL

I dunno, either way, great UI, shitty content meet shitty UI, great content.

JOSH

Good words. I like the detail.

Kendall keen to keep this on track and push his advantage, goes for a very direct love-bomb—

KENDALL

You know I like you. Outside of all this, I really, really like you.

Josh absorbs this. Isn't immediately sure how to respond. Is this a move?

JOSH

Oh yeah—? I fucking like you too, man.

KENDALL

Big fucking nervous breakdown of a party for my fortieth. You've gotta come.

JOSH

Oh wow, great. Who's going?

KENDALL

What, you need the list? You, me and Henry Kissinger! Fuck you, I know everyone, it's gonna be the bomb!

JOSH

Ha! No, man, so cool. Send me the list. I'm kidding. It's so great to see you, man!

But suddenly – the gravity has shifted. Josh's attention is suddenly elsewhere.

Kendall turns to see Logan, passing through the house and now heading outside. He hasn't seen him since that day. They lock eyes but neither gives the other one anything much. (In background – Colin peels away and returns to the car.)

Hey! Captain! My Captain!

Josh greets. Logan is trying to hard to be solicitous but it doesn't come easy. He's still the more substantial figure.

> LOGAN

Josh. How's your daughter?

> JOSH

I think she's going to be fine. Thanks for coming all this way.

> LOGAN

Not at all. I know how it is.

Josh nods. He enjoys having them come all this way, but allowed it to go unspoken.

> JOSH

So? Guys?

Josh is pushing the moment a little. Forefronting the drama: Kendall and Logan haven't said hello. Logan turns to Kendall, frosty.

> LOGAN

Hello, son.

> KENDALL

Hey, Dad.

Josh looks at them. Feeling under his watch, instigated by Logan, they embrace, but it's mechanical and feels completely wrong. We're inside the hug, it's too brief and also too long. Then they break.

How was your call?

Logan doesn't follow.

I was telling Josh, you got delayed on a call—?

Kendall is fucking him.

> LOGAN

It was fine. It was nothing.

Kendall smiles and nods. It feels like the whole thing might be unraveling already. Josh steps in, and guides them over to some seating nearby, where there are drinks. Maybe they sit.

> JOSH

So yeah, I'm sorry, for all this. What a circus huh?

No arguments there. Josh makes a show of humility.

And look I know you're pushed for time . . . I just wanted to check in. As an investor but also, as a—
>   (*he isn't one*)
as a friend.

> LOGAN

Uh-huh. Sure.

Logan isn't enjoying this and it's clear. Kendall clocks it.

> JOSH

You know, I guess I have concerns.

> LOGAN

'Concerns.'

Josh smiles.

> JOSH

Look, Stewy is— I've known Stewy a long time. But they have a good narrative here and the market loves a narrative.

Logan launches into a prepared line.

> LOGAN

Look, I can tell you, hand on heart with fifty years of business experience, that whatever the turbulence short term there is nothing that is a significant issue.

Kendall listens, but also watches Josh. Is this landing?

The core business is the core business and the volatility is priced in now, it's all upside from here so, the safest option, is to back me, sit tight counting your gold in your castle out here while I make you whole, okay?

> JOSH

Uh-huh. Uh-huh. And this thing? Here – this situation?

He looks between them. Kendall hedging – keen to reassure him but also to stake out his own territory.

> LOGAN

All things must pass. Fucking, everything's coming up roses. Right, son?

> KENDALL

Right.

> JOSH

Okay, well that's fine then. I'm reassured. Thanks for coming out.

He looks in earnest for a beat then cracks.

Fuck you. No, come on, can we take a walk?

> LOGAN

Look at this fucking New York wiseacre.

Josh just smiles. He's not the type to get tripped by Logan's microaggressions.

> JOSH

C'mon. It's so beautiful out here it's disgusting. It should be expropriated and given to the people. But the people would ruin it, so I'm the custodian!

> LOGAN

Uh-huh. A walk. How far?

Logan looks at his watch. His displeasure hidden but not very well.

> KENDALL

Come on, Dad, let's walk it out.

Logan doesn't love being pre-empted.

> JOSH

Yeah? Shall I call around for a cart, Logan, or shall we walk?

But he's not about to look weak—

> LOGAN

Sure. Let's take a walk.

> JOSH

Great. Look at this.
>> *(joking but not joking)*
Fucking King Kong come out to dance for me. I'm honored!

Josh heads off to speak to his assistants. Kendall and Logan alone. Who'll break the silence and offer the olive branch? Is it the high-status or low-status thing to do? Some side glances. Silence grows.

Eventually Kendall smiles to himself – it feels high status to be the human being.

                                KENDALL
        You alright?

Logan genuinely doesn't quite hear.

                                 LOGAN
        What?

                                KENDALL
        I said: 'Are you okay?'

                                 LOGAN
        Yeah I'm okay.

Kendall feels like – fine, if you're giving me nothing, fuck you. More silence. It gets quite painful.

        When I got here, what were you talking to him about?

Kendall is enjoying the new dynamic between them.

                                KENDALL
        I just told him the truth. You're toast but we're still the best bet.

                                 LOGAN
        He's watching us.

                                KENDALL
        Well I know he's watching us.

                                 LOGAN
        Yeah well he is.

Kendall looks away.

        The pitch is we both want what's best for the firm. In all families
        there are fights, but this is an opportunity to move forward
        stronger.

                                KENDALL
        So fucking lame.

Josh reappears, now with walking sneakers.

                                 JOSH
        So! Okay. Anyone need emergency footwear or we all good—?

Kendall and Logan are all smiles—

INT. WAYSTAR — MEETING ROOM — DAY

Roman looks at files on Kendall. Hugo enters.

> HUGO
> *(re phone)*
> Okay, they're on their way up.

> ROMAN
> Yeah—? Fucking *Tattoo*-man. This is nuts. Keep a straight face, okay?

He sees a file, Kendall's name on it – surveillance material about Kendall.

> Is this the dirt from the dirtmen?

> HUGO
> I just think we need to be respectful.

> ROMAN
> Oh sure. We should all be upstanding for the guy with my brother's name tattooed on his head.

Roman looks through the file.

> Mm. Looks like Ken's stopped eating again? Wonder if he'll go full anno?
> *(then)*
> Two days – no food. Just sports gloop and apples?

They can see them approaching, escorted by security.

Then, lawyer (Kara, female, thirties) enters, followed by Justin. He has bangs, or a hat, partially covering his forehead.

> Hey. Hey, man.

> JUSTIN
> Hi.

> ROMAN
> How. How you doing? You look good.

> JUSTIN
> I've . . . This is just a suit I have from my friend.

Oh god.

ROMAN

Right sure. Me too. I'm kidding. But, yeah thanks for being here. Thanks.

JUSTIN

Yeah, good to – good to see you again.

ROMAN

Right, yeah.

(*awkward*)

Good to catch up. 'It's been too long.' 'You never call,' et cetera. Hahaha.

Roman is peering at Justin's forehead.

Hugo?

HUGO

So. We wanted to make an offer to Mr Albescu.

KARA

Is this an NDA situation?

Roman is still peering at his forehead—

ROMAN

I'm sorry, and I don't want to be a dick, but I'm looking, and I'll just say, you are the guy, right, is it there?

KARA

After a four-year period he had the um . . . the er, insignia, the design, removed. In order to improve employment potential and social acceptability.

ROMAN

I mean that's a shame, you had something there and it was really working for you. Can I?

Justin sweeps his hair aside. Roman looks very closely. Like Justin is a piece of meat. A very faint outline remains.

(*to Hugo*)

I mean you can kind of see it? Right?

Hugo peers.

HUGO

Um, yeah. Yeah?

> ROMAN
> Crazy idea, never happen in a million years – you wouldn't
> consider having it – done again, would you?

Justin looks like: What?

> Or a recreation in pen for photos?

> JUSTIN
> I don't think so—

Roman thinks. He whispers something in Hugo's ear. Then—

> HUGO
> Do you have any photos of it? We'd arrange a payment for any
> photos you might have?

> JUSTIN
> I'm not super-proud of what I did. So I wouldn't want my
> photos of it out there.

> ROMAN
> Right, and without wishing to make this too transactional –
> how much?? For the photos?

> JUSTIN
> Um? I really – it doesn't feel good. It would feel like going
> backwards.

> ROMAN
> Oh sure. There must be a number though . . .

This is like the conversation they had fifteen years ago.

> JUSTIN
> I guess, I kind of learned my lesson and I wouldn't want my kids
> to see the photos?

> ROMAN
> But maybe they wouldn't see them if you could afford to send
> them to a finishing school in Switzerland?

> JUSTIN
> It's about self-respect.

> ROMAN
> I'm just going to say a million dollars?

Justin wavers, looks at his attorney – it doesn't feel good but he nods. Roman gets his phone out and goes to exit.

EXT. JOSH'S COMPOUND – REAR DECK – DAY

Kendall and Josh descend the stairs leading away from the house. Logan follows, at a remove, on the phone as he walks.

> ROMAN
> *(from phone)*
> I found the guy we tattooed. Justin Albescu. I'm working on photos. I think we got him. I think it really hurts him, Dad.

Logan smiles. He likes it.

> LOGAN
> It's good, son, thank you.

He hangs up. As Logan begins to walk away from the house, a young girl (Kitty, nine) runs out from inside and dive-bombs into the pool. Logan catches up to Kendall and Josh.

They walk away from the house as Kitty splashes and enjoys the pool behind.

Logan is getting pissed off.

> She's feeling better ah?

> JOSH
> Yeah. Thank god. Aren't they amazing? Rubber ball. She was in bed an hour ago.

Logan doesn't like it. Kendall looks back to Kitty, now back out of the pool and diving back in.

> KENDALL
> Love it. Fearless.

> JOSH
> Yes. Love that. We could learn.

Logan wants to get on with it.

> LOGAN
> (*smiling but not*)

So, how about you just tell me what you want and I'll see if
I can give it to you and we can fuck off?

> KENDALL

Low blood sugar.

> JOSH

Oh okay? You want me to run back, grab you a PowerBar?
Because I wouldn't mind getting into it all.

*Kind of a fuck-you. Kind of a real offer. Logan just waves it away,
as they head up some wooden steps at the rear of the property,
disappearing from view—*

EXT. JOSH'S COMPOUND – GROUNDS

*Josh, Kendall and Logan step out onto a coastal trail, and begin to
walk.*

> JOSH

So here's my thing: I've lost ten percent of the value of my four
percent on this. Three hundred and fifty million dollars. So
I guess it comes down to: Are you or Sandy going to get me it
back?

> LOGAN

Stick with us – you stick with the value proposition. This is the
industry vision. Right here.

> JOSH

Uh-huh. But how does it work? The two of you. After what
you've said, how the hell does it work?

His dad is pissed off. Kendall has got a relationship so—

> KENDALL

Well you know, Beatles put out some of their best shit was when
they were suing each other, right?

> JOSH

Good band.

> KENDALL

Uh-huh. Great band.

271

Logan hates it but feels he has to contribute.

>   LOGAN
> Good band.

They all consider how good The Beatles were.

>   JOSH
> Look, honestly I don't love Stewy and Sandy but they offer me a story and a plan.

>   LOGAN
> Has Stewy run many major media companies?

>   JOSH
> Sandy has.

>   LOGAN
> Sandy's mashed potatoes.

>   KENDALL
> Sadly.

>   JOSH
> I like the scale of their ambition.

>   LOGAN
> Ambition? What, buy the company, hacksaw it and sell? Fucking genius.

>   KENDALL
> Stewy's a great guy but he's just numbers. He could run a calculus class at MIT but he'd close a pizza joint in a week.

>   JOSH
> I wouldn't say this, but people are asking, rude people are asking, has Logan Roy still got it?

Josh looks at Kendall. He gives poker face.

> And hey, I'm not expecting you to pitch me but, you know—?

He is expecting Logan to pitch to him. Logan has little choice.

>   LOGAN
> I'm still hungry. Lots of ways through this.

>   JOSH
> Because Ken likes GoJo. Right, Ken?

Kendall looks to Josh. Is he trying to drive a wedge between them here? Logan doesn't take the bait.

> LOGAN
>
> Sure. It's an option. But what I also see is the value in despised assets. That's cream you can get fat on. I'm a printing press for greenbacks and I don't give a fuck what anyone on god's green earth thinks of me.

> KENDALL
>
> Sure. Or maybe he falls on his sword and I win.

Logan smiles. Sounds dangerous to Josh.

> JOSH
>
> I guess honestly, the actual easiest thing for me would be, you know, Kendall, it's probably not too late to back-pedal on all your shit, say you were wrong or just – fuzzle it up, 'more complicated than it looked', back off and cool it down?

Kendall's senses twitch.

> KENDALL
>
> Not possible. That destroys my reputation.

> LOGAN
>
> You should listen to him.

A possibility arises in Kendall's mind.

> KENDALL
>
> Is this what this is? I've been brought out here to be roughed up by the two of you?

> JOSH
>
> Just 'things got out of hand'. You were mistaken. Things went too far?

> KENDALL
>
> Nope.

> JOSH
>
> I'm just saying, maybe quiet it down, at least? You've made your point, can't you close up the outrage shop, leave it to the DOJ to investigate?

Kendall looks between them.

273

> KENDALL
> (*a little hot*)
> Are you trying to fuck me, because, I see this.

> JOSH
> Whoa. Ken. Easy, friend.

Kendall has got a little overheated. Josh walks on and Logan gets a chance to whisper-hiss—

> LOGAN
> You okay, son? Some of those drugs you do can make you paranoid, is that right?

INT. WAYSTAR – BULLPEN – DAY

Shiv walks through the bullpen. She stops at Karl's office – knocks but doesn't wait to enter.

INT. WAYSTAR – KARL'S OFFICE – DAY

Frank and Karl inside. They look up – they weren't expecting an interruption. Karl is eating shrimp with a dipping sauce.

> SHIV
> Hey. Any updates from Dad?

> FRANK
> Radio silence. So, either, all going to plan or they've stabbed each other to death.

Frank gestures: Fifty-fifty. Karl makes the decision to continue eating his shrimp. Shiv nods, taking everything in. Then—

> SHIV
> And where we at with the Sandy and Stewy negotiation?

A weird atmosphere in the room. This isn't strictly protocol.

> KARL
> Oh, uh – broken momentarily.

> SHIV
> Oh yeah—?

She doesn't like the sound of that.

                              FRANK
They're just grabbing a quick bite while they wait on the
turnaround of the document.

Shiv senses the weird atmosphere but just pushes through.

                              SHIV
But in terms of the temperature?

                              KARL
It's attritional.

Shiv nods and smiles. But the details are vague.

                              SHIV
Great, great.
                             (*then*)
But just so I'm clear – we're hung up on what exactly?

Karl turns to a stack of notes, checks it.

                              KARL
Last breakout session was some specifics on the non-
disparagement clause.

                              SHIV
We're still on that? I'm green so, apologies – but aren't there
bigger points like the standstill?

                              KARL
Maybe but— I guess this is— What we're really scoping out is
if there is a deal space. We can figure out all the fixings in three
hours *if* they're serious about settling?

                              SHIV
Sure but do we have time to find out? Or do we maybe send one
of you two big-hitters to bang some heads, pull them out of the
weeds?

                              FRANK
Uh. It's an option. For sure.

                              SHIV
Look. Whatever you think? Let me know how it goes.

Karl just smiles. It's all smiles. Everyone smiles.

Well great. And any big news or vibrations, let me know.

KARL

We absolutely will.

SHIV

Thanks, guys.

A final smile. Shiv exits. Frank and Karl watch her go.

INT. WAYSTAR – GREG'S OFFICE – DAY

Greg at his desk in his windowless office, working hard. Tom enters. He has a cracked energy.

TOM

Knock knock. Is this the home of my distant assistant?!

GREG

Oh. Hey, Tom.

Tom enters, invading the space.

TOM

Terminal Tom calling. The ghost at the feast. The shame sponge.

Greg smiles. Tom seems a little off. Aims for casual.

GREG

I should have the – the – comparison deck with you by the morning.

Tom sits on the corner of Greg's desk. He needs to share.

TOM

Uh-huh, yeah, just got my clock cleaned by Ravenhead. Chewed me the fuck out. It's cool. It's just the job. I only mention to amuse.

GREG

(doesn't find it funny)
Cool, that's funny, that's a funny story.

Greg nods. Tom sees a muffin basket, looks at the card.

TOM

Yeah. And now I'm down here to apply the thumbscrews. Ooh, courtesy pastries.

> GREG

I think I'm being courted?

Tom sits on Greg's desk and starts eating a croissant.

> TOM

Correct.
> *(to muffins)*

Delicious, carby, carrots.
> *(to himself)*

Big fucking stick. So?

> GREG

Well. I guess I'm 'considering my options'.

> TOM

Good. Greg, honestly, you can probably ask for whatever you want.

> GREG

Yeah. It's just sometimes, you know, I love being your chief of staff. But . . . I guess, I've sometimes sustained physical injuries when I've talked about career development?

> TOM

Yeah well, you're an asset now. And I'll have to eat it and like it.
> *(smiles)*

Go on, what do you want?

> GREG

Well, all due respect to ATN, I feel like where my heart is, is parks. Because looking long-view, I guess the experience economy is maybe where it's at. And in a few years we're all gonna be in our pods, juiced up on happy pills, jerking off into the mainframe? Parks, *experiences*, that's the only game in town.

> TOM
> *(kidding)*

Greg, why did I never talk to you before, you're like a real person with your own little insights and opinions! Okay, let's game this—

Greg smiles.

> GREG

I was thinking of asking for operations director. Then kill Ray.

277

                              TOM
Ray's an asshole. But maybe hands-on to start . . .

But Greg already has it all figured out.

                              GREG
Exactly, get in at a tier-two park. Maybe ask for deputy at
Brightstar Buffalo, so I'm home on weekends?

                              TOM
Right. I guess you've already got it gamed?

Tom is staring at Greg. Pride, envy, love, hate, everything.

Heh. Ha!
                             (*beat*)
An amusing notion has occurred to me, Greg!

                              GREG
Yeah?

                              TOM
Yes. You're going to be running a theme park and here's me,
going to prison. You're going to be living in a magical castle
while I'm going to be down in a dungeon, sucking off ogres for
phone cards.

                              GREG
I mean, who even knows? It probably won't work—

Tom looks to Greg.

                              TOM
Greg – what do you know about Nero and Sporus?

                              GREG
Nero and—?

                              TOM
Sporus, Greg. He was a young slave boy. Nero's favorite. You
know what he did to him?

                              GREG
Um, 'Nero and Sporus'. This is not IP that I'm familiar with.

TOM

Nero pushed his wife down the stairs then he had Sporus
castrated and he married him instead. He gave him a ring and
made him dress up like his dead wife.

GREG

Wow. Plot twist. Did not see that coming.

TOM

I bought a book on the Romans, to read in prison. It's a big
book.

GREG

Is it a good book?

TOM

It's a decent book. I'd castrate you and marry you in a heartbeat.

Tom smiles, it's a joke – Greg smiles.

GREG

Are you okay, Tom—?

Tom can't let anybody in, even for a second, or he might die.

TOM

See if you can pull me to the ground, Greg! Let's fight like
chickens! Let's have a punching match.

*Maybe there's a bit of a moment where Greg goes to, or starts to, but
it doesn't feel right. Tom growls back or something and Greg backs
off.*

GREG

I don't want to, man.

TOM

Come on, come at me! Fight me like a rooster, you weakling.

Tom starts circling Greg, trying to grab for his tie.

GREG

Careful, my watch. I just ate a Danish—

TOM

Why are you such a cuck, Greg?

Greg finally snaps.

GREG

I don't want to.

Tom looks at him.

TOM

'I don't want to, I don't want to.' I don't want to either, Greg. It was a joke, *you idiot.* Dude, you are so hard to riff with. Big career obstacle for you there. Big.

EXT. JOSH'S COMPOUND – BLUFF/BBQ AREA – DAY

Josh and Kendall stand at a bluff, with a view out to sea.

JOSH

Good yeah?

KENDALL

Oh yeah.

JOSH

I'm losing some though. Got some erosion. Real estate slipping into the sea. Kinda like legacy media?

KENDALL

Right. But you've held our position for a while?

JOSH
(*a smile; then looks out*)
Uh-huh. It's going to collapse one day, but probably not today. Right? Today we're all good?

Josh jumps, testing the ground. Kendall smiles, distracted, looks down to his dad.

You here? You here with me?

KENDALL

Yeah I'm here.

JOSH

Uh-huh.
(*then*)
You should involve me more, on the deal-flow, you know? The creative. That would be the smart thing to do.

This is a reach by Josh. Kendall has to tread lightly.

> KENDALL

Uh-huh. Absolutely. Be great to get your brain on it.

> JOSH
> (high-handed)

Okay well send me over what you have and I'll get back to you with my thoughts. Pitch, counter-pitch.

Kendall doesn't like the implication that he should be answering to Josh. But he has to swallow it.

> KENDALL

Awesome. Thanks, man.

Josh shrugs – It's nothing.

Eventually they turn away. Nearby, there's a table to sit at. BBQ food available. Some discreet service staff who set up, serve and then disappear on golf carts.

As they cross towards the BBQ area, they see Logan, lagging now.

> JOSH

But your dad is okay?

> KENDALL

He's fine.

> JOSH

Kind of fucking magnificent. The Lion in the Meadow. So come on. What do you have on him? Hard?

A sudden pivot. It takes Kendall by surprise.

> KENDALL

I'd rather not say. Legally.

Kendall doesn't want to get into it. Waits, watching his dad walk towards them. Josh looks hard at Kendall.

> JOSH

I guess it's difficult. If you have jackshit, you look like a fake. If you have really damaging shit, it makes me maybe run away? Right?

> KENDALL

I have – I have things.

Josh looks at him. Kendall thinks how much to say.

Emails. Letters of concern sent directly to him.

> JOSH
> Your dad's smart. I don't think he'd put anything in writing?

Kendall becomes aware of Logan returning. He drops this a little louder, to make sure Logan hears it.

> KENDALL
> He's implicated.

Logan returns to them. He half-hears. He feels pissed off and excluded.

Just riffing.

> LOGAN
> Uh-huh.

> KENDALL
> Pitching our vision.

> LOGAN
> You should tell him about Justin Albescu. That's a funny story. Your brother was just telling me?

This name knocks Kendall. Logan taps his forehead.

> KENDALL
> Right. What? Maybe not now, yeah?

Silence as they look at one another.

Josh clocks the atmosphere. Logged and noted. He motions for them to sit.

Logan's phone goes. He moves away from the BBQ area to take it.

> LOGAN
> Yeah—?

Intercut with:

INT. WAYSTAR – KARL'S OFFICE – DAY

Karl on the phone.

> KARL
> (*into phone*)
> Logan. Sorry to chase, just looking for an update from your end.

Irritated, Logan looks over at Josh and Kendall.

> LOGAN
> I don't know. Maybe.

> KARL
> Great. Great. I'll feed in and we'll keep pushing.

Half-beat. Then, the real reason Karl phoned.

> Um and listen, I just wanted to check in, about Siobhan, and how it's all shaking down here.

Logan unsure he likes the sound of this.

> LOGAN
> Uh-huh.

> KARL
> It feels like she thinks she has been authorized to tell me what to do?

> LOGAN
> I want her looped in to learn the ropes.

> KARL
> Sure. But – fifteen years with the organization and now I have to run her errands? Come on. I can take my licks. But if she can give me marching orders, I have to reconsider my position.

Line goes quiet.

> I mean obviously I don't want to do that, this close to the shareholder meeting, but we are where we are.

Logan takes a steadying breath. The choice is alive in his eyes for a moment. He and Karl both know it. Trusted colleague or daughter? Which way will he decide to . . .

> LOGAN
> Fine. I'll speak with Siobhan.

Karl immediately reverts to being the supplicant.

KARL

Thank you. Major-domo! I'll eat a sausage off the floor for you anytime, you old bastard.

LOGAN

Uh-huh.

INT. WAYSTAR – SHIV'S OFFICE – DAY

Tom comes in to give Shiv an update. It's bad news, he's in a low mood.

TOM

Hey, yeah, so it's a no from Ravenhead. He just doesn't see how he can accommodate the pivot.

She is wary, can see he's low. Shiv's aware of the glass, people passing outside.

SHIV

Okay? Well, that's unfortunate.

TOM

Yeah he was quite unpleasant about it all.

SHIV
(*looking to cheer him*)
But I hear Greg's a lock? He signed the JDA. So – you nailed that?

TOM

Uh-huh. That's my level. 'Tom Wambsgans, minion wrangler and shit-eater.'

SHIV

You okay? Is it the seniority thing?

He shakes his head.

The, the, prison possibility?

He's been having these obsessive thoughts. He wants to share—

TOM

I just keep thinking about, when we get home and before dinner we have that first glass of cold white wine? On an empty stomach, that very cold glass of wine – I just fucking love that.

So I did some research and I got deep into the prison blogs again – about 'toilet wine', but then I got worried I'd forget to 'burp' my bag of 'ketchup hooch' and it would explode.

(*then*)

But the truth is, I'm not going to get wine, of any temperature, in prison. There's no fine wines in prison, Shiv.

SHIV

Tom.

TOM

You don't get to choose what you eat in prison and you don't get to say what you do in prison. And like how late can you read? When is lights-out?

Shiv looks at him. He's on the edge a bit.

I'm fucking terrified, Shiv.

SHIV

Tom. Baby? It'll be okay.

TOM

Uh-huh. Sure, I know.

(*then*)

But what if it isn't? What if I buckle?

She wants to hug him, but also wants to protect him from the gossip if she does – employees pass outside.

SHIV

Tom, I don't know what to say. I haven't got anything to say. Let's talk at home. It won't happen. I'm sorry.

He's still sad. A thing occurs to her – pathetic, but why not?

Listen, one tiny thing. Would it be fun for us to, push 'go' on the vineyard?

TOM

You said it was a money pit?

SHIV

I was in a shitty mood. It might be fun? To have something growing? It could be fun – whatever happens, right?

He looks like: Maybe. Her phone goes. She looks at the display:
'Dad'.

I should— Dad?

Dad is always most important.

> TOM
>
> Uh-huh sure. Sure.

Tom looks at her and leaves, sadly. She watches him go.

Intercut with:

EXT. JOSH'S COMPOUND – BBQ AREA/TRAILS – DAY

> LOGAN
>
> I just spoke to Karl.

> SHIV
>
> Greg's in. We just got signature copies.

> LOGAN
>
> Karl's not happy with your level of input.

> SHIV
>
> Oh, okay well, fuck him, right?

> LOGAN
>
> I don't need another toothache.

> SHIV
>
> But you okayed me to go in and kick some ass and—

> LOGAN
>
> I gave you a destination, I can't walk you there, okay?

> SHIV
>
> You give in to Karl, everyone starts carving me out. This is a
> line, Dad, and—

> LOGAN
>
> Nothing's a line. Everything, everywhere is always moving
> forever, okay? Get used to it.

Shiv realizes she's just going to have to swallow this.

SHIV
Uh-huh. Okay.

Shiv hangs up. Sting of humiliation.

Logan returns to the BBQ area, hanging up his phone as Kendall's phone goes. Logan glowers at Kendall for taking a call at this important time. Kendall looks like: Fuck you, you took your call – as he moves away to take it.

KENDALL
(into phone)
Lisa – hey?

LISA
(from phone)
Ken, where are you?

KENDALL
I'm nowhere. I'm in meetings—

LISA
I know you're with your father, Kendall.

Kendall doesn't even contest it—

They briefed the DOJ, Ken, they told everyone. They played you.

KENDALL
I had to be here. There's a wider view.

LISA
Ken, you don't get to go on TV and call your dad a rapist and then go out on a picnic with him.

KENDALL
Well we lose this shareholder, and lose the vote, I'm fucked so—

LISA
DOJ is re-evaluating. They think you're using them and it's hurt your credibility.

Back with Josh and Logan at the table. Josh spots some nearby plant life. He gets up, or reaches over to it.

JOSH
Beach grass. You know, you can eat this.

(he does)
You want some beach grass, Logan? Tide you over? It's very bitter.

LOGAN

No I don't want to eat the beach grass, thank you, Josh.

Josh smiles. He maybe enjoys prodding at the old man. Kendall returns.

Everything okay?

KENDALL

Uh-huh. All good.

A look between them. Kendall replays Frank's call in his mind. Josh watches.

LOGAN

So, Josh. Where are we on this? Because you know I have a wife at home—

A crooked smile, meant to feel chummy and warm but coming across desperate—

JOSH

Okay. Here's where I'm at – I hear you, on the fundamentals. You're right. Fuck Sandy and Stewy, they're just financial engineering – and I can do that myself right?

KENDALL

Absolutely, yes.

They're getting somewhere—

JOSH

But this. Hand on heart, it still feels off. Ken, it feels like you want your dad to go to jail?

KENDALL

Well that's not for me to say.

JOSH

Kind of is though—? Like if you were a judge, you'd want him to go to prison?

Logan notably silent.

KENDALL

I believed a traditional whistleblowing process would be subverted. So that's why I—

JOSH

Logan, the reputational hit? I mean optically. Maybe you become, you know, a punchline. One of those big guys, who aren't coming back? How does this end? The investigation? The two of you?

LOGAN

It ends with me in control. Slapped wrists and a payout. That stuff—

(*waves at Kendall*)

sea mist. Vapor.

Josh looks at Kendall. Poker face.

JOSH

It's this friction thing you see – I'm hearing separate planes – seems like you kind of hate Kendall, Logan? And maybe that doesn't matter, but I don't like to bet on blood feuds.

LOGAN

Uh-huh. It'll be okay.

JOSH

Sure. Absolutely.

Josh maybe takes a bite, or checks his phone – a subtle gesture to betray confidence, before he casually slides in the blade.

Here's the disconnect. Here's where I think maybe we're bumping. I think that, end of the day, you work for the shareholders. For me. But I think that you think I'm some dipshit who had a lucky night at the casino who acts fancy but then makes you eat fucking rodents for my pleasure, right?

Josh lets it land for a beat. Tense smiles. It's true.

But in this moment I don't like it, I kind of hate it—
(*he loves it*)
But I have my boot on your throat. And what I need to know is that this is a functional situation. I mean you're gonna say it is, but I need to hear you say it anyway.

>   (*then*)
>   So can you work together?

*Josh sits back, or takes a drink. Their move. Logan doesn't like this
dynamic. Dancing to this tune.*

                              LOGAN
>   Uh-huh.

                              KENDALL
>   Sure. Absolutely.

Josh nods. Then—

                              JOSH
>   So tough, though. Because I kind of don't believe you!

                              LOGAN
>   It'll be okay.

                              JOSH
>   Really?

Josh smiles. Logan realizes he needs to work harder to triage this.

                              LOGAN
>   It'll be okay, because he's a good kid.

                              JOSH
>   He's a good kid?

                              LOGAN
>   Yeah he's a good kid.

                              JOSH
>   Okay?

Josh maybe he leans in. An unspoken turn of the screw.

                              LOGAN
>   He did what he thought was best, I think he went too far but
>   he's a good kid.

                              JOSH
>   Right?

                              LOGAN
>   Yeah.

> JOSH

Yeah?

Does Josh still need more? Logan offers it all the same.

> LOGAN

He's a good kid and I love him. There'll be a big number, we'll pay, he'll mew and cry and I get it. It's all okay. And maybe it'll be him, one day, because it's in his blood and he learnt it all from me. He's maybe the best one of all of them. So yeah it's going to be okay.

> JOSH

Wow. Well. So that's nice to hear?

A smile and a look to Kendall. Kendall smiles and shrugs.

Josh looks between them. Maybe it landed with him. Either way he'll push his advantage.

I guess if the psychodrama wasn't going to bump things. I guess to come your way, I have a little wish list. A little EPS-juicing. Some stock buyback. Let me in, you know? I would suggest perhaps the company selling off some real estate and leasing it back?

> LOGAN

Well sounds good. I'd consider all that. Absolutely.

Logan will deign to 'consider' it. Josh nods, allows Logan his dignity.

> JOSH

Well, I'd appreciate that, Logan.

Maybe it's all going to be okay? Josh's phone goes.

I should take this. I want us to get back a little easier.

> LOGAN

Oh yeah? City boy ah? You're a bit far from your nearest coffee and a bagel!? Haha.

Josh exits to take his call.

Logan looks at his food.

Kendall looks at Logan – wants to see what's in his eye. No eye contact available. Looks down.

Kendall glances up again.

But Logan won't look. Kendall looks down.

Logan glances. Kendall doesn't see.

Kendall looks at him more. Did he mean what he said at any level?

Logan feels Kendall's eyes rest on him. He glances. Kendall looks right at him. Logan looks right back. They hold the look – not really willing to give anything to the other one.

No gratitude from Kendall – it's gone too far, and without that, no softness available from Logan.

Kendall looks away.

Kendall is intrigued to know what he means. Did he mean it – did he mean it right out? Probably not? Or was it regret? But somehow masked by the requirement in this moment with Josh to show some conciliation.

Or was it the opposite – disdain.

Logan's not smiling. But is he silent because he means what he says or he doesn't? Kendall looks at him. Eventually—

                    LOGAN
                    (cont'd)
    What?

                    KENDALL
    What what?

Logan will not give him anything.

Kendall stares him back, won't give anything back.

It goes on for a while. Josh returns.

                    JOSH
    Okay. Look, shall we head back? They'll send carts for us. You
    wanna wait or we can go up to—? We can start walking and
    meet them.

Kendall glances to Logan. He's probably tired. Would rather wait.

                    KENDALL
    Wanna rest up, old geezer?

LOGAN

I'm good.

They stand and start walking back. Josh leads them over to a different path, now heading inland. Josh walking out in front, leading the way. Maybe looking at messages on his phone.

Going along the trail. They walk. Josh leading, eventually, through a series of paths.

They walk on.

On their faces . . . Kendall and Logan.

Was it all just total bullshit?

Logan is panting quite heavily.

Kendall smiles.

KENDALL

Nice speeches.

LOGAN

Yeah, well, you'll say anything to get fucked on a date, won't you?

Kendall thinks – fuck him. And Logan thinks – fuck him.

We stay on them in their silence.

They walk on. The going getting a little harder.

You know, Greg's with me now. He tell you that? You're on your own, son.

News to Kendall. He doesn't want to let it show—

KENDALL

Uh-huh. We'll see.

They walk on. Anger bubbling up in Kendall—

Retire now, effective immediately, maybe I go easy, row back.

LOGAN

You'd scuttle the fleet in a month.

                         KENDALL

Dad. You're the silverback but I put you in the ground that day and you don't get to come back, no matter how much you wriggle.

                         LOGAN

You know something, son? I'd rather get fucked by a spic in a shower block than see you have it.

Kendall smiles. Infuriating for Logan.

I've got the Raisin, under my thumb. I've got the family. I've got little Greggy, I've got this fucking tattoo-man in the tank, you're high and dry. Face it son, you lost—
                (*a finger to the lips*)
Sssssssssshhhhhh.

Infuriating to Kendall. Going along the trail. They walk on.

It's heavy-going now. Logan feels less good. He walks on. Josh drops back to join them.

                         JOSH

You okay to keep going? I have visitors arriving so I'll go on ahead. You sure you're okay?

Logan doesn't look so great all of a sudden.

                         LOGAN

I'm great. You go.

Josh goes up ahead to try to intercept the golf carts.

They walk on. Logan's breathing hard. He's not in a good way. They walk on. Logan coughs.

Kendall looks at his dad. Sees he doesn't look great. Kendall calls ahead—

                         KENDALL

Hey, Josh? I think this feels like it's going to the ocean? Can you drop a pin for them?

                         JOSH
                       (*calling back*)
No this is – this is the short way back. I know where we are.

Kendall looks to Logan.

> LOGAN
>
> Stop staring. I'm fine.

> JOSH
> (*calling back*)
> Rough though. You want to wait here for the cart?

> LOGAN
> Huh—? Bumps. I've walked bumps—

Logan looks sweaty. The heat or exertion has taken a toll.

> JOSH
> (*calling back*)
> You sure? Because I can call them.

Logan is too proud to admit weakness. Kendall sees it.

> LOGAN
> No no. Not just for me. Not on my account.
> (*then*)
> Right, Ken—?

Logan looks to Kendall: Help me out.

Kendall thinks. Looks back. The moment hangs.

And he goes in—

> KENDALL
> We're good. He's all good. Let's walk it out. Right, Dad?

Kendall looks to Logan – a vindictive flash.

> He's fine. He's a bear.

Josh sets off. Kendall and Logan left walking behind.

> Can't you even fucking tell him you need a breather?

> LOGAN
> I'm fine—

> KENDALL
> You've lied so much you don't even fucking know anymore.
> Your brain's scrambled egg, look at you.

Logan is becoming steadily out of breath—

LOGAN

I beat you – pipe down.

KENDALL

What's that? I can't hear you—?

LOGAN

You're fucked.

KENDALL

Uh-huh. Look at you, you're six hundred years old and you've pissed off your fucking big brother the president, and he's sending the feds on you and you're wriggling but you're in too deep. Everyone knows, and now you're trying to counter but you've put Shiv in there and she's a fucking dipshit. I hear no one respects her, everyone's digging her out and you're losing control and everyone hates you.

LOGAN
(breathy)

Let's close the deal with Josh—

KENDALL

He fucking hates you too. Your anti-Semitic fucking 'bagel and gold' bullshit.

LOGAN

Fuck off.

KENDALL

You don't know what you're saying half the time. You're off the pace. You're way off it.

Logan struggles on.

LOGAN
(low)

You got – water?

KENDALL
(low)

Ask your fucking iPhone.

They walk on. Logan wheezing now. Josh stands looking out, quite a ways away so Kendall and Logan can talk without being heard. It's increasingly clear that Josh is lost, but he won't admit it.

> JOSH
> (*calling back*)

I'm gonna call the house. This is the quick way, but it can take longer. So I'm checking.

> KENDALL

Okay?

Logan turns away from Josh, so that only Kendall can see.

> LOGAN
> (*low; to Kendall*)

Get me something – in case I puke.

> KENDALL

Catch your breath.

> JOSH
> (*up ahead; into phone*)

Well I know where I am, we don't know where you are. So we're not lost, you're lost. Can you come get us?

Logan's breathing hard. He's not in a good way.

> KENDALL

Dad – come on.

Logan maybe pukes or dry-heaves. He swallows something down or spits out saliva or a little vomit.

> (*reacts*)

Dad—? You okay?

> JOSH
> (*calling over*)

You okay—? Is he okay—?

> LOGAN
> (*low*)

Tell him yeah—

Kendall realizes he needs to cover, for both their sakes.

> KENDALL
> (*calling back*)

All good.

Josh buys it, returns to his call. Logan's wan, sweating.

Are you okay? Are you having a fucking heart attack—?

LOGAN

Fuck off – I know what heart attacks are, this isn't one—

Kendall looks at him and then decides.

Up ahead, Josh back on the phone—

JOSH
(*on the phone*)

We took the quick path from the bluff—

KENDALL
(*to Logan*)

We need a cart and a doctor.

LOGAN

No – we're not getting a fucking doctor – not in front of him—

KENDALL

You're fucking dying here.

LOGAN

I'm not dying – you're trying to fuck me in front of him—

KENDALL

I don't want you on my conscience.

LOGAN

You made me walk the extra— You tried to fuck me—

Josh is now walking back towards them from further along.

JOSH
(*calling out to them*)

So we're not lost – but my guys don't know where we are.

Josh, approaching, maybe starts to clock that something's happening here, as Kendall and Logan try to conceal it—

KENDALL
(*to Logan*)

We need to get you back.

LOGAN
(*to Kendall*)

Fuck off – I just need to have a word.

Logan steels himself and turns to face the approaching Josh. But he falters or falls a little, rolling his ankle. Kendall steadies him.

> KENDALL
> Whoa – okay, Josh—? We need to get my dad back so we're going to have to leave it there.

> JOSH
> Fuck, is he okay? Now I feel bad—

Logan, now unable to put weight on his ankle, retches again. He needs to sit.

> KENDALL
> Oh god, hey, Dad—?

Kendall seems to maybe even angle Logan slightly towards Josh, or exaggerate his reaction just a little so Josh sees the extent of Logan's ill-health.

> JOSH
> Okay, I think maybe we need a doctor—

> KENDALL
> Too much sun. He'll be fine, just a bit too much sun.

Kendall helps Logan sit then makes a move towards Josh, for a connection—

> But hey, listen, man—

> JOSH
> (*cutting across him*)
> I think maybe take care of your dad?

Kendall nods and snaps back to it, as though he were moving that way already, but the snub from Josh is clocked and noted.

Kendall helps Logan get comfortable under the shade of a nearby tree, while they wait for a buggy. Logan tries to resist, but knows he's tapped out, and succumbs.

Kendall and Josh stand waiting.

Eventually we see or hear carts start to arrive.

INT. ATN MEETING ROOM – DAY

Mark Ravenhead, Wanda and staff are in the middle of an editorial meeting. Shiv knocks and enters. All smiles.

SHIV

Hey. Sorry to barge in.

All eyes on her. A sudden shift in the temperature.

Would you prefer for me to wait outside?

Wanda can read the room.

WANDA

Er, we were just breaking up, so—

SHIV

Great.

Wanda is careful in how she couches this – impolitic to raise this with Shiv, but she needs to protect her talent.

WANDA
(quietly; on the side)
Um, you know Mark only discusses editorial with Cyd or Logan, that's just long-standing, but—

SHIV

Oh fine it's not editorial.

Wanda exits. Leaving just Shiv and Mark. A smile between them. It's obvious why she's here.

Shiv smiles. Then—

So yeah it is editorial. I have a line for you, on the president, that we'd like for you to roll out starting immediately. We're open to suggestions but we feel our general ideological sympathy has maybe let them off the hook on too many specifics. Middle East, big tech, green subsidies. We'd like this as a branded, nightly segment, maybe: 'Losing His Grip'.

MARK

'Losing His Grip'. Jesus. You know he's a friend?

SHIV

But with a question mark. Like, 'Is he?'

MARK

Oh with a question mark? Thanks for giving me discretion on the punctuation.

SHIV

This is like our advice to our friend. You know?

MARK

'Losing His Grip'? That's— I mean, he's very sensitive and that plays into the rumors.

SHIV
(*deadpan*)

What rumors?

Mark just watches her.

MARK

You know, I might feel more comfortable doing this with my agent present—?

SHIV

It's okay. I called her already, to let her know we'd be having this conversation.

Quite chilling.

MARK

I have a perspective and a reputation that I have built up over a number of years.

SHIV

Mark – I get it – this is all new to me. I'm feeling my way here. Church and state, there's editorial guardrails in place and I'm kinda merrily skipping over them.

No argument there.

But this is something my dad wants. So, one: He has great antennae and you might like to back his hunches. But two: In a sense this conversation is already over. It's just a question of how many times we scream the word 'fuck' at each other before you do what we want?

Shiv smiles. A sense of nihilistic calm. She's surrendered to it.

301

MARK

What if I walk, right now? Across the street.

SHIV

Yeah, you're under contract so no one will touch you.

MARK

What if I go public about this full-court press? Incredibly embarrassing for you.

SHIV

Yeah the thing about us, Mark – and you really should know this by now – we don't get embarrassed.

Shiv smiles.

INT. WAYSTAR – GERRI'S OFFICE – DAY

Roman enters. Gerri's on the phone.

ROMAN

Hey. How things looking?

GERRI
(*re phone to Roman*)
Conference with lawyers before they head back in. Stewy and Sandy. No progress. Not good.

ROMAN

How was the date? You fuck him or just tug him off between courses?

GERRI
(*into phone*)
Yeah, no that's not going to work for us. At all. That's a red line.

ROMAN

Oh my god you did – you tugged him off under the table, you absolute monster!
(*then*)
Tell me, did you wear your work glasses or your whore glasses—?

Phone down.

GERRI

Enough. Okay? Seriously. No more.

ROMAN

Gerri – are you – flirting with me?

GERRI

What do you want?

Roman has a printout – a photo of Justin, with his tattoo. And a Polaroid of him with Kendall and Roman, drunk and disheveled either side, grinning.

Oh god—

ROMAN

It was so fucking funny, Gerri. I mean, I wanted to cry and be sick too.

GERRI

Uh-huh.

ROMAN

I'm giving them to Dad. He wants to get them out right away.

Gerri has a thought to lay.

GERRI

Rome. Don't use it.

ROMAN

This is a magic bullet. Dad will give me my bedtime bath.

GERRI

Bank the photos. By all means. But don't spread them around. It's great for Logan. Bad for Kendall. But bad for you. 'The Tattoo Brothers'.

Roman sees what's happening here.

ROMAN

Ooooh. Gerri – you – care?

GERRI

Yeah I care. I care about me. And I think I maybe need you, so: 'How does this advance my personal position?' You need to think that twenty-four-seven. You should get *that* tattooed on your head.

Roman thinks on it. Then—

> Keep them as our little secret.

Roman smiles. He likes the way that sounds.

> Did you hear about your dad?

ROMAN

> No, what?

EXT. AIRFIELD — DAY

Later, two identical private jets, lined up, awaiting clearance to take off—

INT. LOGAN'S PRIVATE JET — EVENING

Logan sits, his ankle now supported. He's on the phone.

LOGAN
(into phone)

> Uh-huh. Uh-huh. Well I'm sorry.
>
> (listens)
>
> I don't control them like that. He has editorial freedom.

Logan sits, enjoying the anger from the other end.

> C'mon, this is just rumors. Watch the show, I'm sure it won't be so bad?

Logan listens on. He sees Kerry standing and waiting for him nearby. He covers the phone.

> (to Kerry)
>
> You want to hear what it sounds like when the president loses his temper?

Kerry smiles. Is he serious? Logan gestures: Take the phone. Kerry crosses, and puts her ear to the receiver. She takes it in. Weirdly thrilling. Then—

> (to Kerry whispered)
>
> You want to hang up on him?

Kerry laughs: No way? But Logan takes the phone back.

(*into phone*)
Look, let me investigate. It's just, you know Mark. Very tenacious. Very independent. I dunno, maybe if I wasn't so tied up with this fucking investigation, I could focus on keeping ATN on-message?

Logan hangs up. He feels momentarily better. He relaxes into his seat. A second phone goes. He takes it.

(*into phone*)
Uh-huh?

FRANK
(*from phone*)
Okay. So we just heard back from Josh.

INT. KENDALL'S PRIVATE JET – DAY

Kendall, on the phone.

Intercut with:

INT. WAYSTAR – ROMAN'S OFFICE – DAY

ROMAN
I hear you tried to kill Dad again, fatty.

KENDALL
It was just heat exhaustion—

ROMAN
That's not what we're hearing. We're hearing you took an old man out to die in the sun.

KENDALL
We went for a hike, with Josh—

ROMAN
You tried to assassinate our dad with the sun. Do you have a fetish for *nearly* killing Dad? Like, 'just the tip' but for killing Dad.

KENDALL
Yeah well, it's in hand. The vote. Josh is a lock.

>   ROMAN

Well, no he's out.

>   KENDALL

He's with us.

>   ROMAN

Frank just got off the phone. Dad's freakout gave him the shits.
Weak leadership, fractured at the top. You let him fucking
shrivel, he saw.

Kendall's thrown. Stomach drops.

He has quote, 'zero faith in the post-Dad leadership'. So go eat
a donut, ya jowly fuck. We're gonna lose the company at the
shareholder meet all because you wouldn't give our dad a timely
fucking Evian. Goodnight!

Kendall hangs up on Roman. He stares out.

*Then, he looks out the window – and sees Stewy climbing out of a
helicopter to meet Josh. A warm embrace between the two.*

Episode Five

RETIRED JANITORS OF IDAHO

Written by
Tony Roche & Susan Soon He Stanton
Directed by Kevin Bray

Original air date 14 November 2021

Cast

LOGAN ROY	Brian Cox
KENDALL ROY	Jeremy Strong
GREG HIRSCH	Nicholas Braun
SHIV ROY	Sarah Snook
ROMAN ROY	Kieran Culkin
CONNOR ROY	Alan Ruck
TOM WAMBSGANS	Matthew Macfadyen
FRANK VERNON	Peter Friedman
KARL MULLER	David Rasche
GERRI KELLMAN	J. Smith-Cameron
KAROLINA NOVOTNEY	Dagmara Dominczyk
HUGO BAKER	Fisher Stevens
JESS JORDAN	Juliana Canfield
EWAN ROY	James Cromwell
STEWY HOSSEINI	Arian Moayed
SANDY FURNESS	Larry Pine
SOPHIE ROY	Swayam Bhatia
KERRY CASTELLABATE	Zoë Winters
COLIN STILES	Scott Nicholson
BERRY SCHNEIDER	Jihae
COMFREY PELLITS	Dasha Nekrasova
SANDI	Hope Davis
ROGER PUGH	Peter Riegert
CYD PEACH	Jeannie Berlin
RAY KENNEDY	Patch Darragh
DR TROY JUDITH	John Rue
JOSH AARONSON	Adrien Brody
BIANCA	Hermione Lynch
MAYA BERNARD	Trian Long-Smith
RICHARD	Richard Vernon
SHAREHOLDER 2	Yasu Suzuki
VOICEOVER	Sarah Naughton
STEVE COX	Wayne Pyle
ISABELLE PETERS LYON	Alexandra Foucard
RICHARD MARTINS	John Higgins
REMI BISHOP	KeiLyn Durrel Jones

MARK ROSENSTOCK	Brian Hotaling
SECURITY GUARD	Marvin Johnson
SECURITY GUARD 2	Zachary James

INT. LOGAN'S APARTMENT – LOGAN'S STUDY

A TV has ATN on mute. Chyron reads: 'President's Memory "May Be Suspect"'.

Richard puts on Logan's big medical walking boot.

> LOGAN
> *(winces)*
> Easy, clumsy fucking, donkey—

Richard tries to ignore him, smiles, apologizes.

EXT. LOGAN'S APARTMENT – DAY

Colin and Kerry accompany Logan out, gruff and uncomfortable towards the car.

> LOGAN
> *(to Kerry)*
> Hm. Might need a piss.

> KERRY
> *(a tiny hesitation)*
> Do you want to go back up? You don't want another (infection)—

It's a long way back up.

> LOGAN
> Nah, c'mon, let's get it over with.

Colin comes to help him.

> I can do it.

INT. SHIV AND TOM'S CAR – DAY

Shiv is a mass of nervous energy, dialing on her phone.

> SHIV
>
> Karl. Anything from the negotiations? Any kind of human
> communication would be good.

End of call. Tom massages her shoulders a little.

> TOM
>
> You smell so good.

She shrugs off his touch.

> It's relaxing.

> SHIV
>
> Thanks. I mean it's not. But thanks. I should look at my words.

She looks at papers.

> TOM
>
> Yeah, I asked for some stage time but Logan said he didn't want
> 'the Birdman of Alcatraz flying around the room dropping shit'?

INT. LOGAN'S CAR – DAY

Logan looks out the window.

> LOGAN
>
> What do you think, Colin? Is this it?

> COLIN
>
> Feeling good, Mr Roy, feeling good.

> LOGAN
>
> Uh-huh. Fuck 'em.

Logan looks at Kerry, she smiles supportively. Logan is worried.

INT. VENUE – VARIOUS ROOMS – DAY

Montage. Waystar employees set up for the shareholder meeting.

*Outside the venue: TV vans and some reporters do pieces to camera
and wait for action to start. There are some protestors, some
photographers.*

Reception area: handouts are placed on registration desks (annual reports, proxy statement, ballots and folders containing agenda). The staff set out a couple of ballot boxes in the reception area.

Café: refreshments are laid out.

Onstage: a table and chairs are set up, the lectern mic is tested, Waystar promo video is played on the big screen.

Green room: a big comfortable space backstage.

In there, screens are set up showing the stage and auditorium.

Auditorium: staff put rules, agendas, ballots on seats. The large security team arrives and is briefed.

Marshals put reserved signs on front two rows of seats and area where Sandy's team will sit. Technicians arrange mics for the audience.

Lanyards with 'Shareholder' are placed at the check-in table.

INT. VENUE — UPSTAIRS CORRIDOR — DAY

Kendall and Jess walk down the hotel hallway. Kendall is FaceTiming with his daughter Sophie.

> KENDALL
> Soph? What's going on, Wild Honeypie?

> SOPHIE
> *(from phone)*
> Bianca won't let us feed Megathump a piece of bagel.

> KENDALL
> Put Bianca on.

> BIANCA
> *(from phone)*
> Hi, yeah I'm sorry but I looked it up and rabbits aren't supposed to eat bagels—

> KENDALL
> Bianca. Let the rabbit have some bagel. Those rules are for fuckheads who are going to go to Miami and leave a rabbit with

a Big Gulp and a dozen cinnamon and raisin. One won't hurt okay?

Jess hands him a phone with a PGNB piece he wants to see—

STEVE COX
(*onscreen*)
Our top story this morning is of course, that the fate of media giant Waystar Royco hangs in the balance.

INT. HOTEL SUITE – KENDALL'S HQ – BATHROOM – DAY

Kendall walks out to survey his HQ, a full comms set-up. But also champagne chilling and a weird party vibe. Remi. Comfrey. A couple of their assistants.

KENDALL
Shadow chamber! HQ of the hashtag resistance.
(*to Jess*)
What's his ETA?

JESS
Your dad's still en route.

The story plays on the TV.

STEVE COX
(*onscreen*)
The proxy battle between founder chairman Logan Roy and activist investors under the Maesbury Capital banner is currently, 'too close to call'. The sides have spent close to a hundred million dollars fighting a battle to win the hearts, minds and votes of corporate investors and small shareholders. Positions are entrenched. An eleventh-hour deal looks elusive and all the signals are that the two sides are gritting their teeth to go to a vote at the company's annual shareholders' meeting, being held in New York City today.

Kendall gets a call. He answers. Turns TV off or down.

KENDALL
Yo, are you sweating me, On Golden Pond? Have we got a deal?

Intercut with:

INT. VENUE – GREEN ROOM – DAY

Frank in a private corner of the green room.

> FRANK
> (*on phone*)
> Ken, I would like to privately transmit a certain degree of trepidation.

> KENDALL
> There he is, the panic meister cooking up his sweaty spaghetti. What bullshit you selling me today?

> FRANK
> We haven't had a breakthrough and I think Logan is willing to let this go to a vote.

> KENDALL
> He's not gonna fuck this, is he?

> FRANK
> I'm just thinking, if we need it, is there a back channel here? It might be nice to let Moscow know what Washington's thinking today, so we don't all stumble into armageddon?

> KENDALL
> (*thinks*)
> Uh-huh? Let's keep this channel open. Eagle's Eyrie out!

Kendall looks out the window, thinks.

INT. LOGAN'S CAR – LOADING DOCK – DAY

Down below – Logan is helped out of the car by Kerry.

> LOGAN
> Will you sit out front today, K? I need to know what the temperature is amongst the shit-munchers?

> KERRY
> Sure. Um, in that case, I'll leave these with you? You'll remember, yes? You don't want me to—

She nods to Colin. He's embarrassed, doesn't like discussion of illness.

LOGAN

No. I have it covered.

She slips Logan the pills – his UTI meds – and they go into his jacket pocket discreetly.

INT. VENUE – GREEN ROOM – DAY

Shiv, Tom, Frank, Hugo, Karolina, Cyd, Ray, Mark and various assistants are checking phones. It's tense, downbeat.

This is our arena for much of the day: a semi-private space. Within it there might be an area of couches for the inner-circle, to have private discussions.

Assistants and proxy advisors, etc., work elsewhere. There are some more private rooms and spaces off the green room. Roman arrives, checking his phone. A news website headline reads: 'Questions Grow Over President's "Competence and Capability"'. He shows it to Shiv, who shrugs.

ROMAN

How you feeling?

SHIV

I dunno. Yeah. Terrible. I keep thinking is this real? But it really is real.

ROMAN

I guess, even on your way to the chair you keep thinking, 'It won't happen to little old me.'

CYD

Interesting day. Potentially attending one's own funeral.

FRANK

Tom Sawyer seemed to enjoy it.

Karl and Gerri arrive. They've not had much sleep.

ROMAN

Okay, here they are! Pump and Dump the corporate clowns.

SHIV

How we looking?

> GERRI

Total breakdown. They want the moon on a stick.

> KARL

Two five a.m. nights.

(slumps)

If we lose control wake me up to tell me my career's over, okay?

> SHIV

Fuck. Was there a deal there?

> KARL

I dunno. No concessions. I mean, four board seats? Full-fat for them, toenails and corndogs for us.

> GERRI

I think, end of the day, to settle, the clause Sandy really wants is that Logan Roy henceforth sits on a corkscrew and spins. Hard to give that.

A chill in the room. It's what a lot of people are thinking.

> TOM

Okay well it's down to the vote. We're climbing into the vote boat.

> ROMAN

Great. 'Voting'. Let's throw it open to the fucking retired janitors of Idaho.

Maya Bernard and the rest of the proxy solicitor team sit at a table set up nearby. Gerri calls to them.

> GERRI

Maya, where are we?

> MAYA

Um – too close for us to call. Some shareholders won't vote till they hear your father, so.

> ROMAN

Those pussies won't bail once they hear God speak, right?

> SHIV

We're gonna lose the fucking company. Are we going to lose the fucking company today?

> MAYA

If Josh Aaronson is against? It is hard to see how you win with a clear margin.

A dejected beat. Connor enters and approaches Shiv and Roman.

> CONNOR

Hey! Here I am. Made it.

> ROMAN

The cavalry has arrived! So, Con, the news is – tomorrow we're all gonna try to get jobs in the same branch of Target.

> CONNOR

Where's Dad? I want to spitball.

> SHIV

Yeah, um? Maybe not the best day for chat? No time.

> CONNOR

Oh, bummer. Well then I guess he'll have to make time, Madam Secretary.
> *(then)*
Unless he wants me to go public and take a big blacklight to our semen-stained family scrapbook maybe he should fit me in, yeah?

Connor walks confidently over to the catering table. Shiv and Roman exchange worried glances.

Logan, Colin and Kerry enter. Logan looks frail.

> ROMAN

Okay here he comes! The Big Beast. Ready to kick ass, with his big, ass-kicking shoe.

Logan raises a hand to folks around the room and makes it over to the core team—

> TOM
> *(to Shiv, aside)*

Hitler is in his bunker!

> SHIV

You heard where we're at?

LOGAN

Uh-huh.

SHIV

So?

LOGAN

Gerri, Karl?

He looks around: What's the plan?

KARL

Um, I guess – delay the vote? Squeeze Sandy and Stewy's airtime. Run the long versions of speeches.

GERRI

I've emailed a list of assigned shareholders for last-minute persuasion?

LOGAN

Uh-huh. Okay. Yes.

SHIV

And that's it? No like last-minute—?

LOGAN

What about the Raisin?

SHIV

The White House is shitting fuel rods about the tone change.

TOM

PGN is running with 'Memorygate', and calling for him to release tests.

CYD

Lot of calls incoming. We're sandbagging.

LOGAN

Good. Press for something, a statement. Rumor of a statement. Anything before the vote that looks like a win and turns the DOJ temperature down.

Some doubtful looks. No way that's possible last-minute.

FRANK

Great. Uh-huh. Late in the day, very, late in the day. But potentially, all the more – useful.

Logan nods. A slight look of physical discomfort. Cyd, Ray and Mark head out to prepare their speeches. Kerry settles Logan in, and heads out to the auditorium.

INT. HOTEL SUITE – KENDALL'S HQ – DAY

Stewy enters Kendall's HQ.

> KENDALL
> Yo yo. Come on in. Welcome to the real annual meeting. Leave your fucking, lanyard at the door.

> STEWY
> So what's up, man? Shouldn't you be on a rainbow soapbox somewhere screaming 'Time's up'?

> KENDALL
> Yeah, well. Without family control I can't change things. I'm still here for the victims.

> STEWY
> Save it for *Vanity Fair*, bro. I'm good.

Kendall lets it slide.

> KENDALL
> Whatever, my only agenda today, right now, is to find a deal that works for both of us.

> STEWY
> Cool, okay, bullshit.

> KENDALL
> I'm your most powerful ally in the company. I know your financing's starting to wobble and you don't want to risk everything on the dice roll of a vote any more than we do.

> STEWY
> Meh, we lose, we walk. We just move on to the next company.

> KENDALL
> With a fifty-million hole in your pocket? This has been a fucking march to Moscow. And for what? You want something out of this. And Sandy wants to hurt my dad. So let's figure this out, yeah?

Stewy looks at him. Through the sparring the realization this is important.

> STEWY
>
> Fine. So, what do you have for me? An awesome tweet? 'Yes, all women'?

> KENDALL
>
> I've got an inside track with my dad and he's one hundred percent ready to take this to a vote.

Stewy nods. A little fearful.

> STEWY
>
> Well, okay? That would be very stupid.

> KENDALL
>
> Stewy, I know you guys have been angling for a better deal, and you don't think there's any risk taking this to the brink, but I know for a fact you're not going to get one. He's a psychopathic narcissist and he believes he can take this to the floor, drag back the undecideds with his beefy Logan voodoo and win outright. And, you know, who's to say he can't?

Stewy takes it in. Maybe this was always the way it was going to go?

> At this point, it's managing egos. And if this shakes out – what with the board composition? We could be partners in this shit one day?

> STEWY
>
> Wow, I'd get to be in business with Kendall Roy? Pinch me, I must be dreaming.

Stewy looks at Kendall. But there is a sizzle of mutual usefulness.

INT. VENUE – GREEN ROOM – DAY

Tense silence. Gerri gets a call. She signals to Logan across the room.

> GERRI
>
> Logan. It's Stewy Hosseini? Shall I?

He gives a little nod.

> Stewy? Hey?

> *(listens, then to Logan)*
> They want to meet? They have thoughts.

Logan considers. Everyone is keen. Tom, Shiv, Roman, Frank, Karl look at him. He's unreadable. The beat goes on. He makes a nod.

> Okay, we're on.

She hangs up. The room fills with hope and excitement.

> ROMAN
> They have thoughts? What kind of thoughts?

> SHIV
> We're back on?

> GERRI
> We might be. They have ideas for a deal space for a settlement.

> ROMAN
> Fucking A!

But Logan's thinking . . . and already he's suspicious.

> LOGAN
> Why are they suddenly looking to settle?

> SHIV
> Because they know it's the smart option?

> LOGAN
> Have they had bad news? What do they know that we don't?

> SHIV
> Well let's find out, right?

Logan thinks. Does he smell weakness? Good. But he's suspicious.

> LOGAN
> Uh-huh. But I'm not gonna go do a tap-dance. Shiv. Gerri. Karl.

Roman looks.

> Romulus. Go report back.

> FRANK
> I think that's smart. But Gerri should be helming out front so should I—?

LOGAN

Frank – we nail you to the cross out there.

FRANK

Okay.

LOGAN

Let Sandy do the soft-shoe. He's wriggling! Let's screw them out!

They all know it's just a petty feud between old men now.

INT. HOTEL SUITE – KENDALL'S HQ – DAY

Kendall on the phone.

KENDALL

Hey, sis. Okay, no need to talk. Listen, I'm gonna throw you a bone cos I don't want you to remember your first shareholder meeting as the one where you lost us the company. Whatever the deal space you end up in, Sandy's gonna be too obdurate to say yes. But stay cool, daughter Sandi's confident she can get him to settle. Apparently, *she* knows how to play her dad. Okay. Puppet master out.

INT. LUXURY NEW YORK HOTEL – LOBBY – DAY

Gerri, Roman, Karl and Shiv are in the lobby.

SHIV
(*covering*)
Thanks, I no longer wish to receive these calls.

A sherpa comes and greets Gerri and leads the way.

Roman asks, as they walk in private, or head up an escalator—

ROMAN

Does Sandy really have syphilis? What if he's covered in sores? What if he takes his dick off and waves it around and screams 'Yahtzee'?

GERRI

The syphilis – I think we started the rumor.

KARL

I dunno. Late-stage symptom is dementia I believe.

ROMAN

Been doing some panicky late-night googling, Karl?

Maybe they reach a spot where they are asked to wait. Shiv changes the subject.

INT. LUXURY NEW YORK HOTEL — OUTSIDE SANDY'S SUITE — DAY

In a waiting area outside the inner sanctum. On TV on PGN a chyron: 'Candid Shot Suggests President Can No Longer Spell Simple Words.'

ROMAN

This is good. More pressure on the Raisin. If he can understand what's going on.

SHIV

Look, if it's helpful, I'm happy to talk to Sandi? Maybe there's a connection? The daughter thing.

Gerri and Karl exchange a look. This could be awkward. Roman watches on, savoring everyone's discomfort.

GERRI
(*back the fuck off*)
Uh-huh. Well, that's a kind offer.

KARL
(*yeah back the fuck off*)
Yes it is.

GERRI
(*I'm in charge*)
And it's good for me to have options.

KARL
(*yeah we're in charge*)
Absolutely. If we should need them.

SHIV
(*you've failed so far*)
I just thought, if the traditional channels don't work, maybe you could use me, as a fresh approach?

GERRI
(*alright, that's enough*)
It's a good thought.

KARL
(*no thanks*)
And it's much appreciated.

GERRI
(*we don't need you*)
But if they're serious, hopefully we've done the deal already.

SHIV
Sure. Just an offer.

They force a smile at each other. Beat.

ROMAN
(*stage whisper to Shiv*)
I think Gerri won, Shiv, but nice try.

Stewy comes out.

STEWY
Hey. We ready?

ROMAN
Uh-huh.

They get up.

So, how bad is he? Is it true they're building him a mechanical dick out of Legos?

STEWY
Amazing, mentally. He just can't speak too clearly. So other Sandi will translate.

GERRI
'Translate'?

> STEWY
> (*correcting*)

Transfer. Transmit. Relay.

INT. LUXURY NEW YORK HOTEL – SANDY'S SUITE – DAY

They go in to the inner sanctum and Sandy is in a wheelchair – by his side, daughter Sandi, and a medical attendant nearby. He is physically a little frail. He doesn't react much but it's hard to tell if he is fading from the world or his bright and beady eye is just watching everything.

(He's had a stroke on his left side. He has tissues in his hand, or a handkerchief. The medic makes sure he has water nearby. Occasionally, Sandy might take a few breaths before clearing his throat.)

> SANDI

Hey. Thanks for coming. My father is very excited to see you all.

Sandy just sits, impassive, giving nothing away. They all sit. Sandi nods to Stewy to go.

> STEWY

So, look, after careful consideration, we're willing to agree to a standstill, so no takeover.

Roman and Shiv exchange a look: Good.

And provided we lead on deal-making options going forward we'll accede to a continuation of combined chairman and CEO roles. So, that's yours.

The Waystar team exchange glances. Kendall was right, it sounds good to them.

> GERRI

I think that sounds reasonable.

> STEWY

And the three board seats?

Shiv and Karl and Gerri look at one another.

> SHIV
> *(jumping in)*
Including yours? Sure, we can do that right now, I have my dad's
authorization to go there.

Is that it?

> KARL

Can we sign that off?

*It's all one nod away from happening. Stewy looks to Sandy, who
whispers something to Sandi.*

> SANDI

Um, and he wants our costs covered.

The Waystar team think they can bear that.

And veto right over any Roy family member ever taking over as
CEO.

Not so good.

> SHIV

Those were his exact words?

> SANDI

They were his exact words.

> GERRI

Stewy?

*Stewy in a tough spot here. He has to defer to his partners. It's
bullshit, but he can't say that.*

> STEWY

That's what the man says. We feel it's an important protection.

> ROMAN

And, no offense, I have to ask, he is definitely fully aware of
everything that is at stake and just he is a full – person – here?

> SANDI
> *(to Sandy, as if he's deaf)*
He's asking if you understand what's going on?

Sandy whispers something.

He basically said yes.

> SHIV

'He *basically* said yes'?

> SANDI

He didn't put it that nicely.

> ROMAN

I mean I'm just going to say it right out since there's an eighty-five-billion-dollar baby on the table here – Sandy – how do we know he's not your meat puppet?

> SANDI

I just do what my dad tells me. Like you guys.

A look from Roman: Yeah, right.

> GERRI

Do you mind if we take a beat?

> STEWY

Please. You've got tons of time. Seconds. Whole minutes.

Gerri, Karl, Shiv and Roman move into a quiet huddle. Karl and Gerri like it. Shiv and Roman don't.

> KARL

I mean, other than the new provision it's a very attractive prospect?

> SHIV

There's nothing to discuss. It fucks us and it's designed to humiliate Dad.

> GERRI

Right.

But for Karl and Gerri there's no real downside.

But it's basically optics. I mean I'm not sure it would even stand up.

> KARL

You could probably work around if it ever came to it?

Roman looks at Gerri. She looks at him. He stares her down. A moment of growth—

ROMAN

With all due respect, Ger, get bent.

Gerri relents.

GERRI

Look, okay, sure, it's humiliating. And I'm ninety-nine percent certain your dad will agree. But given where we're at, I will need to check in with him. I'm sorry.

Gerri takes a couple of steps away to make a call, dials.

SHIV

Is she going to fuck us?

ROMAN

What—? No. I don't know. Why the fuck you asking me?

Gerri's got her answer. Shiv and Roman look at her as she prepares to transmit Logan's answer.

GERRI

We'll meet your costs. But no veto.

Sandy whispers something to Sandi.

SANDI

We need the veto.

Tense beat. This is it. Gerri shrugs.

GERRI

I mean is there not an alternative shape here? We're so close?

Sandy whispers something. Sandi listens. Sandi says something back to Sandy – a ruffle. But then . . . Okay! Relief.

SANDI

Look, we're going to have to think.
(*then*)
But we agree, it would be a shame to destroy all the hard work on a detail. Let's let the lawyers get to work. We have a landing space here. We'll be in touch very soon.

The meeting breaks up. Sandi and Sandy head out. Roman and Shiv look at one another.

ROMAN
(*quietly elated*)

Are we good?

SHIV

I think we might be good.

They share a look. They've played this well. Gerri and Stewy are a little ways off and can't be overheard. Roman and Shiv watch them talking.

INT. VENUE — GREEN ROOM — DAY

Logan shifts uncomfortably in his seat. Karolina clocks it. She looks at Colin who responds.

COLIN

You want a water? Kerry says you need to stay hydrated.

Logan waves him away. Connor crosses over to Logan.

CONNOR

Hey, Pop. You got a minute?

LOGAN

It's tight, son. Later.

Connor screws up his courage.

CONNOR

Actually, later's hard. I was thinking some time around now?

Logan looks at him coolly.

LOGAN

What?

CONNOR

Look. Dad. I hear things are shaky at the White House but he'll run again, is that what you hear?

Logan shrugs, not about to say what he knows. Connor has his request—

Sure, so, I wanted to ask you directly for a really significant role within the firm to burnish my reputation, for my future.

> LOGAN

You've never been interested.

> CONNOR

Well, maybe I wasn't really encouraged?

Logan feels the anxiety of a big conversation about feeling coming.

> LOGAN

I can't do ancient history.

> CONNOR

Fine, and—

> (*with a little threat*)

I don't want to get into ancient history either. So? Can we find common ground?

Logan wants to be kind.

> LOGAN

I'm just not sure you have – the track record?

> CONNOR

Roman's a moron, Shiv's a fake, Kendall's screwy. I've seen more than any of them. Why can't I get a shot?

Is this a reference to something? It's tense.

> LOGAN

Like what?

> CONNOR

Europe. Nothing vital. Like cable?

Logan nods, serious, he'll think about it. Then—

> LOGAN
> (*shouting*)

Where's the john?

> KAROLINA

Yeah, so, unfortunately, the nearest is out of use so it's down the hall and up the stairs on the right.

> LOGAN
> (*re his boot*)

Uh-huh. Fucking lucky I'm wearing my sneakers.

But when no one's looking it's clear he's not fine. A call comes in from Shiv.

INT. LUXURY NEW YORK HOTEL – CORRIDOR – DAY

Gerri's with Roman. Karl's up ahead. So is Shiv, on a call.

> GERRI
>
> Sorry about—

> ROMAN
>
> About trying to fuck me over to consolidate your position?

> GERRI
>
> No. It just seemed to make business sense.

> ROMAN
>
> Throwing me overboard to drown?
> (*looks at her*)
> You picked your prince, Gerri. Don't fuck it up now.

Gerri looks unsettled for once. Roman has a slight upper hand. Up ahead, Shiv's got through to Logan.

> SHIV
>
> Dad, they're going to marinate on it, but I think I – we – did it. So, fingers crossed.
> (*hangs up, sees Gerri*)
> You don't mind me relaying the news?

> GERRI
> (*yes, very much*)
>
> No, not at all.

> SHIV
>
> Yeah he's my dad so.

INT. HOTEL SUITE – KENDALL'S HQ – DAY

Kendall is leaving a voicemail for Stewy.

> KENDALL
>
> Stewy. Catching some good vibes. Let me know where your head's at. It's exciting. Let's get this done and pop some corks okay?

He hangs up. He's excited, but maybe also a little anxious.

Jess leads Greg in, he spots Comfrey.

> GREG
>
> Oh hey, yeah. I was wondering if you'd be over here!?

> COMFREY
>
> Yup, doing my job.

> KENDALL
>
> There he is! McGregor. Big day, big dog. C'mon. What's the mood, inside man? Is my dad bugging?

> GREG
>
> Little unsteady I hear. You didn't stamp on his foot did you like people say?

Kendall waves this weird rumor away.

> KENDALL
>
> The big snapping turtle thinks he closed a deal, but I closed the deal. And everyone in the company's going to know it. C'mon, we need to talk—

INT. HOTEL SUITE – KENDALL'S HQ – BEDROOM – DAY

Kendall closes the door. They're alone. Greg is nervous.

> GREG
>
> So, hey, man, I just wanted to say I know you're probably pretty upset with me for going over to Waystar and their joint defense but—

> KENDALL
>
> It's fine, bro.

> GREG
>
> I had no choice, really in terms of—

> KENDALL
>
> Yeah, man. I get it. I get it.

> GREG
>
> Okay, wow. That's a relief! Cos I've been summoned to see my gramps and I don't want to be getting it in both ends because—

KENDALL

But look, I may have to burn you.

GREG

You— I'm sorry, what?

KENDALL

Yeah. I wanted to get you up and give you fair warning as a pal. That okay?

GREG

What, getting 'burned'?

KENDALL

Yeah.

GREG

Well it doesn't sound great?

KENDALL

Yeah, so my dad lands a deal today, that strengthens his position. Lisa says the DOJ is non-committal about the case. I need to throw them red meat. The thought is I give them you, it's not much but it's a morsel. Plus it likely gives them Tom, maybe Bill, it builds the pressure and maybe someone flips on Dad. You see?

GREG

Dude.

KENDALL

It's not my preferred choice.

GREG

Or mine! I thought you said you'd never burn me?

KENDALL

I said I'd try not to burn you.

GREG

Well, no. You said—

Greg looks sad.

KENDALL

Look, I'm still not saying I *will* burn you. All I'm saying is I might burn you.

GREG

And just how bad will the burning be? I mean, even as I ask that, I can tell it's not going to be . . .

KENDALL

You'll probably be fine. They don't want to send bottom-feeders to prison, they'll probably just fuck you and chuck you to get to the red meat.

GREG

Uh-huh. 'Great'.

KENDALL

Or, I mean, you drop from the joint defense?

Greg thinks. Jess enters, gives Kendall a 'now'.

I have to monitor the meeting, but I wanted to give you a heads-up. I like you, Greg. I really like you.

Kendall pats Greg on the shoulder. Greg leaves. As he gets outside—

GREG

Oh fuck, fuck, fuck, fuck, fuck.

Still he finds time to say bye to Comfrey.

INT. VENUE – RECEPTION AREA – DAY

The last few shareholders are heading in. Kerry passes a couple of them who are holding ballots.

KERRY

So. You figured out which way you're leaning yet?

Greg finds Pugh and Ewan sitting outside. Ewan doesn't care for the surroundings. They have a travel word game they are playing between them.

GREG

Hey, hey! Gramps. How you doing? An interesting day ahead! Sorry I'm running a little—

EWAN

Don't try to sweet-talk me, kiddo.

> GREG

Okay, it was just some words of – greeting, and hey, Mr Pugh, how are—?

> EWAN
> (*cuts him off*)

I am not an uncomplicated man, Greg, I know that. Nevertheless I have tried, such as I am able, to show you love and compassion.

> GREG

Are you kidding? You're the best darn gramper out and I wanted therefore to ask you—

> EWAN

You asked me for help. And I took that request seriously. And now I hear you've dispensed with Roger's services, presumably to throw your lot in with my brother and his gang of crapulous shills, without so much as a telephone call?

> GREG

Right. Well, this is funny because I was actually wondering, if I shouldn't, take another turn around the block with old Mr Pugh here because—

> EWAN

I've known Roger Pugh for fifty-five years. You don't take him for a fucking ride anywhere. He's a *friend* of mine.

> GREG
> (*panicky*)

Right, okay. Then I guess the other route is to see if there's any way you might see your way clear to provide a little financial support to help me retain my neutrality—

Disgusted, Ewan nods to Pugh to take it from here.

> EWAN

Roger?

> PUGH

Are you familiar with Gerrard Winstanley, Greg?

> GREG

Uh. Yes. I mean, no, not as in actually.

                    PUGH
He believed in making the Earth 'a common treasury for all'?
The English Civil War provided—

                    GREG
Um, this is – good stuff but – I could be getting burnt or jailed
so—

                    PUGH
I'm helping your grandfather transfer the entirety of his estate to
charitable endeavors.

Greg looks like he's been punched.

                    GREG
As in?

                    EWAN
I'm giving all my money to Greenpeace, Greg.

                    PUGH
It's going in parts, for tax reasons. A Great Unburdening.

                    EWAN
It will take a while to drain the entire estate but the process is
underway.

                    GREG
What, even – my part?

                    EWAN
That's the first part. That part's already been drained.

                    GREG
Why? Why is that the first part? How can you even tell? I mean
why—

                    EWAN
Because, Greg, your life is not a bagatelle. Because you are
putting yourself in the service of a monstrous endeavor. Because
you need to take yourself seriously, kid.

Greg is in shock.

Now, I should go in.

Pugh clears up the game.

INT. VENUE – WINGS – DAY

Hugo walks with Frank.

> HUGO
>
> Okay, so, just whip through it, keep any dissent to a minimum. As soon as the deal's agreed, we'll let you know and you can announce the vote's off. Ger's sent her opening remarks, so we got you covered. Good!

Frank heads out.

INT. VENUE – STAGE/AUDITORIUM – DAY

Frank, at the lectern, looks at the teleprompter. It says, 'Hi I'm Gerri Kellman, the new CEO. And as the new CEO . . .' He takes a breath.

> FRANK
> (*briskly*)
>
> Hi, I'm Frank Vernon, Vice-Chairman. Welcome to Waystar Royco's Forty-sixth Annual Shareholders' Meeting!

Frank looks into the audience, locking eyes with Josh, Ewan and a number of unhappy-looking shareholders.

INT. VENUE – GREEN ROOM – DAY

Everyone's watching the feed of Frank's introduction. Tom whispers to distracted Greg.

> TOM
>
> 'Welcome, one and all! Logan Roy has my tiny wrinkled balls in his coin purse.'

> FRANK
> (*onscreen*)
>
> We're thrilled to be hosting on home turf in New York and delighted to have so many of you joining us. I'm told it's the best-attended annual meeting in Waystar history!

Hugo arrives back.

> HUGO
>
> 'Enjoy the coffee and croissants, try to forget all the sex crimes.'

FRANK
(onscreen)

And I'm so happy to see so many friendly faces!

But Hugo isn't allowed to do those jokes, Tom turns—

TOM

Hey! No.

Tom turns his attention to looking at a vineyard on his iPad. Greg trying to get things straight in his head.

What you think? This is the vineyard I'm thinking of going for?

GREG

Uh-huh. Great. Yeah.

Tom looks at him.

So my grandpa is giving my inheritance to Greenpeace.

TOM

While I'm inside, something will be growing out here. Berries getting round and fat. Don't worry, Daddy's home soon.

GREG

I'm losing twenty-five thousand a day. They're burning my money. That's not eco-friendly.

TOM

They say Riesling is the most misunderstood grape.

GREG

He wants to save the world, but what about me? I'm in the world?

Logan watches the feed of what's happening on stage. He looks physically uncomfortable (from his UTI).

FRANK
(onscreen)

I'd like to invite to join me onstage, some of our senior leadership team, Cyd Peach, Chairman and CEO of ATN, and Ray Kennedy, Chairman, Parks and Cruises, and Mark Rosenstock, Chairman, Waystar Studios. Please give them a warm round of applause.

INT. HOTEL SUITE — KENDALL'S HQ — DAY

Kendall is watching on a live-feed as well.

> KENDALL
>
> Fucking Frank. Humiliating. All these years, he still has to play maître d' at the Bistro of Bullshit.

Kendall's phone buzzes. He looks annoyed, takes the call.

Yeah, what?

> BIANCA
>
> (*from phone*)
>
> Mr Roy, I'm sorry to bother you but the rabbit is sick.

> KENDALL
>
> What kind of sick, call the vet.

> BIANCA
>
> The vet's unavailable. And so is the vet they recommended . . .

> KENDALL
>
> Okay, so, figure it out. Call our doctor.

> BIANCA
>
> But the doctor does – people?

> KENDALL
>
> If he can do people, he can do rabbits. If you call a vet find someone from Rabbit Harvard. The kids can't deal with a bunny corpse right now. Just make sure the rabbit's okay. Seriously, it's a mammal, call the concierge doctor. I'm sure rabbits are just little, hairy, fucking less complicated people.

INT. VENUE — GREEN ROOM — DAY

Shiv, Roman, Gerri and Karl return. Good feeling in the room. Cheers from Connor and Tom.

(*On the monitors, Frank has introduced Ray, Cyd, Mark, Isabelle Peters Lyon, the external lawyer, and Richard Martins, the acting general counsel, to the table on the stage.*)

> CONNOR
>
> All hail the conquering heroes!

SHIV

Well, it's not a done deal yet, Con. But it's close! I think the lawyers can finesse the rest.

ROMAN

Hey, hey, hey! Dad, you would have loved it. Sandy had a guy draining his spit so he didn't choke.

TOM

It's on? You did it?!

SHIV

They have nowhere else to maneuver.

LOGAN

They could've said yes in Greece. Saved us all the ballache.

GERRI

Still. Logan, this is good news.

Logan shifts uncomfortably – pained by the deal and his UTI.

LOGAN

Uh-huh. If it's good for them, maybe it's bad for us?

SHIV

Dad, how can it be bad for us?

It gets chillier in the room.

LOGAN

They were always gonna settle.
(*thinks*)
Something's screwy. Do we give 'em a taste of their own medicine? Make some tweaks – let everyone know they bent for me?

SHIV

Reopen the negotiation? Dad, are you serious? We settle now or we go to the vote and lose.

LOGAN

Tell him he can't set foot in the building?

GERRI

Logan, I know how painful this is, but we need it.

> SHIV
>
> Christ, Dad, you just said it's not far off what you originally offered. We fuck this, there are no more deals . . .

Beat. Logan suddenly can't remember why everyone's looking at him. He feels confused. Sweaty. He covers and makes a non-committal noise.

Everyone breathes easier. They think he's letting it go.

> Thanks, Dad. That's smart. It is.

Tom grabs Shiv and gives her a hug.

> TOM
>
> Well done, well fucking done, honey.

Then he kisses her. On the mouth – they are off in a bit of privacy but it turns into an open-mouthed kiss, over the edge for this public space. Goes on a bit long and eventually Shiv breaks.

Roman looks and looks at Gerri: WTF.

Tom whispers to her.

> Are you wet?

> SHIV
>
> Uhhm?

> TOM
>
> Can I show you something?

Logan turns to Colin.

> LOGAN
>
> Pills.

> COLIN
>
> Sorry, sir? Advil?

Logan watches the feed, worried as Colin gets Advil and water.

> LOGAN
> (*asks Colin, quietly*)
>
> What do you think?

Colin is confused.

COLIN

Sir?

LOGAN

About the deal. Settling?

Colin is taken aback. Why is he asking Colin?

COLIN
(*no idea what to say*)

I don't know. It could be – good?

LOGAN

Uh-huh.

Logan broods on this.

INT. VENUE – HALLWAY – DAY

Tom is walking, leading Shiv. He has the iPad.

TOM

Yeah I just thought, maybe I'd show you this vineyard?

SHIV

What the hell was that?

He opens a door – an unused space. He looks at her.

TOM

You're so sexy when you're winning.

He takes her in his arms but there is slight resistance.

SHIV

Okay. You wanna show me real quick?

He tosses the iPad aside, carefully.

TOM

I've been looking at you.

SHIV

What – like—?

TOM

And I asked you a question. Are you wet?

> SHIV
>
> Why is the shareholder meeting making you so incredibly horny?

> TOM
>
> Kinda hot, right, all the tension, and the votes and the tellers and the—

> SHIV
>
> Someone could walk in.

> TOM
>
> Right. Sexy?

> SHIV
>
> What, some fucking proxy solicitor? We gonna ask some Dunder Mifflin guy to join in?

> TOM
>
> What if I move the desk so it blocks the door?

He presses close to her.

> SHIV
>
> Tom, you're not even hard, what is this?

> TOM
>
> I want to do it.

> SHIV
>
> Sorry, honey. It's just – I'm not in that place. Okay? But I appreciate you are, or want to be, or— I'm really fucking busy and that's just extending from up here all the way down.

She looks at him, it was a weird but sweet idea and she tries to let him down gently as they exit.

> At least I know your kink now. Convene some huge annual meeting, next time I want some action.

INT. VENUE – STAGE – DAY

The audience is watching a montage of families enjoying Waystar theme parks, studio tours, Waystar TV shows; Waystar employees smiling on the job; the Roy family laughing at a photo shoot.

VOICEOVER
For fifty years we've helped bring people together.

A mix of made-up headlines: 'Waystar in trouble', 'Cruises not smooth sailing', 'Company may have had a few bad apples'.

But along the way something went wrong. That's going to change.

Shots of solemn Waystar town halls, theme-park workers helping a lost child, concerned ATN editorial meetings . . .

We're doubling down on the founding principles that have made us the number-one choice for families for five decades.

More happy families loving Waystar products and services.

Waystar. We Get It.

INT. VENUE – GREEN ROOM – DAY

Logan watches the video on a screen – is he okay? Bit glassy. Gerri writing her speech. Karolina's also writing. Shiv comes back in with Tom.

SHIV
How's the release coming?

Karolina indicates it's nearly done.

And who's going to announce?

KARL
I can do it.

GERRI
I'll do it.

Gerri gets a call. Looks at display.

It's Sandi.

CONNOR
Which one?

GERRI
The one who can talk.

She looks: Shall I answer?

Yeah?

(answers)

Hey Sandi?

(listens)

Are you sure about that? Well go on.

(listens)

Alright. But—

(listens)

Seriously? Okay.

She hangs up.

So they have one more proviso. They want to take away the private jets.

ROMAN

The PJs? No.

GERRI

'Elitist and out of touch.'

ROMAN

Well, duh. Look, no. They're trying to humiliate him.

KARL

Was it real or are they just basting the turkey?

SHIV

Dad, let's just eat it, you can tell them to fuck off later . . .

Logan looks confused. He's struggling to think straight.

KARL

We could just offer to cut personal use? Or a mileage cap?

ROMAN

Bullshit. Nah. First they came for the PJs and I said nothing. Then they came for our outsized compensation payments – you know? They'll back down. They won't blow it up over this.

All eyes on Logan. He's actually not totally sure what he's being asked—

Dad? What do you say?

LOGAN

Um? I need a piss. Shiv?

346

>   SHIV
> Oh, sure, you need some help shall I reach out to—?

>   LOGAN
>   (*indicates Tom*)
> You. Let's go.

>   SHIV
> We wanna make the decision now – before or—?

Logan makes a noise that suggests not to ask again.

> We can wait I guess.

Tom helps Logan make his way out of the room.

>   KAROLINA
> Um, Karl, Frank's about to introduce you?

Shiv calls Stewy.

>   KARL
>   (*to his back*)
> Well what the heck am I going to say? Boss?

But Logan is heading out. Karl heads out.

>   SHIV
> Stewy's not picking up. Karl, vamp.

INT. VENUE – CORRIDOR – DAY

Tom helps Logan towards the bathroom.

>   TOM
> Okay. Here we go. Would it be impolitic to ask what you're
> thinking?

*Logan looks at him. It looks scary but actually maybe he doesn't
understand for a beat where he's going.*

> Fine! Understood. Your call.
>   (*after an uncomfy beat, 'Latin?'*)
> Callius, maximus, yourius.

*Logan's phone goes. Michelle-Anne, she's asking if he'll talk to the
president. Tom gives him space.*

> LOGAN

Yeah? Uh-huh. Of course.

He hangs up a beat. Confused for a beat – where is he?

We need to get back.

> TOM

Right you are! Back we go.

INT. VENUE – CORRIDOR – DAY

Karl walks as fast as he can, then breaks into a trot.

INT. VENUE – STAGE – DAY

Karl tries to write a note to an assistant to give to Frank, but Frank sees Karl and introduces him before he can finish it.

> FRANK

So, without further ado, and with interesting things to tell you I believe, please welcome our Chief Financial Officer, Karl Muller.

Applause as Frank and Karl smile and greet each other.

> KARL
> (*in his ear*)

Slow it down. Deal might be off. I'm needed elsewhere. Vamp! Bon chance, Franco!

Frank fixes his smile.

> FRANK
> (*shit*)

Excellent! Wonderful news! Well. In fact, we will be hearing from our CFO a little later. And before that a little further ado, in fact, much ado. Much ado about – something.

> INVESTOR

Get on with it!

> FRANK

Indeed. Yes indeed.

INT. VENUE — GREEN ROOM — DAY

Tom helps Logan back in. Everyone watches.

> GERRI
> Logan. We can't wait any longer. What do we say?

> SHIV
> What's it gonna be, Dad?

> GERRI
> We need an answer.

> LOGAN
> (*no idea*)
> Uh-huh.

> GERRI
> What you think, Logan? Yes or no?

> LOGAN
> Fuck 'em.

Beat. He repeats.

Fuck 'em.

Stunned silence. Even Roman is a little scared.

> SHIV
> Dad, are you sure? You sure you want to do this?

He doesn't quite recall what's going on. But has a vestigial sense that he likes the aggression. He nods to get it over with and stop everyone looking at him.

Karl returns.

> (*quietly*)
> Dad? Are you okay? Do you know something?

Logan makes a noise.

> GERRI
> Okay. I mean, this is a— That's a huge call. We're happy?

Logan walks away to the corner, beckons Colin into a private huddle.

> LOGAN
> (*to Colin, hissed*)

Pills.

> COLIN

I just gave you some, sir? You need something else? Tylenol?

Gerri, Roman, Karl and Shiv take the chance to form a huddle a bit further away. Tom too.

> GERRI

Does this make sense? Is he okay?

> ROMAN

Yes. He's a fucking – badass. He's gambling the company cos he's a fucking baller.

> SHIV

I mean, he did say no, right? That was a clear no? Because—?

They look over to him with Colin, his back turned.

> ROMAN

Shiv, he said no deal.

> SHIV

But did he?

> GERRI

I think it's definitely no deal.

> ROMAN

If we win without a deal, it's all upside.

> KARL

We're really rolling the dice?

> ROMAN

It's fucking classic Dad.

> TOM

I guess, if we come through, it's one for the memoirs. I mean, it's – I guess it is thrilling.

> SHIV

It's a huge fucking gamble. For, what?

> ROMAN

He's trusted his gut before and it's always worked out.

GERRI

I would love to know the thinking. But yeah. I mean, he's been here before. So?

TOM

He did get a call, on the way to the restroom?

GERRI
(good, okay)
Okay, so maybe he knows something?

ROMAN

He fucking always knows something. He's six moves ahead.

SHIV

Alright so we're doing this? We're seriously fucking doing this? Fuck! Fine, I'll make the call.

EXT. VENUE – DAY

Sandi, Sandy, Stewy and their retinue are heading in through the thinned-out gaggle of protestors and press and onlookers.

SANDI

Siobhan?

Intercut with:

INT. VENUE – GREEN ROOM – DAY

Shiv finds an isolated spot.

SHIV

No. So either you fold on the jets or we'll take our chances on the vote?

SANDI

He won't fold on the jets.

SHIV

Then we'll go to the vote.

SANDI

Seriously? Why?

> SHIV
>
> I dunno. 'I just do what my dad tells me.'

Shiv hangs up. She writes a note and hands it to Greg.

> Get this to Frank, now!

INT. VENUE – CORRIDOR/WINGS – DAY

Greg runs flat out, hands the note to a Waystar assistant.

INT. VENUE – STAGE – DAY

Frank, at the lectern, a chart of revenue by division projected behind him. An assistant hands him the note.

> FRANK
>
> With the cruise ship – um – situation – rapidly subsiding, thanks to the far-reaching efforts of management, and after a major overhaul of company policies, we continue to strive to make cruises a safe and special place that provide special memories for all our customers.

He looks at the note: 'Deal's off! Dead slow!'

He tries to swallow his deep disappointment.

> It adds up to a bright future all around.

INT. VENUE – GREEN ROOM – DAY

Shiv returns to Tom.

> SHIV
>
> Fuck. Well. It's done.

> TOM
>
> Good. Decisive. We win, it's all good, right?

Logan from a spot alone talking to Connor, nodding (about European cable), calls over to Gerri, Shiv and Karl.

> LOGAN
>
> What's going on with the—?
> (*indistinct*)
> Reagan.

(then)

The Raisin?

Gerri approaches—

GERRI

I'm sorry? With the president? Um—

LOGAN

Can we get Ravenhead on the air?

SHIV

Dad, Ravenhead? We're in the middle of daytime programming?

LOGAN

Call Michelle-Anne and let's get the SEC to shut this meeting down.

Gerri and Shiv and Karl look at each other. It's crazy.

KARL

Okay, well we'll look into that.

LOGAN
(to Shiv)

Where is he? I need a piss?

TOM

Who? Me? Well sure.

INT. VENUE – CORRIDOR – DAY

Kendall walks quickly down the hall while on the phone.

KENDALL

Look, I don't know their thinking. It's fucked.

Intercut with:

INT. VENUE – AUDITORIUM – DAY

Stewy, Sandy and Sandi are shown to their seats by a marshal. Stewy hangs back a bit. A corporate video is being played on stage.

STEWY

Great. You're supposed to be my inside fucking track?

KENDALL

Uh-huh, where did the plane bullshit come from, it's petty.

STEWY

We're a – complicated coalition. Sandy's the world's angriest vegetable.

KENDALL

Listen, I can salvage this. I'm on my way to talk to them.

STEWY

Well good luck, but the fucking Belligerent Zucchini here is set to close negotiations for good.

KENDALL

Hang tight, motherfucker. Batman's on it.

INT. VENUE – BATHROOM – DAY

Logan is standing in a stall ready to piss in a bowl.

INT. VENUE – CORRIDOR OUTSIDE BATHROOM

Tom's waiting, concerned. Then there's an anguished cry.

TOM

You okay, Logan?

(*beat*)

Need help?

Beat. A thump. Shit! He has to go in. Tom enters. Logan's slumped against the wall a bit.

Hey, you okay, big man? Are you okay? Logan? Did it get caught?

LOGAN

Huh? Give me a hand.

TOM

To like—? Not to—? You don't like need me to, hold the, the scepter do you?

Tom hesitates. Logan grimaces. Wilts a bit. Tom takes his weight a bit and rights him.

No rush. Take your time.

(then)

Are you okay, you're shivering? Logan, I think we need to get you seen by someone.

LOGAN

Thanks, son.

That's kind of nice – but Tom knows something is not right here.

TOM

Anytime, 'Dad'.

INT. VENUE – GREEN ROOM – DAY

Shiv is worried, looking at phone. Incoming call to Karl.

KARL

Hey?

(listens, to Shiv)

Michelle-Anne, she wants to talk to your dad? He's not picking up.

SHIV

More moaning about our coverage. Tell her he's busy.

KARL

She says it's urgent?

SHIV

Yeah, we'll call back.

ROMAN

Tell her he'd have more time if we weren't fighting the DOJ.

Tom helps a lethargic, feverish Logan in and sits him down with Colin. He beckons Shiv over, for a quiet conference.

TOM

Er, Shiv? Your dad's totally out of it.

SHIV

Dad? You okay?

LOGAN

Not now, Marcia. I'm busy, I need to watch this.

Panicked looks. Shiv is already dialing Kerry.

INT. VENUE — AUDITORIUM/RECEPTION AREA — DAY

Kerry's phone rings and she heads outside to take the call.

Intercut with:

INT. VENUE — GREEN ROOM — DAY

Shiv's trying to hide her rising anxiety. Tom is helping him to a seat by the door or off away from the central Waystar hub.

> SHIV
> Kerry, is Dad on any medication?

Everyone stops, clocking the urgency in Shiv's voice.

> KERRY
> He has a UTI, why? Is he alright?

> SHIV
> Could his meds make him confused?

> KERRY
> *(already on her way)*
> Shouldn't. That's what happens if he doesn't take them.

> SHIV
> Where are they? Does he have them?

> KERRY
> I left them with him but I'll be right there, I have shots. And I'm calling his doctor.

Shiv nods for Colin to tend to her dad. Tom stays with him.

Shiv motions for Gerri, Karl, Roman, Karolina. Connor joins. Hugo tries to hover near the central Waystar top-brass hub.

> SHIV
> Okay. He's got a fucking UTI.

> ROMAN
> Seriously? Is that—? That's not bad though, right?

CONNOR

At his age, that can make you crazy. Reagan had one and nearly
nuked Belgium.

A horrible moment of realization and panic.

SHIV

Fuck! How long's he been like this?

KARL

Was he like this when he said no?

GERRI

When he risked the whole company?

HUGO

Was that his bladder talking?

*Gerri looks round the room – doesn't like Hugo weighing in. Waves
him away.*

SHIV

No one hears of this! Look after him! Tom? Tom, what do we
do?

Hugo goes to Logan. Tom comes over.

ROMAN

Should we give him a cranberry juice and ask him again?

TOM

He was asking for Caroline.

SHIV

Oh fuck. He's piss-mad.

CONNOR

Well he was still in good shape when he offered me European
cable.

SHIV

When did he say that? Because he was out of it when he said
that, definitely.

CONNOR

Well no – he was cogent at that point.

SHIV

I can guarantee he wasn't. He's been out of it for a while it sounds.

ROMAN

Well we don't know. What about the phone call he took? The decision might have been a good decision. We don't know when he went piss-mad?

TOM

That? Could have been anything. Robocall? His fucking urologist? No I suspect he's been piss-mad for quite a while.

ROMAN

Oh do you? The fucking Hercule Poirot of piss here.

TOM

Should you overrule him, Shiv? Go back to Sandy and Stewy. Say we've changed our minds?

ROMAN

Yeah, great idea. Dad loves being overruled.

HUGO
(from Logan's side)
He still needs to make his speech. What you think?

KAROLINA

Can he do the speech?

ROMAN

'Can he do the speech?' The piss-mad demented King of England?

SHIV

He could say anything. He could tell everyone he's Barbra Streisand. No, we need to drop it.

GERRI

At the very least he has to be onstage.

KARL

It would be great to get the body up there?

Shiv thinks. Does he? He does. She looks to Maya – right across the room.

358

                         SHIV

Hey? Any progress?

Maya's look says no. Shiv starts writing a note.

We'll push it as late as we can. And maybe if we just get him onstage that'll be enough?

                      CONNOR

Sure. Maybe you can send him up through a trapdoor surrounded by dry ice?

Hugo comes over.

                       HUGO

Um, he's – he – he's concerned there is a dead or dying cat under his chair?

                       SHIV

Okay. Great.

                       HUGO

He's quite insistent. He doesn't want Rose to see it? He wants Colin to take it out?

Roman can't be bothered.

                      ROMAN

Fine, have Colin take it out.

Hugo returns to Logan and talks to Colin. We might glimpse Colin's confused reaction to being asked to take out a bag.

Kerry arrives, opening a small medical kit.

                       KERRY

Hey. The doctor's on his way.

                       SHIV

Why the fuck didn't you tell anyone about this?

                      KERRY
                    (glances at Colin)

He didn't want anyone to know?

                       SHIV

Well that worked out well.

Kerry goes over and prepares to inject Logan. It freaks Roman out. Colin has a brown takeout bag he carries at arm's length.

They see Kendall coming in from the other end of the room.

Oh, Christ.

Shiv and Roman move quick to keep Logan from seeing Kendall.

> KENDALL
> So what the fuck is going on? He's squashing the deal? You have to turn this around, right now.

> SHIV
> We are figuring it out.

Logan yells something incoherent. It's a little scary.

> KENDALL
> (*spooked*)
> What's happening? Is he okay? Where's his doctor? What the fuck's going on?

Colin passes him with the bag, holding it weirdly.

What's that?

> ROMAN
> It's an imaginary cat, now fuck off.

> KENDALL
> Right. You've all gone fucking Hieronymus Bosch. Listen to me carefully, all of you, this is you throwing it away. You think they're bluffing? They're not bluffing, and you're putting everything I've fought and bled for on the fucking edge and I'm not going to let that happen. You understand me? Fucking fix it!

Kendall heads for the exit.

> ROMAN
> (*calling after*)
> Delusional! A delusional man is leaving the room right now!

> KENDALL
> And figure out a fucking doctor or I'm calling mine!

>   ROMAN
>   (after him)
> Like you give a fuck. You probably slipped him something,
> Putin!

*Across the room, Karolina is watching the live-feed. She gestures to
Gerri: You're on.*

INT. VENUE — CORRIDOR — DAY

Gerri runs as fast as her footwear will let her.

INT. VENUE — STAGE — DAY

*An assistant crosses upstage and gives Frank the note: 'Logan ILL,
SLOW DOWN!!!' He sees Gerri in the wings, catching her breath,
gesturing she's not ready.*

>   FRANK
> And now I will hand you over to Gerri Kellman, our interim
> CEO—

Frank gestures to Gerri: Sorry.

*Applause. Gerri looks at the teleprompter. It reads, 'Time is tight, so
I'll keep this brief.' She ignores it.*

>   GERRI
>   (slowly)
> Thank you, Frank. I'd like to begin, if I may, by reflecting on
> some of the changes I've seen in my thirty years at Waystar . . .

INT. VENUE — SMALL ROOM — DAY

*Whatever private space they could find, off the main room. Not ideal
but okay. Shiv watches on. A one-liter bag of IV fluid hangs from a
coat or picture hook.*

Roman, Shiv, Kerry, Doctor Troy Judith and Colin are in there.

>   DOCTOR TROY JUDITH
> He's on fluids and hydrating so it should be pretty quick.

> ROMAN

But he'll definitely be okay?

> SHIV

Like how quick?

> DOCTOR TROY JUDITH

Well, he's not a cup of instant noodles . . .

> SHIV

Can we speed it up? A blood bag, or an adrenalin shot?

> ROMAN

Let's take it easy. You wanna give him the fucking Tabasco suppository?

> SHIV

Fuck you, it's what he'd want.

> ROMAN

The main thing is that we look after him.

> SHIV

Well, obviously, I agree.

> ROMAN

Really? Because it sounded like you want to jump-start our father like a fucking pick-up truck.

Roman walks out . . .

INT. VENUE – GREEN ROOM – DAY

. . . to look at the feed of Gerri's speech. She's pretty good. Comforting.

> GERRI
> (*on screen*)

And we'll be forming a strategic committee looking at new acquisitions to be spearheaded by – our visionary Chief Operating Officer Roman Roy—

Roman likes that. Hint of apology from Gerri. In a quiet corner, Greg's on the phone to his friend a law student.

GREG

Hi. Lia? Yeah I was wondering, in your view, is it possible to sue a person, a grandparent for example in a way which is – like in an affectionate way? That might convey like, 'I love you and I'm glad you're part of my life? But I am taking legal action against you.'

(listens)

Well, yeah, so, I really need my grandpa's money. And I know that sounds bad. But it's to stop me going to prison.

Roman watches more of Gerri.

Maybe we cut back to her live onstage as she starts to take questions.

INT. VENUE – STAGE – DAY

SHAREHOLDER 2

It's been a terrible year PR-wise. How much worse is it going to get?

GERRI

Well I think we're through the worst—

Disquiet from some of the crowd.

INT. VENUE – GREEN ROOM – DAY

Roman anxious, starts pacing. Karolina and Hugo are watching the feed of Gerri fielding questions. Getting rough.

KAROLINA

This is not going to be turning any floating votes our way.

HUGO

Call in a bomb threat?

She smiles at him – it's crazy. But is it?

Shiv comes back in from seeing Logan (leaving him with the doctor, Kerry and Colin). Roman looks at her: How is he?

SHIV

I think his moaning's getting louder so—

CONNOR

That's something?

> SHIV
>
> Is it a wheel-on-and-wave?

> ROMAN
>
> Shiv? We're not going to make the piss-mad bear dance with
> cattle prods? We need to look after him.

They look at her. It's not going to happen. Shiv thinks. Calms herself.

> SHIV
>
> Okay. He's not doing a speech. So – what, we just fucking go
> down – that's it, we give up?

Over to Maya—

> Talk to me.

> MAYA
>
> I would strongly urge you to do whatever you can to settle.

*Shiv, Roman, Tom, Connor, Karl, Frank (who has come back
from stage) start to huddle in the inner-circle area. Hugo edges in,
encouraged by Karolina to keep PR close.*

> SHIV
>
> Okay. Listen. I think we go back to Sandy and Stewy and save
> the deal?

> ROMAN
>
> Well no because Dad said—

> SHIV
>
> Dad didn't say shit. His urethra had wrested control from his
> brain.

*Shiv looks at Roman. They have a conversation between them
looking into one another's eyes.*

> I talk to them at least, right?

Roman knows it's true.

> It goes to a vote, we're probably dead. Rome, you back this?

Roman thinks and nods.

> ROMAN
>
> Go on, go and fuck it up, moron.

Shiv heads for the door, already on the phone.

SHIV
(*on phone*)
Hi. I was hoping we could have another chat, just us, before the vote closes.

INT. HOTEL SUITE – KENDALL'S HQ – BEDROOM – DAY

Kendall is leaving a voicemail for Stewy.

KENDALL
Stewy, call me back. Both ways work here. I can help if you need me to help. But also, you win, there's options. I have a set of golden keys here. Call me.

Kendall hangs up. Nothing to do. Jess looks at him, smiles, supportive.

Enough fucking smiling, get me – get me fucking, rabbit updates, okay?

JESS
I didn't want to bother you.

KENDALL
Christ, Jess, I'm playing nine-dimensional chess here. I can care about the victims, and the DOJ, and Lisa, and the meeting, and what happens to my kids' pet, okay? I can run ten things at once, and I expect you to be able to as well, yeah?
(*then*)
Because I believe in you, okay?

Jess nods and leaves.

INT. VENUE – GREEN ROOM – DAY

Roman, Tom, Connor, Frank, Karl, Hugo and Karolina watch the live-feed as Gerri struggles to stall for time, she introduces a video and exits the stage . . .

KAROLINA
Okay she's dried. She just couldn't do it. She's hit the video. But we're going to have to close the vote. This is it.

Kerry enters, cellphone to her shoulder. She looks spooked.

> KERRY
>
> Um, I've got the White House on the line?

> HUGO
>
> Yeah they've been coming in through every porthole about the ATN pivot.

> KERRY
>
> Not Michelle-Anne, it's the president? He wants an urgent conversation.

That stops them in their tracks.

> FRANK
>
> On that phone now?

> KERRY
>
> Switchboard. He wants Logan?

Shit.

> KAROLINA
>
> Right. Well, that's not ideal?

> ROMAN
>
> Could we tell him to fuck off. By all accounts he won't remember by tomorrow?

> KARL
>
> How do we feel about saying no to the president right now?

> CONNOR
>
> I would love to say no to the president.

> ROMAN
>
> Well he can't talk to Dad. He's still grieving the invisible cat.

> KERRY
>
> I was wondering if it might be about the DOJ and – everything?

> HUGO
>
> I mean it's fucking late, but if the pressure got turned down – and we can leak it and keep Gerri talking?

They look at each other. Who's gonna eat this bullet? Gerri returns from the stage.

> CONNOR

I could do it?

> TOM

Shiv? Can we get her back? Frank?
> (*there she is*)

Gerri! We need someone, sensible to talk to the president about an urgent personal matter.

> CONNOR

I'll do it?

> KAROLINA

I mean, if it's between Roman and Gerri, I'd have to say—?

> CONNOR

I'll talk to him. The little bitch.

> KERRY

Should we hurry?

Roman and Tom and Gerri look at each other.

> GERRI

Um, I can but – Roman. You know him, right? If anyone here is bootleg Logan – Roman.

He looks at her. It's a big vote of confidence. He swallows, time to buckle.

> ROMAN

Gimme.

> FRANK

Just explain it's out of respect – and you can take the message and—

> KERRY

Yeah I'll connect this end.

> ROMAN

He's a prick with a button.

Kerry hands him the phone. Hugo, head in hands—

> HUGO
> (*to Karolina, re Roman*)

This guy? Tony Tourette's? Are you sure?

> KAROLINA
> (*last-minute advice*)
> Don't swear at the president!

> ROMAN
> (*duh*)
> Oh yeah? Not cool to ask him to blow me . . .

Roman without breaking rhythm—

> . . . Hello, Mr President, sir? This—
> (*awkward crosstalk*)
> Yes, hi – it— No, sorry, you go— This is actually, I'm his son,
> Roman?
> (*they have met*)
> Yeah. Roman, exactly. He can't talk now, but – how are – you?
> (*listens*)
> No he's just in the middle of big stuff.
> (*beat, going badly*)
> No, no not hiding, he literally can't.
> (*beat, going worse*)
> Okay, well I'll let him know you're upset, but—

Roman is clearly being yelled at. He grimaces. Tom and Hugo grimace.

> (*the lie*)
> he really does keep a hands-off approach to editorial so . . .

INT. VENUE – CORRIDOR – DAY

Shiv waits in an secluded corridor area of the venue. Sandi walks out and meets her.

> SHIV
> Hey. Thank you. So look. Upon further reflection, we have
> decided to accept your counter. We can eat the jets.

Sandi looks at her.

> SANDI
> Okay. Any context?

                    SHIV
We took another look and felt this was the clearest way
forward.

                    SANDI
And this is what your dad wants?

Beat.

                    SHIV
Yup. It is what my dad wants.

                    SANDI
But he's not going to tell us?

How to cover?

                    SHIV
He's proud. He preferred me to let you know.

                    SANDI
Well, good. This is good.

                    SHIV
Right. But we're good? We're going to be good?

Sandi looks unsure.

                    SANDI
I guess. It's whiplashy. But good. I should get back and pitch it.

                    SHIV
Because we're getting fucking close? So if we're not good, you
should say.

                    SANDI
Sure. Well honestly. Knowing where my dad is coming from.
I do just wonder if there will be – 'one last thing', so don't turn
your phone off.

                    SHIV
Right. I mean, can we figure something out here? It's kind of
now or never.

                    SANDI
I don't know?

                                    SHIV
Look, look, I don't think it's right your dad sidelines you in all
this. Maybe it'd be appropriate for me to have someone like-
minded on the board? So how about—? How about . . .?

Shiv hesitates for a moment. Then goes for it.

How about a fourth seat on the board. For you. Tell him you
screwed it out of us and my dad was losing his shit and it nearly
killed him?

*It's big. Sandi tries her best poker face. But she's wanted something
like this her whole life.*

                                    SANDI
Four seats is a lot of seats. He'll like that.

                                    SHIV
It's one more than three by my count. For balance, Waystar
would get an extra seat – for me.

                                    SANDI
                                    (*ah*)
I see.
                                    (*then*)
He won't love that.

                                    SHIV
If he needs one last push, explain the markets won't ever let me
or my brothers be CEO?

                                    SANDI
Do you believe that?

                                    SHIV
I just care if your dad believes it.

They look at one another.

                                    SANDI
Uh-huh. Look. I should go. See if I can sell it. But this is good –
with Logan.

                                    SHIV
I can sell it. Can you sell it?

They part with a look of mutual understanding.

INT. VENUE – GREEN ROOM – DAY

The stage is clear, a long video is playing on the monitors.

Roman continues talking to the president on the phone.

> ROMAN
> Okay. Well. I'll relay that.
> *(for their benefit)*
> You're not running again and you hope we're happy?

Frank and Karl and Gerri, Karolina, Hugo all react. Look at one another, surprised, unhappy. Connor looks thrilled.

> FRANK
> *(whispered)*
> No.

> GERRI
> *(whispered)*
> We need the access – no. No!

> ROMAN
> And I mean this is decided? Because I think, whatever our –
> our – minor differences we'd urge you, to – to and not to stand
> aside right now?

Thumbs up from the team.

> *(listening)*
> Uh-huh? But, no I'll be the messenger boy, happy to be that—
> *(crosstalk)*
> I just, I think our position would be – speaking for my father
> here, you know good friends can be tough in their constructive
> criticism but, we would say you know and I've seen, you're a
> really, a significant historical figure with so much more to give,
> and the whole – family at ATN would rally round—

*Thumbs up from Frank, Gerri. Karolina looks at Hugo: He's actually
stepping up. He can actually do this.*

> *(listening)*
> Well, it's been a privilege to have this opportunity to—
> *(listening)*
> Okay then. Well, I hear you. All the best and—

The call ends.

Yeah, so, he wanted us to know he's quitting. He's got a 'minor neurological issue' that the media, starting with us, have blown out of all proportion and he doesn't want to put his family through blah blah, fuck Dad, fuck me and Ravenhead, fuck ATN and good luck getting the kind of access he's granted with whoever is the next president. Which, if it's left up to him, could be a chicken.

TOM

Oh fuck.

KAROLINA

Shit.

GERRI

Oh, man.

CONNOR

Boom-shaka-laka! Hell yeah!

It sinks in. They fucked themselves by alienating their most powerful ally.

ROMAN

I mean it's nice to know we can – like – mold the whole American Republic project and all, but—

Elsewhere, Tom takes a call with Shiv, announces to the room—

TOM

Shiv!
(*reporting*)
Four seats, we eat the PJs but we get a board seat too. It took some persuading but Sandi and Sandy are definitely in. Are we good? Gerri?

KARL

Four seats, fuck . . . I'd like to say yes to that. I think we need to say yes to that. Gerri?

GERRI

Okay. Can we say yes to that. Okay, um—

Looks to the room where Logan is – still with the doctor.

ROMAN

I mean, Dad is going to walk out of there at some point . . .

Looks to Roman. Roman nods.

TOM

Are we good?

Gerri decides. Nods.

ROMAN

We're good. We're good. No vote. Hold the voting.

Assent from the group, Frank, Karl, Gerri, Roman.

TOM
(*into phone*)

They're good, it's yes this end. Then we're good?
(*phone down*)
If we're good they're good. It's done.

Relief in the room.

GERRI

Okay! The lawyers will need to plug in the new details and get signatures. And then we can get out there and tell shareholders.

Karl spots an opportunity.

KARL

Well, Frank you've done so much already, I'd be happy to—?

Before anyone else can jump in—

GERRI

Okay. We'll publish the press release as Karl announces.

INT. VENUE – CORRIDOR – DAY

Tom out into the corridor. Shiv is arriving back.

TOM

Fucking superhero!

SHIV

Thank you!

TOM

Amazing. The world's on fire!

He gives her a kiss.

Tonight. Want to get a hotel room?

SHIV

A hotel? I mean – I think there's rooms in the apartment we've never walked all the way into?

He kisses her neck.

TOM

There's just something about how you smell and your body looks at this time of the— You know I'm like a dog.

SHIV

What time—?

TOM

I get most horny, when you're most fertile, that's how it works, right?

SHIV

Is this why you asked when my period was? Babe are you . . . tracking me?

TOM

Nuh— We're a sorority house, we're in sync. I'm just vibing to your sexy window.

SHIV

Are you keeping a shadow log, Tom? Have you been watching the phases of the moon to see when I'm breedable?

TOM

I just counted the days on my iCal. It's not creepy! Come on, I've only got like six more ovulation windows before all sex is prison sex?

SHIV

I said I didn't like the timing.

TOM

I think it's good timing. Nine to twelve months is what I'm hoping I might serve. It's a good . . . slot.

> SHIV
> Put one in, for when you're out?

> TOM
> No! It would keep you not company but— I might need something. Shiv. Otherwise what's the point of all this, where's it heading?

> SHIV
> I don't want to be your fucking incubator while you – do chin-ups and, and, read Knausgård.

> TOM
> You're making it sound horrible but it's not horrible, it's nice. It was meant to be nice.

She walks on out—

INT. VENUE – CORRIDOR – DAY

Kendall walks quickly, trailed by Comfrey and Jess. Comfrey has summoned her boss to deal with Kendall going rogue.

> BERRY
> It's not my place to say no, Ken . . . but my advice is no.

> KENDALL
> We have the deal, Stewy says. It's safe.

Berry and Comfrey look at one another.

> BERRY
> Your very absence has a certain power.

Kendall weighs this, but keeps walking.

> COMFREY
> They won't let you get onto the stage I don't think? So—

> KENDALL
> Maybe. Maybe not.

He smiles. This is what he wants. He walks.

> But if they turn this into fuck-show, let's make sure we have our own footage. Okay?

INT. VENUE – STAGE – DAY

The stage is empty. A video is playing. But Karl comes on and it stops.

> KARL
> Um. Can yes, I er, I interrupt to give the glad tidings! We are
> pleased to report that a settlement has been reached with
> Maesbury Capital and Furness Media Groups, which will
> preclude today's scheduled vote on the election of our board of
> directors. We will now be adjourning this meeting.

The audience reacts.

INT. VENUE – WINGS – DAY

*Kendall is there in the wings. Smiling weirdly, looking at Karl. Behind
him some way, Comfrey is filming. Karl tries to ignore—*

> KARL
> And Logan, Logan Roy desperately wanted to address his
> shareholders, especially at this very, important time, but he has
> been he is, he's a details guy, my friends, and he's been hard at
> work on this and he will be communicating with shareholders
> directly soon with details of this exciting and forward-focussed
> partnership agreement.

INT. VENUE – GREEN ROOM – DAY

*Staff bring champagne in. The entire Waystar team celebrates their
victory. Cheers for Shiv! But Karolina is getting a message.*

> KAROLINA
> Um? So. Kendall's onstage?

> SHIV
> What?

> KAROLINA
> Kendall's about to go onstage.

INT. VENUE – WINGS – DAY

Kendall walks out from the wings.

KENDALL
(to Karl)

Sorry, do you mind?

KARL

Um? Um?

Karl doesn't know what to do, or what Kendall's going to do.

INT. VENUE – GREEN ROOM – DAY

Team Waystar watch on screen.

ROMAN

Stop him. Tase him!

SHIV

Can we take him out? Is there not a guy?

ROMAN

Tackle him, take his legs out!

INT. VENUE – STAGE – DAY

Kendall walks to the podium.

KENDALL

Okay, I'm going to be quick because. The gorillas are going to rush me!

But the security that are there now at the side of the stage are getting messages not to interfere.

INT. VENUE – GREEN ROOM – DAY

They watch on screen. Shiv to Gerri and Karolina.

SHIV

We have to let it go, right, we can't manhandle him, right?

INT. VENUE – STAGE – DAY

But they aren't coming for him . . . Kendall readjusts.

KENDALL

Okay. Well. Actually, you know I'm not scheduled to speak today. But I'd like to say this.

(beat as he readjusts)

I'd like you all to join with me in a moment's silence for all the victims of crimes that took place on our watch.

The mic gets cut. This is more like what he expected.

And I would like to announce that I am launching a foundation to support victims of sexual abuse suffered at the hands of my family's company. Kira Mason, Iris Vesppuci, Kelly Robinson-Kellis, Irma Ivanovic. Lesley Pullis. Not forgotten! Today is a turning point! Thank you!

He leaves the stage to some scattered, confused applause.

INT. VENUE – GREEN ROOM – DAY

Logan has revived now. A bit drained, resting in a chair, but back to his senses. He's looking at the screen, Kendall has been ushered off stage.

He talks to Gerri.

LOGAN

We should have chopped him down.

GERRI

Yeah well. I guess it might have looked suspicious? Kind of like shredding a human document?

LOGAN

Four seats? And the Raisin gone. What if we get a more aggressive DOJ?

GERRI

You feeling better?

Meanwhile, Connor talks to Hugo and Cyd.

CONNOR

And here I was, looking at European cable? And then, boom, open sesame! Can you believe it?

CYD

It is hard to believe.

CONNOR

GOP's wide open now. The bulk of the primaries are over. It's anyone's game and I'm a big fucking anyone.

HUGO

Only three months to the convention? Is now the time?

But Cyd is glad not to have him around.

CYD

Oh sure, he doesn't want to waste his time at Waystar, Hugo!

CONNOR

Exactly. While the party elite scrambles, I sail in like Bonaparte after Egypt and overthrow the Directory.

Elsewhere, Tom is thinking, Greg approaches.

GREG

So apparently I can't technically sue Ewan while he's alive. But, I can sue Greenpeace by dint of a loophole, possibly?

TOM

I'm sorry?

GREG

I might be going to sue Greenpeace.

TOM

You're going to sue Greenpeace? I like your style, Greg. Who you gonna go after next you think? Save the Children?

Frank clinks his glass and interrupts the celebration briefly.

FRANK

Sorry, everyone. I think every attendee of today's shareholder meeting can agree we've heard more than enough out of me today.

Some scattered laughter.

But I just want to say well done to all. Well done to Logan. And well done to Shiv on one hell of a Hail Mary! To us!

Some applause. Shiv smiles and bows ironically.

Logan looks not entirely happy with the attention Shiv is getting.

Shiv sidles over to Logan who is with Gerri. She tries to angle for some praise.

> SHIV
> So, you did it. Congratulations.

> LOGAN
> I need to see all the detail.

> SHIV
> Dad, the detail is good. The seat was the only way.

> LOGAN
> That's what people on the shitty end of a deal always say. Four seats?

> SHIV
> I stipulated we'd add a board seat of our own. We talked about that, right? Adding another person to the board, like me, or—?

Logan looks at her.

> (*backtracking*)
> Or Connor, or whoever?

Logan shakes his head.

> We couldn't risk a vote. You were – you were AWOL. What would you have done?

> LOGAN
> It doesn't matter. Not that.

> SHIV
> Okay? But what would you have done?

> LOGAN
> I'd have figured it out.
> (*to Gerri*)
> Time to think about next moves.

> SHIV
> It's been two minutes. Don't you want to savor the fact we got through this alive?

> LOGAN

There's blood in the water. The sharks are coming. We should hustle on acquisitions.

Shiv hands Logan a glass of champagne.

> SHIV

Dad, take this, just for a toast!

But in her haste she spills a little on Logan.

> LOGAN
> (*loud*)

Shiv, I'm trying to talk to Gerri about something important. Stop fucking buzzing in my ear!

The whole room turns. Shiv tries to cover.

> SHIV
> (*forced cheer*)

Well somebody's feeling better! Here's to us, everyone!

But everyone's clocked her humiliation and she knows it – she walks away.

Tom goes to hug her. She resists.

> TOM

Hey, it's okay. I'm not gonna hump you, okay? It's a hug. It's just a hug.

With everyone looking elsewhere, she briefly lets him give her a hug.

INT. VENUE – CORRIDOR – DAY

Kendall in a back hallway, watched by security now, is conferring with Berry and Comfrey. Looking at photos and social media on phones. Kerry approaches.

> KERRY

Er, Ken. Listen. I'm sorry. Would you mind sticking around?

> KENDALL

Er no. I have things to do.

> KERRY

Because I think your dad would like a word?

> KENDALL
>
> Oh yeah? What's he bringing? The rubber hose or the
> knuckledusters?

Kendall smiles.

INT./EXT. VENUE — VARIOUS — DAY

Waystar staff clear up. People head out.

INT. VENUE — HOLDING ROOM — DAY

A shabby room. Footsteps. Kendall, eager for the confrontation with his dad he knows is coming, full of righteous indignation, stands. The handle turns – he's ready and then . . . Jess comes in.

Kendall recalibrates – looks at her face. He knows something awful has happened.

> KENDALL
>
> The rabbit. It's dead, isn't she? I know.

> JESS
>
> No. The vet said it'll be fine.

> KENDALL
>
> Oh. Okay? Well, that's good.

> JESS
>
> Are you okay?

> KENDALL
>
> Yep, I'm good. I'm good.

Kendall makes a call. To taunt or provoke the old man.

INT. LOGAN'S CAR — DAY

Incoming call: 'Kendall'. Logan hands Kerry his phone.

> LOGAN
>
> Can you block this number for me?

> KERRY
>
> Sure.

LOGAN

                         LOGAN
Permanently.

INT. KENDALL'S APARTMENT — NIGHT

Kendall is with Sophie and Iverson and their giant rabbit. Kendall's giving out a confusing energy.

                        KENDALL
Guys, what you did wasn't wrong. Sometimes animals are weak and they die so you can't feel guilty about that, okay? But this one is strong. We've got to make the world as good as it can be, yeah? Okay? We're going to have a new president, a new attorney general, and your daddy is going to help clean out the bad stuff and win. But in the meantime we've got to be better. I love you. Okay? Shall we get another rabbit?

His kids just sort of stare at him, a little confused.

Come on, bring it in.

His kids come in for a hug.

Kendall stares off, lost in thought. He can still win this. A new path has been cleared to take his dad down.

Episode Six

WHAT IT TAKES

Written by Will Tracy
Directed by Andrij Parekh

Original air date 21 November 2021

Cast

LOGAN ROY	Brian Cox
KENDALL ROY	Jeremy Strong
GREG HIRSCH	Nicholas Braun
SHIV ROY	Sarah Snook
ROMAN ROY	Kieran Culkin
CONNOR ROY	Alan Ruck
TOM WAMBSGANS	Matthew Macfadyen
WILLA FERREYRA	Justine Lupe
JESS JORDAN	Juliana Canfield
COLIN STILES	Scott Nicholson
HUGO BAKER	Fisher Stevens
KERRY CASTELLABATE	Zoë Winters
MICHELLE-ANNE VANDERHOVEN	Linda Emond
COMFREY PELLITS	Dasha Nekrasova
LISA ARTHUR	Sanaa Lathan
MARK RAVENHEAD	Zack Robidas
MAXIM PIERCE	Mark Linn-Baker
KEITH	Jordan Lage
REECE	Drew Ledbetter
CONGRESSMAN JERYD MENCKEN	Justin Kirk
VIC SCHMIDT	Tony Crane
VP DAVID/DAVE BOYER	Reed Birney
SENATOR RICK SALGADO	Yul Vazquez
RON PETKUS	Stephen Root
PETE	Patrick Noonan
GLYN	Julian Elfer
SDNY PROSECUTOR	Twinkle Burke
GUEST	Cullen Wheeler
HEDGE FUND GUY	Nati Rabinowitz
NATURAL GAS EXEC	Fred Inkley
VERY OLD DONOR	Rick Crom
INSURGENT	Austin Wedderburn
GOSSIPY DONOR	Lois Robbins
RIGHT-WING DONOR	Samantha Steinmetz
RIGHT-WING DONOR 2	Gannon McHale
RIGHT-WING DONOR 3	Brian McManamon

LOUD GUY	Douglas Widick
FVA ANCHOR	Lindsay Tuchman
CARTER	Intae Kim
ZACH	John Skelley

DAY ONE

INT. CONFERENCE ROOM – DAY

Kendall is being questioned by Keith. A tense atmosphere. We sense he's been grilled for a while now. Lisa is by his side.

> KEITH
> Mr Roy, we'd like to move on to the matter of these illegal payments?

> KENDALL
> Uh-huh. Fine. I mean we've done that but, uh-huh.

Kendall makes a note.

> KEITH
> Specifically your first-hand knowledge of what happened.

> KENDALL
> Yup. Yup got it.

> KEITH
> What we want you to explain to us, based on what you saw and heard, is how these illegal payments were approved and by whom.

> KENDALL
> Yup. Got it . . . What's next?

He jots notes. It becomes obvious they are at Lisa's office, running a mock Q&A for his SDNY proffer.

> KEITH
> You want to give the answer?

> KENDALL
> I think I'm good.

Then they wait.

Okay, fine uhhhh . . . *I* approved the illegal payments because I love sexual assault and I love to cover it up. How's that? Is that bad?

LISA

Okay we can wrap up. But, you're confident?

Kendall looks at his notes.

KENDALL

Um. Yeah all these are great. I'm good. Thanks, guys, great work. Yeah. I just will privately run the – the timeline at home but yeah I'm good. We're good, right?

The room breaks up.

LISA

Good. And just yeah, humble, straightforward, no agenda. If they feel an agenda is leading this—

KENDALL

Uh-huh

(*smiles*)

'Hide the agenda.'

LISA
(*smiles*)

No agenda.

KENDALL

Sure. They're government employees, I mean, how smart can they be?

She's not crazy about the jokes.

I'm not saying that, I'm saying what you think I think? Right?

They smile. But underneath she's nervous he's a loose cannon. They walk out.

INT. LISA'S OFFICE – CORRIDOR – DAY

Bit more private in the corridor.

KENDALL

And so we're on the same page, in terms of aims, for me, the wish list goes: Immunity for yours truly. Task force for Waystar. My dad deaded.

LISA

Uh-huh. Well, I don't do requests because I'm not a DJ but I hear you.

KENDALL

I think a task force in there it's just very Enron, you know? Huge signal.

LISA

Ken. I'm optimistic. But look, I want to, give you, like, a, not a reality check but— Look, come in here. They're jigsawing all the papers—

INT. LISA'S OFFICE – BIG CONFERENCE ROOM – DAY

They head into the big conference room.

KENDALL

Okay! Hail, paper people!

Lisa nods for them to leave. She has to cool him down.

LISA

You know, Waystar is now, cooperating. 'Helpfully' offering up *one billion pages* of documents. Hiring white-shoe, former-DOJ types to conduct an internal that looks super-scrupulous. Offering up employees for talks with DOJ. New compliance program and worker safety protocols around cruises. Which is all fine. We can adjust. But this isn't a slam-dunk here.

KENDALL

Uh-huh but the papers?

LISA

Yeah. On the emails, contracts, memos, et cetera. You know, once you pull everything out that falls under other jurisdictions, or maritime law – or is privileged or outside the statute of limitations—

KENDALL

But an FCPA angle obviates those objections. Right?

Who's he been talking to? She looks at him.

LISA

Well the stuff that can work for Foreign Corrupt Practices Act is inferential. Waystar was careful.

Kendall doesn't like the implication.

KENDALL

So you're saying the papers are bullshit?

LISA

I'm just saying they lack some of the explosiveness it was suggested they might have.

KENDALL

So you're suggesting that I suggested that, and that was bullshit?

She looks at him. He feels like that guy at the press conference who is under the lights and things aren't quite lining up—

(*a big word vomit*)

Well I can reposition the context in the public arena. Maybe I can flip someone up the tree? Ah? I just feel sometimes we're allowing the tune to be played at my dad's tempo, Lisa, and I'm not sure why. I have the quote unquote best lawyer in town, I have the best story, I have fucking receipts, excuse my language I'm not angry. But honestly I am a little disappointed.

LISA

(*fuck you*)

I hear you're concerned. You have a big day tomorrow. Okay? This happens the night before. Big day. Rest up. Okay?

KENDALL

Thank you. And I really value all the work you do, honestly. But let's try harder. Yeah? Thank you.

He gets a text from Greg: 'Hey dude. Hope ur good. Just checking in. Any update on the burning?'

INT. ROY PRIVATE JET – DAY

Greg is on his phone, waiting for a reply near Tom, typing out a message to Kendall.

Roman and Shiv watch Logan down the plane as he returns from the plane bathroom. He's full of life, invigorated by his victory at the shareholders' meeting. Logan returns and sits near Kerry. Colin at the back.

ROMAN

I'm gonna miss the big boot. At least we could hear him coming.

Logan settles into work, checks his phone. He sees something amusing and smiles. Logan shows Kerry. Kerry smiles at what she sees and chuckles. A small chuckle from Logan.

LOGAN

Yeah? Heheh.

The siblings watch this weird display. They look at one another. Conversation passes between their eyes.

SHIV

Okay? What's—?

ROMAN

Clearly fucking.

SHIV

Dad and Kerry? Please.

ROMAN

Showing memes to a young menial? Tale as old as time.

SHIV

He hates the close-proximity bang.

Up the plane maybe Kerry smiles at Roman or shares another laugh.

ROMAN

I heard he's still really into blowjobs. That's his thing.

SHIV

Ugh. Please. You'd like to give him a blowjob. Stop projecting.

Then, from up the plane—

LOGAN

Hey, Romulus!

Logan beckons his son over to show him the meme. It's old and sour, maybe homophobic or misogynist with culturally insensitive or racist overtones. Roman smiles.

ROMAN

Think that's been around for a while, Pop, but yeah, well played, the internet.

Shiv watches, excluded. Roman smiles at Shiv, does secret 'kissing Dad', 'we're in love' mimes to Shiv out of Logan's eyeline. Logan downs the phone to focus.

LOGAN

Okay!

Motions for Shiv and Tom to come join. They gather—

Hugo?

Hugo starts in as Shiv and Tom arrive.

HUGO

Yeah. Your dad has been drawing up priorities for the weekend. He wants everyone hitting anti-tech positions, hard?

LOGAN

Regulate and strangulate. They're too powerful. Everybody knows it.

Shiv has thoughts, looks at Tom, but—

ROMAN

Oh yeah, we're all slaves on the Zuck plantation. Picking digital cotton for the likes. I can hit it.

LOGAN

Uh-huh. Get your beak out singing that song.

Logan nods to Hugo.

HUGO

And acquisitions. We're back on the front foot.

LOGAN

We kick the tires on GoJo.

> SHIV
>
> Sorry, you want to buy the hot social media streaming platform while railing against big tech?

> LOGAN
>
> I am not saying go back to the fucking abacus, Siobhan, I am saying, fair competition.

> HUGO
> (*ticks the aims off*)
>
> Stop tech eating our lunch. Put a new friend in at the top. One who's not gonna fire up Justice about our 'boring old case'.

> SHIV
>
> And I guess, a bellyful of humble pie about – you know, accidentally knocking over their president and smashing him on the floor?

> ROMAN
>
> Boohoo.

Shiv looks at Roman.

> It's not our fault the president's brain couldn't thunk good no more.

> HUGO
>
> The feeling is – go offense. Spread it round that if the Raisin goes for us, he's politicizing the cruises case. 'It's so sad.' 'His Justice Department has a grudge.'

> LOGAN
>
> I might have heard the DAG has a picture of me on her dartboard, which is disgusting.

> TOM
>
> Have we heard that?

> HUGO
> (*nope, but*)
>
> Well that's the rumor that's going around?

Back with Greg. He sees the three dots – Kendall's replying. It seems to take a long time. Anxiety builds.

'Sorry dude. Still considering options.' Greg creases into anxiety.

EXT. AIRFIELD — RICHMOND, VIRGINIA — DAY

As they divide into the waiting cars, Shiv strides up to her dad.

> SHIV
>
> Dad, can I jump in with you. That okay?

> LOGAN
>
> Uh-oh!

Logan pretends to feel trepidation.

INT. LOGAN'S CAR — DAY

Logan and Shiv in the back, Kerry in the front, a few minutes in. Tension between father and daughter. The first time they've been alone together since the shareholders' meeting.

> SHIV
>
> Can we go up a degree in the back?

She's talking about the temperature, addressing the driver, who complies. Logan looks at her.

> You okay?

Pointless question. Doesn't deserve an answer. She looks out of the window.

> LOGAN
>
> You gonna be a fuckin' sourpuss?

> SHIV
>
> No. Just. The last time we talked properly you were humiliating me at the shareholders' meeting. I thought it would be good to check in.

> LOGAN
>
> It was a long day and I was unwell.

> SHIV
>
> And I'm just going to say. I'm concerned about who you might endorse this weekend. The vice president.

> LOGAN
>
> You're scared of Dave Boyer?!

SHIV

Nothing as dangerous as a second-rate individual who sees his chance. He's a silver-medal snake.

Logan shrugs.

He's a neoliberal posing as a Maniac. He's the nice guy who kills a stripper to fit in with the bros. Why do you even care who they pick?

LOGAN

Well I want them to win. I don't like your bunch of mimsy can't-say-that fucks.

SHIV

C'mon, you're a money guy. What's the difference between us, politically, really? You want marginal tax rates at twenty, twenty-five percent? I want them at thirty, thirty-five?

LOGAN

I need to keep my spoon in the soup.

She looks at him.

SHIV

Fine.

(*then*)

I would also just say. I know you two are having your whatever moment but, this might not be the best place to let Roman be a mouthpiece.

LOGAN

He's maturing.

Logan waves it away.

SHIV

Well, I've been to a heap of these in my time, you need the subtle knife. Not a dirty little pixie with a megaphone.

LOGAN

He's a good kid. He's fun.

SHIV

Well, I love him but he fucked the phone call with the Raisin, that's an existential risk. The only solid thing he ever actioned in LA was *Dr Honk*, the movie about the man who could talk to cars? We're walking into there with a hundred different aims. Some nuance is required—

Logan opens the window a crack. He's warm. Doesn't buy all this about Roman, he sees something but he's not about to get into a fight. So just looks skeptical.

You know, I'm just glad we still have a company to be acting on behalf of, thanks to me.

They pull up.

LOGAN
Kerry. Get Shiv a fucking medal.

But smiles between them.

EXT. RICHMOND — APPROACHING JEFFERSON HOTEL — DAY

The Waystar convoy heads into town.

A heavy amount of security patrols the area.

White-noise machines have also been set up everywhere.

EXT. RICHMOND — OUTSIDE JEFFERSON HOTEL — DAY

A mass of black town cars, SUVs and Hummers are arriving outside a hotel.

Press, if they are there, are in the far distance.

INT. JEFFERSON HOTEL — LOBBY — DAY

Logan and the gang arrive. Hugo and Kerry deal with the signing-in formalities as Logan walks in with Colin.

A reporter or opposition observer is being escorted out by two discreet but no-nonsense security operatives in chinos and polo shirts, but with weapons in holsters.

Roman eyes with interest and takes in the white-noise speakers.

INT. HOTEL – RECEPTION – DAY

Later. People have changed clothes. A large, ornate, gaudy room where guests of the Future Freedom Summit have gathered for drinks.

The guests are skewed white and older.

The servers, who circulate with drinks and hors d'oeuvres, more diverse and younger.

We see a gallery of power conservatives:

Hedge-fund guys (the equivalents in our world of Steve A. Cohen, Robert & Rebekah Mercer and Stephen A. Schwarzman).

Retailers and online sellers (the equivalents in our world of Kenneth Langone and Richard M. DeVos).

Coal, oil and fracking industrialists (the equivalents in our world of the Koch brothers, Corbin Robertson Jr.).

Government contractors (the equivalents in our world of Richard Farmer and Stephen Bechtel Jr.).

TV anchors (our Mark Ravenhead and others male and female ATN anchors and hosts, plus from other further right OAN/Newsmax networks).

Strategists (the equivalents in our world of Steve Bannon and Roger Stone).

Supreme Court Justices (the equivalents in our world of Neil Gorsuch and Amy Coney Barrett).

Politicians (including Jeryd Mencken, Richard Salgado, Dave Boyer and others).

As Greg walks into the room with the other guests, he passes a short old donor, who looks up at Greg and smiles.

                    VERY OLD DONOR
You know, if you were black the Lakers would draft you!

Greg nods and smiles semi-politely as the old-timer walks away.

                         GREG
Right. I have a semi-cavus foot, so probably not.

(downing his drink)
Jesus . . .

We join Shiv, Tom and Roman as they survey the gross scene.

SHIV
You can smell the panic. Berlin-bunker vibes.

TOM
It is rather – pungent.

Roman needles an uncomfortable-looking Shiv.

ROMAN
Heh. Lil Ms Libtard, how you like spelunking in the elephant's asshole?

SHIV
I'm just a corporate observer.

ROMAN
Wait till the weekend's over. We're gonna get our white cis-male stank all over you.

SHIV
This party is falling apart.

Roman has been reading.

ROMAN
Well no, actually, Shiv, the Maniacs are just taking charge.

TOM
Actually, Rome, the wise heads feel the Maniacs are in fact only clinging on. The Maniacs are the moderating influence right now.

SHIV
The Maniacs are the moderating influence?

TOM
Yeah. You have a small country-club rump but the Maniac Majority are really a good option.

ROMAN
'The Maniacs' are actually quite boring, when you look into it.

TOM

If anything we need to bolster the Maniacs. Because they're getting outflanked by the nutjobs, who are losing ground to the full-on shit-flinging fuckheads. Our best hope is finding what I think of as a 'capable maniac'.

ROMAN

Speaking of maniacs. Captain Kook from the SS *Loonitania*.

He gestures over across the room at Connor.

SHIV

Is it just me or in a room full of Timothy McVeighs does Connor suddenly look like a Roosevelt?

We join Connor and Maxim Pierce, who are talking to a donor named Pete, who's a mega-fan. Willa types on her phone.

PETE

It's such a thrill. I'm probably the biggest Conhead in Oklahoma.

CONNOR

Of course. Panhandle Pete! And you've met Maxim Pierce? He's my intellectual heft.
    (*rubs Maxim's belly*)
My Beltway Buddha.

MAXIM

I push him, he pushes me, and around and around we go!

CONNOR

Sweetie, this is Panhandle Pete.

WILLA
    (*barely looking up*)
Uh-huh?

CONNOR

Frowny-face here wanted to stay home and finish her play. But duty calls for my leggy Mary Todd.

WILLA

No, it's fine. I can just write a play on my phone.

PETE

So. And how did you two meet?

Connor and Willa kind of look at each other.

CONNOR

Online.

WILLA

Online.

CONNOR

You know how it goes. She's a writer and I'm a billionaire she's trying to turn into a millionaire with her plays!

A few loud clinks are heard. Mega-donor Ron Petkus (seventies), the organizer of the dinner, is holding his Scotch and soda high.

PETKUS

Folks, if we can quiet down for a sec. I just want to thank you all for being here on such short notice . . . And I want to thank you as well for keeping your attendance private. What we do here at the Future Freedom Summit is of the utmost importance for our party and our country. I've been fighting the fight for over thirty years now. And this is, without doubt, the most pivotal battle of my political life.
(solemn beat)
But friends and patriots, I happen to believe the next President of the United States is somewhere in this very room.

On Logan as he surveys the room. Connor turns to Maxim.

CONNOR

He is, and he's hard as a rock.

Back on Petkus.

PETKUS

May God shepherd this person. The health of our republic depends on it.

A light-hearted jeer from one of the guests.

GUEST

And the health of my portfolio!

But there's some Proud Boy-influenced types in the mix.

INSURGENT

Fuck you!

Uneasy laughs. A shift in the room.

MICHELLE-ANNE

To the Republic!

Roman, Shiv and Tom observe.

ROMAN

Yay. The Republic.

SHIV

Ron Petkus blew his son's archery instructor. True story.

Greg approaches. He looks very uncomfortable.

GREG

Um, some guy with an undercut just called me Soy Boy?

TOM

Don't worry, Greg, it's nice. It's a safe space where you don't have to pretend to like *Hamilton*.

GREG

I like *Hamilton*.

TOM

Sure you do. We all do.

Shiv joins the Tom–Greg huddle.

GREG

So, like, what is it, actually, here?

ROMAN

Here? Just a nice political conference of like-minded donors and intellectuals.

TOM

AKA time to pick the president. Selecto el presidento!

Greg looks intrigued.

SHIV

That's not really how it works.

ROMAN

No sure. But really it is.

GREG

And is that like – constitutional?

TOM

Ooh I don't know, Greg. Maybe we should phone the referee? Is there an ombudsman in the house?

Elsewhere, Michelle-Anne approaches Logan. Shiv and Roman gather around.

MICHELLE-ANNE

Well. Here they are. The family who lost us a presidency.

LOGAN

How is he, the Raisin?

MICHELLE-ANNE

How is he? He's out of a job in six months, lame in the interim and the GOP's in flames. We're all doing backflips.

ROMAN

Yeah, sorry about that.

LOGAN

He's got a serious condition. We felt the country needed to know.

MICHELLE-ANNE

Oh, it's a public service? Your country thanks you. My life is hell.

They smile at each other coldly. Shiv steps in.

SHIV

So what are you hearing?

MICHELLE-ANNE

Well? With the president out we need a nominee. Welcome to clown town. Six months to election day and no candidate. Super Tuesday's gone, ballots are finalized, nowhere to go now but a brokered convention. The delegates will choose at the RNC of course, but I think we can be real and say we need to choose here, first.

HUGO

It's Boyer, right? We're going Boyer.

> MICHELLE-ANNE

Yup. Cleanest option is the vice president. The party needs to be united. So I hope having started this mess you can help us clear it up?

They observe Vice President David Boyer (fifties) across the room.

> LOGAN

Dave is good. I like Dave.

> MICHELLE-ANNE

We all like Dave.

> ROMAN

Dave the steady old plow horse.

> HUGO

He's only polling second or third right now?

> MICHELLE-ANNE

You don't want to be in the lead early.

> SHIV

Correct.

> ROMAN

But at some point you do? I mean eventually you do. Just before you win?

> MICHELLE-ANNE

You don't want to be the hare, you want to be the tortoise.

> ROMAN

Hard shell, stubby legs. Exciting.

Meanwhile Tom talks to Mark Ravenhead and a natural gas exec. Toeing the company line. Greg too.

> TOM

Shame what happened. Although? There is the argument, the prez was no longer in the same place as the party?

> MARK RAVENHEAD

Could be.

> TOM

But he did go very easy on Big Tech. Gotta get a hold of that?

They watch Boyer nibbling on a leafy canapé.

> NATURAL GAS EXEC

I heard his daughter has made him go vegetarian, did you hear that?

> TOM

Really? No, I think I've seen him eat a meatball.

> NATURAL GAS EXEC

Nope. Secret herbivore. I hear. Not a biggie.

They all sit with that. They don't love it.

> MARK RAVENHEAD

But we like Dave.

The Waystar team works the room, spinning and talking shit.

> HUGO

The investigation, such as it is, ever was, is really slowing down, we hear.

Roman talks to another more gossipy donor nearby.

> ROMAN

I mean, between us, I think his brain was shot. So it had to come out. You hear some whackadoo stuff.

> GOSSIPY DONOR

Really?

> ROMAN

Oh yeah. Apparently heads of state would be coming in to the O and everyone would be like, 'Has he got the old hot-dog stand open?' Like check he was zipped up?

> GOSSIPY DONOR

No way.

> ROMAN

Wanted to use the ding-a-ling like it was a pen. Tried to veto bills with it.

> GOSSIPY DONOR

Jesus.

> ROMAN

Some of it is rumors I'm sure. But yeah we had a duty to report it, even if it hurt our interests overall because we loved the guy.

Shiv talks to a hedge fund guy.

> HEDGE FUND GUY
> And so how are you all feeling after your shareholder meeting. Humiliated?

> SHIV
> What, by winning? We threw them some board seats, fine. We're still very much in charge.

Logan chats with Ron Petkus. The wary old allies.

> PETKUS
> Quite an Oswald you pulled on the big guy.

> LOGAN
> More a misunderstanding.

> PETKUS
> Oh sure. I'm sure.

> LOGAN
> But still, for the best. We can't have a president who smells toast and shits in the waste basket.

They survey the landscape of hopefuls, donors and hacks.

> PETKUS
> Boyer though? Good yeah? It's his turn?

> LOGAN
> Mm.

Petkus and Logan nod in agreement for a beat.

> PETKUS
> I don't really mind the lip-licking thing. Do you?

> LOGAN
> No – is it bad?

> PETKUS
> Not really. But once you notice it you definitely notice it.

> LOGAN
> Can he stop?

> PETKUS
> It's unconscious I think. The tongue just creeps out there.

Logan considers.

> As long as he doesn't do it much in the debates we should be fine.

Logan nods. But senses a lack of Boyer fever in the room.

Elsewhere, Roman and a British Tory operative named Glyn. They glance at Boyer.

GLYN
The man must have the wettest lips in North America.

ROMAN
It's like he's a cartoon bear and there's always a picnic hamper nearby.

GLYN
But Dave is great. Have you ever seen him eat a burger?

ROMAN
Umm, I don't rightly know?

GLYN
Congratulations by the way.

ROMAN
Uh-huh. For what? What have I done now?

GLYN
The wedding. Your mother? Your mother is Caroline Collingwood, right? She's getting married, no? To Peter Munion.

ROMAN
Um, no. Nope? She's in a relationship with a canoe-shaped gentleman named Rory.

Glyn searches on his phone.

GLYN
Nope. Pretty . . . Maybe it's another . . . No.

Glyn shows him the invite on his phone. Roman stares.

ROMAN
Uh-huh? Well, this is— Uh-huh. Well, yeah, this seems to be— Okay well, you know how it is, Glyn. Families!

(*then*)
Can you forward this to me?

GLYN

Do you think that's okay?

ROMAN

To my mom's wedding? Yeah I think that's okay, Glyn.

Shiv passes and he pulls her aside.

Hey. So, you know about this, you withholding bitch?

SHIV

What?

Roman shows her his phone.

ROMAN

Glyn the Brexit pervert sent this to me. Mom's getting married.
To 'Peter Munion'.

SHIV

Is this a joke? Who is Peter Onion?

ROMAN

I don't know. I think I remember, is he one of those guys—? A
Sunday-lunch man?

SHIV

She really hasn't fucking told us she's getting married? Call her.

ROMAN

What the fuck. You call her!

SHIV

I don't want to call her. She prefers you.

ROMAN

That's true actually. Why doesn't Mom like you? We should call
her and find out.

SHIV

Yeah I'm kinda curious.

ROMAN
(*pulling out phone*)
It's too late to call her now. She'll freak and get a headache. I bet
the first-born fuck knew.

Roman calls Kendall on speaker.

Intercut with:

INT. KENDALL'S APARTMENT — KITCHEN — DAY

Kendall in his apartment. He's meeting with a couple of older white guys.

> KENDALL
> (*on speaker*)
> Hey. What?

> ROMAN
> Hey, bro. I'm here with Shiv. Just wanted to let you know . . . New dad just dropped.

> KENDALL
> What?

> ROMAN
> Mom's getting remarried, dingus.

> SHIV
> Did you know?

> ROMAN
> Of course he didn't know. Ken bores the shit out of Mom.

> KENDALL
> What are you even talking about? What about – um, Rory?

> SHIV
> I guess she took the view 'fuck Rory'.

It's actually kind of heavy. Feels bad.

> KENDALL
> When did you hear? Was she going to tell her children at some point?

> SHIV
> She was probably too busy throwing away our old finger-paintings.

KENDALL

Hey, Shiv, is it true? You at the hate-fest fest? Burning books and measuring skulls down in Nuremberg, Virginia?

SHIV

Uh-huh, what you doing with your weekend? Plotting to send us all to jail? Your favorite?

ROMAN

Look, we just wanted to let you know Mom still doesn't love you, Ken, bye!

In Kendall's apartment. Back to this other lawyer.

KENDALL

Okay, Paul, say that again.

INT. HOTEL – RECEPTION – DAY

Roman hangs up.

Tom is leaving the reception and Greg sidles up.

GREG

Hey man, so um? I just wanted to broach something with you—?

TOM

Broach away, Greg.

GREG

Yeah, look, I'm pretty anxious. Ken's saying he might burn me.

Tom looks at Greg.

TOM

Are you threatening me? Because you can't threaten me. I'm immune.

GREG

No. No. Tom, I was thinking about advice. Because, I guess I'm obsessing and I wonder how to stop thinking about it?

TOM

Yeah I tried that – it doesn't work. What I'm preferring, is to always think about it. Then when you don't for a moment it's like, 'Oooh, someone's loosened their icy grip on my innards'?

411

Tom smiles and moves on. Greg nods. He looks scared.

Logan is leaving the reception. He sees Boyer across the room chatting to Michelle-Anne. Boyer licks his lips slightly. A face from Logan.

INT. HOTEL – SHIV AND TOM'S SUITE – NIGHT

Tom is in the kitchen of their suite, looking at a case of wine, special delivery. He opens the box, pulls out a bottle.

                              TOM
Uh-huh so, you wanna try? It's the Spätburgunder. From our vineyard.
                    (first disappointment)
Oh. Screwtop?

Shiv is watching a clip of magnetic, aggressive presidential hopeful Jeryd Mencken on Freedom Views America (FVA), an OAN-style further-right-than-ATN news channel. They might talk over some or all of this.

                           MENCKEN
                          (onscreen)
—but there's this myth that we're in power. Even if we keep the White House, that's just us hanging on. We're not in power. Cosmopolitan elites who steer the armada of culture are in power. And they will use their GIFs and their streaming platforms and their token black and brown avatars to smear and vilify our heritage—

                             SHIV
                     (shivers re the clip)
Ugh. He's such a fucking— And now Boyer's losing juice. You hear?

                              TOM
Uh-huh. It's biodynamic, so—
                            (sips)
it has a definite funk to it.

It's not good. Hands her a glass.

                    SHIV
               (*sips, weird taste*)
Mmm. Yeah? Yeah?

                    TOM
Yeah you have to meet it halfway.

                    SHIV
No good. Earthy. Yeah? It's very, Germanic.

She puts her glass down.

                    TOM
Interesting. I feel like it's still unfolding, in my mouth. Yeah,
atmospheric. A little gothic. Definitely Old World. It's old. It's –
it's, it's, it's – it's—
               (*the truth*)
it's not very nice, is it, Shiv?

She looks at the iPad.

                    SHIV
I wonder if Boyer flames out, if it's time to pivot party?

He opens another bottle, in case it was just one that tasted weird . . .

                    TOM
Yeah, my prison consultant called. It's looking like the place
upstate might be full.

Tom is sad. Shiv doesn't really know what to do with that.

                    SHIV
You're tired. It'll feel better tomorrow.

                    TOM
Yeah? One day closer to my incarceration.
               (*sipping*)
They're all the same.
               (*then*)
They say the food is—

                    SHIV
               (*cutting him off*)
Tom, I don't get why you want to keep talking about it? What
else is there to say?

>   TOM
> I'm sorry, does the topic of my imminent imprisonment bore
> you?

>   SHIV
> C'mon. You're obsessing. I can't keep going round and round.

Huh. She realizes that was a little cold. She kisses him.

> Honey. I don't know what to say.

*He kisses back, but dispassionately. She smiles and kisses more
sensually.*

> No?

>   TOM
> Sure.

*They kiss – and maybe move towards the bedroom or somewhere
where things might progress. But then—*

>   (breaking the kiss)
> There just doesn't seem much point?

>   SHIV
> What to – making love?

>   TOM
> If you're still on contraception?
>   (then)
> It's just – throwing so much cake batter at a brick wall?

Okay, that's the end. Shiv goes to her phone.

INT. HOTEL – PETKUS'S PARTY – NIGHT

*Petkus is having a casual gathering in a private area – other friendly
donors. A mixture of millionaires and billionaires.*

*Willa sits in an armchair, next to Petkus, who is charmed by her.
Connor perches on the arm of the chair, thrilled.*

>   WILLA
> I think what I realized is I'm just not that interested in being a
> commercial playwright?

CONNOR

I mean the audience helped you discover that, didn't they?

PETKUS

Beauty and brains! I probably shouldn't say that, will I be canceled??

WILLA

Ha, oh no! No. Who knows. The night is young.

PETKUS

I don't know how you do it. How do you come up with things that aren't already there?

CONNOR

Oh you don't know the half of it. We talk long into the night. Ideas. Literary. Global. Macro. Micro. Cosmo. We bounce off each other.

PETKUS

Oop! Sounds delightful.

CONNOR

Haha, no, but yeah.

WILLA

Con—?

PETKUS

You must come up to Pound Ridge one weekend. Both of you, or if you're busy, or tired, one, one and all.

CONNOR

We'd love that, wouldn't we, chicken?

WILLA

I don't know if you're invited!

CONNOR

Haha!

PETKUS

Haha!

(*then*)

Let me circulate, I'll hydrate this gorgeous creature on my return!

CONNOR

Canceled!

WILLA

Aghh!

Left alone now, Willa vents.

CONNOR

Fun guy.

WILLA

Con, maybe don't abandon me upstate with Larry Lech here. It's weird.

CONNOR

Very influential. We're just showing a bit of leg.

WILLA

Yeah, my leg.

CONNOR

The collective leg. He's a huge donor.

WILLA

We don't have a collective leg. And his aftershave has given me a headache.

INT. HOTEL – GOLD BAR – NIGHT

Roman scrolls through photo after lame photo of Peter Munion.

Congressman Jeryd Mencken approaches the bar with entourage.

MENCKEN

Hey, man, what's up?

ROMAN

Oh okay. Hey, it's the ghost pepper. The spicy new flavor.

They size each other up for a beat. Mencken nods. And then—

MENCKEN

So what's your deal? Most people here want to fuck me or kill me. You?

ROMAN

Me, I always found it hard to care about politics.

MENCKEN

Uh-huh, well listen, here's my party trick: Tell me who your enemy is and I'll tell you who you are.

Roman tingles a little.

ROMAN

I've seen your poll numbers. You're dark-horsin' it. People buying your whole thing, huh?

MENCKEN

Well they better buy it. Or I'll send them to the gulag!

Mencken flashes a mischievous grin. Roman likes it.

ROMAN

Now we're talking!

MENCKEN

No, I'm kidding. No work camps. They'll be like summer camps.

ROMAN

But with beatings?

MENCKEN
(*with a wink*)
No no no. Shhhhh. 'No beatings!'

He smiles and winks. Roman laughs. This is fun!

ROMAN

I like this. Just a couple of cool guys having disgusting fun.

Mencken leans in conspiratorially.

MENCKEN

So do you guys know yet? Who takes over?

ROMAN

What's that?

MENCKEN

When they send the old battletoad off to the hoosegow? Your dad. Admiral Grope Boat.

ROMAN

Oh, yeah, no. He's not— That's not going to happen.

417

> MENCKEN

Hahaha! That's right! That's the line! Gotta stick to the line!

Mencken takes his drink and leaves. Roman watches him go. A twinge of something – excitement?

INT. HOTEL – SHIV AND TOM'S SUITE – NIGHT

Tom and Shiv lie in bed. Shiv is asleep. Tom is wide awake, staring at the ceiling. His eyes filled with fear. A kind of mortal dread.

Carefully, so as not to wake Shiv, Tom takes his phone from the bedside table.

Intercut with:

INT. HOTEL – GREG'S ROOM

Greg is awoken from a deep sleep. He answers his phone.

> GREG

. . . Hello?

> TOM
> (*whispered*)

Waffle time, Sporus. C'mon. I'm gonna teach you about prison.

INT. WAFFLE HUT – NIGHT

Tom and Greg in a booth in a chain waffle establishment. Greg has a big, thick, rubbery, smooth omelette. Tom has eggs, ham and hash browns.

> TOM

So, according to Steven, my prison consultant, apparently this is what the food is like, you know, inside. So I'm in training. How is the omelette?

> GREG

Oh? Making some inroads! So, I actually wanted to talk, Tom—

> TOM

It's like Afghanistan.

(*motions to a spot on the large omelette*)
Establish a base of operation in the center there and work out to
secure more territory.

GREG

Yeah I'm just worried about prison. Because of my physical
length, I could be a target for all kinds of – misadventure.

TOM

It won't be as good as this of course. Take off thirty to fifty
percent of the endless salty gym mat. The camel's labia.

GREG

They wipe their ass on your pillowcase. It's something they like
to do.

TOM

Obviously. I have read all the blogs, Greg.

Tom takes another mouthful – and finally drops his fork.

GREG
(*risks it*)
So um, look? You know how around the office they've been
calling you – that name? The, you know – 'the Christmas tree'?

TOM

What's good is to eradicate hope. Hope is the enemy. If you can
drain that away, then they can't get you, because you've got no
hope, you see?

GREG

I guess it's because – you know – if, one has a crime they need to
unload they can hang it from you? Like an ornament?

TOM

I haven't slept in eight days.

GREG

It's not a nice name. But – I was wondering – I mean, since it
looks like you're going – anyway. Is it possible you might, with
me—?

TOM

Are you asking if you can hook your bauble of corporate
wrongdoing to one of my branches, Greg?

> GREG

I just thought, if it won't make much difference to you?

Tom looks at him for a long time and thinks, then—

> TOM

Fine. Load me up you piece of shit.

> GREG

Really? Tom? No quid pro quo? Just—

Tom nods.

Well that's – that's just incredibly – kind.

> TOM

Giddy up. Load up the crime mule.

> GREG

Can I get this?

> TOM

Nah. Greenpeace stole your inheritance. Besides, all my meals will be free soon.

Greg looks at Tom – he's grateful. Tom can't quite accept the wave of good feeling he has engendered.

DAY TWO

INT. HOTEL – BREAKFAST AREA – MORNING

A new day rises over the hotel complex.

A bunch of Alt-Right types mingle over breakfast buffet.

Shiv eats breakfast. Roman returns from a phone call.

> ROMAN

Okay, so. Mom says it's all fine. She is getting remarried, but we're not to get it out of proportion or cook it up into a whole big thing. It isn't *Romeo and Juliet* but he makes her laugh, he is a little bit awful and vulgar and he wants a huge social wedding to show off in Tuscany and she's sorry for not telling us but she couldn't because Rory doesn't know yet and he might kill himself and he can't because he's building her a new chicken coop but he's got the black dog and it wouldn't be fair right now.

She looks at him. He looks in low spirits.

It's dumb but I guess it kind of makes sense.

SHIV
Jesus. She's cucked you so hard.

Shiv looks at Roman. She sees something. A button to press.

Wait . . . are you sad?

ROMAN
What? No, Shiv, I am not sad. I don't give a hoot.

SHIV
(*looks at him hard as he evades*)
Did you hope Mummy and Daddy would get back together?

ROMAN
No, Shiv, because I'm not eight years old.

SHIV
That's adorable, Rome.

INT./EXT. KENDALL'S SUBURBAN – DAY

Kendall and Lisa head to the SDNY proffer. Kendall is nervous, preparing in his head.

INT. US ATTORNEY'S OFFICE – SDNY CONFERENCE ROOM – DAY

Kendall, Lisa and Keith sit across from two SDNY prosecutors, two from Main Justice and two FBI agents.

It's the end of Kendall's proffer with SDNY. It's been long. Kendall is frustrated but scrupulously polite and careful.

SDNY PROSECUTOR
Okay, Mr Roy . . . Is there any other illegal conduct you are aware of, in connection with what we have been talking about today, that we haven't covered?

It's the kind of question you'd ask a semi-slippery witness.

> KENDALL

Um? No. Not that I can think of now. At the moment.

> SDNY PROSECUTOR

And is there any question you thought I might ask that I did not?

> KENDALL

Uh . . . Well. No.

> (*thinks*)

No I guess not.

A disappointment in Kendall's face. Like he didn't really get what he came for.

INT. US ATTORNEY'S OFFICE – SDNY HALLWAY – DAY

Kendall, Lisa and Keith exit the proffer room. They walk and talk.

> LISA

Good. I think that – you did fine.

> KENDALL

Uh-huh.

> LISA

It's a good start. And they'll have another session.

> KENDALL

We can say it went badly, Lisa. It's okay.

> LISA

Okay. Let's maybe just— We'll do the Monday-morning quarterback in a bit—

> KENDALL

They spent all day trying to find hairline fractures in my story, meanwhile my dad's a fucking tsunami of corruption.

> LISA

They don't do cuddles, Ken.

In the background, the guys come out of the room.

> KENDALL

I know how this works, okay? My dad is drowning them in chicken feed and compliance bullshit, five years go by and it's,

'Hey, whatever happened to that big investigation into the bad people? Oh well!'

                    LISA
Ken.

Lisa tries to move him down the hall toward the elevators. But Kendall stops so he's in earshot of the prosecutors.

                  KENDALL
These guys won't even be here in five years. They'll be at one of the firms who are running this investigation out of my dad's offices. It's a fucking revolving door!

A few of the prosecutors lift their heads.

                (*even louder*)
They're scared of my dad. They pretend they're on the side of the whistleblowers but they're chickenshit!

                    LISA
Ken, shh, c'mon. Stop. Please stop. Ken. Let's go. Please?

They definitely heard it all.

Ken. Not here.

But as he clocks they have gone, Kendall winks at Lisa. Looks over his shoulder.

                  KENDALL
                (*quiet now*)
Should put a rocket up their asses?

She can't believe it. That was for show? She cools her first response, which is call him a rich asshole.

                    LISA
We don't want this to get politicized.

                  KENDALL
Well everything is politics. So.

Lisa walks for a beat, she's really pissed off.

                    LISA
Kendall. Look, do you think you're smarter than me?

> KENDALL

What? Do I—? What?

> (*yes*)

No. No.

> LISA

Because maybe you are. But I am a better lawyer.

> (*stops herself*)

Let's take stock okay? You're right, today was not a good day. You acted high-handed and defensive and then oscillated to wildly overfamiliar and glib. You sometimes undermined my status and didn't appear to be frank about your own involvement.

> (*about to freak out but stops*)

But let's take stock. Okay?

They walk.

INT. HOTEL – HALLWAY – DUSK

Logan and Kerry emerge from Logan's suite and walk through gilded hallways en route to dinner.

> KERRY

Stigwood is angling to get ten?

Logan smiles. A knowing vibe between them. Logan remembers, it's all up there, somewhere.

> LOGAN

Uh-huh? Squinty-face? Ohio fourteenth?

She nods: That's right. They round a corner and run into Boyer.

> BOYER

Oh. Hey – Logan.

> LOGAN

Dave! How are we?

Boyer's air a bit desperate. He knows he's losing steam. Discreetly his security detail are off down the hall.

>   BOYER
> Good! Glad I ran into you. Feels like we've hardly got a chance
> to connect.

>   LOGAN
> Uh-huh? Well here we are?

>   BOYER
> Here we are. You heard, they're calling this the ATN primary?
> Heh.

>   LOGAN
> I wouldn't worry about all that.

>   BOYER
> You know one thing I wanted to discuss with you is – is—
>   (knows this is what he wants to hear)
> controlling tech. That's a big, big plank for me.

>   LOGAN
> Oh that's interesting? That's really interesting?

>   BOYER
> Uh-huh. Sure. Sure. Plus. I can sometimes fear, you know against
> you legacy-media guys, a degree of – of 'legal overreach'.

>   LOGAN
> Uh-huh. You heard this thing, the DAG has a dartboard with my
> face on it?

>   BOYER
> Right, I mean I think that was just a rumor?

Kerry's there and part of it.

>   KERRY
> To me it's one of those things, even if it isn't true, there's a
> reason it feels like it is, right?

*Boyer looks at her – who the fuck are you? But senses he needs to
take her seriously.*

>   BOYER
> Uh-huh. Right.

>   LOGAN
> Okay. Good!

Logan wants to wrap it up, walk on. Boyer's growing more desperate, holds him back.

> BOYER
>
> Look, I'm just going to be straight with you. I need you. I like you. Petkus and the big-dollar guys are on the fence. Let's make it happen yeah? I just need you to push me over the brink here?

> LOGAN
>
> Great. I get it. See you at dinner.

Logan keeps walking.

Once he's out of earshot. Logan turns to Kerry, sotto voce.

> I think he's been waiting there for me for ten fucking minutes!

Logan and Kerry chuckle quietly.

INT. KENDALL'S APARTMENT — LIVING ROOM — DUSK

Hip hop plays somewhere. Kendall's new friends – Reece, Zach, Carter, and off a way a bit Comfrey on a laptop – are there. Kendall comes in from the other room. He's cokey. Everything's falling but he's keeping it all on the rise with a bubble of his own enthusiasm. If he lets it drop – who knows . . .?

> KENDALL
>
> Hey hey hey. So. Comfrey. Lisa's out. Once I sign the new legal A-team we need to get that out with the right context. Okay?

Comfrey looks alarmed.

> Not a big deal. It's an opportunity. We just flip a big name, it's all good.
> (looks at them)
> Okay. Big four-oh. How we looking?

There are design ideas around. Zach is looking at one.

> ZACH
>
> Shit's gonna be lit.

> KENDALL
>
> Yeah. You think?

He looks at him – can he trust him or is he a moron?

Comfrey, is this cool? I mean it's cool. But is it bullshit cool?
How old are you?

(*looks*)

I love the ideas but are they too narrow? Is it just like: hunter-gatherers, herders, agriculture, cities? Guns, germs and steel?

People hate it in the room.

Or – Comfrey? What was the one I liked?

COMFREY

'"End Times": Weimar meets Carthage meets Dante meets
AI and antibiotic-resistant superbugs'?

ZACH

That's kinda dope though?

KENDALL

Uh-huh. I mean I do want it to be a fucking party? Are James
Murphy and Zadie Smith and fucking Chuck D gonna come to
my antibiotics party?

COMFREY
(*looking at list*)
'Last dance of the white man'. Is strong?

KENDALL

And there's a big wicker white man at the end and we all dance
to Genesis or Roxy Music or something fucked up?

Jess comes in the room.

Will he meet?

JESS

He's not picking up to our numbers.

KENDALL

Okay, get me new numbers. Let's keep calling. He is priority
one. Jess.

INT. HOTEL – GRAND BALLROOM – NIGHT

*A grand dinner set-up with tables and tasteful music. Everyone in
formal wear. Post-dinner vibe. We might see a montage of servers
setting down desserts. Guests move freely around and mingle.*

Shiv is returning from the restroom on the raised opera-box level when she is approached by a sharp presidential hopeful named Rick Salgado (late forties).

SALGADO

Is that Shiv Roy? Good to see you here. Does this mean you've come to your senses?

SHIV

Me? Just shopping here in the marketplace of ideas, Rick.

SALGADO

Well step right in, Shiv, the water's fine. Pleased to have you!

He smiles. A reasonable-seeming guy. Shiv likes the flattery.

Look, I don't want to bum-rush you here. But can you help me? There's a feeding frenzy around your dad and I'm trying to stand apart from the – you know—

SHIV

The total fucking whack jobs?

SALGADO

Hey, don't get me wrong now. I'm with the base. The energy is extraordinary. I just also believe conservatism is about – facing facts.

SHIV

You know our internals always said you had the best shot of making the math work.

SALGADO

I like to think I can bring traditional conservatives into a more diverse dialogue.

'Facts'. 'Diverse'. He says the right words.

SHIV

ATN hasn't given you a lot of shine, it's true.

SALGADO

It's a – a – a—

(*terrifying*)

'exciting' time.

> *(with emphasis)*
> And not to be indiscreet but I just feel if I was in the White
> House, you were in the C-suite, we could mold?

SHIV

> Sir, you are very forward!

SALGADO

> That's forward?
> *(comedy 'whispered aside' but also in secret)*
> Hey, get your old man to make me president and I'll figure it out
> that you're CEO – even if I have to send your dad to prison!

Shiv laughs. Salgado laughs.

SHIV

> Oh will you now?

SALGADO

> Who knows?!

SHIV

> Very funny.

SALGADO

> It is funny. But maybe I will!

Shiv looks around and smiles. They carry on the joke.

> So it's decided. You land it for me and I'm sending your dad up
> river?

SHIV

> Unless he resigns in a month!

SALGADO

> Clean kill, baby!

SHIV

> Oh, man. Good stuff. Funny.

*Elsewhere, Tom and Greg chat with a guest named Vic Schmidt, who
served time for white-collar crimes. They look ill.*

VIC SCHMIDT

> Look, you want some advice? Here's a trick I picked up: Hoard
> mackerel tins. Sounds funny, I know. But you'll need them for
> bartering.

                    TOM

Okay. Greg, will you keep a note?

                VIC SCHMIDT

And the toilet. Ah. The toilet bowl. Your toilet is your stair machine, it's your bench, it's your fridge, it's your lover, it's your brother, it's your priest. Also, most important, and sometimes you can almost forget, but it's also your toilet.

                    GREG

Right, uh-huh. So that's, that's a big part of prison – then?

                VIC SCHMIDT

Boys, my toilet saw me more vulnerable than my wife has. He could be a perfect gentleman but he could also be a terrible bastard.

                    TOM

Yeah. Your toilet could be a bastard?

Logan huddles with Petkus, Michelle-Anne and the elite kingmakers of the party.

                  PETKUS

The key is unity. We have to move together on this or it won't work. If we can land on a favorite, I can pool the big money. But I need to know the messaging will be there to back me up?

Instinctively, they look to Logan.

I like him, but a lot of people are asking – is Boyer a fighter?

                   LOGAN

I don't care about the résumé. Or ideological purity. So long as they get it and they pop.

                    PETE

If you want someone who gets it, I've got your man: Connor Roy.

Connor is nearby and overhears. He tries to play it cool as he gravitates.

He's got a brand name, a war chest, populist appeal. And he's a fighter.

Awkward beat. It's Logan's son. How should they react?

> CONNOR

I believe I speak for my father when I offer a firm and robust – no comment!

Some polite laughs. But Logan doesn't laugh. He nods.

> LOGAN

Sure, I could see Connor.

The group quiets. Connor's eyes widen.

> PETKUS

Uh-huh, sure. I agree.

The group murmurs their assent. They go with Logan's flow. Meanwhile, Maxim leans in to Connor.

> MAXIM
> (*whispers*)

The sword has been pulled from the stone, my liege.

Connor smiles. A little scared. But he's vibrating.

Elsewhere, a few of the candidates engage in some jousting while Shiv and Roman watch.

> MENCKEN

Look, I'm a conservative. I like tradition. I doff my cap to Vice President Boyer for his years of loyal service.

> BOYER

Thank you. I believe you used to call me 'Martin Van Boring'?

> MENCKEN

Hey, c'mon, no. I *still* call you that.

A little tense.

> BOYER

Jeryd and I may differ in some areas. But we both agree this is the party of the working class now.

Shiv subtly rolls her eyes.

What? The richest counties in America are all blue. The Democrats and tech hold all the wealth.

Salgado steps in.

> SALGADO

I just think some of us get so high on 'owning the libs' that we forget to talk policy.

Some polite nods.

> MENCKEN

Rick loves to 'talk policy'. What he does is he memorizes a *National Review* issue from 2012 and recites it back to you. Cool policy, bro.

Salgado laughs, a bit rattled.

> SALGADO

And – and Jeryd hates to 'talk policy' because it means, you know – having one!

Roman smirks at Salgado's weak retort.

> ROMAN

Sick burn.

> MENCKEN

We're kidding. We like each other. I listen to his speeches every night. Help me drop off.

> SALGADO

Well maybe it's boring talking about populist solutions for working families but—

> MENCKEN

Rick, c'mon, you've jerked off to Reagan's headshot for thirty years, now you're Tom Joad?

> SHIV

So fucking boring.

> MENKCEN

What's that?

> SHIV

No, nothing. I've just seen your thing quite a lot.

> MENKCEN

What's my thing?

> SHIV

Oh, you know. YouTube provocateur bullshit, aristo-populism, rape is natural, 'it's all red pill, baby.' I'm just over it.

> MENKCEN

You read Plato?

> SHIV

Yeah. I've forgotten it, what happens?

> MENKCEN

Read Plato! Read Plato!

> SHIV

Don't want to! Don't want to!

> SALGADO

See, he's not interested in having a conversation. He just wants to yell loud enough to get on ATN.

> MENCKEN

Nah. Fuck ATN.

Logan is nearby. Some glances to see if he's listening.

> (*raising his voice now*)

No, really. ATN is treated as a bulwark. But it's dead. It's basically a pudding cup at five p.m. in the nursing home.

A few very nervous laughs. Is Logan getting all this?

> Honestly though. It doesn't speak to me. Or the people I talk to. It's status quo bedtime stories to maximize shareholder value. No disrespect, Logan Roy was an icon. But he's no longer relevant.

Logan continues his conversation. But there's no doubt he heard what Mencken said.

Meanwhile in the corner of the room, Greg is surrounded by a bunch of right-wing donors. They appear enthralled with Greg.

> RIGHT-WING DONOR

Fuck, Greg. That's amazing.

> GREG
> (*smiles, flustered*)

I mean, I guess so?

> RIGHT-WING DONOR 2

You have no idea. We've been trying to figure out how to sue Greenpeace for *years*.

> RIGHT-WING DONOR

Years.

> RIGHT-WING DONOR 2

Put the squeeze on those dolphin fuckers.

He slaps Greg's back. Greg is carried by their enthusiasm.

> GREG

Yeah. Ha ha.

> RIGHT-WING DONOR

What's the angle?

> GREG

Um, actually, defamation?

> RIGHT-WING DONOR 3

Interesting! How's that work?

> GREG

Well, my grandpa gave my inheritance to them? And someone posted a comment about it on their website? And it could contain a slight on my character? So my lawyer thinks it could be defamation? So yeah that's how I'm suing Greenpeace.

It's pretty fucking weird. But they nod.

> RIGHT-WING DONOR

I like it!

INT. HOTEL – STAIRWAY – NIGHT

Shiv and Roman make their way to Logan's suite after dinner. Tom and Greg follow.

> ROMAN
> (*off his phone*)

You recognize him? The jelly-boned low-T chinless fuck.

> SHIV

Have you told Dad yet?

> ROMAN

No. We should stop it, right?

> SHIV

Oh my god, can you stop being obsessed with Mom's husband, who cares, get over it.

> ROMAN

Get over it? It just happened. Our mother is getting married to some dickhead crooked-tooth turnip man. What is wrong is how little you care, you frozen bitch.

> SHIV

Poor Rome. His dreams of porking Mom slipping through his lubed-up fingers.

They head into—

INT. HOTEL – LOGAN'S SUITE – NIGHT

Shiv, Roman, join Connor and Hugo in Logan's suite for a late-night election-strategy talk. Colin stands by the door.

Some snacks and drinks and a feel of hunkering down.

> LOGAN

Okay, so. Come in. Come in.

Greg follows with Tom.

> HUGO

Um? Greg? Is Greg necessary?

> LOGAN

Just keep your trap shut. Watch.

> GREG

Yes, sir. Minimizing the Greg window.

Greg makes himself scarce. Logan starts.

> LOGAN

Right. There's a lot of chaff flying, lot of flapping but Ron and me are gonna have brunch and figure out how to pull for the same name. We need one voice on this, or we could fall apart and hand it to the fuck-fuck donkey gang. So. Who do we like?

Okay, is that this? They settle.

> SHIV
>
> Should we not kick it around? I mean – I mean, it feels like it's poised so, if you and Petkus come together and the other donors follow then—

> LOGAN
>
> Exactly. We're picking.

Then, as they weigh—

> We do not have all night.

Logan looks around.

> CONNOR
>
> I like Connor Roy.

People try to look serious about that. Make serious noises of consideration.

Logan looks at Shiv.

> SHIV
>
> Honestly? I think you go Dems.

Sigh of exasperation from Roman, Hugo. Logan looks at Roman.

> ROMAN
>
> I – I kinda like Mencken but, you know, he's been shitty, so if it was now I guess, Boyer. But can I note, I do not like Boyer. So.

Shiv shakes her head.

> What?

> SHIV
>
> Rome. No disrespect. Boyer's yesterday's papers. The Dems will run on change and blow him away.

> ROMAN
>
> Oh Mrs Politics? How many big races did you win as a consultant?

He counts on his fingers down to one – his middle finger giving Shiv the finger.

SHIV

Roman. Boyer's not a winner. We know that.

ROMAN

Then do we talk to Mencken and see if we can deal?

KERRY

The base does like him?

(*is she allowed to speak?*)

Right?

Logan gives her validation. Hugo nods. Shiv looks at Roman.

SHIV

Look. Okay. Can I just say. No. Okay? Mencken is— He's
a nativist integralist fuckhead. He's toxic. 'Medicare for All,
Abortions for None'. His idea of diplomacy is shooting roe
deer with Viktor Orbán and then starting a trade war with
China. I'm tough, I know there's the fucking carnival bark and
then there's the show but, he's outside the American political
tradition. I just think Waystar, we have a certain responsibility,
to, like, the American Republic and for the future of the—

Roman starts humming 'The Star Spangled Banner'.

For kids, and— Fuck you, Roman.

ROMAN

'Four score years and whatever my sister did bring forth from
her bedroom a cup of milky sputum.'

SHIV

He's talked about burning Korans and licensing press
credentials?

ROMAN

He's just shifting the Overton window.

SHIV

He's opening it and throwing union organizers out of it.

ROMAN

Stop Chicken-Littling us, Shiv. It just makes everyone want to
take a nap.

SHIV

Stop being a dirty little pixie whispering swastikas in Dad's ear.

> ROMAN

There you go again. So route one.

> SHIV

I'm not saying it's going to be full Third Reich. But I think there's a genuine possibility we slide into some Russian-Berlusconied-Brazilian fuck-pile.

> ROMAN

You have a trophy husband and several fur coats. You'll be fine.

> LOGAN

Tom? Who do you like?

> TOM

Me, I think – I think Shiv talks a lot of sense. I also jibe with Salgado.

> ROMAN

You do? Can I watch you jibe sometime? At some special jibing club?

Beat. People think.

> GREG

Do I get a vote?

> ROMAN

Sure. You get to vote at the election, with the other folks.

> GREG

Right? I guess it feels like you maybe get a bigger vote in here?

> ROMAN

Easy, Castro.

> SHIV

What about considering the other way though, Dad? The Dems?

Tom's phone buzzes. He looks at the screen: 'Kendall'. A flash of confusion, then worry. Why would Kendall be calling at this hour?

After a beat, he quietly excuses himself from the room.

> TOM

Um, excuse me—

They keep talking, barely aware he left. He finds a secluded area of the suite and hesitantly answers his phone.

                              (*answers*)
   Hello?

Intercut with:

INT. KENDALL'S CAR – LATE NIGHT
                         KENDALL
   Tom.

                         TOM
   Uh-huh?

                         KENDALL
   Where are you?

                         TOM
   Um, Virginia? Why?

                         KENDALL
   No, where are you in the building?

INT. HOTEL – LOGAN'S SUITE – NIGHT

Tom is back with the gang.

                         LOGAN
   Look, end of the day, aside from the business, this crop of
   Dems, they want to pull everything down but that can't put up
   a fucking tent. They're zealots, and they believe in magic, that
   some words are bad magic. Fuck 'em.

Beat.

                         HUGO
   Boyer is likely to be flexible over the DOJ?

                         SHIV
   Not if he doesn't win. Which he won't.

                         CONNOR
   Reeks of 2008. Dripping with MySpace.

SHIV

Did Willa tell you to say that?

HUGO

We're actually hearing murmurs that the DOJ is cooling down. The case is weakening. That no one big is likely to get jail.

It hangs for a beat. Then, he scrambles to correct—

With the notable exception of Tom, obviously. Sorry, Tom.

TOM

Please. Hugo. Understood.

Shiv puts a consoling hand on his hand. But Tom thinks again about what he's heard on the phone from Kendall and texts him a positive, nervously.

SHIV

Look. If you're not going to go blue, then it has to be Salgado?

Roman makes a bored noise.

CONNOR

Señor Dickless. Captain of the Tampa Bay Cuckaneers.

Tom makes his excuses, waves phone, heads out.

TOM

Cyd! Excuse me. Duty calls!

Shiv barely notices, waves him off.

SHIV

Look, I don't like him, he's a neocon pretending to be a paleocon but he talks base and he'll bring new demographics.

ROMAN

Shiv, can I just say I know we have our differences but you are just *so brave* for picking the brown man. Should we send you a particular medal for white women who like brown men?

SHIV

Amazing! Just racist. Just being a racist now?

ROMAN

Oooh oooh, I'm the good girl, I pretend to care about people, because no one ever cared about me!

SHIV
'Mummy loved me too much because I was the runt of the litter.'
Haven't you got a message from Mum for Dad, Rome?

Logan looks at Roman, who decides he might as well just drop the bomb—

ROMAN
Fine fuck you. Yes, I do. Yeah – Mum's getting remarried.

LOGAN
To Bertie Woofter?

ROMAN
No, Peter, Peter Munion?

LOGAN
You're kidding. The fucking seat-sniffer? He's been hanging round for forty years.

ROMAN
Yeah and she – *they* would – love it apparently if you came to their Tuscan wedding?

LOGAN
La-di-dah! And they sent you as the messenger boy?

Logan laughs. He likes that.

He wants my juice ah? Heheh. Who does he want to fuck, her or me?

Logan smiles at Kerry.

EXT. HOTEL – NIGHT

Tom comes out into the dark, looking about.

TOM
(*into phone*)
I can't be seen with you. I know a place—

INT. WAFFLE HUT — NIGHT

Tom enters to see Kendall sitting at a booth, prepared, somewhat ignited. He takes a seat. A waitress immediately joins them. Tom knows what he wants with only a quick glance.

> TOM
>
> Hey. The griddle hero special. Double hash browns, fully loaded. Plain waffle and a large cup of room-temperature water.

Kendall hands his menu back.

> KENDALL
>
> I might just watch him.

Waitress exits.

> TOM
>
> You know Rasputin would take a dose of arsenic with breakfast each morning, to build up tolerance.

Smiles.

> KENDALL
>
> So look, I've always liked you, Tom.

> TOM
>
> I like you too, Kendall. I mean, I have notes.

> KENDALL
>
> Haha, yeah well me too.

> TOM
>
> I think mine might be more extensive.

> KENDALL
>
> But look. I think I can help you, get you out of this mess, where you're going?

> TOM
>
> Uh-huh? Well nothing is certain, so.

> KENDALL
>
> You know they're calling you the Christmas tree?

Tom looks at Kendall. Not about to break cover.

> TOM
>
> Perhaps it's because I'm tall and jolly?

KENDALL

Maybe? You think?

They smile at one another – Tom still not showing any interest yet.

But I think maybe you don't want to be the chit the company offers up when it has no choice?

TOM

Well obviously I'd prefer that not to happen. But it's complicated.

KENDALL

It is. It's complicated. But are you interested in an alternative, theoretically?

TOM

I have, of late, decided not to tarry much with hope.

But Tom's face is not saying no—

KENDALL

Okay. Well, my case is strong, but—
(*then, more honesty*)
No, my case is fine, it has gaps. But if I had someone who could say nothing gets signed off on without my dad's say-so. Which we both know to be true.

TOM

Oh I don't know if I do know that?

KENDALL

Uh-huh?

TOM

I'm just a humble servant.

Kendall nods, sees his shield.

KENDALL

I admire you, man. You're a long way from home. You're far from the tree. You've played your hand well and you're sitting at the top table.

But Tom's not giving him anything.

443

> TOM

Well shucks. Thank you. I fell in love with your sister, is what happened.

> KENDALL

Sure. Sure, man. The country mouse and the hot tamale. And I suppose you're just a long glass of water? No agenda?

> TOM
> (*whatever you want*)

I guess.

> KENDALL

Well. Here's how it goes. I've got new lawyers, who are amazing. I've been in to SDNY, and it's honestly just a huge relief. Don't underestimate the cognitive dissonance you're experiencing – lying, hiding. But pretty soon: granted immunity. And you're not going to prison. Think about that. That's nice? Right?

They look at one another. The waitress brings food for Tom.

Check is on me.

> TOM

Wow. Suddenly everyone wants to buy me dinner?

INT. HOTEL – LOGAN'S SUITE – NIGHT

Logan, Kerry, Hugo, Shiv, Roman and Greg still talking.

> HUGO

I guess. It is tough. Boyer – there's questions on his cut-through. Mencken – we don't know if he'll dance. Salgado is – you know? Meh? I guess, there are other names?

Connor coughs.

> LOGAN

We have to be united. It's a disaster if we splinter.

Connor coughs.

> SHIV

Salgado has a great narrative?

                    ROMAN
Quit butt-huffing Salgado, Shiv. We all agreed to pretend your
political career was real, out of pity, but this actually matters.

                    SHIV
'Ooh I'm Roman, I'm a rebel, except where's a big daddy?
Please rule me, please punish me.'

Connor coughs.

                    LOGAN
What?

                    CONNOR
What? Nothing. No.

                    LOGAN
I mean, what about Con?

                    CONNOR
Interesting. I do think that idea has a good deal of promise. I do.

*Roman and Shiv try to nod and not be too rude right now, need allies
and just don't want to be horrible.*

                    LOGAN
I could see it.

                    CONNOR
If you can see it, should we talk about it?

                    LOGAN
Kids?

                    ROMAN
Sure. I dunno. Yeah.

His dad is looking at him.

I mean *really*? Crap-pants for president?

Logan nods.

Um. I guess. Sure. I dunno. They're all fucking weirdos, I guess,
so why not? No offense, Con.

Connor looks like: Well, bit taken.

> LOGAN

I mean, he's a good-looking kid. He's smart, in his way. Fucking
Joe Kennedy did it for his boys? Get him in there on a smile and
a shoeshine, get Ron and everyone behind him?

> CONNOR

I'd fight so fucking hard for this family, Dad.

> LOGAN

Shiv, as a political consultant how would you rate him?

> SHIV

Con? Um, well, you know?

Deep breath.

> CONNOR

It's okay, Siobhan. I have elephant hide.

> SHIV

Well, not huge name ID but – the family name will be a factor—

> CONNOR

A positive. One of many.

> SHIV

I mean he doesn't have a track record?

> CONNOR

Nothing to beat me with. I'm a clean skin.

> SHIV

I guess, in terms of presentation and connection skills . . .

> CONNOR

Tick. Tick.

Logan seems to be considering it.

> LOGAN

He can walk and chew gum. He pisses pretty straight.

> CONNOR

Straight as an arrow. I piss policy laser.

> ROMAN

I mean is this serious? We're talking about trying to make
Connor president. Of the United States of America?

CONNOR

Rome. Big tent, come on in.

ROMAN

Sure. No, fine. Fine. I might call my dentist. He's a possible?

LOGAN

Reagan was outstanding but it was skin deep. You don't have to
be fucking Thomas Jefferson. Index cards and a team.
(*thinks*)
Greg – would you vote for Connor?

GREG

Me? Would I? Um—

LOGAN

Honestly?

GREG

Honestly. It depends. I could maybe see myself – spoiling my
ballot in his favor, depending on the opposition?

LOGAN

Shiv? What do you think, is it nuts?

SHIV

Look. I love Con, I do. But if we're talking about him seriously
I think we have to look at Salgado. Can I get him up here?

LOGAN

Okay. And I'm still curious about— Hugo? Can you call Boyer?

Hugo dials. Talks to front desk.

ROMAN

If she's bringing in Soggy Salgado I want to see if we can tame
Mencken. Okay?

Hugo nods he has him.

LOGAN

Speakerphone.

BOYER
(*on speakerphone*)

Er? Hello? Logan?

> LOGAN

Dave, it's Logan. How are you?

> BOYER

Oh um, good. Logan. How are you?

> LOGAN

Oh, fine. Listen, I'm in my suite. Would you fancy dropping by?

> BOYER

Um, it's pretty late, Logan.

> LOGAN

Uh-huh.

Silence. Logan lets it hang uncomfortably long. The static buzzes—

> BOYER

But – sure. Sure.

> LOGAN

Great, Dave, and listen. My fridge is bare. Don't suppose you could run me over a Coke?

Boyer can't quite believe it.

> BOYER

A Coke?

> LOGAN

Yeah. Just a Coke.

Beat.

> BOYER

Do you wanna call room service?

Long beat.

> LOGAN

If you don't have a Coke maybe there's something else?

> BOYER

Uh-huh?

> LOGAN

Maybe you could fire the deputy attorney general?

> BOYER

Fire the DAG?

Beat, then, Logan laughs.

>   LOGAN
> I'm kidding, Dave! But listen, would you come over for a chat?
> Is it convenient?

*Logan signals for Hugo and Greg to leave him and Shiv and Roman
and Kerry now. Greg stands to leave. Something is weighing on him.
Takes a breath.*

>   GREG
> Um. I will go, but I just want to say, I think I owe it to my
> country to say – I don't think you should crown, or make,
> Connor president. Sorry, Connor. That's it. Goodnight.

Greg exits with Hugo.

EXT. WAFFLE HUT/PARKING LOT – NIGHT

In the parking lot. Kendall and Tom continue talking.

>   TOM
> So, thanks for the waffles.

He's ready to go, but Kendall walks with him.

>   KENDALL
> Uh-huh. So?

>   TOM
> Let me think.

>   KENDALL
> Fine. Okay. I see. It's tough for you. Shiv seems safe, Dad seems
> powerful but—

Tom stares.

> You think she'll still be there, waiting for you after prison??

This can't help but land a little.

> She's my sister but, man, my family? You've mated with a
> different species. Patience? Selflessness? Monogamy? . . . Not so
> much.

>   TOM
> You know prison was *my* idea. Not Shiv's. Not Logan's. Mine.

449

> KENDALL
>
> And how hard did she try and stop you? Did she cry?

> TOM
>
> Shiv's a warrior.

> KENDALL
>
> I think she would have cried if it had been her?

> TOM
>
> And how exactly do you think it works if I come over? How is it better when I tell my wife, who I love, and this family, that I'm turning against them?

> KENDALL
>
> She'll respect you. Tell her what's she doing. Bring her with us, Logan goes down. And Shiv knows who the fucking man is.

Could be true.

> C'mon, man. Just sack up for once. Nut up.

> TOM
>
> You make some sense.

Tom looks around the quiet dark parking lot in the middle of Virginia.

> But – and I don't want to be insulting, but having been around a bit, my hunch is you're going to get fucked. Because I've seen you get fucked a lot and I've never seen Logan get fucked once.

> KENDALL
>
> So are you really happy to be the Waystar bitch?

> TOM
>
> Would I be happier being yours?

It's over. Tom starts to walk. Kendall takes a photo of Tom as he leaves. Tom sees him clearly, his desperation. It feeds him.

> Great. Classy. I have to get back.
> (then)
> You know what they're doing in his suite? They're picking the next president.

KENDALL
(*after him*)
I like you, man. I like you. I'm here.

INT. HOTEL – LOBBY/BAR – NIGHT

Tom enters, deep in thought.

As he walks through the lobby or up to the elevator bank, there is a commotion in a bar he can just about see into.

He is in a quiet hotel space – just a few stragglers. But in the bar or restaurant area the night is going strong.

He can see some odd flashes of action. The billionaires and donors are mostly elsewhere, this is the fringe folk, the PAC chairs and folk closer to the base. The true-believer consultants.

As he passes by a group of Proud Boy-types are doing shots with Greg. Or perhaps they have hoisted Greg onto their shoulders and are marching him around like a king.

LOUD GUY
Fuck Greenpeace!

GANG
Greg! Greg! Greg! Greg! Greg!

In the center of the gang, or on their shoulders, Greg laughs nervously. But also pretty intoxicated by it all. Tom looks, doesn't have time to fully take in and moves on. Up the stairs. Thinking.

INT. HOTEL – CORRIDOR OUTSIDE LOGAN'S SUITE – NIGHT

Tom approaches as Salgado is leaving with his chief aide. A Secret Service security detail is outside befitting the presence of the vice president inside.

INT. HOTEL – LOGAN'S SUITE – NIGHT

Tom re-enters the room. Shiv and Connor and Logan are there with Boyer. Boyer has a political aide.

> BOYER

So yeah. On tech I mean the strategy is clear. And I hear you on GoJo, I personally don't see that there would be any regulatory issues.

Logan nods, ending this part of the evening.

> LOGAN

Uh-huh. Well thanks, Dave. You've certainly given us a lot to think about.

He's drawing things to a close.

Boyer and his acolytes start to leave.

> CONNOR

Still no one really tackling microplastics? Interesting. Well great to see you, my very good adversaries.

Connor guides them to the door, shaking hands. Boyer wonders how it has come to this. – Tom regards the scene. Power being exercised.

Across the room, Logan clocks him and gives him a wink and pats a cushion or nods for him to come and sit nearby.

> LOGAN

Tom. You're a good Midwestern mulch cow, who do you like?

Boyer might still be there just in earshot, so this is playful, Tom smiles as they smile at him.

> TOM

Let me ponder a moment.

Tom sits. Shiv looks at him questioningly – where has he been? Can tell he's not quite the same Tom anymore.

INT. HOTEL – LOGAN'S SUITE – BATHROOM – NIGHT

Meanwhile: Mencken and Roman in a large marble-and-glass hotel bathroom.

> ROMAN

Fun shit before. Tripping the light fantastic on the grandpappy's ballsacks.

They have a good vibe between them. Jamming on the same cultural frequency.

MENCKEN

What about when I called your dad bullshit? Did that bump?

ROMAN

I mean, sure. Whatever. Hardcore.

MENCKEN

Because the thing is, this monkey don't dance.

ROMAN

Nope. No. No dancing here. Not in Pappy's bathroom.

Roman smiles. Mencken smiles: How was my dance? Did you like it?

I guess the thing is. I'm just going to say it. Fascists are kind of cool, but not really you know, so is that a thing? A problem.

MENCKEN

Seriously? Me? I just don't have a lot of boundaries. St Augustine. Thomas Aquinas, Schumacher, I'll borrow from anyone. And if Franco or H or Carl Schmitt had a good pitch, fuck it, I'm a Man for All Seasons.

ROMAN

Uh-huh? 'H'? You know there was a very naughty boy called H who—

MENCKEN

I'm a fully fledged, Democrat. A well-regulated election is a transmission frequency for God's grace.

ROMAN

You really are a Christian aren't you?

MENCKEN

My only thing is, who's a stakeholder? Like, I've been tending my little garden for a hundred years and then forty new guys roll in on the back of a truck playing their boombox and it's put to a vote and they decide to give my farm to them. I'm like, 'Sorry, what happened?' Maybe you have to put in before you get to take out?

ROMAN

And who gets to – to join?

453

> MENCKEN

Well. People trust people who look like them. That's just a
scientific fact. They'll give more tax dollars to help them. Now
you can integrate new elements, of course, but c'mon, *slowly*.
I mean, fuck, why not? I like this country, let's just take a beat
before we fundamentally alter its composition? What is wrong
with an abundance of caution?

Roman looks at him.

> ROMAN

And in terms of this here. There's a thing, right? I mean I get it,
you're 6G, we're Betamax. But you need us, right? Our news,
viewers. The almost-deads. Big slice of pie.

> MENCKEN

If I'm the nominee are any of them really gonna vote against
me?

Roman weighs it. Fair point.

> ROMAN

This is going to be a shit show going into the convention. You
need our push.

> MENCKEN

Or maybe you need mine?

> ROMAN

Uh-huh?

> MENCKEN

And where are you in all this?

> ROMAN

Me? I'm creeping on the come-up.

> MENCKEN

Oh yeah?

> ROMAN

I've got plans for ATN. Sluice out the oatmeal, add some
sriracha. No more 'Dave Plain-Penis and here's what the Dow
did today'. I want to make it more like . . . you?

> MENCKEN

Like?

ROMAN

My vision? Um . . . Smash the system. Fresh faces. Poach a couple TikTok psychos. E-girls with guns and Juul pods. Get me some straight-shot blacks and Latinos. Brain science and strength training for the working-class coalition. No more pillows and bedpans, we're strictly bone broth and dick pills. Deep-state conspiracy hour but with a fucking wink, funny. And it's all kinda set for the star of the show: President Jeryd Mencken.

Mencken considers. Roman isn't bad at this.

MENCKEN

Look, bottom line is I do think your dad is bullshit.

ROMAN

My dad's a Titan.

MENCKEN

But, if anything, it's him who doesn't like me. So look. I'm not going to jump through any hoops for the guy?

INT. HOTEL — LOGAN'S SUITE — NIGHT

Jeryd and Roman appear from the bathroom.

Everyone looks at them.

Jeryd walks towards Logan.

Pulls a can of Coke from his pocket. Kisses it. Cracks it and puts it on a side table next to Logan.

MENCKEN

Heard you wanted one.

LOGAN

Thank you.

MENCKEN

Anointed with a Coke.

Gives a little nod, almost a bow of appreciation and heads on out. He leaves. They all watch.

LOGAN

That was nice.

ROMAN

He's nice.

SHIV

He is not nice.

ROMAN

Look, Dad. We came to market to buy you a nice milk cow but we found ourselves a fucking T-Rex. Okay? He's box office. The guy's diesel. He's good on camera. He's fun. He'll fight. Viewers will eat from his hand. No downside.

SHIV

Yeah, Dad. Let's invade Poland. No downside.

ROMAN

Oh please.

SHIV

His chief of staff broke a kid's jaw at a rally.

ROMAN

Meh meh. If we don't come to an accommodation, we get outflanked and we lose the ATN fucking dollar machine when we need cash to fight tech.

(*then*)

Look. I guess Shiv wants her way, and I want my way, and Connor wants his way, so it's even and you have to—

SHIV

It is not even! I'm sorry. But my opinion counts more, okay? It does. It just does. I know this. Okay? I know.

(*then*)

People hate the guy. *Hate* him. You need to look at the climate—

As Shiv talks Logan looks over to Kerry. She looks like: Go for it. Roman is right. Logan interrupts—

LOGAN

The climate said I was going down. The climate said I should just step aside.

(*shrugs*)

I guess I'm a climate denier.

Logan gets up. End of the night.

456

> SHIV

Seriously, is this how it happens? Dad. C'mon. Seriously, he's just – he's fucking dangerous.

> LOGAN

Goodnight.

Logan gets up and Kerry leads him through from the living room of his suite towards the bedroom.

It could just be her helping him but she goes on into the bedroom. Shiv looks at Roman.

> ROMAN

Your polling was off again, Shiv. Definitely fucking.

Roman heads out, sensing he's victorious.

DAY THREE

INT. HOTEL – PALM COURT/LOBBY – LATE MORNING

A large buffet brunch service has been set up in a dining room, perhaps spilling into an outdoor seating area as well. The Future Freedom Summit guests have gathered for an end-of-the-weekend farewell brunch.

Willa and Connor nurse his wounds.

> CONNOR

Well. It was close. It was very close. But the money's on Mencken now. Donor class, the establishment.

> WILLA

Well I got a lot done on the play?

> CONNOR

Great. That's great. No that's the big takeaway from the weekend.

> WILLA

It's a satire. This place is actually great, for material.

> CONNOR

Oh a satire? On here? No! That's the one thing these people fear!

> WILLA

Yeah?

> CONNOR

What I'm actually thinking now though is do I march the Conheads off third party? The whole two-party horse race stinks. Maybe me and my merry band are the ones to blow it up?

Elsewhere Logan, who huddles with Kerry.

> KERRY

Mencken's going to take the weekend straw poll and Petkus has confirmed he's backing.

> LOGAN

Good. Sunday show pushed him this morning. Let's see if this horse can run.

> KERRY

Also CAA is calling?

> LOGAN

Uh-huh.

> KERRY

They're saying Michelle-Anne has lots of options but feels like ATN is home.

> LOGAN

Fine. Yeah, get Tom on it.

He leans into her ear.

Tell him to fill the trough for all the little piggies.

Tom is serving up food for himself, with Greg alongside. They move along the breakfast buffet with a hint of prison.

> TOM

So I saw you. You looked like you were having a whale of a time up there? Flying on the wings of white power?

> GREG

Yeah, I was commandeered.

> TOM

Did it feel good, when the fascists hoisted you up like the Stanley Cup?

> GREG

They're not good guys. I should have said something.

> TOM

I'm kidding, Greg. You can't. You can't change people's minds.

> GREG

Sure.

Greg swallows, looks at Tom. Maybe they do change people's minds. Tom looks at him.

> TOM

Greg, shut up. Give people what they want, then walk away. After that, it's their shit.

Meanwhile Shiv chats with Salgado.

> SHIV

It's funny, here I thought you were gonna be the guy who put my dad in prison?

> SALGADO

Ha. Yeah, right. That was funny.

We hear Logan across the patio calling for Shiv. It draws the attention of numerous others.

> LOGAN
> (*waving her over*)

Siobhan!

Shiv excuses herself and walks over to Roman, who's with a smiling Logan.

> ROMAN

We're doing a photo.

> SHIV

Um. Right?

> LOGAN

Family photo.

459

Shiv sees Mencken gathering with Tom.

SHIV

With him? Um, No.

LOGAN

We're all going to be in it. Let's go.

SHIV

We've got enough people in the shot. I'm good.

LOGAN

Get in the photo, please.

Logan is trying to contain his anger. He doesn't want to be part of another family scene in public.

Siobhan, are you a part of this family or not?

Shiv thinks. Is she one of them? She hesitates for a moment. Quietly. Mencken is motioning for her to come next to him.

SHIV

Look, I'm not standing next to him. I'll be in the photo, but not right by him?

Logan considers this and nods. He'll let her think she's won a little victory.

LOGAN

Fine. You win, Pinky. You win.

Shiv walks over pointedly to the other side of the group to pose for a photo that will live on the internet forever.

As they get in place, Logan leans into Roman, ruffles his hair or chucks his cheek.

Nice going this weekend, son.

Roman smiles, bathed for once in his father's validation.

Logan, Roman, Tom and Shiv join Mencken. They 'walk and talk' with Mencken as a photographer snaps some 'candid' shots of the group.

Shiv now stands two feet away from the new face of conservatism, trying to get her face to look right.

Episode Seven
TOO MUCH BIRTHDAY

Written by Georgia Pritchett & Tony Roche
Directed by Lorene Scafaria

Original air date 28 November 2021

Cast

LOGAN ROY	Brian Cox
KENDALL ROY	Jeremy Strong
GREG HIRSCH	Nicholas Braun
SHIV ROY	Sarah Snook
ROMAN ROY	Kieran Culkin
CONNOR ROY	Alan Ruck
TOM WAMBSGANS	Matthew Macfadyen
FRANK VERNON	Peter Friedman
COLIN STILES	Scott Nicholson
KARL MULLER	David Rasche
GERRI KELLMAN	J. Smith-Cameron
WILLA FERREYRA	Justine Lupe
KERRY CASTELLABATE	Zoë Winters
BERRY SCHNEIDER	Jihae
COMFREY PELLITS	Dasha Nekrasova
RAVA	Natalie Gold
NAOMI PIERCE	Annabelle Dexter-Jones
ATTENDANT	Kyra Weeks
NURSE	Aisling Halpin
WAITER	Charlie Franklin
BOUNCER	Gordon Tashjian
LUKAS MATSSON	Alexander Skarsgård
SERVER	Isabel Pask
TECHNICAL DIRECTOR	Ted Koch
COMPLIMENTER 1	Hope Ward
COMPLIMENTER 2	Marchael Giles
COMPLIMENTER 3	Sean Bell
REECE	Drew Ledbetter
ZACH	John Skelley
CARTER	Intae Kim
GARY	Greg Brostrom
ASSISTANT	Grace Dumdaw

INT. KENDALL'S PARTY – BIG ROOM – DAY

Kendall is pre-party in relaxed clothing, holding a mic.

Naomi is there and, beyond, is Comfrey, who is covering the party while her boss does bigger stuff. A chief party planner and a number of helpers.

Kendall listens as the opening bars of 'Honesty' by Billy Joel play. He comes in with the vocal and sings the first few lines pretty well . . .

After a bit he's heard enough and gives thumbs up to sound engineer, who gives him a thumbs up, and then Kendall nods to the party planner who nods to technicians in a control booth and the music goes off.

Kendall looks at Naomi.

> KENDALL
> Yeah?

> NAOMI
> Yeah. Yeah. I mean, yeah. Pretty good, man.

> KENDALL
> Yeah. Funny, right. Good?

> NAOMI
> I think good. And you're gonna do the . . .

She motions. He discussed some pretty mad stuff. Maybe we can see some props, a crucifix being wheeled in or adjusted.

> . . . your, whole – thing?

> KENDALL
> Yeah I mean, fuck it, right? I think, balls to the wall, just fucking, nut-nut. Pure – excess. Full bore, yeah?

She's pretty sure it's good. But is it?

NAOMI

Yeah.

KENDALL

No?

NAOMI

No, yeah I think.

KENDALL

It's like, just: bleurggh! 'I'm throwing the grossest, bestest freakout fuckalalooza and it's bonkers' and I own it because if you don't give a fuck, no one can hurt you. I've gone Anti-Fragile. I can accommodate anything. If I start second-guessing, it collapses.

NAOMI

Right. No, I think that is right.

She does think he's probably right. He can see her scintilla of doubt – but he can roll over it.

KENDALL

Fuck you, c'mon, Nay! What do I want like forty buddies in St Barts with pills, and we all go home with headaches? Nah, this is, like, it's the full fucking thing.

A large prop or sculpture or a lighting balloon might be being brought through.

INT. WAYSTAR – ROMAN'S OFFICE/BULLPEN – DAY

Shiv and Roman, Tom. Reviewing some documents in Roman's office. Roman is on edge, he's been working hard. Couple of Roman's assistants and colleagues are packing up.

Meanwhile Tom flicks through photos on his phone of different prisons, again, distracted.

ROMAN

Okay. We got this. Right? This all makes sense? He has some binders on how to make an acquisition of GoJo work.

Shiv flicks. It's good work but she sees another angle.

> SHIV

Uh-huh. I think this is—
> *(flicks dismissively)*

great work, Rome. But obviously the main thing is, the
organizational–cultural thing.

He bites his lip and winces but she spots it.

I think everyone agrees GoJo makes sense. No one needs
persuading of that.

> ROMAN

Well, kind of regret staying up all night with my assholes then?!

He nods to the last of his departing team.

> SHIV

It's just about us here who get it—
> *(re the three of them)*

oiling the wheels and making sure – there's no friction.

Roman looks at her. She's patronizing him, again.

> ROMAN

Well. Of course. I mean, I would say we can handle the human
stuff without too much issue. That needn't concern us, it comes
naturally, to some of us—
> *(me!)*

which is why I have focussed so much work on the integration
benefits, and deal detail.

He nods to the binders.

> SHIV

Great. I'm just saying, big picture.

> ROMAN

Well the big picture is made from small details?

> TOM

Guys? Honestly, this is nerves. You've done great work. Let's go
help your dad make the deal, okay?

They head out towards Logan's office.

> ROMAN

And you going tonight?

> SHIV

Ken Fest? I wouldn't think so. I mean maybe if Matsson does, for follow-up?

> TOM

Gonna be pretty horrific. Your brother in a porta potty rolling down a hill.

> ROMAN
> (*wants to go*)
> I might have to go, just to see how bad it is.

But she can see he wants to go and see him.

> SHIV

Aww. 'Brudders'.

> ROMAN

Fuck you. It's pure rubbernecking.

Up ahead they see Kerry closing the blinds in Logan's office.

> TOM

Okay? What's this?

> SHIV

Is Matsson here already?

> ROMAN

Or she's about to give birth to Dad's baby while we chant a Satanic mass?

> SHIV
> (*re Kerry*)
> It's like he's having a midlife crisis aged eighty.

> ROMAN

It's fine.

> SHIV

Rome, he's fucking an assistant who's fifty years younger than him?

> ROMAN

That's not a crisis. That's normal. That's the opposite of a crisis.

INT. WAYSTAR – LOGAN'S OFFICE – DAY

Logan, Kerry, Karl, Frank, Gerri are gathered. Logan, Gerri and Kerry are high on secret news.

Shiv and Roman, Tom join as champagne is passed around.

> ROMAN
> Hi. Oh, okay? Champagne?

> SHIV
> Did you do it already, Dad? You didn't land GoJo already without us?

Kerry hands Roman one. And Shiv.

> GERRI
> We're not celebrating.

> LOGAN
> 'Long road ahead'.

> FRANK
> Lovely long open road. Wind in our hair!

> ROMAN
> Okay, Boxcar Willie, what the fuck's going on?

Logan looks at Gerri: You say.

> GERRI
> We've had a vibration. I've been speaking to a contact with connections at the DOJ—

> ROMAN
> Laurie?

> GERRI
> *(not telling)*
> We have a number of friends. And, the word is, on the down-low: they've seen everything now and reviewed and they're happy with how we're engaging and they are coming to the view that Kendall overpromised. And – perhaps – some men were terribly naughty back in the day but . . . nothing systemic, and nothing sanctioned!

                              KARL

Lots and lots of breaches. Terrible breaches, regrettable
breaches. Of codes and regulations and little bitty laws but—

                              LOGAN

It's going to be a number.

                              ROMAN

Just a number?

                              GERRI

Nothing custodial. For anyone.

                              TOM

No – prison?

                              GERRI

Nuh-huh. Nope, we don't think so.

*Delight all round. People congratulate Tom, who can't quite take it in.
After a moment, Shiv remembers to offer a gesture to Tom – a hand
on his arm or kiss his cheek or something.*

                              FRANK

Here's to us!

                              ALL

To us!

                              LOGAN

And to justice!

*This is done head on, no irony, Logan doesn't believe any of them
have ever really done anything wrong.*

                              ALL

To justice!

*They raise their glasses and drink. Logan touches Tom on his arm,
shoulder, whispers.*

                              LOGAN
                       (*with a wink and a squeeze*)

I'll remember.

This goes through Tom like a huge voltage of electricity.

Shiv clocks. Mixed feelings. Relief but also annoyance that her dad can get away with anything.

Plus – she's recalibrating. Didn't want him to suffer but she'd made peace with Tom going away.

Roman looks at her, he can see she's got ever so slightly mixed feelings. She clocks him watching her and responds.

> SHIV
> Well, congratulations, Dad. You've done it again.
> *(then)*
> It's great. But let's try hard not to do it again, right? But no. Lessons learned. Here's to Tom!

> GERRI
> Long road ahead. No premature celebrations.

> ROMAN
> Amen to that!
> *(finishes his glass; to Kerry)*
> Top me up, wontcha?

> KARL
> Take me home, country roads!

> GERRI
> We will continue to work with our friends at Vincent, Hertz and Voss to help the DOJ find that accursed piece of paper where a naughty minion wrote down the wrong piece of corporate guidance!

> KARL
> Gosh darn that guy!

> FRANK
> Fiddlesticks!

> KARL
> And here's to the friendships we'll make along the way!

> TOM
> Just need to pay a visit to the little boys' room.

As he heads out . . .

LOGAN

Okay! Enough mooning. Enough backslapping. GoJo! GoJo
GoJo GoJo.

*Tom walks out of Logan's towards the elevators, a lot of emotions
simmering just under the surface.*

INT. WAYSTAR – GREG'S OFFICE – DAY

*Greg's at his desk typing an email. Tom comes in bursting with
happiness—*

TOM

Hello-oh-oh-oh-oh-oh!

GREG

Hello?

TOM

Greg – can you—? Scoot over a little please?

Tom comes round to Greg's side of the desk.

Greg makes way as Tom positions himself behind the desk.

(*merry*)

I thank you!

*Then. Tom checks his position, takes the strain and feel of the desk's
weight, prepares himself, and then – flips the whole thing over in one,
crashing the monitors and all the stuff off the desk away from him.
And issuing a great bellow of relief:*

AAAGHHHHHHHHHHHH!!!!!!

Greg watches, inching back.

Yes! Yes yes yes yes fucking yes!

*Now Tom kicks and swipes and punches a few things, swiping stuff
off surfaces, kicks hard a trash basket, all in joyful abandon, a dance
of destruction.*

Greg watches, grinning, fearful, perplexed.

*Tom might punch a wall in final celebration, denting the plasterboard
and exiting.*

Fuck yeah!

He maybe actually beats his chest in triumph and joy.

> GREG
> Tom, what is it, are you okay?

> TOM
> Apologies, Greg, I may have gotten a little carried away. I just popped by to say: No one is going to jail! The Waystar Two are free!

Then with a sound effect of popping his lips for each motion he playfully slaps Greg on each cheek, left then right, then mimes punching him in the groin.

Then Tom walks out.

We stay with Greg as he looks at the contents of his room. What the fuck was that?

. . . Slowly he starts to pick things up.

INT. KENDALL'S APARTMENT — DAY

Kendall is at his place with Naomi, a few other friends, including Zach, Reece, Carter and a couple of others. It's the pre-party.

Kendall is looking down at the venue on FaceTime on an iPad, he's got a drink on the go. Maybe there's a blunt on the go that he gets offered at some point.

Comfrey, in the venue in a back area, is showing him stuff from his party, Kendall enjoys it.

> KENDALL
> Yeah. Yeah. Oh yeah. Show me the cross again. Oh yeah. Looks good, Comfrey-dumphrey.
> (calling)
> Nay! Come look at my cross. Look. Look at this shit. Hahaha!

Comfrey tries to show something but it's indistinct.

> It's fucking bananas. Zach, look.

> ZACH
> Shit's gonna be lit!

KENDALL

And what are we looking at, what are the responses looking like?

COMFREY
(*onscreen*)

Um, good, yeah, I think about eighty percent of your A-list are yesses. Fifteen percent are maybes.

KENDALL

Maybes are nos, let's not live in a dreamworld. But who's in?

COMFREY

Um, off the top of my head, it's great: Diane, Barry, JP, David, Anna, Tom, Tory, Lauren, Aerin, Ashley and MK, Zara, Jessica and Jerry, Andy C., Jeff, Elon, Lukas, Jennifer and Emma yesses. Chloe is maybe. Do you want me to message you this?

KENDALL

Uh-huh and the sibs?

COMFREY
(*no answer*)

Um. Yeah – um—?

KENDALL

Whatever. Fine. This is fucking cool, Comfrey, and you have a good time too yeah? Everyone. Servers, fucking, the imagineers, the DJ crew, this is highly egalitarian, like: 'Do your job, but fucking get your drink on, get your buzz on.' Okay? There's no boundaries if you're cool. Mission control out!

INT. WAYSTAR – BULLPEN/LOGAN'S OFFICE – DAY

Tom walks back through the bullpen, straightening himself up, patting himself down. Happiness and relief coursing through him.

Back outside Logan's office, a gang of GoJo emissaries wait, three or four of them. He nods a hello.

Shiv and Roman are in Logan's office, giving Logan space.

Kerry is elsewhere in the room. Karl, Frank and Gerri on their phones hang back too. They are all around the conference table. Tom's all high.

TOM

Hey!

But he clocks Logan glowering and joins Roman and Shiv – anxious.

All this is whispered/low so as not to annoy Logan.

GERRI

There might be a problem.

TOM

Where's Matsson?

SHIV

He's sent sherpas. He's not coming.

TOM

Okay. I mean, is that okay? Because he's a bit—? Doesn't love meetings, right?

ROMAN

Uh-huh. Dad's thinking.

Everyone is silent while they wait and occasionally steal glances at the big man behind his desk.

TOM
(*whispers*)
But he knows how important this is in terms of . . .

ROMAN

He knows everything.

Beat more then finally . . . Logan nods to Kerry.

KERRY

Okay.

They come through.

LOGAN

Yeah, it's off. Tell these kids to fuck off. Meeting's cancelled.

SHIV

What's the downside – meet this guy, could read petulant not to?

LOGAN

If he wants to send a nobody.

> KARL

Well, his CFO and a team of . . .

> LOGAN

He's going to this fucking party, isn't he? Ah? Where is he? Getting his nails done, asshole whitened?

> ROMAN

We kind of might need to court them a little though?

> LOGAN

Everyone's telling him he's hot. He thinks he's it. Nah, it's bad fucking juju to start like this.

> ROMAN

Can we not at least . . .?

> LOGAN

No. We've got options.

> SHIV

But have we? It might be our last chance to avoid the legacy-media graveyard.

> LOGAN

Frank's reached out to Nan about Pierce.

Shiv lets her head fall and bang on the table.

> SHIV

Seriously? We're going after Pierce again?

> FRANK

It's exciting.

But he doesn't sound excited. The room feels a little flat.

> LOGAN

Alright. Enough. Everyone back to work!

Tom, Frank, Karl leave.

Kerry goes to give the GoJo emissaries the news that the meeting is cancelled.

Shiv stays. Roman clocks. He stays too. And Gerri lingers.

> The deal makes sense. I like the deal. But he won't make the deal because he's an arrogant prick.

Shiv and Roman share a look.

> SHIV
> Fine. Matsson is an asshole. Of course he is. So we should burn our life raft over *that*?

> LOGAN
> It's just smart business, Shiv. I don't want to pay over the odds. And eventually the market will make him make the deal.

Kerry re-enters.

> ROMAN
> Unless someone else makes a better offer first?

> SHIV
> Dad, this is it. We have a scale issue. Our streaming platform is for shit. We have nothing which looks like growth. This gets us consequentially into streaming, it gets us into social media, sports betting and turbo-boosts our AI. We have a *little* window. Back out now and we end up a pilot fish nibbling the leftovers from between Bezos's fucking teeth.

Logan can see it. But he's not ready to give up his grumble.

> LOGAN
> Kerry? What was it, the thing you said about Matsson?

> KERRY
> (*shrugs*)
> He thinks he's a genius. He's made one good piece of tech. Fuck him.

A glance from Shiv and Roman. Kerry has become a problem.

> SHIV
> We appreciate your input, Kerry, but 'fuck him' is not good tactics.

> LOGAN
> It's good tactics.

> SHIV
> Dad, if you don't want to talk to him, fine. But let me. Please.

Logan thinks.

                              ROMAN
                          (*makes a face*)
          We can *both* talk to him. He'll be there tonight?

                              LOGAN

          You're going?

They look at one another.

          Fine. But – do not overplay. This thing is a black box. I don't
          want to overpay.

                              SHIV

          On it.

                              ROMAN

          I'll reorganize my diary.

Shiv heads out. Roman stays.

                              LOGAN
          Since you're going – you can give him the card in person.

Roman checks that Shiv can't hear.

                              ROMAN
          Cool. What you think? Do you think he'll like it?

They smile at one another. Roman heads out.

INT./EXT. KENDALL'S PARTY – DUSK

Montage.

Last-minute preparations for Kendall's party.

Maybe Kendall runs a loop of the big room.

Extra supplies of food and drink being taken in.

The last few servers arriving.

A security guard giving a briefing to the security team.

*A sign being finalized above the entrance – 'The Notorious KEN –
Ready to Die'.*

EXT. KENDALL'S PARTY – NIGHT

Party guests arriving. It's a mix of elites – we might not recognize anyone but we feel the types – big hitters in the business world, sports stars, models, artists, TV and film people, rappers. Each with their own little entourage.

There's heavy security around the courtyard holding media well back. There's also security around the entrance.

Shiv and Tom are out of the car and heading to the entrance.

> TOM
>
> I feel amazing. It's like – all my senses are heightened. The air smells sweeter. I can sort of like see the poetry in the little mundane things.
>
> (*looks around, musing*)
> I am going to get *so* fucked up. Okay? Is that okay?

> SHIV
>
> Hey, you don't need my permission.
> (*then*)
> Like how fucked up?

> TOM
>
> Just clear my airways if I look like I might choke on my vomit. And block my airwaves if I start shouting that I'm a sexy girlboss? Maybe I should give you my wallet?

They join Roman, Connor and Willa, who saw them arrive and waited by the entrance for them.

> WILLA
>
> Hey there.

> TOM
>
> 'Hi, Tom Wambsgans! Not going to prison!'

He shakes her hand playfully. Everyone's looking sharp, but Connor's also wearing a light coat and has his arm in a sling. As they head in—

INT. KENDALL'S PARTY – ENTRANCE/CLOAKROOM – NIGHT

The sounds of a womb are being played in.

On various screens are shots of wriggling sperms.

> ROMAN
> This is even worse-slash-better than I'd imagined.
>> *(to Connor, re arm)*
> What happened?

> CONNOR
> Ranch stuff.

> ROMAN
> Uh-huh? Horse didn't want you to fuck it?

> WILLA
> He had a fall.

> CONNOR
> Well don't say 'had a fall', that sounds like I'm eighty-nine! No, Maxim and I actually got some poll results and we shared a cognac and I slipped while dancing a little Irish jig.

> ROMAN
> Classic ranch action. Real cowboy.

> SHIV
> Um. Can we leave already? Do a FaceTime with Matsson instead?

> ROMAN
> Sure. Go. I can do it.

He looks at her.

Assistants check names off lists. They all hand off gifts to assistants.

Shiv, Tom, Connor, Willa and Roman are in a queue which leads past the coat check to a staircase into the party.

> ATTENDANT
> Hi, we're asking everyone to hand in their coats and phones. Kendall would like his present to be everyone being 'present'.

> ROMAN
> Yeah, fuck off, I'm not doing that.

> SHIV
> Sorry. Gross. You're gonna need to tase us.

ATTENDANT

And your coat?

CONNOR

Nuh-huh. I will remain coated thank you. As is my right.

Attendant lets it go. Connor winks at Willa. Beat the system.

INT. KENDALL'S PARTY – PASSAGEWAY – NIGHT

Another attendant ushers Shiv, Roman, Tom, Connor and Willa towards some stairs dressed with red material and looking like some kind of biological passageway. Another attendant is allowing people down in small groups.

SHIV

So where's Tabs?

ROMAN

Busy.

SHIV

'Busy'? Again. Uh-huh. Did you kill her?

ROMAN

It's going great. It's just when you get to know her she's actually quite boring.

SHIV

Oh yeah? That beautiful fascinating blonde VC, she's boring you?

ROMAN

She's fine, she's just a bit boring is all. That's all I'm saying.

SHIV

Okay? But the relationship was fine, sexually, and you were loving the *intimacy* and all.

She looks at him but he stares her down.

ROMAN

Yes. Loved the intimacy. Love people really getting to know me.

SHIV

Uh-huh?

She's smiling annoyingly.

> ROMAN
> Like you're the fucking catch of the day, you're more fucked up
> than me!

INT. KENDALL'S PARTY — PASSAGEWAY/DELIVERY ROOM —
NIGHT

*They emerge into a recreation of a delivery room from a New York
hospital circa 1980. They're greeted by an actor playing a nurse.*

> NURSE
> Congratulations! You've just been born into the world of
> Kendall Roy!

> WILLA
> Oh! Immersive!

> SHIV
> Oh Jesus.

> ROMAN
> So, if we've just been born then—

*He turns to look back the way they came and sees a giant version of
Caroline's legs spread to give birth to guests.*

> Okay?

He goes back to the passageway. Touches the inside of it.

> So this is . . .

He goes back into the passageway.

> So I'm inserting myself into my mother's vagina right now?

> SHIV
> (*tapping walls*)
> Cold and inhospitable. Which seems to check out.

He steps out, then goes back in, then steps out.

> ROMAN
> I'm repeatedly entering my own mother? That is, not right.

(*to the nurse*)
That's my mom's cooch, so you know. And you're implying it's massive. I think you should tighten my mom's vagina.

They are handed a map/brochure of the party layout.

CONNOR
A map? A map to a party? I feel tired.

ROMAN
Nothing says party like a stack of literature.

Tom grabs some maps from a pile and hands them out.

SHIV
Do they show where the fun is?

Tom spots Greg looking lost.

TOM
'Tom Wambsgans, free man, how you doing?'

GREG
'Gregory Hirsch, not going to prison, pleased to meet you!'

They laugh and shake.

TOM
Look at you all gussied up, you slick little fuck.

GREG
Well thank you.
(*looks round*)
Say have you seen Comfrey—? PR who works for Ken? With the hair, in a kind of – like—

Tom takes this in—

TOM
Gregory John Hirsch – do you have a crush?! Oh my god.

GREG
What? She seems like a nice person.

TOM
I mean, obviously it's absurd. She's way out of your league, man. It's like a haunted scarecrow asking out Jackie Onassis. It's a suicide mission.

Greg smiles, like it's all a big joke—

GREG

Uh-huh, sure, Tom—

TOM

This is not a razz, Greg. She's a goddess and you're a nine-foot Cro-Magnon man. I mean, you shouldn't even be thinking about her. You're going to put her in a really tough spot. It's not fair.

GREG

Look I'm not unaware of the discrepancy, in terms of our physical circumstances.

TOM

It's a chasm. This is Evel Knievel trying to jump the Grand Canyon on a penny-farthing.

GREG

I have one initial approach like, 'You're like a fascinating book I'd like to crack open'?

TOM

Right, what do you call that, 'the perverted professor'?

Greg's a little pissed off now.

GREG

I mean how did you get with Shiv? She's out of your league?

TOM

Oooh! Testy! Well, Greg, I have a dick the size of a red sequoia and I fuck like a bullet train. Satisfied?

INT. KENDALL'S PARTY – CHILDHOOD ROOM – NIGHT

An impressionistic representation of Kendall's childhood. Maybe his nursery. Maybe some giant mobiles. Some outsized toys and furniture. Maybe some baby photos around.

Connor, Willa, Shiv, Roman and Tom and Greg take it in.

WILLA

Is this how you remember it?

CONNOR

Well, I wasn't invited over so much during this period, so.

Willa stops by a mirror. It has a sign next to it, explaining what it is. Shiv and Roman catch up.

Okay. 'The Silly Mirror'?

SHIV

What's it say?

WILLA
(*reads*)
That when you cried as kids your dad would make you look in the silly mirror to show you how silly and ugly you looked crying to make you stop?

SHIV

Well no, that wasn't Dad. That was Mom.

INT. KENDALL'S PARTY — SCHOOLROOM — NIGHT

Bar staff and servers dressed in school uniforms from Kendall's old school. On a blackboard: 'Kendall Roy is not a narcissist' written over and over.

They walk on—

ROMAN

Ken, pumping out the anti-Dad propaganda.

CONNOR

No, it was Dad.

SHIV

No, the mirror was Mom. Dad was never there to see us cry.

CONNOR

Okay, well your mum may have been an enthusiastic adopter. But Dad was the inventor.

Connor sees a waiter passing with plates of egg pastries.

GREG

Sorry, what is this?

WAITER

Lord Woolton's Egg Pie? It's based on a recipe Caroline Collingwood's . . .

But Connor has taken a bite.

CONNOR

Oh no, this is no Lord Woolton's Egg Pie, my friend.

The waiter has been given a speech for guests.

WAITER

It's actually a recreation of a modified wartime dish created by Kendall's grandmother and . . .

CONNOR

Um, no. This is more like a quiche. Nope, sorry to say this egg pie is bullshit.

Connor places his napkin back on the tray with a bright smile.

They walk on into—

INT. KENDALL'S PARTY — BIG ROOM — NIGHT

A DJ's onstage and the room's filling up. They look around.

SHIV

Okay, so where's Matsson?

ROMAN

Probably standing in a corner monitoring his biometrics on his watch. Maybe let's just say a quick hello to Ken??

They spot Berry.

SHIV

Hi. Um, do you know where Ken is?

Berry indicates the upper floor overlooking the dance area. She's surprised to see them. Could be something to handle.

BERRY

VIP. Um, I'll have someone take you up.

TOM
(whispers to Shiv)

Listen, Shiv, may I be excused from the table? I think I'm going to devolve into a disgusting drugs pig!

She gives him a kiss on the cheek.

SHIV

Take care!

INT. KENDALL'S PARTY – ESCALATOR – NIGHT

A party organizer stands with Shiv, Roman and Connor, Willa as they go up the escalator. It feels weird. Cool partygoers, drinks in hand, standing still and some chatting, many in silence.

INT. KENDALL'S PARTY – UPSTAIRS VIP AREA – NIGHT

Up above the big room.

Kendall looks out on his party. He's nodding to the beat – yeah this is good, I'm happy, he thinks. Naomi comes over, looking at her phone.

NAOMI

So listen, I'll give you your real present later—

KENDALL
(*interrupting*)

Oh! Okay, what is it?

NAOMI

It's – nothing. It's—
(*why do you care?*)
But to tide you over . . . did you know your dad's reached out to Nan again?

KENDALL

Haha, what? Ahab's back on that white-whale grind?! Oh Jesus. The suspense! Who will gain control of the gold mine, the fucking – Omaha Butter Churner? Who'll get to print next week's strips? What shall become of Beetle Bailey? The Battle for Marmaduke is upon us! Jesus.

Kendall looks over and clocks Shiv and Roman arriving. Connor and Willa stop to talk to someone.

Kendall stops speaking when he sees them – eye contact from across the room. How's this going to play out?

Shiv, Kendall and Roman face to face for the first time in a while. They trade blows but it's mostly light-hearted banter.

Wait, who let you in? This is friends-only.

SHIV

Shouldn't it be empty then? Happy birthday, old man.

ROMAN

(*hand up; confessing*)

Okay. Just to say, I am only here because I've heard it's going to be a five-dimensional catastrophe and I want to see you crash and burn. Also, I've just farted. So yeah – happy birthday.

Roman wafts the fart in Kendall's direction.

KENDALL

Thanks. You shouldn't have.

Kendall hugs Roman. In the hug—

ROMAN

My god, it's like you *feel* old. It's like hugging a leather satchel filled with human remains.

Kendall looks at Shiv.

KENDALL

No card? I'm disappointed, cos you normally write me such lovely letters.

SHIV

Couldn't find one that said, 'Happy Fortieth' *and* 'Get Well Soon'.

KENDALL

Well, I'm glad you came. Says a lot.

SHIV

It's a ten-minute drive.

KENDALL

Uh-huh.

But he is maybe more pleased than he expected and she can see.

SHIV

Okay, hug before you start weeping?

They hug. Kendall sees Connor and Willa approaching.

> KENDALL

Holy shit. Gang's all here, huh?
> (*re the coat*)

What's this, Con? What happened?

> CONNOR

Overexcited about a political breakthrough.

> KENDALL

Okay. But what's with—?
> (*the coat*)

You not staying?

> CONNOR

Listen, you – might wanna chat to your team about the egg pie?

> KENDALL

Hilarious, right?

> CONNOR

It's a lot of things brother. But it's ain't Lord Woolton's Egg Pie.

> KENDALL

Well, we're making Auntie Nora's Pink Shape for dessert. And Gully Mixture. Remember, yeah?

> ROMAN

Cough syrup and space dust, shoved down the gullet on a bed of spoon.

Kendall smiles, overexcited.

> KENDALL
> (*re the party*)

So what do you think?

> ROMAN

Uh-huh. And tell me, did you get Mom's permission, for the use of her—?

Roman whistles, gestures back to the entrance hall.

> KENDALL

What, from a copyright perspective?

                              ROMAN
Call me old fashioned – I just feel like you should ask before
you construct a giant replica of someone's vagina?

                              KENDALL
Roman, relax. Yes – you can take it home with you.

                              SHIV
So. Go on, who's here?

                              KENDALL
Who isn't?

                              ROMAN
Your dad.

                              SHIV
Your mom.

                              CONNOR
Your wife and kids.

                              ROMAN
Any real friends?

Kendall smiles. He's missed the sparring, the connection.

                              SHIV
Business folks? Stewy? Honestly, we could do with building
some bridges. Lawrence Yee?
                    (*thrown away*)
Lukas Matsson?

                              KENDALL
Sure, somewhere.

Momentary eye contact between Roman and Shiv.

Hey I've got something to show here. This way.

As they go, Roman angles so Shiv doesn't see—

                              ROMAN
From Dad.

Roman hands Kendall the card.

                              KENDALL
What is it—?

ROMAN
Um, I think it's all your milk teeth and an iTunes gift card. No,
I'm kidding. It's nice. It's a nice thing. We hope you'll like it.

Kendall's surprised and pockets the envelope, walks on.

KENDALL
Let me show you some shit.

INT. KENDALL'S PARTY – THE FUTURE ROOM – NIGHT

Kendall guides them to the cusp of the Future Room.

KENDALL
Yeah so I consulted with Gladwell and Harari, Lovelock and
Popcorn and this, it's pretty technical, but this is the best we
could come up with on the likely directions of society so a little
dry but—

*They enter to find – on the wall, four enormous mocked-up
newspaper covers.*

*On one, a photo of Kendall. Headline reads: 'Waystar Chairman,
Kendall Roy elected President of World Federation'.*

*Another, a photo of Roman. Headline reads: 'Failed sibling dies in
tragic jerk-off accident'.*

*Another, a photo of Shiv. Headline reads: 'Wife of Tom Wambsgans
arrested in sweep of city streetwalkers'.*

*Another, a photo of Connor. Headline reads: 'Connor Roy elected
President (of shitting his bag)'.*

ROMAN
Well, everyone in this room is now thinking about me jacking
off. So who's the real winner?

Connor stands in front of his poster.

CONNOR
Oh, man. What if, McCartney tweets this? This is not— I mean,
jokes are all very well but, c'mon, man? I'm breaking through.

> WILLA

Ken. I don't know if you're aware but right now Con's actually polling near enough one percent?

> ROMAN

One percent? Congratulations.

> CONNOR

Well that's four million people and enough to sway the race, so. I am a significant figure. I'm interested to see who comes crawling first? Merkel, begging for me to save democracy or Soros serenading me from the trees.

> KENDALL
> (to passing functionary)

Hey can we take down the crap-sack Connor piece please?
> (a nod; they move on)

Come on, man, unwrap, loosen up.

He beckons an attendant over.

Listen I gotta circulate. Anna will show you round. But let's check in later, yeah? I'd like that.

No one's quite sure what do with that.

> SHIV
> (feels bad lying)

Sure. That'd be nice.

After he's gone—

Does he seem okay to you?

Roman's a bit disturbed by how Kendall's doing but trying to hide it.

> ROMAN
> (no)

Like I give a fuck.

INT. KENDALL'S PARTY – WAYSTAR ROOM – NIGHT

Kendall enters. He stands in the middle of a fiery hell-like version of Waystar. He looks at the party. Watches for a beat. Then, takes out the envelope.

Inside, a generic birthday card. We may or may not be able to read in full – 'This entitles Kendall Roy to the value of his share in the holding company – $2bn.'

On the card Logan has crossed out the printed words 'Happy Birthday!' and written 'Cash out and fuck off.'

There's a printed term sheet in there too.

Kendall takes this in. He smiles. Puts the card back in the envelope and the envelope back in his pocket.

On the far side of the room, Greg lingers. He sees Comfrey on the other side of the room on her phone. Greg braces, and crosses to her.

> GREG

Hey. So what's up?

> COMFREY
> *(on her phone)*

Hey.

> *(to party planner)*

Think there's a line at the treehouse, can you fix? Hey, um, Greg, I'm glad I ran into you . . .

> GREG

Me too!

> COMFREY

Right, because I might have to brief the press against you?

> GREG

Oh. Right? The whole press?

> COMFREY

Just because, Kendall's going balls to the wall and – you're on the other team. I mean, I'll see if I can keep it, targeted, rather than terminal but—

> GREG

Oh.

He takes it on board and tries to stay positive.

Well, um, thank you kindly, ma'am. That's very kind of you! How can I possibly repay you . . .?

And she has to head off, summoned by a party organizer she's liasing with. He calls after her—

You are a very fair maiden. An even-handed maiden.

Greg stands.

INT. KENDALL'S PARTY – DRUG ROOM – NIGHT

With Kendall, now with Naomi. The card has bumped him, but he's turning the energy positive, maybe with drink and drugs but mainly the power of his mind.

KENDALL

So. Dad's sent me something for my birthday.

NAOMI

Okay?

KENDALL

Yeah. A Trojan mind-fuck. Trying to slip a maggot in the candy apple. He's offering to buy me out of my share in the company.

NAOMI

Oh—? Okay—? Wow.
(*then*)
And what is that? In terms of a number?

KENDALL

Two bil? But, it's a mind-game. He's worried I'm not gonna let him keep on living rent-free up here.

Taps head.

NAOMI

And?

KENDALL

And fuck him! Maybe I refuse to engage. Mind-game that, motherfucker!

NAOMI

That's great. But I mean maybe you do, take it?

KENDALL

Maybe, I dunno, maybe I buy you a – a diamond the size of the Ritz Carlton and a few illustrious newspapers – the *Globe* and *Mail* and the *LA Times* – and I print a front page of my dad eating dog dick every day for a year. And I'm living in Marrakesh just fucking you and smoking hash and learning how to turn a lathe?

He kisses her.

In another part of the room (or another room), Greg is with Tom.

> GREG
>
> Yeah. She might be spinning against me. Which, I dunno, feels kind of – vibey? Right, 'I spin against you, you spin against me.' Yeah?

Tom bangs back a champagne.

> TOM
>
> Just ask around, Greg.

> GREG
>
> I don't want to ask strangers for drugs. What if I get in trouble?

> TOM
>
> Oh come on please, don't be so provincial. Ask him. He looks like an asshole. Or go to the bathroom and listen for sniffing?

> GREG
>
> Well what drugs do you want? I can't just ask for generic 'drugs'.

> TOM
>
> Cocaine, Greg, your favorite! I want to get coke-loading. Packing my cheeks for winter like a fucking Bolivian coke squirrel!

INT. KENDALL'S PARTY – ON WAY TO TREEHOUSE – NIGHT

Kendall is walking with Naomi and Comfrey and a party planner.

> KENDALL
>
> Do I buy a diamond mine and make it a co-op? Or just fucking – give two bil to UNICEF and make Dad look like a fuckhead?

> COMFREY

Um all great but sorry, do we know where Lukas Matsson is right now—?

> NAOMI

I still think you should just give it all to me?

> COMFREY

Just Roman and Shiv have been asking staff if we have a location for Matsson? And enquiring discreetly about a private space? Is that okay?

Kendall takes this in. He sees the significance of this. It sinks in. Then—

> KENDALL

Okay.

> (*then*)

Okay, Comfrey, can the party team get eyes on Matsson and ask him to meet me in the treehouse?

Kendall's arrived at the treehouse. He takes a drink as he moves past security and enters.

INT. KENDALL'S PARTY — HALLWAY — NIGHT

Photos and video of Kendall on the walls. Performers wearing Kendall masks. Roman is standing looking at all the Kendall masks.

Shiv approaches.

> SHIV

Okay, I have a location.

> ROMAN

Well, okay. Let's go!

They pass through rooms we haven't seen.

> SHIV

Okay. But easy. Do not fuck this.

> ROMAN

Shiv? Please.

SHIV

If we miss this, in eighteen months we'll be dead, begging some rinky-dink Facebook whistleblower to redesign our whole bullshit from the bottom up.

ROMAN

Sure, but maybe leave the talking to me?

SHIV

Right. The gentle touch. Profanasaurus Rex. Might be safest if it's me?

ROMAN

That's funny because lately everything I touch turns to gold and everything you touch withers and dies.

SHIV

Well maybe knuckle-dragging white nationalists are your intellectual level. And maybe I should talk to Matsson.

ROMAN

Fine, we double-team him. You do the charm and I'll do the offensive.

INT. KENDALL'S PARTY – OUTSIDE TREEHOUSE – NIGHT

Continuous – a few guests wait outside a large fabricated 'treehouse'-style room, fake tree branches sticking out.

Lots of security outside. This is the most VIP of the VIP rooms.

Shiv and Roman arrive at the door.

ROMAN

Okay? A forty-year-old man rebuilding his childhood treehouse should instantly go on the sex offender registry.

SHIV

'Come play in my treehouse, Drake.'
                    (*then inspecting*)
Which one is this based on?

ROMAN
                    (*remembers it well*)
Um? The ranch? Montana? Is it?

> SHIV

Right. Where he got so mad when we got in that he pinned you down and had Ray Raleigh spit in your mouth?

Roman shrugs. They reach the security. They try to move past.

Hey—

Bouncer stops them.

> BOUNCER

Um, do you have a rainbow band?

> ROMAN

Sure, man, I'm a walking rainbow band.

He holds them up as Kendall approaches from inside and steps out.

> KENDALL

Oh, hey. Okay? You done downstairs?

> ROMAN

Yeah hey, Ken. May we please step inside your mental disorder?

> KENDALL

Good one. Hehe.

Shiv shifts towards the entrance but Kendall doesn't move.

Um, look. I know why you guys are here.

> ROMAN

Yeah we're here to do body shots off McCartney. Can we come on in?

> KENDALL

Um, sure. Sure.
> 		(*thinks, serious*)
Oh. Except. Um? Actually. Sorry. Shit, sorry, that's not possible.

> ROMAN

Why?

> KENDALL

Yeah. No because the thing is. The treehouse is cool. And you're not cool?

> SHIV

Ha. Sure. It's the coolest grown man's treehouse I've seen in quite a while.

> KENDALL

No, okay, come in. Just give the password. You do know the password don't you?

> SHIV

Is it 'borderline personality disorder'?

Roman moves for the door. Kendall blocks him.

> ROMAN

'Colossal dick-cheese'? All lowercase? C'mon, fatty. Heave-ho.

> SHIV

Ken? C'mon.

> KENDALL

No, okay. Okay. NO seriously, guys, come over here.

He looks serious.

Sorry but joking aside there is actually a real issue here and I need to be discreet but there's a lot of celebrities around and there is just one significant issue. Which is the issue of—
> (*holds nose, waves air*)

PHEW-WEE! We're trying to keep the stink out. And you guys stink.

> ROMAN

Ken, don't be a fucking moron.

> KENDALL

I'm sorry. It's just, if you guys were in the treehouse, it kinda wouldn't feel like the treehouse, you know?
> (*to Roman*)

You're a Nazi lover—
> (*to Shiv*)

and you're a Nazi lover and I'm a defender of liberal democracy. And this is made from George Washington's cherry tree, so?

They look at him. He's not joking?

ROMAN

You're actually not going to let us in?

KENDALL

To see Matsson?
(*looks at them*)
That's why you're here? For him? You're trying to push a deal
here?

They're busted a little.

High-quality personal conduct. Really top-rank.

Roman owns it.

ROMAN

Okay, so what? We just wanna talk to him. What's the
difference?

SHIV

You know what happens if you let us in? And we talk to him?
Either we strike out and – nothing. Or we succeed and Waystar
benefits and your net worth goes up by several hundred million
dollars.

KENDALL

Right. But I have to weigh that against the consideration that
'no losers are allowed'.

ROMAN
(*losing it*)
LET US THE FUCK IN.

KENDALL

Bro, calm down. You're crying about a treehouse. Do you have
any idea how ridiculous that is?

A guest approaches.

Hey, man! Come on in. Wristband him.

ROMAN

Who's that?

KENDALL

No idea.

        (to bouncer, pointing at Shiv and Roman)
Don't let these two in, okay? This is my space you shouldn't be anywhere near here!

        (to Roman)
And thanks for the offer, Rome. Really cool, great headfuck from you and Dad, thanks.

Kendall walks back into the treehouse. Shiv and Roman are alone now. Shiv pondering something that got mentioned.

ROMAN

Unbelievable. I genuinely hope his kidneys fail.

SHIV

Uh-huh, and a butt infection. What offer? What's he talking about?

ROMAN

What? That's nothing.

She looks like: Well tell me.

Just a little move, to ease him out of the holding company.

SHIV

You and Dad?

ROMAN

Well, he can only sell to family, right, and yeah I think Dad put me on there. It's housekeeping.

SHIV

Right. You '*think*'?

ROMAN

It's a name on a piece of paper, Shiv.

SHIV

Okay. So can I be the name on the piece of paper instead?

ROMAN

I can't even do anything with it, it's musical chairs.

SHIV

Right I just guess who owns the company has historically been of some interest?

ROMAN

Dad and I handled it. You wanna figure out the financing?

Shiv doesn't like that at all—

SHIV

'Dad and I handled it.' That's cute. Love that.
(*then; shrugging*)
You know what, great. It's all fucking great.

Shiv walks off.

INT. KENDALL'S PARTY – BIG ROOM – NIGHT

Connor's with Willa. He's looking at his phone.

Willa's anxious.

WILLA

So, Con, you know your percent?

CONNOR

The four million souls in my ass pocket? I have some awareness, sure.

He smiles. She smiles along, as Connor looks out.

Five states where the parties are within one percent of each other. I'm like climate change, Willa – I must be reckoned with.

WILLA

But now you're on the radar I guess people are gonna start digging, right?

CONNOR

The ponytail photo? Oh I don't think that plays anymore. Let them dig. I'm seventy inches of rich, pH-balanced, loam.

WILLA

Uh-huh. And what about our – arrangement?

CONNOR

Well, we've moved past that.

WILLA

Mmm.

(then)
But the direct deposits are still?

CONNOR
That's for housekeeping. That's normal in a lot of – marriages.

She blanches slightly at the word.

And relationships. What I mean is a few hundred thousand per financial quarter isn't anything to do with how we feel.

Willa makes a non-committal noise. Connor reacts—

CONNOR
I mean I want to do that. But we'd be together whatever. Right?

WILLA
(as close to a yes as she can muster)
Hmmm-hm.

CONNOR
Right?

WILLA
Well, I don't know. Yeah. Sure.

CONNOR
We met, we had an arrangement, the arrangement – over time – transmogrified into a relationship.

Willa reaches out to him, to try to be honest because she owes him that.

WILLA
Connor. Well, honestly—? I like you. I didn't always like you but I do like you. But. Um. Yeah?

Connor takes this in. A million different responses flash through his brain. Denial seems to be the most convenient.

CONNOR
Well thank you, I appreciate that.

Connor tries not to look too hurt by Willa's reaction. Willa feels bad.

WILLA
You okay?

                                        CONNOR
Mm-huh. Little chilly.

He goes back to looking at his phone.

INT. KENDALL'S PARTY – THE TREEHOUSE – NIGHT

Kendall comes into the treehouse, finds Matsson—

                                        KENDALL
Okay! Lukas Matsson! My man, my myth, my motherfucker!

Matsson looks around.

                                        MATSSON
Hey. Excited to be here. I hate parties.

                                        KENDALL
Still not figured out the socials? You should get your algo guy to
fix your code.

                                        MATSSON
So what happens in the treehouse? Do we tell ghost stories? Do
you show me your winkie?

                                        KENDALL
Listen, you know my siblings are looking for you now.

                                        MATSSON
Okay. Is there a more exclusive area? A crawl space maybe?

                                        KENDALL
Emissaries from the Grand Old Duke of Old. Dad wants to buy
you so he sent his winged dildos to schmooze.

                                        MATSSON
Okay well I shouldn't say anything. Even the look on my face is
commercially sensitive.

He pulls a 'maybe I don't give a fuck' face.

                                        KENDALL
But it makes no sense, correct? Amtrak buys Tesla. If anything
you should buy him!

                                        MATSSON
Uh-huh. Great to get your impartial read.

Comfrey interjects.

> COMFREY
> Um, Rava wanted to say hi?

> KENDALL
> (*dismissive*)
> Sure. When I'm ready. Listen, stay up here, okay? So you don't
> get networked to fuck. What can I get you?

> MATSSON
> Um. Privacy. Pussy. And maybe pasta?

> KENDALL
> Reece can help you out. Pussy, coke, wristwatches – he's a one-
> man dark web.
> (*calling out*)
> Yo Reece, customer for your candy store!
> (*whispers*)
> He's not a good guy. Enjoy.

INT. KENDALL'S PARTY – DRUG ROOM – NIGHT

*Tom and Greg sit on a couch. Tom is pretty fucked up now. But the
drugs have sharpened his edge.*

> TOM
> This is good. I am on cocaine, Greg. I am very happy.

> GREG
> Yeah? Feels good?

> TOM
> Oh yeah. Sure. It's lovely.
> (*grits teeth*)
> How would you kill a man, Greg? What would be your
> preferred method?

> GREG
> Oh, I really don't know, Tom.

> TOM
> (*cokey stream*)

Bag on head? How would you kill someone like Nate for instance? You could cut off his dick and let him bleed out or make him eat it?

> GREG

What happened, Tom? You were so happy?

> TOM

I am happy, Greg. I'm very happy.

> GREG
> (*boisterous*)

C'mon, Tom. Smile!

> TOM
> (*a little spooked*)

Don't do that. I don't like that. You're scaring me, Greg. You don't realize you're a scary individual, okay? We need to get more drugs.

INT. KENDALL'S PARTY – HIP-HOP ROOM – NIGHT

An attendant shows Kendall over to Rava. They hug. Things are starting to get to Kendall. Too much stuff going on now.

> RAVA

Hey, Ken. Just wanted to say hi before everyone's too high. We might go soon so?

> KENDALL

Well you can't go. I'm doing a thing.
> (*he wants her to see*)

And we got the Tiny Wu-Tang Clan. These kids we found that do Wu-Tang covers.

> RAVA

Okay?

> KENDALL

It's better than it sounds. Are you not enjoying it?

> RAVA

No, sure, lot of people. It's huge.

He clocks there's no compliment there.

>   KENDALL
>   (*playful but maybe hurt*)
> Uh-huh. Savage. What you gonna do for yours? Just Sarah and
> Orla and some pasta alfredo? Three glasses of Chablis if you're
> feeling 'naughty' and lights out by eleven?

>   RAVA
> That actually sounds nice to me.

*Kendall clocks a guy chatting to some guests behind Rava who's
looking over from time to time.*

> But listen yeah Gary, you know Gary—

>   KENDALL
> I know Gary. Nice little poseable action figure. Does he have any
> genitals?

>   RAVA
> Yes, yes he does. Gary has an early start, so.

>   KENDALL
> Oh, okay. Gary's gotta be fresh for the big meet!

>   RAVA
> Okay well, good luck. And did you get the kids' present?

>   KENDALL
> No. What?

>   RAVA
> We left it with one of the people – they said they'd get it to you?

>   KENDALL
> When? When you arrived? That didn't get to me. Do you know
> who you gave it to?

*She doesn't. Kendall feels sick. What's the point of this whole fucking
party if he doesn't even get his kids' present which is the only thing
that really matters?*

>   RAVA
> Umm. No. No, a person.

> KENDALL

Fine. Okay, I'll find it. I'm gonna find it. It'll be logged. What did it look like?

> RAVA

Um, like a present? It had rabbit paper?

> KENDALL

Alright, got it. Yeah okay.

He's bumped by the encounter and wants to regain something before they part.

Okay well. Fine. Thanks for coming. I might be getting out, from the firm, so – we'll talk more.

> RAVA
> *(heard it a few times)*

Oh, okay? Good. I mean great. Maybe they'll stop sending goons to talk to the nanny in the park about how often you lose your temper with the kids?

He'd suspected these things, but that's nasty. He shakes his head, then—

> KENDALL

Dad's offered two bil to buy me out. He thinks it's a fuck-you but I might just take the money. Put it into something better than Waystar. Like human trafficking.

She smiles.

> RAVA

Sounds good.

> KENDALL

Okay. Rabbits. Rabbit paper. Got it. Give my love to Kevin. Gary.

They both know the game he's playing and they smile as they part, but Kendall's feeling things dropping away inside . . .

INT. KENDALL'S PARTY — HALLWAY AND ESCALATOR —
NIGHT

*Kendall with Berry and Comfrey and his entourage on the move. The
vibe has soured for Kendall now. The start of a sugar crash. He's got
a weird amoral edge. Drops acid comments with a smile. Are they
jokes? As he passes someone—*

KENDALL

Hey. Love the shoes. Are you being ironic? Or am I?
(*to Berry and Comfrey*)
Can we trace that gift please. Priority one. Who are those
people?

BERRY

These are – as discussed – they're some of the artists who
worked on the rooms, and their plus-ones. For economic and
cultural diversity.

KENDALL

I wanted nice people who would bring a cool vibe, these – these
are not what I envisioned. Can we thin them out? They're
hogging servers. It's cool but it's not cool.

*This is below Berry's pay grade. She kicks it across to Comfrey with a
nod, who makes a note.*

Kendall comments to someone as he passes.

Are they playing from the approved playlists in the main room
because my thing was all bangers all the time, yeah?
(*then to Berry and Comfrey*)
Plus and this is nothing, but can we get Connor to lose his coat?

BERRY

Sure.

KENDALL

It's nothing. He's souring the vibe. The fucking arm thing?
It's fine but— Yeah? Fucking disabled vibes. And he's making
everyone feel cold. It's not cold. Is it?

COMFREY

It's at a good level.

> KENDALL

Exactly so let's encourage him to remove his coat, if he wants, loosen this thing up.

> BERRY

No problem.

He enjoys the music for a beat. Then walks on.

> KENDALL

Look. It just feels like an asshole's birthday party. And my one thing from the very first meeting was that it shouldn't feel like an asshole's birthday party.

> BERRY

No sure.

> KENDALL

Could we lower the ceiling? In the big room? It's fucking ridiculous in there. Or give the impression at least?

> (*then*)

And the coat, yeah?

He walks off. Greg approaches.

Hey, Greg! The snitch bitch.

> GREG

Great party. Can I have one moment?

> KENDALL

Um, I'm about to do my set. Walk with me – what is it?

> GREG

Yeah, um, I was wondering about something because I just was about to ask Comfrey out, and then she said this slightly worrying thing about how she might have to—

> KENDALL

You were gonna ask Comfrey out? Comfrey, my employee Comfrey?

Greg checks again to see she's not in earshot.

GREG

Um, yeah? But is that right, do you have to spin against me because as I hear, things are kind of slowing down in that regard, right?

KENDALL

No. And she's out of your league, man.

GREG

Yeah well?

KENDALL

What if I want to ask her out?

GREG

Er.

KENDALL

Inappropriate. But no. It's best you don't, okay? Too complicated. She works for me. Clean lines. Church and state. Okay?

GREG

Okay? I mean, I don't think it would cause many problems because . . .?

KENDALL

Well I said no, Greg. Jesus. Dude. Duh? You're like the world's biggest parasite. You're a fucking human tapeworm. Maybe stop feeding on your own fucking family and try sucking some blood elsewhere, yeah?

(then)

I'm kidding.

Kendall walks away. Greg might make a face, as if to say, 'That's not very fucking fair, is it?'

INT. KENDALL'S PARTY – DRUG ROOM – NIGHT

Tom and Shiv at the bar. He's not smiling.

TOM

Look at their faces. So fucking, dour. It's a festivity, people should be . . . festive!

SHIV
(*in her own head*)
Yeah it's bullshit. Roman and Dad necking in the catbird seat.
Did you hear any whispers about this buyout thing?

TOM
(*why aren't* you *happy*)
Why is no one happy? What is this?

SHIV
You're harshing your own mellow, babe. I think I'm just gonna
hit Matsson on the way out. I have eyes on it and—

Rava passes.

RAVA
Hey.

SHIV
Rava? Hey. My god, an actual person!

They hug. A smile. Tom moves off with a smile.

RAVA
Yeah. It's a – wild one, right?

SHIV
I came in through my mother's pussy so, yeah. That was fun.

They smile.

Are you going, are you coming to my mom's wedding?

RAVA
Oh, yeah, well, got the invite, but, yeah, got a request to maybe
not?

Kendall's a dick they both agree with their looks.

SHIV
Okay, well. Listen, we should do a lunch – it was always fun
when we—

RAVA
I would actually really like that. Are we allowed?

SHIV
Oh we're allowed! I'll allow it.

RAVA

That would be great. I mean we might have to meet in secret.

Shiv looks a little blank.

So I don't – you know, get the anti-fascist Twitter fascists after me.

SHIV

Uh-huh? As in—?

RAVA

No I'm kidding – that photo? And the memes and—? You're okay?

SHIV

Oh Mencken? Yeah, no I'm okay. Yeah no.

RAVA

The left, huh? Eating their own! 'Nazi arm candy'. Yeah fuck off, man! After your career with Joyce and – everything— One picture, c'mon?!

SHIV

Oh right. I just keep off the social media I guess. 'Nazi arm candy'?

RAVA

It's so disgusting.

SHIV

I was there to help my dad, and keep us honest.

RAVA

Sure. I thought, 'Well there's no way Shiv wanted to do that.' Most people I know said that.

SHIV

It wasn't a big deal so—

RAVA

Oh, sure. No. Nope.

SHIV

Well listen, let's be in touch. We can have our secret underground lunch yeah?

Shiv walks off – her insides flipping.

INT. KENDALL'S PARTY – BIG ROOM – NIGHT

Back with Willa and Connor.

Comfrey joins them – she smiles uncomfortably.

> COMFREY
> So um, Connor, we'd like to offer you a complimentary cashmere sweater . . . We're handing them out to prestige guests.

> CONNOR
> I've got my coat. I'm fine.

> COMFREY
> Well the coat check should have taken that. But I'd be happy to take it—?

Connor smiles, indulgently. He's been here before.

> CONNOR
> Respectfully, I don't trust those things. I lost a Norwegian wool in a fusion restaurant in Vancouver.

Comfrey smiles and nods. She has her orders.

> COMFREY
> Kendall would really appreciate it if you'd take the sweater?

> CONNOR
> (*genuinely confused*)
> What? What's wrong with this coat—?

> WILLA
> (*to Comfrey*)
> My partner is cold and he'd like to keep his fucking coat on. And you know what? He's running to be the next President of the United States of America so maybe you should show some fucking respect.

Comfrey heads off – long night.

Connor looks at Willa and smiles. He feels like they're a team again. Maybe he even feels a little warmer.

INT. KENDALL'S PARTY – OUTSIDE TREEHOUSE – NIGHT

Roman approaches the bouncer again. No sign of Kendall.

ROMAN

Okay. Clown time's over. Let me in.

BOUNCER

Um. Sorry, sir. I really can't. He said—

ROMAN

He was *joking*. I'm his fucking brother. Google it. Do you know what I could do to you?

The bouncer is in a tough spot. Kendall could ruin his life too. Roman heads in and the bouncer puts a hand on his arm.

BOUNCER
(gently reaching out)

If you could just—

ROMAN

Hey WHOA! Are you touching me?! You're touching me! What the fuck?!
(yells out)
This guy's touching the fucking guests! *Why* are you being so gropey and racist?!

The bouncer sort of backs up. He's nervous now.

Roman walks into the treehouse and the bouncer does nothing to stop him, but talks into a mic.

INT. KENDALL'S PARTY – THE TREEHOUSE – NIGHT

Roman finds Matsson. Playing something on his phone.

ROMAN

Hey there you are! Hiding away like a human VPN! How's it going, dude?

MATSSON

Hey there. I'm just – you know – you can fill in the blanks. I'm too – whatever.

Roman makes a face.

ROMAN

Oh. I hear you. 'Life'. Exhausting.

MADDEN

I just want to find the good pussy and get out. Mission, side mission.

ROMAN

I hear you. Love pussy. You see my mom's?

Matsson smiles but then—

MATSSON

You seen *my* mom's?

Roman doesn't get it, but he laughs, they're both laughing.

ROMAN

Pussy. Huh. Yeah.
(*then*)
So, look, my old man, he got grumpy this morning, but you weren't trying to humiliate him, were you? I mean everyone says, everyone, last big legacy-content library – last fucking super-app streaming platform. We fit right?

MATSSON

Well everyone says we fit. I guess I do have one question?

ROMAN

Hit me.

MATSSON

When will your father die?

Roman blanches a bit.

ROMAN

When will he *die*?

MATSSON

Yeah. I mean, like roughly. What's your estimate?

ROMAN
(*gulp*)
Um, well? I couldn't rightly say!

MATSSON

I don't want to be rude but what shape is he in, not a year? Five years? I hope not five years. It would be better sooner, right?

Matsson laughs a little, winks.

ROMAN
(*offended and angry but burying it*)
Hehehe. Yeah I mean we're laughing but he is my dad, so
that's – pretty— You know, 'Go easy there chief!'

MATSSON
I'm sorry if this is weird? I guess the deal obviously is maybe
cool, but I just don't like the idea of a man hanging over me.

ROMAN
No, I can understand that.

MATSSON
The guru guy who is bullshit – you know? It's not my world.
Media. So, his death would clear space. With due respect.

Roman doesn't like it but he rolls with it.

ROMAN
Sure. Well, look, we're all obviously—
(*swallows*)
hugely looking forward to my father dying.
(*then*)
But there's another shape to this.

MATSSON
Oooh, exciting. Is it the shape of my butt?

ROMAN
Good, yeah. How about you never have to talk to him. You can
work out of Austin, London, Berlin, Geneva. Totally separate
corporate identity. StarGo we burn obviously.

MATSSON
You should. You should burn the code and fucking acid-bath
those servers!

ROMAN
GoJo full bore. Our library, our firepower and relationships for
content. Good shit, not fucking, all gay moms and wheelchair
kids, popular shit. And on the occasion you need to send up a
smoke signal from Geneva it can all go through me. Cos we get
each other.

Matsson ponders.

517

> MATSSON

You know StarGo truly is a piece of shit.

They've done this, but Roman's happy to do it again.

> ROMAN
> (*smiles*)

Oh boy is it ever!

> MATSSON

I like how it randomly makes me do a full email login again for no apparent fucking reason? Sometimes I open it and just see how long it takes for the landing page to load.

Roman has looked into this.

> ROMAN

Yeah well a lot of that is upstream of our software and the login is—?

> MATSSON

They're bullshitting you.

Roman isn't about to argue though.

> ROMAN

Right. No sure. Sure.

Matsson shakes his head. Roman tries to get into it too.

You know what? Let's take my phone to the bathroom and fucking piss on our app? Shall we stream piss on our streaming platform?

Matsson laughs. They walk towards the toilet.

INT. KENDALL'S PARTY – BATHROOM – NIGHT

They head into the bathroom.

> MATSSON
> (*looks at Roman's phone*)

Twenty-two seconds!

Roman throws his phone in the urinal.

Look, I can't piss near other men due to we don't know what
reason, but please – go ahead.

*Matsson smiles and approaches the urinal. Roman talks to him as he
unzips.*

Look. GoJo is your baby and we don't want to interfere with
what you do. You're the genius. So, bearing that in mind, would
you consider meeting with my dad?

Well, yes. I would.

And you'd be interested in selling to us?

If this is all true then maybe yeah, I would.

Monday?

Sure.

And if I shake your hand now will I be able to tell my dad
I basically just bought GoJo for him?

Haha. No. But you can tell him I'm in the conversation!

Alright!

They shake hands.

Are we amazing? I think I might be the best businessman in
America.

(looking at phone in urinal)

Still loading!

INT. KENDALL'S PARTY — TREEHOUSE — NIGHT

They walk out of the bathroom.

> ROMAN
> (*to a member of nearby staff*)
> Um, so I dropped my phone in the urinal – oops! – would you retrieve and rice it for me? Thanks.
> (*to a passing waiter*)
> Can you do us a bottle train, we're celebrating?

> SERVER
> I'm sorry, sir?

> ROMAN
> A 'bottle train' with the – the sparklers and the fireworks and the hot girls and the whole – 'yay I won, capitalism!'

> SERVER
> Um, I don't think we're doing a bottle train, sir.

> ROMAN
> No bottle train? Then you know what, bring me some tater tots because apparently I'm in a fucking Cheesecake Factory!

INT. KENDALL'S PARTY — BACKSTAGE — NIGHT

Kendall's in his party clothes.

There is a crucifix ready to be hoisted up onto the stage.

Straps and braces to hold him in place, a ledge for his feet. Microphone headset equipment, safety stuff is all around.

We're on Kendall as he watches the technical crew look at winches and straps, buckles, microphones. He looks at Naomi. Does he start to feel what a calamitous misfire his idea could be?

The technical director has a harness for him to put on. There is also a tux and dress shirt ready for him. Four or five prop and sound guys, stagehands are working. As a party planner, Naomi, Comfrey and Berry watch.

> TECHNICAL DIRECTOR
> Okay, if you want to put on the harness you can tuxedo up, and step up onto the footrest we can strap you up then we'll

have thirty seconds and the rig will fly you up and into position, you'll have a three-two-one, you'll see the green light which counts you down to the intro.

Berry can't quite believe she is here and has her own private thoughts about the wisdom of this big number but Kendall looks weird, so she sprinkles some sugar—

BERRY
You ready to crucify Billy Joel?

KENDALL
Yeah, yeah.

BERRY
I'm kidding. You'll be great.

NAOMI
Remember what the guy said about the rig spiraling, keep still, yeah? That sounded serious.

TECHNICAL DIRECTOR
Okay. Harness, then mic? Shall we strap you in?

COMFREY
You ready to rock? You wanna get changed?

KENDALL
Uh-huh, you know what? I'm not gonna do it.

COMFREY
You don't want to do it?

KENDALL
No. It's bullshit. No.

BERRY
Because your thing was it could come over dumb if you don't lean right in?

KENDALL
Uh-huh.

COMFREY
And your speech kind of tees it up, the ironic kind of, 'This is the culmination of my life's journey? To be crucified to save you morons and . . .'

> KENDALL

I'm not doing it. It's overdetermined fifteen-layers master's degree fucking hokum let's pull it. Dressed in a tuxedo, nailed to a cross, singing Billy Joel? It doesn't make any fucking sense.

> COMFREY

What about the Tiny Wu-Tang?

> KENDALL

I don't know. I don't think so. Let them know it's not their fault, it's my fault. We'll pay them up.

He looks angsty and pained and heads out as Comfrey and Berry talk to the technical gang.

INT. KENDALL'S PARTY – BIG ROOM – NIGHT

Shiv goes up to the bar and orders.

> SHIV

Give me a Negroni.

She looks miserable and heads to the dance floor.

INT. KENDALL'S PARTY – UPSTAIRS VIP AREA – NIGHT

Greg is grabbing a drink. In sight of the dance floor.

Then, there is Comfrey passing.

> GREG

Hey? How's it going?

She has a lot on her plate.

> COMFREY

Um. Yeah good. Good. Um, Ken had me try to call Springsteen to rescue the vibe but that's been countermanded, and we're looking at a – a jetpack for him to leave through the retractable roof which takes at least forty-eight hours to move.

> GREG

Okay?

> COMFREY

I mean a lot of the ideas are jokes, but some aren't so—

GREG

Very weird. Yes indeed.

He looks at her. Leave a beat, swallows.

COMFREY

What?

GREG

Me. No nothing, yeah.
                    (*then*)
Yeah, it's – stupid but earlier before I heard you were going to
be orchestrating a smear campaign against me, I actually was
going to – to ask you if you wanted to grab a drink sometime?

*Okay? She could see this might come, from his vibes. It's hardly her
heart's desire but he's interesting and weird and harmless enough.*

COMFREY

Oh. Okay?

GREG

But then . . .

COMFREY

What?

GREG

Um, Kendall, he said—

COMFREY
            (*getting potentially pissed off now*)
He said what?

GREG

Oh, nothing. No, he just said – maybe not? Clean lines. Church
and state. Wrong place, wrong time. But maybe. One day when
you're no longer working for him and trying to destroy my
reputation—

This has been building for her—

COMFREY

You know I spent a week researching where to buy lunchboxes
from the eighties for him? To serve canapés from? Like the one
he took to school? Then he decided he didn't want lunchboxes.
So now I have all these He-Man lunchboxes in my apartment

and I have to try to resell them on eBay and his office wants the receipts.

                        (*then*)

If you wanna ask me out ask me out.

                       GREG

Do you wanna go out sometime?

                  COMFREY

Yes.

                       GREG

Great!

Greg looks over and sees Shiv dancing.

Wow. She's really dancing there. Very, emancipated.

                  COMFREY

Yeah it's like she's dancing *at* something.

                       GREG

Should I help her stop?

                  COMFREY

Maybe some water? But you don't want her to over-hydrate. Do you know what she's taken?

                       GREG

Um, I don't think she's taken anything?

As they watch Tom approaches Shiv and whispers in her ear (the location of Matsson). Shiv stops. Listens. Thinks, leaves.

INT. KENDALL'S PARTY — TREEHOUSE — NIGHT

Kendall and Naomi head through the treehouse and out through a back entrance towards a corridor/backstage area.

INT. KENDALL'S PARTY — GIFT ROOM — NIGHT

A backstage boring cinder-block room where all the gifts have been gathered.

Kendall comes in with Naomi.

> KENDALL
You found the one, from my kids?

> ASSISSTANT
Um, I don't believe so.

> KENDALL
Uh-huh. Well. Okay. That's not good.
> (then)
Will you give us a moment?

The assistants depart.

Most of the gifts are wrapped and we don't clock the contents.

But if we see unwrapped gifts they might include top-of-the-range limited-edition bottles of champagne and spirits, luxury watches, pens, lamps, vases, art pieces, first editions of novels and comic books, movie and sports merchandise and framed memorabilia. Maybe a Triumph or other desirable motorcycle.

Kendall's overwrought, he starts looking through the piles. Looking for the gift from his kids.

> NAOMI
It'll turn up, Ken.

> KENDALL
Uh-huh. Well it won't turn up if we don't look for it?

> NAOMI
Well I know that.

> KENDALL
I'm sorry, I'm just saying, Nay.
> (looks)
So where the fuck is it?

He's getting more agitated.

> NAOMI
Take a break. Would you like my gift?

She focusses him on her.

> KENDALL
Yeah. Yes I would. I would love that.

She gives it to him. Either she knows where it is or has it right there with her. A small box. He opens it.

Okay. Wow. Wow.

NAOMI

It's a watch.

KENDALL

Yeah. Thanks.

NAOMI

No? I'm terrible at presents.

KENDALL

No it's nice. It is. Thanks so much.

NAOMI

It's fine. I'm sorry I didn't know and it was supposed to be nice.

KENDALL

It's great.

NAOMI

It's fine, give it back to me.

KENDALL

I like it. Thanks, Nay, is it inscribed or—?

NAOMI

It's just a stupid watch, I'll get you something else.
(*brightly, kidding*)
Do you want a blowjob?

KENDALL

Ha. Yeah.
(*then*)
No it's just, why would you get me a watch? It's fine but.

NAOMI

Ken?

KENDALL

No. I don't want to be a dick but I have a watch you know I have my watch and like— Just another watch.

NAOMI

It's a shitty gift and I hate buying gifts.

KENDALL

No, it's just apart from my kids you're the only person in the world who gives a fuck about me and this is what you get me?

NAOMI

I dunno, Ken. Maybe I'm a dumb person.

KENDALL

Well no you're not, no, so I'm just trying to get inside your head and figure out why you would give me this gift? It's fine.

He goes back to looking through the gifts, maybe he starts doing it a little manically, he's hiding from Naomi, but as he goes . . . he starts maybe to get to a peak of lostness, a feeling that nothing at all is right and he maybe starts to cry. Or lose control.

NAOMI

Ken? Hey, Ken, come on?

He keeps going. She tries to stop him. Maybe he breaks away from her and carries on until she stands in front of him or yells at him or grabs him and hugs him and makes him stop. He surrenders, broken.

Sorry, Ken. But yeah? You know.

KENDALL
(crying or undone)
No. It's fine. It's fine. I don't know I just thought it might be something. Because I'm you know, I'm spinning, out here. And I thought, I just thought it might be something.

NAOMI

Like what?

KENDALL

Like I don't know, something, else.

NAOMI

Uh-huh.

KENDALL

I want something that might make things good, you know? Something nice.

NAOMI

It's okay, honey.

527

> KENDALL

This is so – pathetic. This – thing is fucking vainglorious bullshit and I – I can't do it I don't want anything to do with any of this fucking shit, it's just nothing and I wish I was – I wish I was home.

> NAOMI

Let's go home.

INT. KENDALL'S PARTY – COMPLIMENTS TUNNEL – NIGHT

Greg is with Tom. Near the compliment tunnel. Tom is cokey, jaw grinding. Feeling powerful but on edge.

> GREG

Hey hey hey hey!
> (*then he sees Tom's grinding jaw*)

You okay, man?

> TOM

Yes I am okay, Greg. Why do you keep asking me if I'm okay?

> GREG

Well I just haven't see you smile in like six hours?

He leads him towards the compliment tunnel.

> TOM

You do not have to smile to be happy. I'm enjoying very much thinking about myself and my various skills and abilities.

> GREG

You wanna try the compliment tunnel?

They head into the tunnel.

> TOM
> (*suspiciously*)

Why are you so happy?

> GREG

Me? Well, actually because I've met the most wonderful girl in the world!

COMPLIMENTER I
(*calling through*)
You're just fantastic.

They walk through.

TOM
(*yes*)
Uh-huh. I'm amazing.

GREG
I mean it's possible she's only going out with me due to, you
know, rancor or pique.

They pass further through.

COMPLIMENTER 2
You're so full of grace!

Tom didn't totally hear and reacts.

TOM
What's that?

Tom stops them.

GREG
Um, I think she said 'you're full of grace.'

TOM
Well that's a weird thing to say. Is she being sarcastic?
(*to the actor*)
Are you being sarcastic?

GREG
(*to the actor*)
It's okay – he's had a lot of cocaine, I think he's feeling a little
paranoid.

TOM
Well don't tell them that! I'm a public figure who could one day
run for high office or lead a Fortune 500!

GREG
(*smoothing over*)
He's a lovely guy, you're doing great work.

They walk on.

> TOM
> (*darkly*)

You're very merry.

> GREG

I'm just – I'm excited about my date. I like her, what can I say? It's exciting!

> COMPLIMENTER 3

You're the best!

> TOM
> (*coldly*)

Thank you.

> GREG
> (*warmly*)

Thank you.

Tom looks at Greg suspiciously.

> TOM

You seem to be happier than me, Greg.

> GREG

It's not a finite pie, Tom, we can both be happy.

> TOM
> (*doubts it*)

Uh-huh, sure.

> (*then*)

It's supposed to be me who's happy, but it's you. How did that happen? I took the wrong drugs in the wrong order and I can't get happy again.

> GREG

I guess this is a cautionary tale?

> TOM

Do not turn me into anti-drug ad, Greg.

INT. KENDALL'S PARTY – TREEHOUSE – NIGHT

Roman is talking to some folks as Shiv barrels up. (She's got in – maybe we see security in the distance pointing her out to one another and deciding whether to take any action.)

ROMAN

Okay, here she is! Are you okay?

SHIV

What are you up to? What's going on, did you get to Matsson?
I heard you were speaking?

ROMAN

Onlookers reported you having some kind of breakdown?
People were anxious in case you swallowed your tongue?

SHIV

Yeah I was dancing.

ROMAN

I heard it looked like a cry for help. 'The Dance of the Sugar
Plum Failure'.

SHIV

You spoke to him though?

ROMAN

Yup.

SHIV

And?

ROMAN

Um, do you mind if I don't say?

SHIV
(lightly)

Fuck you, c'mon.

ROMAN

Don't worry about it, Shivvy. Go cut a rug, I'll handle the
business.

SHIV

Hey come on, seriously, Rome.

*The tone changes. He looks at her and doesn't look away. He stares
her down.*

ROMAN

I am being serious. I'll talk to Dad, see if he wants to loop you
in? He often does like to loop you in.

> SHIV

Roman, just, fucking, I want to know what was said because this is important. I might need to finesse.

> ROMAN

Oh you'd finesse? Thank you! But how can you finesse something that's already done? By ruining it maybe?

> SHIV

No by making sure—

> ROMAN

Thing is Lukas and I have a connection and I don't actually see how you fit into this?

She looks at him.

> SHIV

Dude, if you want to show off maybe do it to someone who gives a shit. Like your girlfriend? Oh no, wait, has she left you?

> ROMAN

Look, I know it's been a bad day for you, what with hearing you've got to carry on sharing your apartment with the old meat wardrobe but try to keep your wig on, yeah?

> SHIV

Dude, I'm the one in a functioning relationship.

> ROMAN

Right. I saw you, sipping Dad's champagne. You looked like you were sucking a lemon.

> SHIV

I don't drink on work days. I have self-control.

> ROMAN

Uh-huh. Were you thinking about all the dick you were going to ride while he was inside?

> SHIV

No one likes talking about me fucking guys as much as you, you know that? Why is that? Is it cos you're the COO who can't fuck?

ROMAN

Did you think Tommy was going to jail? And Daddy was going to jail and I was going to jail and Kendall's looney tunes? Did you think it was ladies' night and they were playing your song? Because you were wrong. All the men have got together in man club and decided *everything's fine*, so just *shut up*.

SHIV

He's using you as the messenger boy because you're easily controlled. But as usual, you're too dumb to see it.

ROMAN

Look I know it's difficult for you. You don't want to have to do the dance for Daddy, cos you are not a good dancer.

SHIV

You're a real piece of shit, you know that?

ROMAN

Turns out he loves it when I do the daddy dance. But I guess that's just because he loves me. He loves fucking me and he won't fuck you.

SHIV

You're fucking gross and you betrayed me.

ROMAN

Daddy doesn't love his carrot-top anymore, even when she does her little daddy dance.

Roman does a little dance.

As Kendall is being led through by Naomi, broken. Roman spots him. Sees his vulnerability – can't let it pass without a poke—

Happy birthday, motherfucker!

Naomi tries to shield Kendall.

NAOMI

Enough yeah?

But Roman waves provocatively and shouts.

ROMAN

Goodnight!

Kendall wants out but some child part inside is provoked—

533

> KENDALL

Neither of you should be in here.

> ROMAN

Oh no? Call the cops! Intruders have breached the masturbatorium!

> KENDALL

You came here to fuck me. You're ghouls and you're disgusting.

> ROMAN

'Sorry'!!

> KENDALL
> (to a member of staff or Naomi)

Can we get them out?

Naomi grabs a party organizer to figure out the cleanest way to get Kendall out, they discuss for a beat.

> ROMAN

Oh dude, it's too late, I already spoke to Matsson, who hates you by the way, and laughs at you constantly.

Shiv can see Kendall's kind of broken.

> SHIV

Rome, c'mon?

> ROMAN

Oh what 'go gentle on birthday boy'?

> KENDALL

You didn't come to see me, did you, Shiv. You came to chase a deal for Dad?

> SHIV

Yeah, well, we haven't been getting on very well lately, have we?

> KENDALL

GoJo was my idea.

> ROMAN

What are you, fucking six? You lost. No need to be a baby about it.

> KENDALL

You like the spying, Shiv? On your niece, on our nanny? You like that?

> SHIV

Lay off the drugs, Ken.
    (*but she picks up a vibration from Roman*)
We're not are we, Rome?

> ROMAN

It's a fucking party game! He's in Dad's shit, we're in his grill, everyone's in the shit so don't act clean.

> SHIV

Well, that *is* disgusting.

> ROMAN

Oh you're siding with traitor now?

> SHIV

No, I'm just saying there's a fucking line.

Typical. They can send letters and do press conferences but Roman can't?!

> ROMAN

Oh there's a line now? No line for him, no line for you. But there's a line for me? You're a pair of stuck-up cunts who can't fucking bear to see me win.

Naomi has a plan and tries to lead Kendall on but there is a bit of residual pain in his tank—

> KENDALL

You're not a real person. YOU'RE NOT A REAL PERSON. YOU'RE NOT REAL.

Roman steps toward Kendall, sensing he's on the edge.

> ROMAN

Come on, Shitty Jesus, hit me! Punch me, Jesus! C'mon. You know you want to. Fucking prick.

But there's nothing there from Kendall. He retreats.

Roman goads and trips Kendall as he retreats out of the room and down and out where he encounters Connor coming to say farewell—

535

Happy fucking birthday, man!

CONNOR
Hey. What's this? Easy, everybody calm down, okay?

Kendall passes Connor but then can't let it go—

KENDALL
Take your coat off. I invited you. I tried to be fucking kind to you monsters. Take your fucking coat off. Take your fucking coat off!!!

Shiv and Roman watch him go, led away by Naomi.

INT. KENDALL'S PARTY — KENDALL'S CHILDHOOD
BEDROOM — NIGHT

Kendall's there with Naomi and Comfrey. Staff have closed off the area.

Kendall points out a few things, a comforter he wants collected.

A book, maybe Too Much Birthday, *the* Berenstain Bears *or* Goodnight Mo*on.*

INT. SHIV AND TOM'S CAR — NIGHT

Tom and Shiv are as far apart as it's possible to be, both staring out the window. Tom's jaw is still going.

TOM
You wanna go someplace else? Like go out out?

SHIV
Um, no. No thanks.

EXT. STREET — NIGHT

Maybe Roman's walking because he's on a high. He wants the fresh air and he's calling his dad. His chauffeur might be following with his car.

ROMAN
Hey, Dad. Nailed him. I am the only child you'll ever need. You can kill the others. Love you.

EXT. KENDALL'S APARTMENT – NIGHT

Kendall has his comforter wrapped around his shoulders.

He's trying to feel the beat.

> KENDALL
> Shall I tell them to stop the party?

> NAOMI
> It's just a party, Ken. Just let it fizzle, yeah? C'mon.

She leads him back to the chairs and table. They sit and she puts a hand on his arm.

Episode Eight
CHIANTISHIRE

Written by Jesse Armstrong
Directed by Mark Mylod

Original air date 5 December 2021

Cast

LOGAN ROY	Brian Cox
KENDALL ROY	Jeremy Strong
MARCIA ROY	Hiam Abbass
GREG HIRSCH	Nicholas Braun
SHIV ROY	Sarah Snook
ROMAN ROY	Kieran Culkin
CONNOR ROY	Alan Ruck
TOM WAMBSGANS	Matthew Macfadyen
FRANK VERNON	Peter Friedman
KARL MULLER	David Rasche
GERRI KELLMAN	J. Smith-Cameron
WILLA FERREYRA	Justine Lupe
RAVA	Natalie Gold
SOPHIE ROY	Swayam Bhatia
IVERSON ROY	Quentin Morales
COLIN STILES	Scott Nicholson
STEWY HOSSEINI	Arian Moayed
SANDI	Hope Davis
CAROLINE COLLINGWOOD	Harriet Walter
KERRY CASTELLABATE	Zoë Winters
COMFREY PELLITS	Dasha Nekrasova
BIANCA	Hermione Lynch
LUKAS MATSSON	Alexander Skarsgård
DEWI SWANN	Robert S. Gregory
SAMIA SARPONG	Faye Yvette McQueen
SIMON EDGERTON	Jeff Blumenkrantz
LAURIE	Tomas Arana
PETER MUNION	Pip Torrens
THE CONTESSA	Ella Rumpf
GAVIN BENTNER	Jeffrey Grover
WEDDING PLANNER	Angeliqa Devi

DAY ONE

EXT. WAYSTAR – DAY

The many discreet cars of directors are arriving.

INT. WAYSTAR – PARKING GARAGE – DAY

Cars pull into the underground car park.

INT. WAYSTAR – DAY

In elevators and through corridors, the directors are gathering.

We might see: Stewy's nominee – Samia Sarpong, Dewi Swann (independent), Simon Edgerton (lead independent director).

Some of them walk through the reception area. Security and Waystar flacks there to keep the entrance gates open and ease their passage as they step into elevators and stand in groups, chatting with assistants.

INT. WAYSTAR – BOARDROOM – DAY

The Waystar directors assemble.

Frank Vernon welcomes them.

INT. WAYSTAR – ELEVATORS – DAY

As Sandi and Stewy emerge from an elevator, Kerry is there to greet them, they expect to go one way but . . .

KERRY

Um, could Logan just get five?

Sandi and Stewy look at one another: Interesting.

INT. WAYSTAR – LOGAN'S OFFICE – DAY

Logan, Gerri and Roman are there as Stewy and Sandi are shown in. Tom has observer status. He has Logan's trust and Logan occasionally checks his responses.

>   GERRI
> Good morning, sorry to delay you. Thank you for this.

>   ROMAN
> Just a little pre-meet!

>   LOGAN
> Welcome. How you doing?
>   *(to Sandi, apparently friendly)*
> How's your dad?

>   SANDI
> He's good, he hopes to make it in person to the next one.

Never going to happen.

>   LOGAN
> Sure. Send him my best.

Logan smiles, unreadable.

> Finally made it into my fucking castle and he's too sick to show up, huh? Still.
>   *(also unreadable)*
> You're here, so that's nice.

>   SANDI
> Thanks, I feel the same way.

>   STEWY
> Great, we're all over the fucking moon. What is this?

>   GERRI
> Well, we just wanted to give you the courtesy, as key partners, of an advance warning – so it didn't come out of the blue at the board meeting.

Sandi and Stewy are suddenly super-alert.

>   STEWY
> What? What are you going to show me, dead babies?

> GERRI

Relax. Roman?

> ROMAN

Uh, yeah, yeah, so.
> (then)

We're in discussions to acquire GoJo.

Sandi processes as a million thoughts occur to Stewy – but he has one question right away—

> STEWY

Okay. How advanced?

> ROMAN

Um . . .
> (very advanced)

not that advanced.
> (checks with Logan and Gerri)

Just getting to outline terms.

> STEWY

So pretty fucking advanced?

> LOGAN

I didn't want to bother you until there was some protein. I know how busy you both are, with all your—
> (bullshit)

various activities.

> GERRI

But, we didn't want to ambush you in the boardroom. We wanted to let you know here.

> SANDI

But you are still ambushing us.

> LOGAN

We're not ambushing you we're—

> STEWY
> (cutting in)

Well no, I mean, if you jump out on someone on the road in the middle of the night and hit them on the head and shout 'I'm not ambushing you!' that's still a fucking ambush.

ROMAN

Yeah, except we're not bopping you over the head, are we?
We're handing you a massively value-enhancing business-
transformative acquisition. So, relax and think about the fucking
honey, ah?

Stewy and Sandi look at one another.

SANDI

Oh thanks, sweetheart, yeah cos I just walked in here from the
hay barn and I have no concerns so sign us up.

STEWY

I'm thinking forty-eight fucking things here, man. Can we get a
little more detail?

ROMAN

Well? We're doing the dance, we're nearly there on headline
terms, and we'll obviously value your input.

STEWY

Oh, we get input? That's exciting. Do we get to sign our names
and put little smiley faces in the dots over the i's? That's my
fucking favorite.

LOGAN

I love my business but we've had our throats slit on ads for
twenty years. We're bleeding out. Another five of cord-cutting
and we'll be dead on the fucking carpet. This is a transformative
deal.

*Logan looks out to Kerry – he wants to be interrupted soon. They've
done the business.*

SANDI
(*without even looking at Stewy*)
I mean, just, obviously, this is not okay. We were supposed to be
inside deal-making.

*But Stewy likes the deal in his bones. Sandi's obstructiveness makes
him squirm.*

LOGAN

Things moved very fast. It's all very sensitive but from now on
we'll be sure to keep you—

Kerry comes in.

> **KERRY**
> Um, I think they are assembling?

> **LOGAN**
> Okay, shall we?

Logan tries to lead them out but Sandi stops things—

> **SANDI**
> How will you feel if Matsson starts – microdosing and tweeting about angels again?

> **LOGAN**
> Matsson is a visionary.

> **STEWY**
> Sure. Cos he's tripping balls. And pumping his stock price.

> **LOGAN**
> He has a team we can do business with.

> **SANDI**
> My dad is worried their valuation is frothy. Their subscriber growth in Asia is padded. Their US growth is flatlining.

> **ROMAN**
> Uh-huh. Position A is he's the bomb. Position B is 'Oooh, twiddle my hispter's tash maybe he's *not* the bomb??' But *yes* he's the fucking bomb. Their tech stack is sharp fucking cheddar. Their AI is terrifying. It'll take a look at your lunch and give you six perfect suggestions for what to watch tonight with the wife the app is gonna match you with next fucking week.

> **GERRI**
> Okay! Shall we? We really ought to . . .

> **SANDI**
> Look. I am just very alarmed at how this is being presented here. Waystar is a somewhat languishing but very profitable business, and yes you need to assess how you meet the challenges of DTC but this is far bigger than anything you've ever contemplated. It will reshape the company entirely.

Sandi looks at Stewy but he's looking away. He does like this deal. Logan clocks the difference of opinion between Sandi and Stewy. He has a tactic—

> LOGAN
>
> Well look, if you guys really don't like it, sure, kill it.

> STEWY
>
> Well we didn't say that . . .

Big smile as he gets up to take them up to the boardroom.

> SANDI
>
> And where's Shiv on this? Why isn't Shiv here?

Sandi looks at Tom.

> ROMAN
>
> Here? Oh this is just inner circle.

She looks at him.

> I'm kidding. 'The President' will meet us up there I guess!

INT. SHIV AND TOM'S APARTMENT – BEDROOM – DAY

She is in sweatpants and a T-shirt. Laptop open. But scrolling her phone. Her phone goes.

Intercut with:

INT. WAYSTAR – DAY

Tom walks behind the rest of the gang towards the elevators on his phone. Gerri is sweet-talking Sandi. Roman going to work on Stewy.

> TOM
>
> Hey. You want the briefing?

> SHIV
> (*looking at screen*)
>
> Uh-huh.

> TOM
>
> I think they'll eat it. Sandi's processing, Stewy loves it. Roman led. No Frank, no Karl. Sandi wants your take. Gerri's trying to

fill your boots but I'm not sure Sandi's buying it. Just walking them up to the boardroom. You in the car?

SHIV

No. I'm gonna call in.

He knew it was possible but it's worrying.

TOM

Oh, okay? You okay?

SHIV
(*fuck off*)

Yesss.

TOM
(*what?*)
Oh. Okay. Good. Well that works.
(*then*)
Everything okay, sweetheart?

SHIV
(*no*)
Yes. I just still feel how I was feeling. So.

TOM

Okay. Right. And, so what about your mom's wedding?

SHIV

I need Fatima to pack for me, I can't face packing but yes. Can you message Fatima to pack when she comes?

TOM

Do you want to talk?

SHIV

I'm not feeling great. There's nothing really to say.

TOM

Okay. Okay. I mean do you even need to go?

SHIV

Oh yeah! Can you imagine? Fuck that. I'd never hear the end of it.

INT. WAYSTAR – BOARDROOM – DAY

Now everyone is gathering around the big table.

> FRANK
> Um, so, the board members not physically available will be joining by phone including: Siobhan Roy who sends apologies, she's working on – strategy.

> SHIV
> *(on speakerphone)*
> Hey.

> FRANK
> And Kendall Roy who is not attending due to—
> *(the agreed line)*
> illness.

> KENDALL
> *(on speakerphone, but he's changed his mind)*
> Not true.

> FRANK
> *(ignores)*
> And we're going to lead off with an update on the promising developments in the ongoing investigation from which portion of the meeting Kendall and Logan Roy are recused. Hence—

He nods to outside – where—

INT. WAYSTAR – OUTSIDE THE BOARDROOM – DAY

Logan looms close to the glass, staring in to the fish bowl, with Kerry behind. Tom looking at his phone on a couch.

INT. WAYSTAR – BOARDROOM – DAY

Inside the boardroom, board members look out—

> SIMON
> Is he going to watch?

Logan stares in.

> STEWY
> I feel like I'm taking a shit in the Guggenheim.

INT. SHIV AND TOM'S APARTMENT — BEDROOM — DAY

She is listening on her phone.

INT. WAYSTAR — BOARDROOM — DAY

Back in the room – the last of the board are leaving.

LOGAN
Wonderful, great thoughts. Very helpful perspective. You've given us lots to think about. Many thanks.

KENDALL
(*on speakerphone*)
I have a number of other points to make.

LOGAN
(*into phone*)
Yeah, fuck off, ghost.

He hits a button. Kendall is gone.

As they depart, Logan gives tight smiles and farewells to the board members.

As the directors pass, Tom catches Stewy and Sandi.

TOM
How you guys feeling?

STEWY
Yeah. It's big. But I guess Grandpa learned how to program the VCR and we should all be glad, right? You been putting ginkgo in his oatmeal.

Tom smiles, then—

TOM
(*to Sandi*)
Shiv sends her regards.

SANDI
Fine. Great. Gerri's looping me in.

TOM
Great. Great stuff.

(*unreadably straight*)
Gerri's the best.

Tom smiles them off and heads to the door of the boardroom.

Sandi and Stewy good?

ROMAN
Uh-huh. I think that all worked.

LOGAN
Yup, Gerri, will you give them some plastic sheriff badges and send them off to eat beans and fart somewhere, yeah?
(*to the group*)
Okay. So, look, I like the shape of this. But if we're going for it, I don't have a relationship with Matsson. I don't like him and he doesn't like me. So, Roman, I need you as the pointman because every other person here is one million years old, right, Ger?

She looks like: Well thanks.

Can you do it? Can you land this fucking fish for me?

ROMAN
I can do it.

Logan looks at him.

LOGAN
No little jokes?

ROMAN
No little jokes. I can do it.

LOGAN
Good.
(*can't let it go without*)
And get a fucking haircut.

Roman heads out.

ROMAN
Uh-huh. Thanks, Dad. And so you want me to send your apologies to Mom?

LOGAN
No. No. I'm coming. We're going.

ROMAN

Oh? Right. Yeah? I thought Peter could suck your – and she could eat your – whatever?

Surprising. Roman can't see what's brought this on.

LOGAN

Nah, I'm coming. Why not? I'm probably paying for the fucking thing!

Roman heads out pondering.

DAY TWO

EXT. RAVA'S PLACE – DAY

Kendall is there with a car big enough for all of them. Bianca, the nanny, is in the car. The kids climb in.

RAVA

Have fun!

KENDALL

Okay. Well, here we go.

He smiles farewell. Not in a great way.

RAVA

You okay?

He nods: Uh-huh.

Great, and um watch them in the pool okay?

KENDALL

Well what's that supposed to mean?

RAVA

It means watch them in the pool.

KENDALL

I'm fine, Rava.

RAVA

Naomi not with you?

KENDALL

I haven't been feeling great. But I'm feeling a lot better. And she's grabbing some time to check in on herself. That okay?

RAVA

Fine, I was just asking.

KENDALL

Sure. Look. I have Bianca and I'm fine, this will be good.

RAVA

Okay, right.
(*been on her mind*)
Um, so maybe I should just say. I had a weird thing where, they kind of said your hot nanny had been shouting, and making Iverson cry Sophie says. And he said maybe taking cash from wallets?

KENDALL

What? I'm sorry? What's 'hot'—?

RAVA

Does it seem right? It didn't seem right. They were laughing but I thought I should say?

KENDALL
(*scrambled*)
Oh, man. Should I take her? Shall I fire her? Why didn't you call?

RAVA

I did call.
(*then*)
It sounded weird. I don't think she's gonna 'do' anything. I think it's fine. It's up to you.

KENDALL

Is this a thing? Can I just get a read, am I going to read about this in court papers? This isn't – leverage is it, Rav?

RAVA

Ken? I am just telling you.

KENDALL

Fine. Just, I have a lot going on. I'm going to speak with my father. About— And Naomi. So this just feels like you're doing a number.

RAVA

It's not a number.

KENDALL

Okay.

(*thinks*)

I don't think it tracks . . . she's stealing a hundred bucks? She's on a hundred grand a year. They like her.

RAVA

It's fine. I think. Say hello to your mom and to Shiv.

He nods, sure. He gets in

KENDALL

(*to kids*)

Hey, hey, hey! We ready or what?

Smiles at Bianca who smiles back.

EXT. AIRFIELD – DAY

Shiv and Tom arrive as other cars leave.

INT. ROY PRIVATE JET – DAY

Shiv and Tom board. Roman is working at a table.

ROMAN

Hey. I know you.

(*then*)

Didn't you used to be Shiv Roy?

SHIV

You sounded dumb at the board meeting.

ROMAN

Yeah at least I showed up, what were you doing? Brunching with some other sock-puppet girlboss presidents?

                              SHIV
Uh-huh, where's Tabitha? Has she found someone a little more
emotionally available? Like a stick of Wrigley's Spearmint gum?

She sits. He waits a beat, has something serious to ask.

                              ROMAN
So, listen. Just to say, I've had Peter Onions rat-fucked.

                              SHIV
What a lovely wedding present.

                              ROMAN
The guy's a tweedy little slime-badger. Three bankruptcies, two
marriages, four kids, five shell companies. Big investor in shitty
care homes. Tipping apple sauce down their gullets and telling
them they had a four-course dinner.

                              TOM
Sounds lovely.

                              ROMAN
So I've asked Mum if we can talk to her, and I think we should
do it together.

                              SHIV
Do what?

                              ROMAN
Well, ask if she should be doing this? It's like five months since
'Rory' was going to move in?

                              SHIV
Whatever.

                              ROMAN
At least check she has a prenup. You know, she's got all the stuff
from the divorce in there, the holding company and everything
and this guy is clearly on the make. So, yeah?

                              SHIV
Fuck it.

                              ROMAN
'Fuck it'?

SHIV
(taunting him)

She's probably in sexual thrall to him. He's driving her crazy with his sugar dick and there's nothing we can do?

ROMAN

Fine. Let him kill her for her emeralds and screw us out of the firm, see if I care.

TOM

Um, Rome, on the deal, I was talking to Karl and Frank . . .

ROMAN

Yeah well, you're not really a part of that, either of you.

SHIV

Well, yes I am.

ROMAN

I mean I can't quite fire you yet, Shiv, because I'm still a little scared of you. But what I'm thinking is, when I take over maybe I put you in the office next to mine and make you my sexy secretary? Sorry, Tom.

TOM

Obviously it should be a lowball because their board will come back but it can't be insulting. It needs to be a subtle number.

ROMAN

Or I might make you my boss. And then whenever you tell me what to do I'll tell you to fuck off.

DAY THREE

EXT. ITALY – CAROLINE'S WEDDING COMPLEX – DAY

Kids, Kendall and Bianca all get out. Staff there for the luggage.

Kendall is maybe subtly watching Bianca.

EXT. CAROLINE'S WEDDING VILLAS – TERRACE

Kendall and the kids meet Caroline on a terrace. Kendall with a new buzzcut.

                              CAROLINE
Hello, all! Hello. Welcome, all.
                        (*looks at his hair*)
Oooh. Back from the front? No, it's nice.

                              KENDALL
Yeah, just stripping down.

Maybe they embrace. The kids are shy but say hello.

                              CAROLINE
                          (*to the kids*)
Look at you. Lovely!

                              KENDALL
You wanted a word?

                              CAROLINE
Yes. Yes. Um, the – people – can show them up if you like?
There's a pool up at your house.

The kids head off to their villa and pool with Bianca and staff.

                        (*to kids as they go*)
You're probably used to pools absolutely everywhere, but
nevertheless.
                          (*after them*)
Don't drown!
                        (*looks at Kendall*)
You look tired.

                              KENDALL
Sure. You look good actually.
                             (*then*)
So? What was it?

                              CAROLINE
Right. Yes. So. Listen, what I wanted to ask is – you'll see up at
your villa, Peter, has had printed this awful sort of itinerary of
events – all the welcomes and rehearsals, the ceremonies and
grisly post-mortem brunches.

                              KENDALL
Uh-huh?

CAROLINE

And yes – without it being too definitive, I was wondering if we could slightly divvy them up?

KENDALL

As in?

CAROLINE

As in, your father would rather not – as I understand it – be together with you, as far as possible.

He looks at her.

Oh god no, don't look like that it's too awful. I can't do it. Never mind.

KENDALL

No go on—

CAROLINE

Well the idea was just to ask you not to come to a couple of the hundreds of events?

KENDALL

And so what is your son getting? And what is your ex-husband, who you hate, getting?

CAROLINE

Oh don't get on your high horse! I don't care. It's 'Bridezilla', he's set his heart on having all the important people at his wedding? He's such a little tart.

KENDALL

Jesus, Mom. I don't know if that works. I actually was planning on talking, so—

Kendall has something he wants to say to his dad – Caroline sees trouble brewing.

CAROLINE

Well yes, exactly, you see I'd love to keep it all nice? So, have a think. I'll see you tons.
                    (*sees Peter, and potential escape*)
Peter! Come and see Kendall.

PETER

Ah! Kendall. Like the mint cake!

> (*aiming at disarming*)

You don't look loony to me!

                    KENDALL
> (*whatever*)

Yeah, pleased to meet you.

                    PETER

Absolutely, we've actually met at lunch a few times and when you were scoping out Dativa, I was part of that whole gang, in those meetings?

                    KENDALL

Right. Yeah, I do a lot of meetings.

                    PETER
> (*unreadable parry*)

Of course. You're very important.
> (*then*)

So. How's it all going? How's the campaign? What have you got up your sleeve? What happens next?

Kendall feels very tired. He tries telling the truth to see how that feels—

                    KENDALL

Yeah, I don't know.
> (*then, fuck you, try the truth*)

I actually might be getting out of the whole business so. Yeah. Spread it around.
> (*heads off*)

Mom, I'll check the schedule, maybe see you next month?

And he's off.

                    CAROLINE
> (*after him*)

Very dramatic! I think it's about four hours.

EXT. CAROLINE'S WEDDING VILLAS — DAY

Shiv and Tom arrive.

And Roman.

Gerri and Laurie. He has painting stuff with him.

Comfrey takes some business cases into Kendall's.

Connor is looking at his phone as people unpack. Willa takes in the view. Connor gets a message. A little troubling.

> WILLA
>
> Wow. What a place. Italy! Pizza, pasta and popes. You ever met the Pope, Con?

> CONNOR
> *(distracted, looking at message)*
>
> Uh-huh. Sure. I met one – couple of popes back. With Dad. He was a real full-fat Pope Classic Pope. Very religious.

> WILLA
>
> Guess he'd drunk the Kool-Aid huh? Everything okay, Con?

> CONNOR
>
> Yup. Yeah. Just – the guy from Politico, asking, regarding his piece, for your full name and like, your, employment history and whatnot?

> WILLA
>
> Oh, right. You think he's digging?

> CONNOR
>
> It might be friendly. But yeah. Probably not. What do you think?

> WILLA
>
> What do I think? I think you'd better not get too attached to your one percent!
> *(then)*
> I'm kidding. We've got nothing to hide. Right?

She smiles and heads on in. He watches, troubled.

EXT. CAROLINE'S WEDDING VILLAS – DAY

People settle into their rooms.

EXT. CAROLINE'S WEDDING VILLAS – GERRI'S ROOM – DAY

Roman comes knocking.

> ROMAN

Hey, you going to the welcome drinks because I'm going to hit it then I'm on with the banks, are you joining?

Maybe Gerri blocks Roman from coming in subtly.

> GERRI

Sure, let me just check on Laurie and then let's put our heads together on the GoJo price.

Roman looks at her.

It's ticking up but nothing scary.

> ROMAN

Laurie Laurie Laurie. Will you *stop* going on about him? You're obsessed with him and it's frankly disgusting.

Roman might try to peer in.

> GERRI

I may need you to check in with Matsson. We don't want to lose momentum and he's gone a little fucking quiet.

> ROMAN

Sure. I'll give the Swede a rub. Defrost the fucking meatball.

Laurie appears, to pick up a box of art equipment left by the door.

> LAURIE

Hi. Roman?

> ROMAN

Laurie! What you got there, buddy?

> LAURIE

My watercolors. Amazing light here.

> ROMAN

Oh fuck yeah, tell me about it.

> GERRI

Roman and I have been working closely on the huge thing I can't talk to you about.

Laurie smiles and takes his stuff back to unpack.

> ROMAN

He seems great. Does he paint with a brush or his dick?

(*then*)
Oh sorry, they're watercolors, he doesn't have a dick, right?

GERRI
(*calling back*)
Laurie, we're going to walk down, will you catch up?

Then as they get away . . .

So, I want to ask you something. To stop sending me the –
'items'.

ROMAN
Which?
(*looks*)
The dick pics. You don't want pictures of my dick?

GERRI
No.

ROMAN
Oh. I'm offended. Are you sure?

GERRI
Yes I am sure.

ROMAN
Hm. Well I'm not sure. I think you do like them but you're being
kind of typically minxy.

GERRI
I think perhaps it's when you're under pressure? But you need to
find another outlet, okay?

ROMAN
Oooh. Look at you, getting inside my head!
(*knocks on his head*)
Locked box, baby. Temple of Doom. Malice in the Palace.

*Roman and Gerri make it to an area where the inner circle of fifty or
so guests are mingling. In summer party wear, blazers, open shirts,
sundresses.*

EXT. CAROLINE'S VILLA – DAY

Roman approaches Caroline with Peter, who's chatting to other guests nearby.

> ROMAN
>
> Hey, Mom.

> CAROLINE
>
> Roman! I think you've met Peter – Peter, Roman is worried in case I'm rushing in to something. He thinks I'm in thrall to you.

> PETER
>
> Other way around!

> ROMAN
>
> Hey how you doing?

> PETER
>
> Oh good. Very excited for all this.

> ROMAN
>
> Sure. Of course. And how's business? I hear you're big into the old silvery gulags?

> PETER
>
> Hehe. Yes helping to turn around a nursing-home group. Very rewarding. We come in and look at operations and trim the fat.

> CAROLINE
> (*whispered*)
>
> He means the nurses.

> PETER
>
> Hehe. She's very rude. I don't know why I put up with it.

Maybe he whispers something in her ear we can almost hear about 'but then I'm very rude to you'.

Roman looks on in disgust as Peter walks off.

> CAROLINE
>
> He is awful, I can obviously can see that.

> ROMAN
>
> Nah just your type. Another in the line of post-Dad posh, English phonies.

> CAROLINE

He's not posh! His father was a doctor. He bought all his own furniture. He's a grasping little scholarship boy.

> ROMAN

Easy, that's my stepfather you're talking about there!

> CAROLINE

He's forcing me into it. 'Toscana'. Maybe he'll wear white for the wedding? But he is tremendous fun. Look at him, fizzing away there like a bottle of cheap prosecco!

Peter is being friendly with another knot of guests.

> ROMAN

Look, Mom, I'm not a big one for – you know, 'saying things' – But I'm just going to say: Are you sure about this? You know he has – like four kids?

> CAROLINE

Oh he has more than that darling!

> ROMAN

But do you have a prenup?

> CAROLINE
> (*teasing*)

So unromantic.

> ROMAN

I'm just – a little concerned, Mom, are you rushing this?

> CAROLINE

What do you expect me to survive on, macaroni and memorial services?

She walks off to join Peter.

Shiv, wary of talking to her mom, joins Roman once she has gone.

> ROMAN

She 'doesn't want to live off macaroni and memorial services'?

> SHIV

What, poor old Eleanor Rigby wants to eat dick and drink champagne for the rest of her life instead?

> ROMAN

And apparently we're meant to hate Peter because he was smart enough to get a scholarship and he bought his own furniture?

> SHIV

You ask about the prenup?

> ROMAN

Oh now you're interested? She's playing dumb. But she needs one. He's a fucking – cad. He may be the world's last remaining 'bounder'.

On to another part of the terrace, Kendall is arriving with Comfrey and the kids.

> SHIV

Oooh. Here he is. Full Metal Kendall. Back from birthday 'Nam.

Over with Kendall – he sees Roman and Shiv but isn't going to go over. Comfrey is briefing him.

> COMFREY

In terms of media to keep you aware of, there's a piece sourced close to the investigation confirming the DOJ expects to settle with Waystar.

> KENDALL

Saw it on the plane. You're such a shitty flack, Comfrey. Requests?

> COMFREY

Um, not much.

They've dried up and he doesn't love it.

Sit down with a podcast, it's basically it's ex-*Globe* journalists, a sort of like, like the Kennedys – 'Curse of the Roys', deep-dive, Connor's mom? Your dad and 'Rose'? The Tabloid Suicides, and they have the thing a kid who was bullied and 'was it an accident?', 'did he kill himself?' – the caterer at your sister's wedding? You know this story?

> KENDALL

Uh-huh. Sure.

> COMFREY

Right. They're spraying requests around the whole family? So?

His dials are all off so he says—

KENDALL

Sure. Fine.

COMFREY

Yeah? You'll do it?

She makes a face.

KENDALL

No. I mean, no. Fuck that why would I give them free content?
(*then*)
But keep tabs on that shit. Okay? Fucking bottom-feeders.

COMFREY

Sure. Okay. And, so, unless it's weird, I might clock off now?

KENDALL

Whatever, clock the fuck off.

She walks over to Greg, pointedly pecks him on the cheek.

GREG

Hey. Hey! How we doing?

COMFREY

Great. Great, you know? It's 'not work' but it's work?

Her phone explodes.

Ugh. I should. Sorry.

She leaves Greg and Shiv and Tom.

TOM

Well, congratulations, Greg.

SHIV

Punching above your weight there?

GREG

Comfrey? Yeah. I like her enough.
(*looks over*)
But I do wonder, is there real depth there? Like – substance?

TOM

Oh my god! The man dying of thirst is suddenly a mineral-
water critic? You want depth? Comfrey can't sate your lust for

wisdom? If only Sontag were still alive so you could take her to the drive-in!

GREG

I dunno, maybe I'm just looking for problems? Because I think she may only be dating me in retaliation.

SHIV

Spite date?

GREG

She's pissed at Kendall and I'm worried when that runs out or she gets to know the quote unquote real me, will she stick around?

SHIV

Well even if it doesn't work out I guess she's a great date ladder?

GREG

Excuse me? As in—?

SHIV

Well because people will look at her, with you and, no offense, they will say, 'What's going on there?'

TOM

Like, 'How did *he* get *her*?'

GREG

Yes I'm aware what you're saying.

SHIV

So it's a good moment. Tom, like honestly I might not have looked twice if it wasn't for Deana.

Greg looks around.

GREG

Okay, well I guess she looks nice?

They look over at a stylish young woman, the Contessa.

TOM

Oh sure! Sure! Why not!

SHIV

I think she's a princess or a duchess or something.

GREG

Too far up the date ladder? Maybe I have a big ladder? I mean why not?

TOM

Sure, why not! I mean we put a man on the moon!

As they watch, Roman moves in and says hi to her in the distance.

GREG

Oh. Okay?

Roman says something to her and she laughs.

SHIV

Oh god. Poor woman. Look at that. She probably thinks she's met a 'fun guy' at a wedding.

They clink drinks, it's a fun little interaction, a hint of flirtiness over the scene.

TOM

Someone should say something.

SHIV

He should have to ring a bell as he walks, or emit a stench.

TOM

He should be colored red like a dangerous lizard.

SHIV

He should have 'Just a Husk' tattooed on his forehead.

Caroline mingles through the party, might be heading over . . .

Okay. Scary Poppins is on maneuvers. Don't let her be nice to me. She knows I'm not in a great place and then, it's House of Flying Daggers. She's gonna wanna know how my marriage is going. And if I'm gonna have kids and—

TOM

How is your marriage going? Are you gonna have kids?

SHIV

'Haha.'

Then Shiv has got the same messages as Comfrey.

Oh fuck. Tom? Matsson.

She shows him as Roman comes over.

ROMAN

What do you think? Is he fucking—?

We see the Twitter post. Matsson in a limo. Maybe he has a TikTok filter so that after a beat he opens his mouth and spews coins—

TOM

'Going to Macao, feeling lucky'? What is that? What does it mean?

Tom looks at Roman. Gerri comes over, with her phone.

GERRI

Have you seen? Off the radar then this? Is this a move?

ROMAN

Could be nothing. Could be just— I think it's just fucking social media fireworks.

GERRI

'To Macao'. 'Feeling lucky'? What is it?
  (peers at the tweet hoping to understand the meaning)
Is he trying to boost his price?

SHIV

Is he rocking the boat?
  (looks at Roman)
Is he trying to blow up the deal? What does it mean? Has he got good subscriber numbers coming?

TOM

Maybe he's just going to Macao and feeling lucky?

Roman is calling Matsson.

SHIV

What the fuck is this?

ROMAN

Hey, Lukas, call me. Are you high? Put the fucking venti ayahuasca Big Gulp down and call me, we need to be inside-track on this tweet, okay?
  (looks at Shiv)
I dunno. It's his thing. He's a trickster.

Over in another part of the party Caroline is having a discreet word with Kendall.

SHIV

Sounds cool. Is he going to steal our watches while he saws the fucking deal in half?

Kendall walks past, he's had twenty alerts already, phone in evidence.

KENDALL

Matsson gone nut-nut? Nice work, Rome. Enjoy the ride! Keep hold of that shit, bro.

ROMAN

All under control, bro. Where you going, Naples to score junk?

KENDALL
(*to them and others standing around*)
Nah, just my mother throwing me out of her party.
(*then*)
Hey, kids! C'mon. We're heading out!

With Connor and Willa looking around at Kendall leaving.

WILLA

What's up? It looks like something's up?

CONNOR

So look, I've been thinking. Who knows what will happen. Maybe I won't ignite? Maybe the two-party system isn't as rotten as it looks. But I have to plan for success. So, Willa, this is a difficult conversation to have.

Does Willa's heart lift a little right away.

WILLA

Oh. Okay?

CONNOR

Yeah. So— Are you okay?

She's on tenterhooks.

WILLA

Yeah it's just. No go on. I'm just – what are you going to say?

Willa is on the cusp. Is her relationship with Connor at an end? How does she feel? Many thoughts go through her head. Freedom. But also the end of certain freedoms.

I mean, we could go back – 'underground' – me in my apartment in the city. You come visit. Kinda romantic?

CONNOR

That doesn't work for me. No, Maxim had an idea. Which is . . .

He gets down on one knee.

Will you make me the most-happiest-man-slash-most-bullet-proof-candidate in the world?

WILLA

Oh, um, okay?

CONNOR

'Okay'?

WILLA

No – I mean. I mean, shit a pony—

He's wobbling on one knee. She doesn't know what to say.

CONNOR

People are looking, Willa?

They are.

WILLA

Well, then I'd be pleased to say . . . Yes. Yes, can I have a think about it?

He gets up and smiles at other guests who look over.

CONNOR
(*to Willa, smiling round at the people watching*)
If it's okay, I'm smiling now, like you've said yes. But take your time. Run the numbers on it.

EXT. KENDALL'S VILLA – DAY

We see the sad sight of Kendall walking up towards his villa. Humiliating. Sophie goes on ahead racing up. Iverson plods, tired.

Kendall is on the phone to Rava.

KENDALL

Hi, yeah, I'm gonna get her thoroughly backgrounded. Well,
Rav, I don't want to have to ask the kids direct in case it
becomes a thing and they feel blamed and then they don't tell
me shit next time you hire some pedo guy to teach them flute,
okay?

(listen)

No I'm not scared. I'm thinking ahead. Yeah fuck you, Rav.
Goodbye, I was looping you in but goodbye.

*He puts the phone down. Calls Iverson to stop and sit on a step while
he asks the question.*

Hey, kiddo, listen. So, I'm just trying to figure something out.
Your mom says that you said that Bianca has been being weird
and taking money and she made you cry? But when I really
spoke to Sophie she said maybe it was a game? Was it a game?

Iverson feels trapped. He looks down and mumbles.

IVERSON

She did call you bad names.

KENDALL

What? Like?

IVERSON

I don't want to say. But she ate my Easter candy.

KENDALL

Did she? Really? Did she make you cry? Ivey?

(then)

I'm not angry.

IVERSON

I don't know. I do like her though. It was supposed to be fun.

KENDALL

Uh-huh.

Kendall thinks he knows what's going on.

Listen. We'll figure this out. Okay?

He's distracted by the party below.

Ivey. Run – go get Soph – this is bullshit, come on, let's go down and see Grandpa.

Iverson looks at him.

It's fine. Go get her. It's okay. I got you.

EXT. CAROLINE'S WEDDING COMPLEX – GARDENS – DAY

Tom and Shiv, Roman and Gerri are together speculating and looking at Twitter and emails on their phones.

GERRI
Okay, well, the GoJo price is moving. Up and fucking up.

SHIV
I think he's played you, Rome?

GERRI
The SEC will be all over this.

ROMAN
Ooh my god, a gummy lovebite from those fucking toddlers. I think he likes us. I think he does, I feel that in my gut.

Shiv's phone goes. New alert about a tweet from Matsson. Three emojis: a gaming controller, crossed fingers, eggplant.

SHIV
Okay! New one. Emojis: Controller. Fingers crossed. Eggplant.

They all look at their phones.

TOM
He hopes to—
(*figuring it out*)
fuck a gaming company?

ROMAN
Esports?

SHIV
I think it's betting. It's a betting firm tie-up or something.

ROMAN
Which is gravy. It's good. This is fireworks gravy.

GERRI
(*looks and interprets*)
Or – I think – could this mean, he's played – or he's playing –
the market or—?

ROMAN
Fucking – Professor Murder She Wrote, here.

SHIV
Keep decoding the hieroglyphics, Gerri.
(*then*)
This is bad, Rome.

ROMAN
I think we're good.

SHIV
Yeah because, he blows the deal up, who is left for us,
exactly? We could become the fucking Pan-American Waystar-
Blockbuster Video Dial-up Corporation?

*Just then (with Colin going ahead, scoping out that Kendall's not
around), Logan and Marcia arrive.*

ROMAN
Okay. Here they come.

*Logan holds Marcia's hand – quite courtly and semi-regal, accepting
the smiles and benediction from around him.*

SHIV
And here she comes.

Discreetly, Kerry goes to Colin and makes an arrangement.

Little Miss Steamed Spinach. The side dish.

Looking over at his dad.

ROMAN
He just does not give a single solitary fuck.

TOM
I mean maybe it's fine? Maybe they all sleep in a big bed
together and watch *Friends* reruns and drink milkshakes?

Caroline comes towards them, smiling. Tom alerts Shiv—

CAROLINE

Your father's made it then?

Shiv and Roman and Gerri still checking phones.

SHIV

And you know the story?

CAROLINE

The skunk, the porcupine and the concubine? It's possibly the best wedding present anybody could have brought me. It's just *so* disgusting. Is he still fucking Marcia do we think?

Shiv and Rome shrug, don't want to comment.

TOM

I think not is the word but . . .

CAROLINE

I do hope not, poor old fella could wear himself out!

They look over as Kerry makes her way out.

And it's her – that hard little piece with the fringe?

TOM

That is correct.

CAROLINE

Well listen I'm going to make sure everyone knows to be 'very discreet', but, Shiv, you've heard about this awful thing tonight?

SHIV

Um. Yeah, me and Rome are kind of working on a big deal and we've just got hit with a kind of a torpedo so . . .

ROMAN

Shiv, don't be silly, you have fun with Mom! I can manage, you're not even that involved!

Over with Marcia and Logan. Peter approaches.

PETER

Logan! You came!

MARCIA

We didn't want you to cry on your wedding day.

Logan is happy to spare some honey for Peter. He might need his help one way or another . . .

> LOGAN
>
> How you doing? Staying ahead of the Inland Revenue?

> PETER
>
> Haha. Welcome to Toscana!

> LOGAN
>
> Glad to be here. Anything I can do, just let me know.

Logan smiles at Peter.

> PETER
>
> How kind. Nothing required. Just your presence! And I suppose the 'secrets of the Caroline'?

> LOGAN
>
> Wonderful woman. Don't give her access to your noggin, or your accountant.

> MARCIA
>
> Enjoy the adventure.

> PETER
>
> Ha! And when we can, I also wanted to talk to you discreetly about your contacts in UK government?

> LOGAN
>
> Uh-huh?

> PETER
>
> Just I'd like to give something back, you know. 'The chance to serve.'

With a smile and a nod, Logan backs away to get a phone from Kerry, where's she's prepped some information. Another one full of emails. She gives him a health drink too. A shot of smoothie that he downs, winces.

Roman approaches.

> ROMAN
>
> Hey – what did he want?

LOGAN
(looking at phone)
Him? He wants me to get the dipshits of Downing Street to
make him Lord fucking Seat-Sniffer of Pantyhose.
(then)
You see the tweet? Have you spoken?

ROMAN
I've tried but, no.

LOGAN
What's the decode. What's his game? Is he trying to make us pay
more.

ROMAN
I think – just bored. I mean does it change anything?

LOGAN
Yeah well I'm not used to negotiating via eggplant. I'm not sure
he wants the deal. He might just want a fucking moussaka.

ROMAN
You want me to call again?

*There's a frisson and people look over. Then, all of a sudden. There
is . . . Kendall. Walking through the crowd, making a beeline for
Logan.*

Does Logan look a little scared?

Roman kind of steps across to shield his dad as Kendall approaches.

Hey. You okay?

KENDALL
Yeah I'm okay. Hey, Dad?

ROMAN
Ken, he doesn't want to see you. He doesn't want to talk to you.

KENDALL
Yeah well this is all total horseshit. Let's just have it out, okay?
I want to see you, Dad. I want to see you for dinner and let's just
nail this, okay? Eight. On your own. Yeah?

Logan considers. Then, to get rid of Kendall—

ROMAN

He's busy.

KENDALL

Sure.

LOGAN
(*to Roman*)

We'll get back to him.

Kendall shakes his head: So pathetic. Then—

KENDALL
(*to Roman*)

And thanks for teaching them the nanny game.

ROMAN

No worries. Fun for all the family.

KENDALL

Prick. They're good kids.

ROMAN

Maybe? I think the boy one's coming for you. That's traditional.

Kendall shakes his head, disdainful, walks off.

LOGAN

Should I go?

ROMAN

Sure. No. Or, I dunno. Maybe wear a stab vest?

Logan smiles but underneath he is a bit scared of what might happen, physically or emotionally.

I mean, it'd be okay. Maybe you should go? Get him out of the firm?

Is Logan scared?

You want me to come?

LOGAN

Fuck off I'm not scared.
(*then to Kerry*)

Can we get rooms? I want to get Matsson on the phone.

EXT. CORTONA — EVENING

A group of woman make the passeggiata *through the streets of an Italian hill town.*

Amongst others: Shiv and Caroline. Willa and the Contessa. Gerri and others.

They look at the Italians who in return check them out.

EXT. CORTONA RESTAURANT — NIGHT

Later, bit drunk, Caroline is having a cigarette outside the restaurant. Shiv comes out too to check her phone and sees her mom.

> SHIV
>
> Oh? Sorry. Lot going on.

She sends a message. Then scrolls Twitter regarding Matsson.

> CAROLINE
>
> Of course. So. What do you make of Peter's daughters? They're both in 'interior design'. I think I'd rather work in an abattoir.

Shiv still has her phone and is working away at messages but they look inside at Peter's daughters.

> SHIV
>
> They offered to take photos and I think they took a screenshot of my address book.

> CAROLINE
>
> A 'bachelorette party'. My mother would turn in her grave.

Maybe Caroline gets some comfort from that. Shiv is still emailing and messaging.

> SHIV
>
> So listen. Rome's concerned. You do have a watertight prenup, right?

> CAROLINE
>
> Do you think he's going to 'do me in' for Granny's fake Rubens?

> SHIV
>
> You have a good lawyer at least?

CAROLINE
Well yes I am having to open up the divorce agreement with your father. Peter loves the Eaton Square flat.

SHIV
Has he not got one?

CAROLINE
He had some bad luck with a salmon-smoking business and lost his place in Pimlico.

SHIV
Quite the business brain.

CAROLINE
He's very trusting, they were these awful boys who sold him on a dream. He has a very big heart.

SHIV
Well – I guess opposites attract.

She's offering a joke but Caroline doesn't quite hear it, on the defensive, looking at Shiv's phone—

CAROLINE
Shall we just enjoy a cigarette and not get all snipey. Or are you just after some attention?

SHIV
Me, get your attention? I think that ship sailed a long while ago.

CAROLINE
I may have been a bit of a spotty mother but you've been a shitty daughter, so.

SHIV
You weren't a spotty mother. You were just – an absence. But I'm fine.

CAROLINE
I moved to bloody New York. But I never fucking saw you.

SHIV
Mum, it's okay. You let Dad take us and that was probably best.

CAROLINE
I gave him custody so you could keep your shares and I could protect your interests! You chose!

> SHIV

Sure. I didn't choose anything.

> CAROLINE

Well, you tend to get what you want.

> SHIV

And you don't?

> CAROLINE

I don't believe I've ever won a single battle in my whole life.

Shiv looks at her.

> SHIV

I was ten, Mom. I was a fucking kid.

> CAROLINE

You were thirteen and you knew how to twist the knife then and you know now, and I might cry.

> SHIV

Yeah? Where's the onion?

> CAROLINE

You were quite a little piece of work. You're the onion. You're my onion.

> SHIV

Well you're my fucking onion too.

A certain truce.

> CAROLINE

The truth is I probably shouldn't have had children. You've made the right decision. Some people aren't meant to be mothers. I should have had dogs.

> SHIV

Well you could have had dogs?

> CAROLINE

No. Your father. He never saw something he loved that he didn't want to kick to see if it would still come back.

And with a smile that says she knows there is quite a lot to unpack there, but she doesn't care to.

Something clicks for Shiv.

They look round as Gerri makes it out, on her phone. And down below Gerri heads to the center of the square.

Roman comes out from a bar across the square to meet her.

EXT. CORTONA – NIGHT

Roman and Gerri, in the distance, maybe unaware of being watched.

ROMAN

Okay what is it?

GERRI

Okay, so. Your dad has called a bunch, he won't take the calls.

ROMAN

Well he hates the phone, that doesn't mean anything. I told Dad he hates the phone. He left me a voice memo. The tweets were fucking around. His lawyers have given him the Reg FD scares. He's flying back to his Swiss place. There's clarification coming.

GERRI

Yeah well your dad thinks Matsson's trying to humiliate him.

ROMAN

Well he's not. He just needs to ride it out. We don't want to panic, Gerri, okay?

GERRI

I am not panicking.

ROMAN

Well you are because you're interrupting a great night, I'm getting very pally with Laurie. I might try to fuck him, see how that fits into our whole disgusting mess.

GERRI

Do *not* try to fuck Laurie. What do you think about going to see Matsson?

ROMAN

Well sure. Does Dad want me to?

> GERRI

Yes. Your dad wants the deal. But they need a translator. Logan needs reassurance before the banker meet.

> ROMAN

Oh, you want me to save the deal? Why didn't you say? Piece of fucking cake.
> *(ticking off list on fingers as he backs away)*
Save the deal. Fuck Laurie. Lead company into promised land. Fuck Gerri. Gonna be a great week!

Gerri heads off but maybe we stay with Roman looking around. Lot on his shoulders.

EXT. KENDALL'S VILLA — TERRACE — NIGHT

The table is set for two. Kendall is with the cook inside. He looks out – Logan arrives, with Colin and Kerry.

> KENDALL

Hey.

Colin and Kerry are there with bags, including cooler bags.

I thought this was going to be private?

> LOGAN

I'm across a lot of shit. She's monitoring.

> KENDALL

Uh-huh?
> *(to Colin and Kerry)*
Well. Hang out wherever – you can wait inside.

They look to Logan and he nods. Logan and Kendall go to sit.

Kendall knows Logan doesn't like being off his turf. Has heard Logan is anxious about his food being tampered with.

So I hear you were asking all about the menu and my chef?

Whispers of weakness. Logan is embarrassed.

> LOGAN

Few things off the menu for me, health-wise.

> KENDALL

Sure. Scared I'm gonna try and fucking Jim Jones you with an olive?

> LOGAN

I think we brought some dishes over that are good for me?

> KENDALL

Yeah, seems a shame. So we checked in with your doc and got the requirements.

He looks inside to staff to let them know they can eat. Logan slightly bumped.

> LOGAN

So. What is this? Because I have things to do.

> KENDALL

As ever.

> LOGAN

GoJo price is spiking. Your pal Matsson's got a screw loose.

> KENDALL

You think we're gonna miss our chance to dance and end up going Kodak?

> LOGAN

Your whole generation is kaput. All about the clicks. You need to put your phones away, make some money and shut the fuck up.

> KENDALL

I'm sure you'll figure it out.
> (*smiles*)
So. Can we talk?

> LOGAN

Well, I can't get into everything now, so if it's going to be a lot of bullshit I'll just go. Let's be civil and not pull our guts out all over the table alright?

Two plates of antipasti are brought out.

> KENDALL

That one's for him.

*The server puts it down. They look identical. Logan looks at his.
Kendall is amused by his fear.*

LOGAN

Where are the kids?

KENDALL

Inside.

LOGAN
(*shouts for him*)

Iverson!

(*then*)

I'd like to say hello.

But they both know it's not true.

KENDALL

Sure.

Iverson comes out.

LOGAN

Hey, kiddo. How you doing? Do you like mozzarella?

IVERSON

Um, not much.

LOGAN

Here. Try this.

He looks at Kendall as he gives the boy a slice.

IVERSON

Um, thanks.

LOGAN

There you go, kiddo. Try that.

*He doesn't want to but, with both men watching, it goes to his lips.
Logan looks at Kendall. Iverson eats it.*

IVERSON

Yeah. It's okay?

LOGAN

Off you go. Go on. Kerry's got something for you in there
I think.

They watch him go. Kendall is incredulous.

KENDALL

Jesus Christ. Who do you think I am? I don't want you dead. I'll be broken when you die.

LOGAN

Uh-huh. How is the boy. Is he, better?

KENDALL

He's fine. Roman taught them the fucking nanny game but—

LOGAN

The nanny game?

KENDALL

Shiv and Rome—

(and Kendall)

There was a thing, when— On vacation they'd try to make up shit to get the nanny fired. For a prize or whatever.

LOGAN

Little shits.

(then)

Did I know that?

KENDALL

(yes)

Look. So. My thing is, I want out.

LOGAN

Okay?

KENDALL

Yeah. Yeah. I think I thought I was a knight on horseback. But— Yeah.

LOGAN

Life isn't knights on horseback. It's a number on a piece of paper. It's a fight for a knife in the mud.

KENDALL

I don't know. But yeah, look, you've won. I think you've won.

LOGAN

Uh-huh.

KENDALL

So I guess there's a couple of ways my life goes from here: Move to Europe, drink or drugs, do cars or beats. Or I fucking do myself in, mort porte it.

LOGAN

Uh-huh.

KENDALL

But I can't do jackshit. So, I want to get a premium payout from the holding, two bil. And a chunky asset, something you can realize without shareholder input – maybe outdoor advertizing, podcasts. I keep Fikret, Jess and I'm gone, divested, off the board, complete disinheritance. I won't even speak at your memorial. We're done.

Logan looks at him.

LOGAN

I'll have to think.

KENDALL

Well you offered, at my birthday, so . . . ?

LOGAN

Well, that was for – fun.

KENDALL

C'mon. Dad, we don't want this bullshit forever.

Logan toys with him.

LOGAN

It doesn't necessarily work for me. It doesn't look good, maybe, you leaving.

KENDALL

What do you care?

LOGAN

Maybe I want you around, you can do the mail. Keep you rattling around?

KENDALL

Look. I tried, but— I thought that things had changed. But I'm not as— There's things you are able to do I can't, maybe.

LOGAN

Maybe.

KENDALL

You've won.
                (*can't quite leave it there*)
Because you're corrupt and so is the world.

LOGAN

Hm, well?

KENDALL

I'm better than you. You're – you know, I love you but you're
kind of – evil.

LOGAN

Don't talk about what you don't understand.

KENDALL

Well you're smart but what you've done is you – you've
monetized all the fucking, the, whatever the American
resentments of class and race and, and—

LOGAN

And I thought I was just telling folks the weather?

KENDALL

You've turned black bile into silver dollars.

LOGAN

Just notice, did you?

KENDALL

Yeah maybe I did.

LOGAN

Fuck off.

KENDALL

Fine, you know what, I don't give a fuck.

LOGAN

Not everyone can live this life.
                (*motions – Italy, servants*)
I'm a great revolutionary. A – a – bit of fucking spice. A bit of
fun, a bit of truth.

                                KENDALL
—Truth, okay?

                                LOGAN
I fucking know things about the world, or I wouldn't turn a
buck.

                                KENDALL
Maybe.

                                LOGAN
Not necessarily nice things.

                                KENDALL
Real world? When was the last day you had a beer, when was
the last time your feet touched the sidewalk?

                                LOGAN
Uh-huh.

                                KENDALL
Look, whatever, I don't want to be you. Let me out? Okay. Pay
up and let me out. I'm a good guy.

*That still actually hurts Logan. He doesn't believe that he isn't. Long
beat.*

                                LOGAN
How long was that kid alive before he started sucking in water,
do you think? Couple of minutes? Three, four, five minutes in
there? Long time, two minutes.

*Kendall looks around to see no one can hear. He's been stabbed in the
gut.*

    What were you even doing? Chasing a piece of tail? Are you
    queer? Were you gonna fuck him? Or was it just for drugs?

                                KENDALL
                               (*quietly*)
I'm better than you.

                                LOGAN
Sure.

                                KENDALL
You know I'm right.

                              LOGAN
   You're my son and I did my best and whenever you fucked up
   I've cleaned your shit, but I'm the bad guy? Yeah fuck off, kiddo.

Logan gets up.

   Goodnight.

INT. SHIV AND TOM'S ROOM – NIGHT

*Tom watches a news report on the Matsson tweet story and the
fallout. We get a sense of the scale of the GoJo empire.*

Shiv is back all fired up. Hot, drunk, angry, but alive.

                              TOM
   Hey. How was your night?

                              SHIV
   Awful. You?

                              TOM
   Yeah, Roman implied Peter might have killed his first wife and
   tried to goad Laurie into talking indelicately about Gerri.

She kisses him hard.

                              SHIV
   Let's have a baby.

                              TOM
   Yeah?

Maybe she gets a drink.

                              SHIV
   I'm gonna fucking fight, Tom.

                              TOM
   Oh, okay?

                              SHIV
   You don't just get given these things at a house in the fucking
   Hamptons.

                              TOM
   Right—

SHIV

I'm not gonna get given the top job, or ATN. You have to fight!
I have to fight Gerri and Roman and Ken. But I can, because I'm
smarter than them.

TOM

You are.

SHIV

I'm going to do it. And fuck Dad, it doesn't matter how often
he kicks me. Ten years or five, get rid of Cyd. Remake ATN,
destroy it, raze everything there.

TOM

Right. I mean, except me?

SHIV
(sure)

Yeah except you. Dad's got spooked by Matsson. I need to find
another deal. A bigger deal. Fucking nail it.

TOM

And what about me?

SHIV

Together. We can't let the dirty little pixie become king. Blow up
Roman, I'm the only candidate left.

She kisses him.

Let's do anything. Let's— What do you want to do to me?
Anything.

TOM

You're so fucking hot.

SHIV

C'mon. Tell me anything, do anything.

TOM

Say anything to me. Go on. Mistress Siobhan Roy.

SHIV

You're not good enough for me.

She kisses him. Bit of a smile, like he can take it, like he likes it. It's a
game.

> TOM
>
> Oh! Right! Come on then! Let's see!

> SHIV
>
> I'm way out of your fucking league!

It's a game, isn't it?

> TOM
>
> You think so? Yeah?!

> SHIV
>
> That's why you love me.

> TOM
>
> Maybe?

> SHIV
>
> That's why you want me.

> TOM
>
> Fuck you.

> SHIV
> *(hard but playfully)*
>
> Even though I don't love you.

A bump but he swallows his reaction.

> TOM
>
> Uh-huh.

> SHIV
>
> But you want me anyway!

DAY FOUR

EXT. CAROLINE'S WEDDING VILLA — TERRACE — DAY

On the terrace, breakfast things are laid out.

Willa is breakfasting alone. Connor joins, only has one thing on his mind.

> CONNOR
>
> Hey! You crept out! Sleep well?

> WILLA
> (*no*)
> Oh hey! Yeah. Really good. Lot of sleep.

> CONNOR
> Sorry about waking you to ask. I'm just curious obviously.

> WILLA
> Yeah. No worries.

He looks at her like: Well?

> Yeah still thinking.

> CONNOR
> *Still* thinking?

> WILLA
> Well yeah, thinking hard!

> CONNOR
> It's just the old thinking cap has been on your head quite a while now. Can't be too comfortable?

> WILLA
> Right, well, big decision. Just thinking away here!

> CONNOR
> Right. Just, this much thinking could start to get unromantic!

She smiles.

Nearby Comfrey is reading.

Greg is at the breakfast buffet when the Contessa appears.

Greg spots his chance. Smiles.

> GREG
> Hey. Oh wow, is that the time?

He shoots out his watch.

> CONTESSA
> Excuse me?

> GREG
> Gah, just checking my old watch here. What you up to today?

CONTESSA

Um, my room doesn't have good Wi-Fi so, I dunno. Work shit.

GREG

Okay, because, I thought, not to intrude, but I understood, you were part of the whole, the titled, monarchical, sort of situation if that isn't too bold to say?

CONTESSA

No, sure, but I do a bit of— I'm an online brand ambassador. A fermented yogurt drink.

GREG

Fermented yogurt? Cool. Very cool. Gut health. Love it.

But then Roman comes through. Looking at his phone. Thinking, ready for business, anxious about his mission.

ROMAN

Hey dipshit.
(*leans in*)
Hands off.
(*to the Contessa*)
Just off to save the world. Should be back for dinner.
(*to Greg but so she can hear*)
Greg, make sure the Contessa is kept occupied. But don't look at her, everyone can see what you're thinking and it's disgusting.

And he's gone with a wave.

GREG

Yeah. My cousin. A very rude man. Well, looks like the time, sponsored by Rolex, is time to get back to the old 'ball and chain'. 'The missus'!

CONTESSA

Okay, have a good wedding.

Greg points out Comfrey reading – his date ladder.

GREG

I'm kidding. She's amazing. It's just not serious. 'Fun but not the one' as they say? I believe?

CONTESSA

Okay well it was nice to meet you. And your wristwatch.

EXT. PERUGIA – DAY

Tom and Shiv have had breakfast out in a square. Shiv in dark glasses. A little hungover. Tom pays.

> SHIV
>
> Well, GoJo price has lurched up. And held.

> TOM
> (*depressed*)
> Uh-huh. Power of the tweet.

> SHIV
> (*swipes*)
> Keeps going, by midweek their market cap is gonna be close to ours. Roman's not gonna find the landing zone for this.

Tom gives a minimal response. They get up and walk the city streets.

> You okay?

> TOM
> Uh-huh. Just that was some pretty spicy pillow talk last night?

Great sex. She kisses him.

> But like it got pretty—

She looks at him.

> When I said, you know, 'say something filthy, do something dirty' and—

> SHIV
> I was just being horrible – for fun? Dirty fun.

> TOM
> No. It was dirty.
> (*then*)
> Just I feel a little – this morning, you know. Bit of afterburn.
> (*then*)
> I guess I was thinking more like, love beads – or I'd be a sexy fireman or—?
> (*then*)
> But it was more in the realm of, that you don't love me.

> SHIV

Come on, what happens in Sex Vegas?

> TOM

Right but sometimes I think, should I maybe listen to the things that you say directly in my face when we're at our most intimate?

> SHIV

Tom, you can't ask someone to say terrible things and then get all— That's a bit – manipulative?

> TOM

But did you mean it, the baby?

> SHIV

Yeah. Yes, I think.

(*then*)

One way or another. No?

He looks at her.

Let's freeze at least.

> TOM

Yeah?

> SHIV

Embryos survive way better than eggs. So we could put it together and have that, for whenever . . .?

> TOM

And when's that do you think?

> SHIV

Well, Tom, it's important . . . the host chamber is willing!

He smiles, come on.

They keep them ten years, then – you know. You can work something out. It's different if one of us dies, or if you are in a long-term coma, you can decide what should happen. I wouldn't just automatically get them, if we divorced or something. If that's what – concerns you?

Tom tries to absorb this overly googled information.

>   TOM
> I wouldn't necessarily have thought about that.

Silence.

>   SHIV
> I just think it's smart to bank some embryos, see where we are.

>   TOM
> But we could be looking at ten years? That's two-and-a-half
> Olympics?

>   SHIV
> It'll get clearer. It's just the option. And if something happens,
> or *you* change your mind, they can destroy them, it doesn't bind
> you.

>   TOM
> I'd want you to have my babies if I died.

>   SHIV
> Oh, okay. Well, thank you.

>   TOM
> And if you – died?

Shiv thinks. Finds her own death too hard to imagine.

>   SHIV
> Would I want you to—? Um. Can I think?

>   TOM
> Sure.

>   SHIV
>   *(jokey)*
> Look, I may not love you but I do love you, you know?

*Tom feels vaguely he has been the victim of a vast swindle but he
can't quite recall what exactly happened.*

>   TOM
> I know. I do know.

So he is on board with the whole thing?

>   SHIV
> Okay?

Um, yes. What is it again?

TOM

Okay.

Kiss.

SHIV

Baby popsicles, baby!

TOM

Baby popsicles.

EXT. HELIPAD – DAY

Roman gets out of a helicopter into a car.

EXT. LAKE MAGGIORE – LANDING STAGE OF MATTSON'S HOUSE – DAY

Roman arrives at the little dock of a house on the lake.

The boat is rocking. Hard to judge the getting out. Matsson is there waiting, watching.

MATSSON

Do you want me to hold your hand?

ROMAN

Fuck you.

MATSSON

Come on. I'll hold your hand.

ROMAN

Fuck you.

Roman leaps and makes it.

EXT. LAKE MAGGIORE – MATTSON'S HOUSE – DAY

They are in the gardens walking. Matsson needs lots of input. Checks his phone. When he's engaged, he's very engaged, when he's not – a loss of connection.

> ROMAN

Amazing place.

> MATSSON

I guess?

> ROMAN

No?

> MATSSON

It kind of freaks me out to be honest.

Roman looks at him.

When I got it and my idea was – *everything*, perfect. And now –
I'm sleeping on basically a camping mat until I get a deep-dive
on the best mattress in the world.
> (*then*)

It's great. I'm just not feeling, great you know? I mean I'm okay.
> (*maybe with a smile*)

But not really.

> ROMAN

Well don't start telling me real shit, man, because I'm giving you
nothing!

Matsson likes it, smiles.

> MATSSON

So what are you worst at?

> ROMAN

Me? Worst?

> MATSSON

Yeah. Success has stopped interesting me altogether, it's easy.
Analysis, plus capital, plus execution. No, the secret is as much
failure as possible as fast as possible, just burn that shit off.

> ROMAN

Well I'm definitely not telling you a single one of my weaknesses,
ever.

> MATSSON

Smart. Because I fucking ream people. I juice 'em like oranges,
I get way into people and they disappoint me. I'm thinking of
doing like quarterly up-or-outs at the company.

ROMAN

Right. Know that one. So listen, the tweet? Seriously, what was that?

Matsson isn't telling.

MATSSON
(*lying*)

That was just a tweet. I was feeling lucky. I got bored.

ROMAN

But like, what you got cooking? Anything big coming out for you?

MATSSON

Dude, are you asking for material non-public information?

ROMAN

I mean were you trying to give your share price a pop by tweeting unverifiable information outside normal disclosure channels?

Matsson makes a crying motion – waggling his knuckles at his eyes. Roman smiles.

(*the nub*)

But look, what I need to know is do you want this deal? Are you into the deal?

MATSSON

Yeah. I'm just a little Swedish you know. I'm into equality.

Roman looks at him. He gets it.

ROMAN

Okay. Because, I'm going to Milan to lock things down with Dad and the bankers – and the tweeting didn't feel great, if you're trying to blow this up, you can tell me. Yeah?

MATSSON

I just want to get myself the best of everything, you know?

ROMAN
(*looks at him*)

Okay. I get that. Well look, let's take another walk around this old hellhole, shall we?

Smiles. Roman thinks he gets him. It was a move, a strategy.

INT. KENDALL'S VILLA – DAY*

Kendall is drinking in an indoor room.

> KENDALL
>
> Hey B? Bianca. Can we have that talk please?

She comes through, wet from playing in the pool with the kids, maybe she has a shift or gown for indoors and to feel a little protected.

> So, hey, um, sit.
>
> *(then)*
>
> Yeah this is a tough one and it's hard but I'm afraid I'm going to have to let you go.

> BIANCA
>
> I'm sorry, what?

> KENDALL
>
> You've probably noticed the tension—

> BIANCA
>
> The tension? No?

> KENDALL
>
> Yeah so, I'm sorry.

> BIANCA
>
> What? Can you tell me why?

> KENDALL
>
> I can't really say. To protect the children. But yeah, your references will be fine and I should say I like you, so I'm sorry. Things could just be weird.

He drinks.

> BIANCA
>
> Okay.
>
> *(but she can't leave it)*
>
> I mean – but why? I do feel like you owe me—

---

* We had to cut the whole nanny-firing-game strand from the episode. It was a tough one to see go but the episode was just too long.

> KENDALL

Why? Why because you're too hot, my wife thinks you're too hot.

He smiles, as if this was meant to be nice. But it's not nice and she feels vulnerable.

> BIANCA

Okay well, I guess I should go. Okay. Shit.

He sees how affected she is. Head down. Might she cry?

> KENDALL

I'm kidding. It's shitty, I'm sorry, I don't want to make you feel bad.
> > (*maybe he feels he owes her this*)

The kids said some things and now it feels like it's too weird, around them, okay? So, they need to learn. But, yeah, that's on me. I want them to be really good people.

> BIANCA

Right? And do you think—?

> KENDALL

I don't know. It's a mess. And listen if you want, stay. As my guest. Just don't see the kids. Stay in the annex. I mean if Rava is going to complain, let's give her something to worry about?

She doesn't know how to look. He leaves it a little too long.

I'm kidding! Like 'what a creep would say'. Look. I know cool people, really chill people so we'll set you up, don't sweat it okay? This is great for you. Okay?
> > (*now he doesn't want her near him*)

Go on. Fuck off to some other asshole kids!

He smiles, drinks.

EXT. MILAN ARRIVALS — DAY

Logan's jet arrives. He comes down the steps with Tom and Shiv and Gerri.

EXT. MILAN STREETS — DAY

Limos through the traffic to a business HQ/business hotel.

Roman inside one of them, anxious.

INT. INVESTMENT BANK — DAY

Roman heads towards a meeting room. Logan, Shiv, Tom, Kerry inside. Nearby investment banker and lawyers waiting to join. Shiv is looking at him, knowing he's on a tightrope.

Gerri is at the door.

> GERRI

Hey. So?

> ROMAN

I think it's over.

> GERRI

What?

> ROMAN

Yeah, I'm not sure he is interested in getting acquired. I think he's angling for a merger of equals.

> GERRI

Okay. Fuck. Well?

> ROMAN

So it's dead. Right?

> GERRI

Are you sure? Because I don't want to pile the pressure on, Roman, and obviously there are always multiple ways forward and I don't want to overcook this . . . but, in terms of deals that make sense, if we don't beef up, soon, I think we end up someone's lunch.

> ROMAN

Well thanks, Ger. I'm already so fucking stressed I'm jerking dust.

> *(then)*

Shall we tell him together?

GERRI
(*fuck you*)
I'm not really inside the detail so?

Thanks. He's alone as he goes in. Ball of nerves.

INT. INVESTMENT BANK OFFICES – DAY

Logan, Gerri, Shiv, Roman, Tom.

On screens: Frank and Karl.

LOGAN
So. Before we get the whole three-ring circus in here, just amongst friends I wanted to get a sense of what's going on? Is he a Twitter panty-flasher? Or is he a serious person?

ROMAN
Well, he's a serious person.

Logan looks dubious. Shiv sees a way to earn points.

SHIV
You're certain?

ROMAN
Yes, Shiv, he's serious. But. Dad, he thinks there's value that isn't priced in yet. Matsson's gunning for a for a – merger of equals. So. I guess. You know? That probably—

He doesn't need to say 'kills this'.

SHIV
Merger of equals?

ROMAN
He's got twelve of the prime Asian sports leagues signed up for GoJo. He's gonna fold it all in to the platform: live sports, games and betting. It's a growth bomb.

SHIV
But the full – fifty-fifty board, all stock. Dad splits control?

Never going to happen and Roman kind of has to own it.

ROMAN
Yes, Siobhan.

                                   SHIV
         Right well, I don't think— Dad?

*Gerri, Karl, Frank shift uneasily. A merger of equals will mean they
are in precarious positions.*

Logan waits and thinks.

                                   LOGAN
         But the guy isn't a fuckhead?

                                   ROMAN
         No. The tweeting was a move.

Logan likes that more. He thinks.

                                   LOGAN
         He's not a big baby who shits for clicks?

Roman sees how Logan is thinking. Glimmer of hope.

                                   ROMAN
         No. He's on the snake. I know people. I'm a people-sniffer.

Logan thinks.

                                   LOGAN
         Cos I can win any bout with a boxer fuck but I don't know how
         to knock out a clown.

                                   ROMAN
         He's not a clown. He's a motherfucker. It's what you would have
         done. Right? He's maximized leverage.

                                   SHIV
         But, Dad, yeah, 'merger of equals'?

                                   LOGAN
         No such thing.

                                   TOM
         Always a top dog, right?

Shiv looks at Tom: Is that helpful? He looks back: It's true.

                                   ROMAN
         Sure and I mean he wants the label but I think we could still be
         the puppy-fuckers here?

> KARL

The family stake would be seriously diluted.

> LOGAN

Hm.

> ROMAN

I think he'd let us craft it so we keep the balance of the board.
I think he wants the freedom and he wants the status. GoJo
Royco. Who gives a fuck? Give him the logo, we take the wheel.

*Shiv does see the business sense. This is a company that would be
exciting to run. No question.*

> SHIV

It would be real scale. It's a legitimate shot at staying relevant.

> FRANK

Big upheaval?

> SHIV
> (*sees Karl's anxiety*)

I mean the top team will obviously— You'll be fighting for your
lives?

> ROMAN

But I'm sure you can trust Dad, guys?

> KARL

Obviously.

> ROMAN

'Merger' is really a state of mind, right? Dad, Gerri, you stay
with your hands on the tiller.

*Everyone looks at Logan. How does he feel? Roman and Shiv are
excited.*

Their price rise is real. Proper fucking streamer. The future is
movies, TV, music, games, sports, esports, AR, VR, betting –
everything, to everyone. Matsson knows how to get there.

Logan considers.

> GERRI

Logan?

LOGAN
(*to Roman*)

We can't afford to walk away right now. Got to be worth a conversation, son.

ROMAN

Okay!

LOGAN

Bring them in. Let's get the fucking bankers in here on this.

Kerry ushers in bankers from outside. Two senior bankers and their underlings. One senior lawyer. American and Swiss.

Roman looks down. He has a message from Gerri. He selects a dick pic.

We might or might not see but his dad is writing something on his phone.

Roman writes: 'Dinner to celebrate Gerri? Eat this.'

Then a message comes in from his dad: 'Good work kid.'

Almost at the same time, Roman hits send. Looks at Gerri.

Her phone is there on the table. Nothing. Nothing. Roman smiles at her then with a sickening chirrup his dad's phone buzzes.

His dad looks at his phone. Dick pic. 'Dinner to celebrate Gerri? Eat this.'

Logan is confused. Looks at Roman.

The world freezes for Roman for a beat before he thinks how he can explain it away – as he feels caught by his dad, a bottomless pit drops away in his stomach.

Then he starts to rationalize and – smiles. It's nothing.

But Logan still looks puzzled, like he can't even tell what it is or what it means yet.

As the bankers come in, Shiv spots something uncomfortable has gone on.

                    LOGAN
                    (*cont'd*)
    I need five.

INT. MILAN — DAY

Another room.

Shiv and Logan. She is handing him back his phone.

                    SHIV
    Yeah that's his dick. He's sent you a photo of his dick. By
    mistake.

                    LOGAN
    Yeah well, that's obvious.

                    SHIV
    He meant to send it to Gerri.

                    LOGAN
    I don't get it?

                    SHIV
    Well, honestly . . .

Logan looks at her. She kind of has Roman at her mercy.

    Look, he's weird about Gerri, everyone knows it. And to be
    honest I think it's fucking disgusting.

                    LOGAN
    Yeah?

                    SHIV
    Gerri's probably not stopping it for leverage. Banking it as
    ammo.

                    LOGAN
    Is he just—? Is it just – Roman being Roman?

                    SHIV
    No. No, I'm afraid not.

Logan doesn't like it.

It's a potential problem. There's issues. He used to get jacked off by his personal trainer. There's something going on with Gerri— He's an unexploded bomb. So as we move forward—

LOGAN

Uh-huh. Sure. Sure, Pinky. Go on.
                    (*shouts*)
Roman!

But Shiv knows she's ahead. As she leaves, she gives Roman a wink as he passes.

SHIV

Put in a good word for you.

INT. MILAN ROOM – DAY

Roman enters and closes the door.

LOGAN

Are you a sicko? What is this? Why do you send them?

ROMAN

No, Dad, it's just like – 'Here's my dick.'

LOGAN

Uh-huh – as a – as a fuck you?

Logan doesn't mind it so long as it is aggressive and mocking, but if it suggests vulnerability or kinkiness it freaks him out.

ROMAN

People just send each other pics of their dicks?

LOGAN

People send each other pics of their dicks?

Roman doesn't want to have this conversation.

ROMAN

Have you heard of dick pics?

LOGAN

We publish a number of popular newspapers, so yes, son, we probably invented the fucking words. But why?

ROMAN

I dunno. It's like, 'here's my dick,' I guess.

LOGAN

Uh-huh?

(*then*)

Have you got a problem?

Roman shrugs, feeling twelve again.

What aren't you with that nice piece of tail?

ROMAN

Tabitha? She's amazing. But we're having some issues.

(*pulling it back*)

And I hope this isn't going to effect how we structure the negotiations going forward because I am inside this with Matsson and—

LOGAN

What interests you in Gerri exactly?

ROMAN

I'm just screwing around!

LOGAN

I don't like things going on I don't know about. She's a million years old. It's fucking disgusting. You're a laughing stock. Go on, fuck off.

Roman gets up.

ROMAN

What happens now?

LOGAN

Well I don't want her hanging round like frozen fucking piss.

ROMAN

Gerri? Look, I'm not a radical feminist but I think maybe we shouldn't fire her for receiving my dick pic?

INT. MILAN ROOM — DAY

Outside the room with the bankers. Shiv is with Gerri. Full of 'concern'. She's seen an opportunity.

                                SHIV
Sorry about all this, Gerri. I just want to get things clear about
what's going on? And most importantly, if you're okay?

                                GERRI
Uh-huh. It's not a big deal.

                                SHIV
I just want to get things clear for my dad. This must be really
hard.

                                GERRI
It's fine.

                                SHIV
Okay. And has this or something like this ever happened before?

                                GERRI
                          (*not going to lie*)
I can't recall.

                                SHIV
If it did, did you ask him to stop?

                                GERRI
Let's talk about this tomorrow, okay? I want to check in with
some people.

                                SHIV
I mean, you weren't – welcoming – these items, were you, Gerri?

She just looks at Shiv, her face says: Come on.

It's just something for your well-being we need to be really clear
about. With all this potential upheaval, and at such a delicate
time, career-wise, for you as interim CEO, if you can't deal with
your own sexual harassment, not a good look.

                                GERRI
I can cope.

                                SHIV
Uh-huh and would you like to make an official complaint
against him regarding this?

*Gerri sees a trap opening up. If she does, that's kind of going to create
a paper trail—*

> GERRI

Well that's for me to decide.

But if she doesn't—

> SHIV

I just think you should report him to HR, Gerri, or it could kind of be argued you welcomed these photos, it undermines your position. That's my concern for you here. I wonder if we shouldn't just kick this all up to the board?

They look at one another.

EXT. KENDALL'S VILLA – POOL – DAY

The sun beats down.

Kids are on devices round the pool. The nanny hasn't been on duty so there are clumps of wet towels and soda cans, wasps buzzing over sticky treats, bomboloni donuts and melted ice creams.

Kendall is on an inflatable lilo in the pool, face-down. A bottle of beer wedged in there.

In the far distance, Bianca leaves.

> BIANCA

Okay. I'm going now?!

> KENDALL

Okay. Bye.

> BIANCA

Bye, kids!

They don't react that much. Seen a lot of staff come and go.

> SOPHIE

Bye.

> IVERSON

Bye.

Then—

> BIANCA

Thanks. Goodbye.

She heads off. So fucking horrible and confusing. She maybe sheds a tear as she goes.

From the kids iPads and their earbuds, the tinny sound of YouTube. They are quickly absorbed again. Burying whatever thoughts or feelings they have about Bianca's departure.

Kendall floats, has a drink, in heaven. And in hell. His face close to the water. He looks at his phone. No messages.

Maybe after a little while his kids head inside, leaving him alone, drunk, and his eyes fluttering asleep there.

Episode Nine

ALL THE BELLS SAY

Written by Jesse Armstrong
Directed by Mark Mylod

Original air date 12 December 2021

Cast

LOGAN ROY	Brian Cox
KENDALL ROY	Jeremy Strong
MARCIA ROY	Hiam Abbass
GREG HIRSCH	Nicholas Braun
SHIV ROY	Sarah Snook
ROMAN ROY	Kieran Culkin
CONNOR ROY	Alan Ruck
TOM WAMBSGANS	Matthew Macfadyen
FRANK VERNON	Peter Friedman
COLIN STILES	Scott Nicholson
KARL MULLER	David Rasche
GERRI KELLMAN	J. Smith-Cameron
WILLA FERREYRA	Justine Lupe
SOPHIE ROY	Swayam Bhatia
IVERSON ROY	Quentin Morales
CAROLINE COLLINGWOOD	Harriet Walter
KERRY CASTELLABATE	Zoë Winters
COMFREY PELLITS	Dasha Nekrasova
LUKAS MATSSON	Alexander Skarsgård
PETER MUNION	Pip Torrens
THE CONTESSA	Ella Rumpf
LAWYER	Filippo Valle
WEDDING OFFICIANT	Simonetta Solder
WEDDING PLANNER	Angeliqa Devi

DAY ONE

EXT. LOGAN'S VILLA – DAY

Something heavy hangs over the day.

Iverson is on a piece of wicker or garden furniture. Logan has his arm round the boy. He's reading to him from a book, Goodbye Mog.

> LOGAN
> 'Mog was tired. She was dead tired. Her head was dead tired. Her paws were dead tired. Mog thought, "I want to sleep forever."'

Logan looks at the page. He is filled with disquiet.

> Isn't this a bit young for you?

> IVERSON
> Umm?

Sophie is down further away looking at her phone. She's heard.

> SOPHIE
> Sometimes he still likes it.

> IVERSON
> Sometimes I still like it.

Logan flicks through the book. Doesn't like where it's headed.

> LOGAN
> I think this is a bit kiddie for you. This isn't for grown-up boys. Let's get you a proper book.

Logan gets up. Iverson takes it on the chin.

> You alright, kiddo? Your dad was okay, you know? He's okay.

> IVERSON
> Yeah.

> LOGAN

Kerry! Can you bring us a book, something with some action!

Logan's phone goes.

> *(into phone)*

What?

> *(to kids as he walks away)*

Careful now.

> *(then into phone)*

Talk to me.

> *(shouts out for assistance)*

Gerri! Where are you, Gerri!

Logan paces. Troubled. Up under a veranda or sunshade, the assembled family members are aware of this disturbance. Logan rolls around the swimming pool like a thundercloud they try to ignore.

Roman, Shiv, Connor, Tom, Willa, Greg all play Monopoly.

They all watch Gerri head down to attend to the king's displeasure. Roman says as she passes.

> ROMAN

Yeah, Ger, you jump on the grenade. Thanks, pal.

He's making out it's a choice to be cut out. But Shiv and Tom and Greg and Con can all see what's going on and Roman avoids their eyes.

The dice clack. A long sticky afternoon.

> CONNOR

Willa, you need to decide.

> WILLA

I'm thinking.

> *(then)*

No. It doesn't make sense right now. I don't want Tennessee Avenue.

Roman shakes. Roman moves his piece, it lands on Shiv's property.

She holds out her hand. A smile from Shiv.

> ROMAN

Why do you love trying to hurt me do you think?

SHIV
It's something to pass the time I guess?

As he counts—

ROMAN
I do know what you tried to do, you know, with Dad?

SHIV
What? I thought that would kinda be your dream, Rome? Me fucking Gerri, with your dick.

People look down.

ROMAN
Yeah once I explained it was just a fun tactic to undermine a female colleague he was actually really into it. He wants me to teach him.

SHIV
Sure.

ROMAN
Dad's whole career is kind of one big dick pic sent to Western civilization, so?

SHIV
Come on, BPD, pay up.

Tom shakes and lands.

TOM
Ha. Get Out of Jail Free. Another.

GREG
Or. Or should that be, Get out of Jail—?
                    (hunting for the joke)
Due to, due to the, the overly cozy relationships between the –
DOJ and the er, revolving door at the the big legal firms. Right?

SHIV
Such a cynic.

Kerry goes past taking a special smoothie, a little bowl of walnuts and some other pills and a couple of older children's books out to Logan.

ROMAN
Oooh. Waitress service.

(*to Kerry*)
Can I get a Cuba Libre and a club sandwich?

KERRY
(*with a 'fuck off' smile and nod to Logan*)
Talk to my manager.

Connor clocks the tray then looks at Willa.

CONNOR
You still into this, Will? Wanna take a turn around the gardens?

WILLA
Mmm? I'm good.

ROMAN
Go on, Willa, marry him! He'll probably only last like ten years then it's all gravy.

CONNOR
I do not wish my private affairs to become the subject of table chat, okay?

SHIV
Yeah. So rude. Marry him, Willa. Go on. Think of the fun you'll have with his motorized wheelchair once he's gone?

Greg gets a text. Smiles.

ROMAN
Greg, please concentrate. Your smile makes you look like a simpleton. Who's that from?

GREG
Just a new friend.

ROMAN
Do not try to compete with me, Greg, I will destroy you. I will strip you down and sell you to an ostrich farm.

Roman has half an eye on the game, half an eye on Logan with Gerri. Shiv clocks his anxieties.

TOM
Okay. I gotta go. Can I give my properties to Shiv?

ROMAN

Absolutely not. You have to auction. Where you going? Off to munch the farmer's turnips with the rest of the herd?

Willa spots Shiv sliding some money out of the bank next to her, quite subtly.

TOM

Um, that little Forbes-profile silly thing. ATN Citizens is a cash machine and they wanna hear how I did it I guess?

SHIV

By turning on the bigot spigot to full gush?

TOM

Well the 'bigot spigot' is kinda reductive but—

WILLA

Um? Shiv?

Shiv looks innocent.

I think you might have accidentally been cheating?

SHIV

Fine. Okay.

She hands the money back. Willa and Greg look shocked.

What? I'm only stealing so I can win?

CONNOR
(*matter of fact*)

Cheating is part of it.

ROMAN

Jesus. Look at her. Do you think good people cheat at *Monopoly*, Shiv?

He slips a couple of notes while people look at Shiv.

SHIV
(*to Roman*)

Never finished a book.

> ROMAN

'Ooooh I'm Shiv, I'm having a nervie B – I can't get out of bed, bring more jello, Poppa's gonna merge and leave me out in the cold.'

> SHIV

'Oh I'm Roman in a shame spiral because my jerk matron has met an age-appropriate attorney.'

They hear car doors opening and closing.

Okay, here he comes, nice, yeah?

Roman looks like: Well, yeah, I'm not a monster. But then mumbles, because he can't stand the sonorous atmosphere—

> ROMAN

Kurt Cobain of the fucking floaties.

They all prepare themselves.

But first to appear is – Comfrey.

> COMFREY

He's just coming – but he's a bit, um, yeah.

> SHIV

Thanks. And we appreciate what you did.

> COMFREY

It was nothing.

> ROMAN

Sure. But listen, if you find him in the pool again, there's a C-note in it if you let him sink.

Shaking of heads.

> COMFREY

I think he's fine. They just kept him in overnight to, you know – I don't know why actually. My Italian isn't great. But no media pick-up, so all—
> (*realizes it really isn't*)
> 'good'.

Then Kendall appears. Shades on, disconnected. Broken but just about able to keep up a facade for his siblings. Comfrey retreats in the background.

ROMAN

Hey.

KENDALL

Hey.

CONNOR

You okay, brother?

KENDALL

Uh-huh, let's not make a song and dance okay?

CONNOR

Well, I think we will make a song and dance, you nearly
drowned, Ken?

SHIV

He fell off an air bed, he's fine.

KENDALL

One too many limoncellos. No biggie.

They all nod.

Okay I'm gonna grab the kids. I guess, thanks. I'll see you
around.

SHIV

I'm sure, they can stay the night if you like?

KENDALL

I'm not leaving them with him.

*Logan is pacing by the pool talking animatedly. Gerri and Kerry in
attendance. He drinks from the smoothie. Not good.*

ROMAN

Oh, come on.

SHIV

Are you – driving?

KENDALL

Why? No, I don't drive.
                    (*then, shouts*)
Kids, hey! In the car, please!

ROMAN

Well. Okay. See you at the royal wedding.

                    KENDALL
Maybe. I dunno. We might jet. We might go join Nay. I don't
know. She has her own shit but – I might need to get home. I'm
talking to new lawyers, so.

                    ROMAN
New new lawyers?

                    KENDALL
I can't say. But, so you know we're discussing putting
everything, all the papers and all my communications for the
last five years up on my Insta.

He nods to Comfrey – who tries to assent but looks queasy.

                    SHIV
Jesus, Ken.

                    KENDALL
Maybe I make my life worthwhile.

                    ROMAN
Mmm. Good instinct.

                    KENDALL
I dunno. Hive-mind it. Radical transparency. So, fair warning.
And *Vanity Fair* might be doing a big piece with me. So.
I dunno. Whatever. I'm ready to really get into it all. But. Um,
yeah, thanks.
                    (*calls again*)
Kids, let's go!! Comfrey, will you—?

*He walks off, but it doesn't feel good. They wait a beat before
commenting.*

                    GREG
He seems – good?

                    ROMAN
Oh, man.

Before she goes—

                    COMFREY
Um, so you know, we were in touch with *Vanity Fair* but I don't
think— It's mostly us calling them?

> SHIV

Thanks, Comfrey. Listen, we might wanna do something with him, before he goes. We might need you to nudge, okay?

Comfrey backs off as Logan comes stomping down the path. He has the phone at his ear.

> ROMAN

Hey, Dad, all good?

> LOGAN

No.

> ROMAN

Should I jump on this or—?

Logan gestures to Roman: Not now. Roman nods: All good.

> LOGAN
> (*then into phone*)

Go on, Karl, what?

Logan marches inside. Gerri is following, stops in for a briefing.

> GERRI

Wobbles. DOJ is gonna likely hit us with a historic fine. I mean – like approaching twenty billion sorries. GoJo market cap has overtaken ours.

Roman is keen to maintain the appearance that he's still inside this thing.

> ROMAN

Okay well, sure. It was heading that way.

> GERRI

GoJo board might be entertaining other options.

> SHIV

Is Dad gonna pull the plug? Is GoJo? Rome—? He swallowed the merger, I'm not sure how much more fucking around he'll eat?

Shiv enjoys putting Roman under the microscope on this, he's anxious.

> ROMAN
>
> Hey, don't get sweaty, Betty. I'll figure it all out and drop you an email.

Logan comes out onto a balcony, or calls out.

> LOGAN
>
> I'm gonna go see Matsson and get inside this!

> ROMAN
> (*calling up*)
>
> You want me to come, Dad?

> LOGAN
>
> No, you stay here and play with your dick.

Uncomfortable, round the table. Gerri and him pained.

> SHIV
> (*calls*)
>
> Dad, if you want—?

> LOGAN
>
> I'm kidding. No c'mon, Tumbledown. He's your pal. Let's go see Hans Christian Anderfuck, see if he's been telling us fucking fairytales.

DAY TWO

EXT. ITALIAN COUNTRYSIDE – DAY

Logan's helicopter flies.

EXT. LAKE MAGGIORE – BOAT – DAY

Logan and Roman. Kerry is up front.

As he sits, Logan seems to inch himself very slightly away from Roman. Roman clocks it. Might be nothing.

> ROMAN
>
> Okay, Dad?

Logan looks towards Kerry enjoying the wind in her hair. Logan gives Roman a look: She's a good-looking woman, right?

LOGAN
Uh-huh. Good-looking woman, ah?

ROMAN
Oh sure. Yeah. Yup.

Beat of uncomfortableness. Little cringey to have that look shared with your dad. Logan has had something on his mind. Asks—

LOGAN
So, look, what is it, son? Are you scared of pussy? Is it all screens or up the ass with you or what?

Roman feels unable to summon the weapons to defend himself.

ROMAN
No, Dad. Jesus. Do we have to—?
(then)
The thing – I was just being horrible. It's all good.

LOGAN
Yeah well just, fucking, if you need to get straightened out, get straightened out. Okay? I don't wanna know.

They travel on. It's uncomfortable.

EXT. LAKE MAGGIORE – LANDING STAGE OF MATSSON'S HOUSE – DAY

Matsson is with his CFO and COO, who greet Roman, Logan and Kerry as they arrive. Roman is first to disembark. Logan up next.

ROMAN
Hey, Dad—?

Roman offers a hand to help Logan. Logan seems to ignore him, and instead accepts the offer from one of Matsson's staff.

Roman clocks it. Logan crosses to Matsson.

MATSSON
Hello. Really pleased to meet you in person finally, sir.

LOGAN
Likewise.

Roman stands. A spare prick or the deal-maker?

INT./EXT. LAKE MAGGIORE – MATSSON'S HOUSE – DAY

Matsson and Logan walk through the house, out into and around the grounds.

>   MATSSON
> Thank you so much for coming to me.

All through, we see these two big beasts from Roman's point of view, as, at first, he tries to keep things on track, but then starts to feel the dynamic shift—

>   LOGAN
> Oh, not at all.
>   (*quick beat*)
> So. What you think?
>   (*then*)
> Are we doing this fucking merger or not?

>   MATSSON
> Oh wow, man, just straight in there!

Roman looks at Matsson: Is this going to be okay?

>   LOGAN
> Yeah well. You know. I'm old. What? You want a bit of 'nice house you got here'?

>   MATSSON
> No. It's good I get bored easily.

Logan smiles.

>   LOGAN
> Well, everything's fucking boring isn't it?

>   MATSSON
> Everything is pretty boring.

Against his expectations, Logan doesn't hate this kid. Roman can sense it. Good. Logan gives a sprinkle of his sugar. A sly smile—

>   LOGAN
> Except this.

>   MATSSON
> Yeah well you've got me interested.

> LOGAN
>
> Yeah but how interested?

Matsson gives a 'little bit' face. Roman thinks – so far so good. Matsson shepherds them out into the grounds.

> Look, I just don't want to fuck around forever with this. I've seen what's happening to your price. And I understand your board will need to look at all the options. But if we stay tight we can work this, so—
>
> *(beat)*
>
> shall we dance, or what?

> MATSSON
>
> Well. Sure and I don't want to be an asshole and trail shit I can't talk about but, everything good you might have heard about us?

> LOGAN
>
> Betting? Subscription numbers?

> MATSSON
>
> All true.

> ROMAN
>
> And I told Dad gaming, the cloud gaming?

Matsson makes a gesture as if to say: Sure, of course.

> LOGAN
>
> So what does that mean?

> MATSSON
>
> Mark – you know Mark? Mark told me this thing, in Rome, at one point, they wanted to make all the slaves wear something to identify them. A cloak or whatever.

> LOGAN
>
> Uh-huh.

> MATSSON
>
> But they decided not to. You know why? Because if all the slaves dressed the same they'd see how many there were of them, and then they'd kill the masters.

Logan shrugs, a little dismissive.

ROMAN

Yeah we don't love Mark.

LOGAN

Uh-huh. Got a kid in Malaysia reading history for him now?

MATSSON

Haha I don't know. But look, to survive, you, me, we're gonna
need a hell of a lot of little folks running around shitting us
data. For the eyeballs, for the revenue, for the scale. And I don't
think you have the technology or orientation to get there.

LOGAN

And you don't have the content.

MATSSON

Yeah but, we're flying like a fucking rocket ship and you're
sinking like a lead balloon. I mean big picture.

Logan isn't about to lie down—

LOGAN

What's your churn like?

ROMAN

We hear you have problems with binge and burn. We've got the
good stuff.

MATSSON

Sure, some of your content is cool but, honestly, business-wise
it's time for you to beef up or sell out. And honestly, you can't
become a tech player because you and the business are just too
damn old!

ROMAN

He's in great shape. You know who he's fucking?

Roman's pushing it, Logan looks like: Easy.

MATSSON

I don't want to be rude because you're a legend okay. You're
bullet-proof. Tank man!

Logan kind of likes this kid.

LOGAN
You want me to get in your sauna and tell you what a pretty pecker you got?

MATSSON
I'm just really excited about the future.

LOGAN
Well me too.

MATSSON
Yeah? But really?

LOGAN
(with a bit of self-knowledge)
Well it's something you say isn't it?
(then)
No. I am excited but—
(then)
America. I dunno. When I arrived, they were these gentle giants smelling of fucking gold and milk, and they could do anything. Now you look at them, fat as fuck or scrawny on meth or yoga. They pissed it all away. I don't know.
(then)
Go on. Talk to me.

They have a connection. Does Roman start to feel eased out?

MATSSON
I think we fit. Your company and mine, but I think, you know, the Street loves us, we're a strong buy. We're up and we're staying there. You have this fine, all this bullshit. You're hurt, you're maybe tired. I make sense as the person, to take over.

That's big. What will Logan do? Nothing, soaks it up, for now. Considering.

LOGAN
Uh-huh.

MATSSON
So, if that is possible. That you would consider selling up. We can walk around. But if you want to tell me to fuck off, tell me to fuck off?

LOGAN

You're not fucking serious.

Huge. Roman looks at his dad. Studies him as Logan feeds this new piece of data into his vast model of the world.

MATSSON

I'd make everything nice. We could we could pay you out – or if you wanted control – inside or outside – of the assets you love? I would want you to maintain prestige. I'm not about making you small.

LOGAN

But you'd rule the roost and it would be your board?

MATSSON

But we'd structure it so fucking nice for you.

LOGAN

Uh-huh.

MATSSON

I notice you're not punching me in the nose?

Logan sits, thinking. Roman feels like he's awake on the table and watching himself being operated on—

ROMAN

Hey, Dad—?

LOGAN

It's okay, son.

MATSSON

What are you thinking?

LOGAN

I'm not telling you what I'm fucking thinking!

MATSSON

I know what you're thinking.

Logan nods: Go on.

You're thinking, 'Every bit of me wants to tell him to fuck off and eat shit except for the bit that knows every word he says is true.'

> LOGAN

I don't see it. I don't see how I swallow this.

Roman feels a flush of relief.

> MATSSON

You know, if this is a family thing I get it. Appreciate the anxieties. And in terms of your son—
> > (*re Roman*)

he'd be absolutely essential to the integration process. Key element, one hundred percent. Face of the family. Crucial.

Matsson looks to him. Roman smiles. He wants it to feel true.

As for the rest, your top team – I'd be happy to assess each according to their abilities.

Logan is thinking. Then—

> LOGAN

Yeah. This is not happening.

But Matsson can sense something. Logan is uncomfortable in front of Roman. There's another layer. He lays some cover—

> MATSSON

Okay, well I see that. Understood.
> > (*then*)

It was worth asking.

Logan smiles.

But listen. You want to stick around? See if the old deal has a shape? Or side snacks? You have the Israeli AI operation that I might like. Asset-swap sort of thing?

> LOGAN

Why not.

There is something understood between them from which Roman is excluded.

Rome, you should head back, for your mom and everything.

> ROMAN

Uh-huh. Sure thing. Sure thing, Dad.

> (*a joke to cover his discomfort*)
> Hate to miss the big nuptials!
> (*to Matsson*)
> My mom's marrying this great guy and we all love him a lot.
> So . . . yeah. I'll just go do that then.

Roman heads off as, after a beat, Logan goes to look out over the lake. Matsson checks in with an assistant.

Logan looks out. Feeling conflicted. Feeling tired.

EXT. LAKE MAGGIORE — EVENING

Roman alone in the back of the launch. Evening is coming. He is small, alone on the big lake.

He looks at his phone. Lot of messages from Shiv and Gerri checking in. He would like to make a call for advice.

Gerri? Shiv?? Kendall??? No one to call.

DAY THREE

INT. PIENZA RESTAURANT — DAY

The next day. Shiv, Connor wait, nervous. Breakfast things on the table. Roman sits.

> SHIV

So?

> ROMAN

So – how was the *Monopoly*? Did you get to pay some income tax for the novelty value?

> SHIV

Merger of equals?

Roman makes a face: I know things.

> CONNOR

Merger of equals?!

Roman and Shiv make patronizing eye contact. Connor clocks, it's infuriating. But he eats it. Again.

SHIV

Is it happening?

CONNOR

Was not alerted to the 'merger of equals' possibility. Matsson wants to deplatform guys like me. Round up the maverick thinkers into his digital gulag.

Shiv looks at Roman as they see Kendall arrive. Making the long walk, sensing something is up.

ROMAN

Do you mind? I'm just all churned up about my big bro and I can't think about that shit?

Roman smiles, the insider — but can Shiv sense it's not real? Kendall arrives.

KENDALL

Hey. Hello? So what is this?

SHIV

Ken. Take a seat.

He looks around and makes a decision. Okay.

Look, Ken, we all just wanted to get together here to tell you that we love you.

Roman struggles but doesn't make a joke or do a fake puke.

KENDALL

What?

SHIV

Right?

CONNOR

I love you. Straight up.

ROMAN

Sure. No, I don't want you to die— Yeah. So.

KENDALL

What is this? What's the angle?

> CONNOR

No angle. We're worried you tried consciously or subconsciously to—

> KENDALL

Are you trying to shut me down?

> ROMAN

Dude, you kind of tried to kill yourself and that's not cool.

> KENDALL

I fell off an inflatable.

> ROMAN

Oh sure.

> KENDALL

Is this an 'intervention'?

> SHIV

We just wanted to say we— A lot has been said – but we do all want you to be – okay. Basically, okay? We want that.

> KENDALL

Why do you get to do an intervention on me?
> (*to each of them*)
You need an intervention. You need an intervention. You need an intervention.

> ROMAN

Well that may well be true, but you're top of the pile right now, we'll do mine tomorrow.

> SHIV

Suicides jump the line.

> KENDALL

I fell off my fucking floatie!

> SHIV

You're an addict. You're addicted to booze and drugs and to relationships and to sex and to work, and to the family drama.

> KENDALL

Well, no, sorry, look who's fucking here? I don't see it. You don't have any standing.

SHIV

Legal papers on Instagram? Another fucking tell-all interview they don't even want?

KENDALL

I have to put out those papers in order to complete my exit strategy from the firm.

ROME

You tried to fuck your nanny, Ken, what part of your MBA is that?

KENDALL

Not true. No, so you can take this little committee of public fucking safety and fuck off.

CONNOR

You need to stop trying to kill Dad. You're selfish and self-centered.

ROMAN

Hey, Con?

CONNOR

What? I can't say my piece?

Shiv and Roman look at him like: Cool it. Infuriating.

SHIV
(*aside to him*)

I'll lead, yeah?

Connor takes a steak knife and starts drawing geometric patterns on the table with it, stewing.

Kendall musters his response. Tries, even, to hear them. Though he can't really bear to hear them through all the layers of mixed feelings and suspicions—

KENDALL

Okay. Look. I hear you. But I feel like everything I have done has been with good intentions. And I do think this is actually about all of you more than me. But listen, I feel like I'm sounding defensive when I'm not – I'm hearing you.

ROMAN

But we're not saying anything.

639

KENDALL

Well I know what you would be saying and if you want to say it, say it. But I've thought about this all a lot.

But the emotion has got to Kendall. He looks down.

ROMAN

It's okay.

KENDALL

Pricks.

(*beat*)

Look. I dunno. Things went off-course, maybe. But can you imagine how it felt? As the eldest son – I mean – to be promised something and then. You know?

They all nod. Beat of quiet.

Just have it taken?

SHIV

Sure, man.

Connor has been stewing, dragging the cutlery around.

CONNOR
(*inaudible – a very low murmur*)

I'm the eldest son.

ROMAN

What's that?

CONNOR

I am the eldest son.

SHIV

Sure, obviously, Con. But you know what he means?

CONNOR

I'm the eldest son, and no one even told me about this merger of fucking equals and what if I want to take over because *I am the eldest son*!!

SHIV

Hey, easy. It's okay.

> CONNOR

I am the eldest son and I must be considered! I need to be taken into account!

> KENDALL

Con. We're talking about what I actually lost . . .

> CONNOR

Shut up!!

> (*to Ken*)

You're hurt?! I didn't see Dad for three years!!! But your spoon wasn't fucking shiny enough? Ah?? Fuck you.

> KENDALL

I thought you 'loved me'?

> CONNOR

I do love you, you fucking prick, but what do I get from you chumps? Chump change. Fucking chump change? Well fuck you!

He gets up.

I'm here for your mom's wedding, and I proposed to my fiancée and *no one* has said congratulations – but I am the eldest son of our father I am – I AM – ME!

He starts to leave. A little away—

> ROMAN
> (*quietly*)

He's him.

But Connor hears.

> CONNOR
> (*departing*)

Fuck you!

Beat after he's gone.

> KENDALL

Seriously. I think, I'm fucked, but I'm okay you know? What if I'm not the fucking problem huh? What then?

He gets up.

EXT. CAROLINE'S WEDDING COMPLEX – DAY

Later. Wedding-day preparations. People are getting into cars.

Connor is about to get into one with Willa.

                    WILLA
You okay, Con?

                    CONNOR
Yeah. Yeah. Just a little tired. Sorry about tossing and turning.
Couldn't get the AC right you know?

                    WILLA
Sure. The AC.

                    CONNOR
Plus my family hates me and I'm gonna lose ATN to a Swede
and so my campaign is fucked and you're gonna leave me. And
I love you so fucking much. So, yeah. That and the AC.

She looks at him.

                    WILLA
Oh, Con?

                    CONNOR
What?

                    WILLA
You're a nice man.

                    CONNOR
Right, thanks.

                    WILLA
And you know what? Fuck it.

                    CONNOR
Fuck it?

                    WILLA
Fuck it!

                    CONNOR
As in—?

                    WILLA
Fuck it, c'mon! How bad can it be?

                    CONNOR
Really?

                    WILLA
Yeah why not, we'll have fun. Fuck it, right?

                    CONNOR
Hell yeah! Fuck it! Fuck it!

                    WILLA
I. Love. You.

Con gets into the car. Top of the world. How quick do the mixed feelings hit Willa? Pretty fast?

Cars leave.

EXT. LOGAN'S VILLA – DAY

Cars are arriving. Bankers and lawyers and assistants pour in.

EXT. WEDDING VENUE – DAY

Everyone is gathering outside.

                    SHIV
Where is Dad? Is he just not going to come? I mean, what the fuck? Rome? Where is he? Is the deal good?

On the side, Roman checks his phone. He's freaking too.

                    ROMAN
All will be revealed. All will be revealed.

                    SHIV
What the fuck does that mean? Who made you the Wizard of Fuck?

But Roman's looking over at Peter, now approaching.

                    ROMAN
And do you not think, maybe one last check with Mom?

                    SHIV
Rome. We're about to go in.

ROMAN

Right. I just don't know if he – you know? (Loves Mom.)

SHIV

You're not sure if he's 'the one'?

ROMAN

I am worried about the prenup.

SHIV

She has a prenup, she had her lawyer on it because she wants to keep the London flat she got from Dad.

ROMAN

But what if he poisons her, what if he pushes her down the stairs to get this flat he so loves?

SHIV

And what about, even worse, what if he fucks her? With his dick? What if he fucks her so good she dies?

Nearby, Tom is with Greg. Comfrey is around too.

GREG

Um, Tom, would you consider chatting with Comfrey? I want to check in on the Princess?

TOM

The Princess now? I thought she was a Contessa?

GREG

Um, yeah. But through her dad, she's actually like eighth in line to the throne of Luxembourg.

TOM

Eighth in line? Greg, marry her and you're a plane crash from becoming Europe's weirdest king!

GREG

Tch. Don't be silly.

TOM

Have you seen *King Ralph*? Off a handful of hemophiliacs, and you'll be the King of Luxembourg. You'd sound like a fancy cookie!

> GREG

It's actually a grand duchy, it's to do with the Congress of
Vienna. It's all really complicated and she doesn't like talking
about it, although we did talk about it quite a lot.

> (*then*)

Oh see, now, Roman! Shit!

Roman has gotten in there to talk to the Contessa.

> TOM

Get in there, Greg, if Roman marries her he'll invade France.

INT. LOGAN'S VILLA – DAY

*Logan is on a call in a big and shaded room. Frank and Karl. Many
others in the room on laptops.*

*Kerry brings in a tray with a smoothie. It makes Logan wince to
drink.*

Marcia passes through.

> MARCIA

I'll send your regrets.

*Logan puts his finger to his lips. Shush. Marcia nods and heads out
past Kerry. Who has papers.*

Kerry, I won't eat down there, I'll take my omelette in my room,
on my return. Thank you.

> KERRY

Of course. I'll let them know.

*Smiles. They have some complicated level of understanding and even,
respect, these two. Marcia heads out.*

As Kerry joins Logan with the papers, he motions for her to talk—

I've marked up some concerns. But yeah, all makes sense.

INT. WEDDING VENUE – DAY

Guests are mostly in place. But still no Logan.

Caroline and Peter are ready to make their processional. Kendall makes it in without kids.

>   KENDALL
> Sorry. I didn't delay things did I?

>   PETER
> No worries, Kendall – we're just missing a couple of people actually. You don't know where – where—?

>   CAROLINE
> Peter, I don't know if Logan's going to make it. You might have to make do with me, is that alright, darling?

Peter smiles. Kendall heads in.

Now Caroline and Peter start their processional. As Kendall makes it to the end of the row next to Tom. In their row it goes: Kendall, Tom, Shiv, Roman, Contessa, Greg, Comfrey.

>   SHIV
> Hey, Rome. I have an idea—

He looks at her.

> When she comes past, why don't you tell her you love her?

>   ROMAN
> Yeah, fuck off.

>   SHIV
> Imagine how romantic it would be if you could marry Mummy today, on her wedding day!

>   ROMAN
> Yeah yeah.

>   SHIV
> Tell them you know a reason they can't be married. She's the only one who makes her son's peepee go boom-boom.

They look over. Willa is by Connor, crying.

>   GREG
>   (*to Contessa*)
> Wow, she's really feeling it huh?

The Contessa looks at the bride and groom. Makes a face: So romantic. Greg smiles back: Lovely.

Beat later Comfrey looks at Greg: Such hypocritical bullshit. Greg looks back: Fuck yeah. Kill me now.

The celebrants calls for them all to be seated.

EXT. WEDDING RECEPTION – DAY

Shiv is doing a speech for her mom.

> SHIV
> So my mom's just asked me to say a few words. Like just this second. And the first words that sprang to mind are – 'shit', 'what', 'no', 'bitch!' Along with the words 'totally' and 'unprepared'. But I guess Mom likes to rush into things. Right, Peter? So what can I say about Mom?
> *(long beat, then)*
> Well . . . she's been a constant in my life. A constant pain in the— But I love her anyway. Which I guess is testament to what a remarkable, complicated . . . interesting person she is. And Peter, there is one thing I'm certain of – you will not be bored in the brief time you're together. That's a joke.

She throws a look and smile to Tom. Who smiles back.

> But in all seriousness – there is no one like my mom. And you're a lucky man. And I'm jealous that you'll get so much of her company. We all are.
> *(picking up a glass)*
> I hope you have a marriage that's as happy and fulfilling and rich and rewarding as mine.
> *(raising her glass)*
> To the bride and groom!

EXT. WEDDING RECEPTION – DAY

Later. Shiv and Roman regard Marcia making the rounds as Peter speaks.

PETER

As some of you may know, I've been pursuing Caroline on and off for a number of years. Thirty-four years. Not that I've been counting. (I have been counting.) Now, I love the thrill of the chase. But you want to have a bit of puff left at the end. Luckily, I think I have a tiny bit of puff left. Although I'll let Caroline be the judge of that later!

Roman gags.

Anyway, the point is, I've waited a long time. And I had some very stiff competition – from some very handsome, very rich men – and Rory – but my god it was worth it. Because this woman is a very special prize. Beautiful, funny, surprising, clever and delightful. Caroline, ti adoro. I hope I can make you happy. It's all I care about in the world. Apart from my children and my businesses and racing and cricket and a peerage. But apart from that, she's all I care about in the world. Truly.

At a certain point, under this, Shiv and Roman start discussing, looking over at Marcia, who gets up—

SHIV

Do you think she knows something? What if it's all fallen apart? I hear he's back. Why hasn't he come down?

ROMAN

Relax. It's – cool beans.

SHIV

'Cool beans'? Since when do you say cool beans? You're bebopping cos you have no fucking clue, do you?

Then Connor bounces up.

CONNOR

Hey hey hey!

SHIV

Um, so listen I think we should say sorry and—

CONNOR

So, guess who's getting married to the best darn gal in the world?!

                          SHIV
  Oh. She said yes?

                          ROMAN
  Hey congrats, man.
                    (*with a smile, not unkind*)
  Finally ground her down.

Connor also has something he knows might hurt . . .

                          CONNOR
  And also. Willa's been talking to Kerry?

                          SHIV
  Does she know where Dad is?

                          CONNOR
  She's sandbagging. But you know what this is?

He opens his palm. A shriveled root. Roman looks.

                          ROMAN
  Is it the dried penis of one of the great men of history? Genghis
  Khan? Bing Crosby?

                          CONNOR
  Maca root. For Dad's smoothie.

                          SHIV
  So why is Kerry sandbagging?

They look at him, blank.

                          CONNOR
  He's working on his baby batter.

                          ROMAN
  Excuse me?

                          CONNOR
  Maca root. Almond butter. Dad's working on a more adhesive
  and potent gloop.

                          ROMAN
  Dad is—? Dad's working on his jissom? Are you fucking
  kidding me?

CONNOR

Have you not noticed all the walnuts he's been munching? He's gonna be rocking sperms like little catfish. Tadpoles like Navy SEALs.

ROMAN

Are you serious? Dad's scrambling the fighters?

CONNOR

That maca root – not good. Nope, you don't tangle with the root unless you're firing up the siege engine.

SHIV

Jesus Christ.

CONNOR

I guess he really doesn't rate you guys. Instead he's activating the bat sperm hanging in the far recesses of his testes.

Connor walks off with a smile. Tom joins them.

ROMAN

Okay well we need a plan to kill this baby.

SHIV

Finally you've found a worthy adversary.
(to Tom)
Bullshit rumors that Dad's trying to – to raise the Titanic. Cranking the trebuchet. Trying for a baby.
(to Roman, ninety percent kidding)
Maybe that's where he is?

ROMAN

What, in the spawn chamber, issuing his hellseed? Sure.

Tom looks at Shiv.

TOM

Maybe we should get cracking? Space race?

ROMAN

You two? Tom, you know her ovaries are covered in teeth, right? Her womb isn't a womb, it's a spiritual vacuum. She has canines where the eggs should be.

> TOM
> (*to Shiv*)

Can I say?

Roman looks between them.

> ROMAN

No, I think if Shiv could have kids it would have happened by now. Because she's had a lot of sex with a lot of men.

> SHIV
> (*to Tom*)

Okay well if you wanna do the public announcement, I guess you've got me.

> TOM

We might be freezing!

> ROMAN

You're freezing? You know what she's waiting for, don't you, Tom? She's gonna make you carry it.

> TOM

Yeah 'ha ha'.

> ROMAN

Seriously you're gonna have to shit your own baby. Then squeeze your Tommy tits for man-milk.

Gerri approaches—

> GERRI

Listen, I've just heard Larry Vansitart's PJ landed at Linate and he was headed for Lake Maggiore.

> SHIV

Larry Vansitart? To Matsson? Why does—? That would mean financing? Why does Matsson need financing if we're doing an all-stock deal?

> GERRI
> (*cards close*)

I'm trying to get a fix. Greg's been contacted by some assistants. Let's split and pool, okay?

They watch her go. Shiv looks at Roman.

ROMAN

Could be a number of things.

SHIV

What the fuck, Roman? I thought you were inside this?

Roman is rattled but tries not to show it.

ROMAN

This is fine, this is good.

As Roman tries to call Logan—

But look. I'll hit Kerry – will you take Marcia? Find out who's up with Dad?

SHIV

Okay. Sure, scale the fucking north face of the Eiger.

They split.

Greg is with the Contessa.

CONTESSA

Everyone who thinks it's easy, I would like them to look through my comments for one day and still be able to keep ahold of themselves, you know, it's mentally draining. Do I sound terrible?

GREG

No, it's good, Maria. I mean, my central work task right now is to try to help keep old people from changing channels by making them scared or angry, so?

CONTESSA

I mean, I guess, I try to feel better by giving a lot to environmental charities.

GREG

Oh. Okay? Like to—? To which? Not Greenpeace?

CONTESSA

No, Friends of the Earth.

GREG

Oh yeah, that's a good one. No I just have beef with Greenpeace. Long story, but they're bad. One guy in Greenland cashing the checks and just – eating penguin and stubbing cigarettes on glaciers. Is what I hear.

Roman walks past, to the Contessa.

ROMAN
Feel free to cut him dead by the way.

CONTESSA
We're having an interesting talk.

ROMAN
Sure, I don't want to be rude but he's what we call in our land 'an irrelevant pauper'. You don't need to listen to the pauper. It's not for your royal ears.

GREG
Ha. Well. No. No-de-no, my friend.
(*to the Contessa*)
I'm sorry. He's widely known, I think you'd agree, Roman, you're a self-admitted – sexual, a – I don't know what you'd say in your language – but he is a – you're a pervert or a deviant?

CONTESSA
Well I knew there must be some interesting people here somewhere!

Roman smiles and switches focus to Greg.

ROMAN
Yeah so listen, kidding aside, I hear you might have been getting some tremors on the assistant loop?

GREG
Me? Um, just some discreet requests I'll keep discreet if that's cool?

ROMAN
Uh-huh? And when the company merges would you like to be inside or would you maybe like to be back at the turkey farm, taking the blind ones out to shit?

Greg weighs. No dog in the fight, why not keep Roman sweet?

GREG
Well, okay, yeah a call went out on Lackey Slack – because there are a number of advisors from LionTree in town, apparently and

they are finding the Italian pillows a little hard, but it's a private sort of thing so—

ROMAN

Thank you.
(*whispers in Greg's ear*)
I'm going to have vaginal sex in the missionary position with her, like a total fucking normo so leave well alone.

Roman moves on to talk, looks for Gerri or Kerry.

GREG
(*after him*)
We're literally having a glass of wine!

*Shiv moves in on Marcia.**

SHIV

Hey. How you doing there?

MARCIA

Oh, fine thank you. I like Italy.

SHIV

Right. Um, I heard, I heard you might be— Do you know where my dad might be at? And what he's doing?

MARCIA

Me?

She looks at Shiv, does she care to give her anything?

No.

But Shiv can see she knows more.

SHIV

Right?

Normally this would be the end of things but Shiv is going to try to go further—

And so, what's going on for you?

---

* I would love to have included this Marcia–Shiv exchange, but the velocity required by the gathering storm of the end of the episode meant we had to lose it.

MARCIA

I am well thank you. And yourself?

Shiv sighs, she's going to try to be open, or at least give the impression of being open.

SHIV

Um, yeah, tough, I don't know, tough, you know, fitting in at work, I'm trying but it can be difficult sometimes to feel I am really progressing, it's a tough environment.

MARCIA

That must be difficult.

SHIV

It is, it is difficult, it is.
(then)
But – I mean how you finding it, the new 'set-up' sort of thing?

She's not about to say.

MARCIA

I am very lucky.

SHIV

Uh-huh.
(then)
Yeah?
('let me in')
I'm just saying hi, Marcia, and if you ever want to talk, you can talk to me. I'm here.

MARCIA
(giving nothing)
You are very kind.

Shiv wants to say 'fuck you' then, but swallows it and persists.

SHIV

I'm just – I'm sorry, we never talked, or really connected and—
You know, I hardly know anything about you and – everything, you know?

MARCIA

You never asked.

655

> SHIV
> (*trying*)
> Right. Well. I mean. Can I ask now? I mean. I know, obviously you grew up – in what in – in Israel and – then in Lebanon, in the seventies and eighties? What was that all like?

Marcia looks at her.

> MARCIA
> It was no teddy bears' picnic.

Shiv is getting exasperated.

> SHIV
> I'm trying to be real here. I can be open, I can tell you my shit if you want, I've got a ton of shit I am happy to unload for you.
> (*then one last try*)
> C'mon though. Was it tough? Did you see a lot of – suffering?

Shiv feels she has put herself out there. Marcia finds her infuriating. But then—

> MARCIA
> So. Okay. I was raised in a refugee camp with a father who died for his religion and my mother sold her body for guns, so it is very difficult for me to talk of these things.

> SHIV
> Fuck. Okay. I'm sorry. Really?

Marcia looks at her coolly for a beat.

> MARCIA
> No. My mother was a doctor and my father was a businessman. My first lover was a Jewish boy and until I was twelve we had more servants than you can imagine.
> (*then*)
> You have no idea even of what it is you don't know.

> SHIV
> Well okay, I'm sorry.

> MARCIA
> How am I supposed to answer these questions if you can dare to ask them?

Shiv looks as Kerry arrives to get Gerri. Says something and Gerri departs – what the fuck?

Shiv looks at Marcia, things are moving. Let's get real.

SHIV

Okay. Look, I really want to know what my dad is up to. And I think you've been kind of screwed by my dad, so? Right? No?

MARCIA

You see now I understand you.
                    (*shockingly frank*)
So, what are you offering me?

SHIV

Offering. Um? I dunno. What have you got?

Then, Marcia weighs – no advantage here. She closes down.

MARCIA

Nothing. No. No. I think, you kids, you cook up nothing into something. It's a wedding day, relax.

A cold smile ends things.

Roman is nearby. Catches Kerry—

ROMAN

Hey so excuse me but what did you say to Gerri just there?

KERRY

Um, nothing.

He looks at her. Hard. Lying.

ROMAN

Uh-huh? And why are you lying? Did he tell you to lie?

KERRY

I have no idea what you're talking about.

Kerry heads off.

ROMAN

(*as she goes*)
Are you trying to have my dad's baby? Because that's an incredibly bad idea. It would be born old, attached to a walker.

Shiv joins Roman. He has his update—

So – I think Karl and Frank are in Europe. There's a bunch of new M&A advisors in Chianciano.

SHIV

What the fuck is happening, Roman? Are we being fucked? Karl? Really?

Roman is already back on the phone. Hears the ring tone.

ROMAN
(*to Shiv*)

Euro ring.
(*into phone*)
Hey Karlo! How you doing? Where are you, man?
(*listens*)
At – the office yeah? In your office? Great, well I'll leave you to get on with your office job.

End of call.

Motherfucker. Marcia?

SHIV

We need to put a penny in the slot to make her talk. She's throwing out bullshit. And where the fuck did Gerri go, you see that?

Panic is rising. Something is stirring beneath the water.

This is fucking ugly, Roman, can you see what I can see?

Roman is quiet. Thinks.

ROMAN

Look, um – so I should probably say, in terms of the meeting—?

Shiv looks at him.

Matsson did kind of float, as an idea – maybe they buy us?

SHIV

Uh-huh. And what did Dad say?

ROMAN

No I mean, yeah. He was like 'no way, fuck you'.

SHIV

Oh Jesus Christ.

She spots Kendall. He's been trying to disengage at the edge of the party.

Ken. Hey, Ken!? We might need to talk. Company stuff.

> KENDALL
> I don't— I'm not interested, Shiv.

Shiv has no time to fuck around.

> SHIV
> Ken – five please. It's fucking important. We might need your line to Frank or Stewy, okay?

He looks at a loss but as they depart – the Contessa gets up to speak.

> CONTESSA
> My new cousin Peter has asked if I will say a few words to give their wedding a 'royal seal of approval'. The truth is they're the real royalty here. Peter is a generous-hearted king, providing care homes for his elderly subjects. Caroline is his beautiful and supportive queen, and like any supportive queen, the one who's really in charge.

Greg watches on admiringly. Maybe does a little clap.

> GREG
> Brava!
>
> (*aside to Tom*)
> She's so personable. It's why her content is so engaging. She's been talking to a company that makes tooth-whitening strips and I don't know why but I'm really excited! I think the influencer has influenced me, Tom!

EXT. CAR PARK – DAY

Shiv, Roman and Kendall have retreated somewhere quiet to confer. A car park. Entrances and exits of staff are ongoing.

Kendall watching the wheels go round. But he's getting bad vibrations from the caterers, the feeling of a family wedding.

> SHIV
> Ken, Dad's doing us dirty.

ROMAN

Can we not make it a thing right away? We don't know.
(*to Ken*)
Matsson pitched Dad the idea of them eating us, but I think he
was flying a kite and Dad kind of shut it down.

SHIV

He 'kind of shut it down'? Cos a minute ago he told him 'fuck
off'.

ROMAN

I can't remember the exact number of expletives, Siobhan. I'm
not a fuckometer.

Shiv has put it all together—

SHIV

Larry Vansitart is in Switzerland with Matsson, so he's looking
for financing. Dad's huddled with Karl and Frank who have
flown in. Our market caps have tipped. The local town has been
bought out by a new set of advisors, something's flipped. I hear
the deal code names have even changed.

ROMAN

Ken, what you think, he would never sell, would he?

Kendall shrugs.

SHIV

I mean – would he?

ROMAN

Ken?

SHIV

And if he did, would we get— I don't know—
(*obviously not*)
protection?

Roman knows he's got something in the bank in that regard.

KENDALL

I can't get into this.

SHIV

Wait—? Do you have an angle on this, Ken? Are you speaking
with Matsson?

Kendall provoked to laughter in spite of himself. She's so far off. Maybe walks away. Shiv looks at her phone.

Laird called me. What's that?

Roman's eye is drawn over to Kendall, now crouching nearby.

ROMAN

Is he shitting?

SHIV

I think, I mean it feels like we're the target, Rome, it just does, right?

Roman makes a face. Like he isn't sure. She walks over.

Ken. We have to go and stop this.

KENDALL

Shiv. I'm not here.

He's crouched or defended and, maybe sensing how far away he is, Shiv gives him a touch. It's something, the touch. First contact for a while and it is small but some molecules realign.

I don't know what the fuck is wrong with me.

SHIV

Are you okay?

ROMAN

It's okay, Ken.

They're there and he is able to try to just say a bit of what he feels.

KENDALL

I'm just not feeling very connected to my children or my – endeavors, right now. I can't get one thing right with another, you know?

SHIV

It's okay.

KENDALL

I'm fucking . . . I tried to do something, I tried.

ROMAN

I know, man. I know. You fucked it.

The touch, the place, just the talking, something is cracking and maybe there's a half-cry, half-laugh or just a noise then—

> KENDALL
>
> Fuck you.
>
> (*then*)
>
> I took a shot and I think, I think I fucking hit—

> ROMAN
>
> It's just business. We're all fucked, it's okay. We're all fucked. It all just got mixed up.

> KENDALL
>
> I had an out, I could see it. I could see the waymarkers and – and I dunno—

It's true for Kendall. But for the other two? Little whiff of self-serving in there? But they're not gonna call it now.

> ROMAN
>
> Uh-huh.

> KENDALL
>
> But I dunno. I'm not a good person.

> ROMAN
>
> Well, whatever, you're – fine.

> KENDALL
>
> I'm bad. I'm evil.

> ROMAN
>
> Oh come on, we're kids. You're not—

> KENDALL
>
> I killed a kid.

> SHIV
>
> Uh-huh. What?

Roman looks around where they are – is this real? Quite possibly.

> KENDALL
>
> I killed a kid and they're coming for me. They'll come for me.

> SHIV
>
> Is this – is this real. What?

KENDALL
At your wedding.

SHIV
What?

ROMAN
Bullshit. C'mon. Bullshit.

KENDALL
The kid. That kid.

SHIV
What – the kid? That waiter kid who—? Really, Ken?

KENDALL
I was in the car but I got out and I killed him.

SHIV
Oh fuck. What?

KENDALL
I was high and I was looking for— I was fucked up but I drove, and he saw something and snatched at the wheel and we went into the water and then I left him in there and ran.

SHIV
Let's get out of here. Let's get you out of here, okay?

Kendall is all broken. She puts an arm round him.

Ken. It's okay. It's okay.

Beat of silence as something grows in Roman's mind.

He looks around. The sun beating down. Looks at his brother and sister. Kendall broken, Shiv comforting him.

ROMAN
I mean, if it pleases the court, you didn't kill him, I mean sounds like he – killed him?

KENDALL
It's fucking lonely. I'm – all, apart.

ROMAN
I mean the road killed him? The road and the water killed him?

> KENDALL

Nah. Man, don't.

> ROMAN

I mean so you, crashed, and you— What, then you, ran?

> KENDALL

No, I mean I tried to get him.

> SHIV

Okay?

> ROMAN

Well, see?

> KENDALL

I dived a few times, I think I did. I did. I remember I did. A couple of times.

> ROMAN

You dived? Like twice?

He looks at Shiv. Trying to be nice, but also this is how it sounds to him—

I mean, that is actually kind of the story of a hero? I woulda been straight out of there? I woulda been out of that water like a fucking tabby cat out the bath, bro!

Maybe Kendall can fix himself enough to say—

> KENDALL

Rome. Don't, man. I'm a killer.

> ROMAN

Bullshit. Nah, sounds like you're at worst you're an – irresponsibler. At very worst. You're being very self-dramatizing with the murderer talk, actually. You're bigging yourself up. At worst you're a manslaughter-er.

Kendall sort of appreciates what they're trying to do but he's a long way down.

> KENDALL

I don't know. I don't know what's fucking . . . I'm blown into a million pieces.

> SHIV

What we gonna do? Where do we go?

They look around.

> ROMAN

Let's get him back into the chapel, stuff him in a confessional and fix this.

Shiv picks up her phone.

Who are you calling?

Shiv looks at him.

> SHIV

Laird called back. One minute.

She nods for Roman to attend to Kendall.

> ROMAN

Oh great. Leave me with all the feeling. Thanks.

Kendall and him connect with a look. Then. Roman consoles the only way he can think, back to kids—

What? I mean who hasn't clipped the odd kid with a Porsche? It's a rite of passage. I've killed a kid.
> (*calls*)
Have you killed a kid, Shiv?

> SHIV
> (*hand over phone*)

Oh yeah I've killed a coupla kids. Sure. Just little ones.
> (*then*)
You ruined my wedding so many ways.

Kendall sits on the verge in the dusty car park. Can't believe he's said the worst thing and he's still there. Saying it all has taken him to a different place. He's able to offer—

> KENDALL

'Sorry'.

Shiv connects. She starts to talk. Circles, getting the full picture, quite focussed all of a sudden.

ROMAN

See, one waiter down. That's why it took so long to get a fucking drink at her wedding.

KENDALL

Please. I can't do the—? He was— You know?

ROMAN

No sure. I get it.

(then)

I'm just saying, I'm the real victim here, I waited three-quarters of an hour for a gin and tonic.

It is so dark that it is kind of funny.

Roman maybe puts his hand on Kendall's shoulder for a touch.

They haven't touched for a long time. Maybe Kendall feels tired or exhausted or back in some family place enough to tip his head and rest it there on his brother's hand just for a second.

Shiv has news. She's shocked.

SHIV

Okay. Okay. Okay. I'm sorry, Ken – but – but I do have to just say, confirmed. Laird's inside the deal. But he's been cucked out of the lead. So he's bitter and bleating. GoJo buys Waystar. They pay a premium. Dad cashes out. Cash and stock. Maybe he keeps a title or takes some assets but it's Matsson's board.

ROMAN

Can we trust that?

SHIV

Ken, I mean, I know it's not ideal, I know. But we need to talk. Can we talk?

KENDALL

I can't talk about that now.

SHIV

C'mon. I've called a car, let's get out of here.

Shiv leads them, starting to walk, she has a plan. Roman makes a call.

EXT. WEDDING VENUE — DAY

They have walked to a pick-up spot. Just around the corner. Roman phone down. Shiv looks at him.

> SHIV
>
> Daddy explain it all?

Roman looks like: Fuck you.

> ROMAN
>
> Nothing.
>
> (*then*)
>
> I just don't see a sale because, how would Dad be in charge?

> SHIV
>
> He wouldn't be in charge.

> ROMAN
>
> Okay so how does that work? How would he stay in charge?

> SHIV
>
> Well he wouldn't be in charge, Rome.

Roman frowns. It doesn't compute.

> ROMAN
>
> I just don't see it.

> SHIV
>
> Well it's hard for you to see anything, because you're still so 'deep inside the deal'.

> ROMAN
>
> No way he fucks us.

> SHIV
>
> Why?

> ROMAN
>
> Because. I think, I think he kind of does love us?

> SHIV
>
> Mm?

Kendall a little reactivated by this claim.

> KENDALL

He calls it loving. But y'know if I call my dick an oboe they still won't let me in the orchestra?

Smiles. Kendall back, a bit. At some point the car shows up.

> SHIV

Okay. Look, we need to go stop him. So, Ken. Where do you wanna be?

> KENDALL

Um, I dunno. I'm pretty— I don't mind. Can I be with you guys?

Shiv says from outside the car—

> SHIV
> (*to driver*)

Villa Castelluccio.
> (*then*)

We go see him and tell him we just won't have it, right?

They climb in.

INT. CAR – EVENING

Inside the car—

> ROMAN

This is rumors. I will need to talk to him direct, just me.

They settle.

> SHIV

You think you're close to him? You're just his – little rat-fucker.

> ROMAN

I am just saying as a matter of fact Dad and I have been working closely lately. I don't wanna go in too aggressive.

Roman looks away, hard to read.

Shiv looks to them both – Kendall broken, Roman on the fence.

> SHIV

Why is it I'm getting Normandy beach vibes here? Looking around the landing craft and I'm in with a load of fucking balloon animals?

> ROMAN

I'm not busting in there crying with Team Shiv. Okay? We have no idea how this will play out.

> SHIV

You think Daddy's protecting you?

He shrugs.

We let Matsson take control, that's Dad slamming the door. It means he doesn't think any of us can, should, or will ever take over.

Roman absorbs.

> ROMAN

I just don't think we go in aggressive. I mean can we even actually stop him?

> KENDALL

Yes. A change of control needs a supermajority in the holding company. Mom got us that in the divorce. He'd need us on board.

> ROMAN

I'm not sure I want to pull out something like that. Maybe I stick with what I have?

> SHIV

Which is what? A hard drive full of dick pics?

> ROMAN

I think with Dad pulling strings—

> SHIV

Where do you think we fit on Matsson's new org chart?

> KENDALL

He'll Romanov us. He'll take us all to the cellar and that's that.

> ROMAN

You see I want to disagree.
> *(feeling cornered)*
But I'm scared, if I do, he'll just off me. Drive us all into the sea.

> SHIV

Man? C'mon.

> ROMAN
>
> What, too soon?

Roman looks unpersuaded.

> SHIV
>
> Dad's not going to choose you, Rome, because he thinks there's something wrong with you.

That seems to land. Something he's thought about before. Shiv knows a line has been crossed.

> And I'm sorry but maybe it's time we said these things, to each other? Instead of talking it all out to Vanity Fair.

Roman sits, head hung. Shiv wants to share too, to take the sting away from him.

> Because this is going to be a moment of huge leverage but, Ken, if we're going to work together you can't ever be the boss of me. It just does things to me when you start using that voice and acting – all, I'm sorry but I can't have that.

> KENDALL
>
> And you can't be the boss of me.

Roman thinks.

> ROMAN
>
> And the holding-company move. That's real?

> KENDALL
>
> He can't sanction a deal without us, that's a legal fact. Block him and he's fucked.

> SHIV
>
> Right. Uh-huh. Time to rip off the Band-Aid. Push him out. Just get him on his own and say, fucking – urinary tract, the shareholder meeting?

> KENDALL
>
> He nearly fucking croaked at Josh's.

> SHIV
>
> He's out of it, he's fucking a twenty-year-old, planning for babies in jars? He's gone loopy and tried to sell the shop. Seriously, just fucking his assistant, if we tell that to the board? He's toast.

670

KENDALL

Full coup.

SHIV

Right. Slide him out. Say, Ken Chair? Me or you CEO, Rome. Other one takes, like, whatever they want, the studio, movies, TV, all media, the streamer. Equal.

ROMAN

But really equal? You two cunts don't fucking big brother me out of my fucking piece here, okay?

SHIV

Yes. We can fucking fight it out. It'll be fun!

KENDALL

That will be fun.

Roman looks at them – is it good for him?

Fucking take Mussolini away in a van to the hospital. Take over the radio stations.

SHIV

I think we can get Marcia to fuck him on his health. For a price.

ROMAN

And the old guard?

SHIV

I have Gerri in my pocket. Thanks, Rome.

KENDALL

I can always talk to Frank. There's deep cable.

ROMAN

And I have like four pieces of rat-fuck that kill Karl.

There are levels but they do look at one another like something is coming together, even if Roman is still most wobbly.

I do think. That – although this literally makes me want to puke and I will want to kill you both every day and it all will end horribly – nevertheless, I do think we could, puke, make a, quote, pretty good team.

SHIV

And how do we feel about killing Dad? Mixed feelings right?

> KENDALL

Pass me the shotgun.

> SHIV

Okay.

> (*to Roman*)

Okay?

> ROMAN

Okay. Fuck. Okay.

They all pull out phones.

EXT. CAR — EVENING

The kids' car drives through the evening.

INT. CAR — EVENING

Shiv on the phone to Tom. Kendall on to a lawyer. Roman, on the filling Connor in.

> ROMAN

Well, Con, this *is* me layering you in. I can't explain everything because it's complicated and there's no time and you're a little slow – I'm kidding! But we wanted to tell you because you're big brother and all.

> (*listens*)

Well I understand . . .

Kendall on his call.

> KENDALL

Yeah, thanks for talking, I just want to triple-check the holding company by-law shit.

Shiv on her call.

> SHIV

Yeah. We've talked. We're going, together.

> (*then*)

No, we have a weapon. Veto on a change of control. It's from the divorce. So we stop that. He's impotent. Deal collapses. We're going to force him out.

Intercut with:

EXT. WEDDING RECEPTION – NIGHT

Tom is still at the wedding reception. Peering backstage at two young caterers slacking off and whipping each other with tea towels.

> TOM
> Fuck. Uh-huh. Okay. And where do I fit in, Shiv?

Tom has a number of feelings going on. But Shiv is all wrapped up in the momentum of the moment.

> SHIV
> High up. There's a lot going on, Tom. We'll figure that out.

> TOM
> Okay. No, sure. Sure. But high?

> SHIV
> But, Tom? Once we do it, right away, we're gonna offer him the medical card, secure the imperial guard. Tell him he needs some rest. And sourced to us kids, we get ATN to confirm. 'Founder Logan Roy ailing'. 'Prayers for the big man'. 'Thinking of taking a step back'.

> TOM
> Yeah? We can source you?

> SHIV
> Yeah. We'll stand it up. So get ready, okay?

> TOM
> Jesus. Okay? Good luck.

End of call. We stay with Tom. As he thinks. Thinks hard. Is this a final moment of decision for him?

Greg approaches.

> GREG
> So, hey, Tom? Say hello to someone who *could be* Logan's ex-wife's step-cousin-in-law. *And* heir apparent to the Grand Duchy of Luxembourg twelve times removed or some shit and potential count of somewhere and legitimate claimant to the dormant throne of Italy!

TOM

What, Greg?

GREG

I'm going for a walk with the Contessa! We're hitting it off! She's having an existential crisis about being a brand ambassador. And I'm right in there. To wheedle away!

TOM

What about—?

GREG

Comfrey? Comfrey might be helping her refresh her personal branding!? She's not even that into me, we're separate bedding! It could be a guilt-free switch-up!

Tom's thinking.

Case closed. Slam it shut. The verdict is love, your honor.

TOM

Greg, listen, things maybe in motion.

Never good news.

GREG

As in—? Is anyone going to jail?

TOM

No! So. Do you wanna come with me? Sporus?

GREG

Can I ask for a little more information?

TOM

No. I don't think so. I might need you as my attack dog. My Gregweiler.

GREG

Right. 'Tom's attack dog'. I mean I have Brightstar Buffalo in my hip pocket? I'm kind of a big deal.

TOM

You fucked yourself before Congress, Greg.

GREG

That's quite a harsh assessment.

> TOM
> (*mocking Greg from Congress*)
> 'Bbebeb if I wish that it might please the court sire'. You're a fucking joke.
> (*then*)
> Who's ever looked after you in this fucking family? Ah?

But it does land.

> GREG
> And in terms of – where I could be looking at – like getting to with you.

> TOM
> You could be heading away from the endless middle, and towards – the bottom of the top.

> GREG
> The bottom of the top? And could I have my own – my own like—

> TOM
> Your own Greg?

> GREG
> Yeah?

> TOM
> You can have twenty! Look, I have things to do. You want a deal with the devil?

> GREG
> Um, well. What am I going to do with a soul anyways? Souls are boring. Boooo, souls!

They shake, smiling.

EXT. LOGAN'S VILLA – NIGHT

The kids' car approaches.

EXT. LOGAN'S VILLA – ENTRANCE – NIGHT

The three of them walk up towards the villa.

They can see the villa some way away. Outside are the many cars of advisors and lawyers.

Lights blaze from many windows. Lots of activity in the villa.

                    SHIV
   We good?

They're united but still a little jostle there. Who is the leader of this pack?

Roman is keeping it together. Shiv can't believe what's happening. Kendall a sort of calm. But they are warmed by each other's presence. The physical reassurance of their bodies.

                    KENDALL
   I'm good. You good?

                    ROMAN
                   (to Ken)
   You can handle this?

                    KENDALL
   Been basically planning it since we were four.

                    SHIV
   What if Dad flutters his eyes at you, Rome? You gonna melt?

                    ROMAN
   Me? No, as long as you bitches don't go waterpistols in Bali?

                    SHIV
   'Waterpistols in Bali'?

                    ROMAN
   We were all gonna go in and squirt? Dad, under his canopy? I went and you fucks left me for dead?

                    SHIV
   Don't recall.

                    ROMAN
   Convenient.

                    KENDALL
   He'll pull the dentist's chair, that's what he'll pull. Divide and rule.

They arrive at a door. There are staff or security but they're not about to stop the kids—

> SHIV

Hey. Shiv Roy. We're going up.

INT. LOGAN'S VILLA – NIGHT

They head in, Kendall calls out.

> KENDALL

Hey, Dad!?

They are followed by staff or security who try to guide them and get ahead.

They reach the first floor and Roman turns right.

There's a lawyer who's coming out of a room with a piece of paper, shirtsleeves in the heat.

> ROMAN

Hey, you, lawyery man, what's that?
> (goes to look at the paper)
Where's Logan Roy?

The lawyer keeps the paper.

> LAWYER

I don't know.

They walk on.

Across the way, Colin looks out. The kids advance.

INT. LOGAN'S VILLA – LOGAN'S OFFICE – NIGHT

Colin is at the threshold, barring entry. Kendall looks at him.

> KENDALL

Hey.

> COLIN

Hey.

They eye one another. Maybe Kendall can almost meet his gaze.

                            LOGAN
                            (off)

Send them in!

They go in. Gerri and Karl and Frank and Kerry in there too.

Hey. Hello hello! What's all this then?

Looks – who's going to go?

                            ROMAN

Um, hey. Hey, all?

The old guard say hello.

Just feeling a bit out of the loop, Dad?

                            LOGAN

Of course! Things have moved fast. Come in, come in.

                            ROMAN

Yeah, um, we might have this wrong but we heard rumors about
GoJo?

                            SHIV

Yeah, that we're the target now?

                            LOGAN

Look at you three. Why so grave? The three little piggies. Come
on, we're family, take a seat.

They might move, but maybe don't sit.

                            SHIV

Is that right, Dad?

                            LOGAN

Okay well, I'm looking at a few options. Let's settle down and
I can explain.

                            SHIV

Right, it could just affect our positions – so we wanted to get
some clarity?

Kendall is glowering. Logan looks at him.

LOGAN

Absolutely. I was about to be in touch. But do you mind – not with him in here giving me the fucking doggy-evils? Can you take him out, Romulus?

(*dismisses Kendall with hand*)

I'll fill your sister in then give you the angles. I can't trust him.

A moment – will Roman guide him out?

Roman?

Maybe there is some quaking but they don't accept his invitation to leave.

KENDALL

You can tell us together, Dad.

Logan looks at the kids – they seem to be united.

LOGAN

(*to Roman*)

I thought we had this figured out?

ROMAN

It might be better – to – just so we all hear.

Logan makes a calculation. Then, trying to make it as businesslike as possible, launches in—

LOGAN

Okay. So. The market capitalizations of our firms have been on the move.

(*because . . .*)

The DOJ fine is going to be very very large – thanks, Ken.

(*then big picture*)

We are a declining business and there are a wave of consolidations happening that mean this is the optimal moment, in my opinion, to make a deal with a serious tech operation like GoJo.

(*that's all folks*)

So that is what I am exploring. Okay?

KENDALL

And they take over?

LOGAN

(*yes*)

That's a long way down the road. It's a merger.

                    SHIV

Someone's always on top.

                    LOGAN

Well, it's maybe more complicated in this case. But yeah, the
numbers might mean I relinquish control of certain elements.

                    SHIV

And so I think we would say, can you ease up and let us in? Stop
this until we see how exactly we're impacted?

                    LOGAN

Well, no, it needs to be now.

                    SHIV

Why?

                    LOGAN

Because I feel it in my bones.

                    SHIV

Right. Well, no arguing with that?

                    LOGAN

Yeah well, end of the day that's all I've fucking got.

                    SHIV

Well—

                    LOGAN

This is the best moment to sell and if I don't do the best deal at
any given point, what's the point of anything, ah?
                    (looks at them)
I don't get out now, I leave several billion on the table.

                    SHIV

Right, that, versus your kids?

                    LOGAN

I'm confused, Pinky, because I thought we were dead if we didn't
make a deal?

She looks unhappy.

See this is why I had to keep you outside. Too much, hot blood
and cold piss sloshing around.

KENDALL

And what are you going to do with your 'several' bil? Put it on a pile with your other several bil?

LOGAN

Yeah. Why?

KENDALL

And what are we supposed to do?

LOGAN

Make your own fucking pile.
(*switches back to ameliorative*)
Look. I know this is a readjustment. But our blood's in the water and I need to make moves fast if I want to stay in control of the situation and get myself – and you – assurances – about the future.

SHIV

Dad, once Matsson is calling the shots, we're fucked.

LOGAN

No! Nah. He rates you. This is an opportunity for you kids to get an education in real life.

The kids look at one another.

KENDALL

No.

LOGAN

Well maybe not you, Ken. But, Rome, Shiv. In five, ten years . . .

SHIV

So why are we not inside this? If it's so exciting?

LOGAN

Trust me. I'll still be in the mix. I can pull the strings. I'm gonna be around for a decade. Don't burn any bridges, okay? Don't listen to the Whisky Sour here, Santa Claus will figure it out for you.

Logan's looking at Shiv and Roman. They look at each other. Water-pistol time. Is anyone gonna back down?

SHIV

We're gonna get fucked, Dad. With you at the top we can take over. Without you, we get fucked.

Shiv's gone, Logan focusses on Roman.

>   LOGAN
> Roman. C'mon, let's get away from the fucking Jacobins, let's
> discuss, I've got you. C'mon.

He tries to take Roman away.

>   ROMAN
> I know what he said, Dad, but, really? Once Matsson's calling
> the shots, we're strung up in the town square.

Logan looks direct to Roman. Full powers trained on him.

>   LOGAN
> He rates you. You have my word. This is an opportunity, son.
> Bit of fucking grit. Adversity. Like me.

Moment of choice for Roman.

> You can trust me.

>   SHIV
> You can't trust him.

*Roman looks from Shiv to Kendall, who gives his brother a look.
One that reaches back. Really? You know you can't trust him.*

Hard for Roman. Can he do it?

>   ROMAN
> Dad, we are here to say, the three of us to ask, and to say: Please
> do not do this.

A little sad for Logan, though he is careful not to let it show.

>   LOGAN
> And what will you do if I decide I can't listen to you?

>   SHIV
> We can stop you. We will stop you and blow this up.

>   ROMAN
> You need our vote for a change of control.

>   SHIV
> You need all of us, you need a supermajority and we will kill it.

Now Logan turns. The soft-soap is over.

LOGAN

You're playing toy fucking soldiers! Go on, fuck off, all of you.
I have you beat, you morons.

SHIV

Well no because you have to—

LOGAN
(*mimicks*)

'Well no because . . . '

That's rude, it stings Shiv. Logan looks to Kerry.

She still on—?

Kerry shakes her head.

KERRY

It's all done.

LOGAN

Can we get her back?

*Kendall, Roman, Shiv share a look: What's happening? Kerry dials
and turns away as she connects.*

ROMAN

Dad—?

Logan just waits until Kerry gestures: She's ready. Hands him the phone.

LOGAN
(*into phone*)

Hello—?

He hits speakerphone and puts her on the table.

CAROLINE
(*on speakerphone*)

Hello—? Logan?

Kendall, Roman and Shiv: What the fuck?

LOGAN

Caroline, you're on with Kendall, Roman and Siobhan.

A distant beat.

> CAROLINE

I don't necessarily want to do any more tonight, Logan. Can you say?

> LOGAN

I thought we should have a brief family conversation, about the accommodations we've come to.

Silence in the room. On Kendall, Roman and Shiv. A painful, wrenching silence. Like the heaviness of children being told their parents are divorcing.

Shall I speak on our behalf—?

> CAROLINE

Go ahead—

Logan looks up to Roman, Siobhan and Kendall.

> LOGAN

Your mother and I have reviewed the terms of the divorce agreement—

Kendall sees what's happening—

> KENDALL

You've fucked us—

> LOGAN

and we've agreed that some of the arrangements were a little, antiquated—

> ROMAN

Oh fuck, Mom – he got to you?

Shiv leans in, right into the speakerphone—

> SHIV

Mom—? Are you serious, already?

> CAROLINE

I can't get into it all, I think everything will be fine—

> SHIV

Mom, you just slit our throats—

CAROLINE

Please don't be angry. I think this is for the best. Peter's – so excited and I'm not sure it's been good for you, all the— You know?

(*signing off*)

I'm sorry.

The below could be over Caroline's farewells.

KENDALL

Okay. We walked in on Mum and Dad fucking us.

ROMAN

Dad, please?

LOGAN

'Please'? The seat-sniffer gets his fucking leg up. That's a deal. What have you got in your fucking hand?

ROMAN

Dad, please. I dunno. Love?

LOGAN

'Love'. You're coming for me with love? You bust in here with guns in your hand but now you find they're fucking sausages you want to talk about 'love'? You should have trusted me. I'm a lamb, I'm a fucking lamb.

Roman is falling to pieces.

ROMAN

Dad, why?

LOGAN

'Why'? Because it works. I fucking win. Come on, fuck off out, you nosey fucking pedestrians!

He walks to usher them out.

Kendall gets right up close to Logan. Eyeballs him direct. Logan meets it as he passes.

SHIV

(*to Rome*)

Who told him? Who told him we were coming so he got to Mom before we could—

> ROMAN
> (*defeated*)

Con? Was it Con?

Logan walks out onto the balcony.

They are left with Frank and Karl and Gerri.

Kendall and Shiv – lost in their own thoughts?

Help us, Gerri. He's not well. Help us stop him.

> GERRI

Why?

> ROMAN

Why? Because you're Shiv's fucking godmother.

> GERRI

Well I'm focussed on whatever outcome serves the best financial interests of the shareholders of the company.

> ROMAN

Why, because I trust you. I fucking like you.

> GERRI

Sure. But it doesn't serve my interests, how does it serve my interests?

He looks to Karl.

> KARL

Sorry, friend. Golden handshake. *Big* fucking golden handshake.

Roman looks to Frank.

> ROMAN

Frank?
> (*but Frank's look is cold*)

Fine, fuck you. You bitter, fucking shoe.

> FRANK
> (*quite quiet and calm*)

I was here when you were a kid throwing tantrums on the carpet and I'm going to watch you out the door.

> ROMAN

I know you think I'm dumb. But you can't see what I've got—

> FRANK

I don't think you're dumb. I would not think anything at all about you if I didn't have to.

> ROMAN

Fuck you.

> FRANK

You and your brother and sister are perfectly fine. Young men and women of quite adequate ability. But, you are careless and you have been cruel and vain and wanton.
> (*leaning in so only Roman can hear*)
I've eaten a bellyful for you, son. Go fuck yourself.

Roman heads towards Kendall and Shiv. In their own private worlds of betrayal and pain. But they are together.

From outside, comes Tom.

> TOM

Shiv? You okay, Shiv?

Before he can get in, Tom passes Logan out on the balcony.

They catch each other's eye. Logan gives a nod of appreciation. Squeezes Tom's shoulder. A wink.

Tom takes it. Can anyone see?

Yes. Shiv sees the squeeze and things fall into place, quite horribly. Shiv's face falls. She crumples, emotionally. Kendall sees. He supports her.

Tom heads on in to find the three siblings together. A hand held here. A bit of support there. Broken but together.*

---

* The end of this episode is a good example of how scripted scenes get improved by the opportunities afforded on set. At script, I didn't know what the final image would be. On set, we found a better sequence for the dialogue and action. Then Mark Mylod, in collaboration with Sarah and Matthew, found a much stronger final image than that gestured at here.

Acknowledgements

The story of the show is one of a series of very fortunate collaborations. I can't list them all, but some key thanks I owe include:

Frank Rich – my friend and fellow executive producer, frequent first reader, who originally championed my work at HBO and got me to meet Richard Plepler who was so encouraging of my working there. Meanwhile, Kevin Messick, with a keen eye for a script and a sharp edit, first commissioned me to write about US politics and opened up the path to a relationship with Adam McKay.

These relationships came together for the pilot which Adam shot, and through which he has had such a wide and long-lasting influence on the show – bringing in all the excellent pilot heads of departments – and leading us, in conjunction with the brilliant Francine Maisler, to much of the main cast. Adam has carried on being the most generous executive producer, supporting me in becoming a showrunner when I didn't even really know what one was.

The unbelievably talented and collaborative cast, including: Brian, Hiam, Jeremy, Peter, Rob, Nick, Kieran, Sarah, Matthew, Alan, Scott, Natalie, Swayam & Quentin, Juliana, JSC, David, Dag, Justine, Arian, Ash, Larry, Zack, James, Eric, Caitlin, Harriet, Danny, Jeannie, Patch, Holly, Cherry, Annabelle, Fisher, Zoë, Jihae, Dasha, Sanaa, Hope, Justin, Alexander, Pip. Neither I nor my fellow writers could or would have written what we did without knowing that they would be receptive. Their notes and thoughts and comments, not to say improvisations and freestylings, have enriched the show at every turn.

Adam McKay also brought Nicholas Britell, genius musician and composer, to the *Succession* party. Even if the show is decent, people think it is 58% better than it is because of the brilliance and depth of the work of Nick and his colleagues, Todd Kasow and John Finklea.

Simon Chin encouraged me to write something about Rupert Murdoch. Leanne Klein at Wall to Wall offered unstinting enthusiasm even when it became time to stint. Liza Marshall at Channel 4 was supportive, but we could just never make it happen. Gregory McKnight was the first person who suggested there was perhaps something in a fictional media-family show. He and my UK agent Cathy King and US TV agent Dan Erlij have supported me throughout.

Mark Mylod – the time we've spent! The care he takes! The way he marshals a set! To have seventeen things going on, to be thinking about twenty others, and then, when I appear at his shoulder with my little clutch of thoughts and adjustments, to meet each one – not without ego or a proprietorial pride, but to feel those things and ride them and still listen and adjust.

His fellow directors – Andrij Parekh, Bob Pulcini & Shari Springer Berman, Lorene Scafaria, Adam Arkin, Becky Martin, Kevin Bray, Miguel Arteta, S. J. Clarkson, Matt Shakman, Cathy Yan.

Lisa Molinaro and Holly Unterberger – constant monitor companions and friends and creative advisors. Sharp eyes, warm hearts.

Amy Lauritsen, Christo Morse, John Silvestri, Michelle Flevotomas – assistant directors who kept the train running and the mood up. And coped with changes, late and big beyond the call of duty, with barely a flinch.

Most of the writers who've worked on the show are recorded herein on episode titles: Tony Roche, Jon Brown, Lucy Prebble, Will Tracy, Georgia Pritchett, Susan Soon He Stanton, Ted Cohen, Will Arbery, Mary Laws, Anna Jordan, Jonathan Glatzer. But not all of them. My friend Simon Blackwell had just enough time to write 'alts' for the pilot before disappearing to meatier things. We also got to work in the room with Alice Birch, Miriam Battye, Francesca Gardiner, Cord Jefferson, Lucy Kirkwood, Gary Shteyngart. All brilliant. All good things sprang from the rooms where we all sat together and plotted and laughed.

Tony and Lucy, Jon and Will Tracy I've leant on most heavily to help me write – and to rewrite – when we had an episode that wasn't firing. And Tony and Lucy were most often at hand through the long months of the shoots as good companions and stout hearts. I've leant on them for creative wisdom and valued their kindness and friendship.

Beth Gorman, Ed Cripps, Jamie Carragher, Siobhan James-Elliott kept the notes in our UK rooms. Jamie for the longest stretch. He stayed up many a night transcribing and ordering and filtering, and still found time to chime in and add a thought or a historical or literary reference that left the rest of us agog at his breadth of knowledge.

Callie Hersheway Love, who I met on *Veep* and has been a constant help, guide, aide, friend and protector of my time and concentration, and has been intimately across every nook and cranny of these scripts, lately with the help of Terry McGrath. Also, Nate Elston who at first I thought I didn't need but soon discovered I was unable to function without, it's been the greatest pleasure to have his company and friendship. Ali Reilly and Danny Klain are also amongst the best of the best.

At HBO: Casey Bloys to whom I first pitched the show, Frannie Orsi, Nora Skinner and Max Hollman, Sally Harvey. HBO could not have been a happier or more supportive home, and they are brilliant and subtle executives whose guidance and support has been steadfast and sustaining.

Jane Tranter, who guided me through the US system and reassured my American partners that we were in the writers' room, not in the pub. Ilene Landress, who produced the pilot, and Jonathan Filley, the first season, and Scott Ferguson – indefatigable producer who got us on to yachts and into nations at short notice and kept the show on the road, with Gabrielle Mahon, when we could have come off the rails.

Our DPs – Pat Capone, who once made me cry with his call to arms amidst the myriad problems of shooting through Covid, Andrij, Chris, Kate. And the camera operators – who dance with the actors, Gregor and Ethan. They are the silent scene partners and need emotional intelligence that matches their iron grip and falcon's eye.

Stephen Carter, head of an art department of obsessive attention to detail matched only by his flexibility and good humour. Also my friends George DeTitta Jr., Katrina Whalen, Ben Relf, Andre Azevedo, Monica Jacobs, Alley O'Shea.

Ken Ishii, Pete and Ethan, Billy Sarokin, Andy Kris, Nicholas Renbeck – for keeping us sounding good against the odds. To catch on the fly every beat and every late-added line and improvisation clean enough to use. Extraordinary.

Merissa Marr has been my guide through the business moves from the first season and guided us towards some excellent areas and away from corporate faux pas. Brilliant on technical detail but also attuned to what we might need and what might work. Likewise Jon Klein on media. Jesse Eisinger and Matt Friedrich on legal matters. Tracey Pruzan and Derek Blasberg on society and New York. Faisal A. Quereshi on

691

oddities, curios, cultural updates and sex parties. Eric Schultz and Ben Ginsberg on politics, and Justin Geldzahler on everything all together all at once. All invaluable.

Doug Aibel and Henry Russell Bergstein, and Avy Kaufman, who helped find and land so many remarkable acting talents.

Angel DeAngelis, Nuria Sitja, Michelle Johnson, Patricia Regan, kind, talented and warm bosses of hair and make-up.

Michelle Matland, Jon Schwartz, Midge and Danny. Costume department of dedication and flair and good humour and hard work.

Paul Eskenazi, who has helped us into and out of our many and ever-evolving list of locations.

Ken Eluto, Jane Rizzo, Bill Henry, Anne McCabe, Brian Kates, Ellen Tam and Venya Bruk – editors of subtlety and wisdom. Who made a thousand good choices before we ever started on the ones we got to worry over together. Dara Schnapper who, with Val, James and Genevieve, presided over post-production with such attention to detail and allowed me such room for manoeuvre.

To Alex Bowler at Faber & Faber who was generous enough to think it was worth starting this scriptbook ball rolling, and his colleague Steve King who has edited this volume with care and sensitivity under a ticking clock, and Jodi Gray for setting it with precision.

To the folks at HBO responsible for enabling this book to come together: Michele Caruso, Tara Bonner, Stacey Abiraj, Arielle Mauge and Andrew Kelley.

And to my support network. Sam Bain, my kind and thoughtful compadre, with or from whom I've learnt everything I know about writing film and TV.

To Pat Halpin and Phillip Rossini. For getting me in and out and putting me up.

To everyone at First Touch FC, especially Mikey, Keith, Euan, Case and John C. for keeping me roughly in shape and pretty much sane. Likewise Chelsey Kapuscinski.

To Ju, Jas, Rob, Mark, Will, Andy & Andy Yates. Rock-solid old pals.

Chris (with whom some of the thoughts about satire in the introduction to the fourth volume were discussed (i.e. he said them and I basically wrote them down)), Jo and all the family and friends who sustained my most important people while I was often absent.

And my family. I don't think I had any idea going into this how consuming it would be and how much it would take me away. The pandemic was particularly tough. I couldn't and wouldn't have done it without your love and support. M, A&A, I love you. My mum and dad and sister and her family, too. Thank you.

Jesse Armstrong